Neither Civil nor Servant

Twenty four years in the
Immigration Service.

Martin Lloyd.

Queen Anne's Fan

First published in hardback in 2014 by Queen Anne's Fan
PO Box 883 • Canterbury • Kent CT1 3WJ
Reprinted 2015
This paperback edition published 2017
Reprinted 2018

ISBN 9780 9573 639-4-6

A CIP record of this book can be obtained from the British Library.

Set in New Baskerville 11pt.

www.queenannesfan.com

Printed in England

Preface

If there is one thing that really annoys me it is a book which opens with an author's declaration that he only wrote the work for his own amusement, this followed by a false apology for inflicting the modest tome upon the public and concluding with a justification of the crime by divulging that his friends had read the manuscript and persuaded him against his better judgment to get it published.

You will not find that here.

The stimulus for my writing *Neither Civil nor Servant* was to record for my children what their father had been doing all the time that he had been absent from their lives. It is neither an autobiography nor a work of fiction. It all happened. It is a record without reverence built along an autobiographical thread and it certainly displays the prejudices and inaccuracies that such works always contain but rarely admit to. Official records exist but they will not tell you what it was like to work in the Immigration Service of the late twentieth century. My book will.

One can always challenge the interpretation of events and I warn you now that this is how I saw them.

THE ILLUSTRATIONS

Wherever I went I carried my drawing pen or pencil and I often found myself sketching what I could see from my desk. Occasionally I used my camera. The chapter numbers are taken from the date line of an immigration officer's embarkation stamp. The odd pieces of ephemera illustrated are those contemporary witnesses that I picked up at random to use as bookmarks and which, years later, still surprise me by leaping out of books in my library.

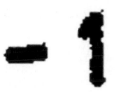

I stare at the name in the book on my desk and then check again in the red passport that the young Swiss man has given me. It is the same name. Involuntarily I glance at the passenger standing before me. He has blue eyes and frizzy untidy hair. My mouth goes dry. 'Stay calm', they had said on the training course, 'stay calm and follow the instruction against the name in the book.'

It was my second day 'on the desk' at London Heathrow Terminal Three and I had caught somebody in the suspect index – the book of naughty names that was issued to all immigration officers. My second day! Some officers served five years before catching anybody.

'Richard Auf der Mauer, born 10.8.52. Swiss. Unlikely to qualify for leave to enter.'

Panic.

All that I had learned so far on the first three weeks of my training course had just left for some distant destination like the thundering jet behind me. Help! I need help. My mentor is tantalisingly out of reach, leaning on an unoccupied desk between us two trainees. Perry Humber, his name is. Been in the Service twenty years. A senior IO. (immigration officer). He is puzzling over the *Telegraph* crossword with the other trainee's mentor.

'H... how long are you staying?' I manage to stutter through the gluten on my glottis, praying that Perry will turn around and take some interest in his ward.

Richard Auf der Mauer, Swiss and only a few years younger than me rubs his nose. 'About two weeks.'

I try to look confident as I flick over the pages of his passport. He had been landed at Luton airport three times in the last year. Straightforward visitor. No restrictions. He was Swiss for Heaven's sake. Who the devil bothers to look up Swiss passengers in the book? Trainees do. Trainees have to look up every passenger they deal with for the first two years – the time required for them to pass their probation and become 'proper' immigration officers. I swallow hard, trying to get my vocal cords to work.

'And er... what are you going to do here?'

I was falling back on the training template. 'How long are you staying? What will you do here? How much money have you got? Have you got a return ticket?'

Perry's grey sports jacket juts out behind him as he pores over the newspaper on the desk top. I still cannot catch his attention.

'I will visit a friend.'

Whilst the passenger adjusts the strap of his backpack, I scrawl, *'he's in the book'* on a landing card and flip it onto Perry's newspaper.

'How much money have you got?' I ask.

I glance across at the two crossword addicts. Perry reads the card, grins at me and turns back to the newspaper. He doesn't believe me.

'About fifty pounds.'

'Perry!' I hiss.

'Repeat please,' the Swiss says.

'I was talking to... er him.' Oh God what do I do now? I've only got one question left before I start asking real questions. 'Do you have a return ticket? May I see it please?' He swings his backpack to the floor and disappears below the front of my desk as he rummages in it. I leap from my stool and poke my mentor in the ribs with my Stationery Office ball point pen. 'He's in the bloody book!'

This time Perry reacts. His eyes start out like golf balls in blancmange. He sweeps me aside and grabs my book. I put my finger on the name and he agrees with me. He writes on a self-duplicating form, tears off the top sheet and gives it to the passenger.

'Sit down over there,' he says and then turns to me. 'Grab your stuff.' I snatch up my book and stamps from the desk and follow Perry through the solid door into the general office. One wall of the office accommodation is glass and gives glimpses of airliners on stands and, further away, the hairline streak of Runway 28 Right. Suddenly Perry stops and *click, click, click*, deploys a telescope which he trains on a craft which is taxiing on the other side of the field. 'Hmm. 707. Woolly Tops,' he mutters and then collapses the telescope back into his pocket.

'Woolly Tops?'

'Nigeria Airways. Their flight prefix is 'WT''

'So why do you call them Woolly Tops?'

He pulls a face and tries to decide whether or not I am stupid. 'Work it out for yourself,' he says. 'Quick, bag that empty table. I'll go and get the suspect circular on this pax. You've got your first refusal.'

I sit down and spread out my stuff. 'This will jolly well show them.'

I think to myself. I had been struggling through the training course with difficulty. We were a mixed bunch of recruit IOs. At twenty-four I seemed to be senior to most of them. Some had already been working at a port, under supervision of course, for several months. I envied them their familiarity with the different rubber stamps and their ease with the jargon. Others had come straight from university with the study ethos still in their blood. I envied them their facility to comprehend the most complex instructions at the first explanation. Pete and I had only been at our port for a couple of weeks before being sent on this course and we knew nothing. He had come from five years living in the Netherlands; I had come from three years in Paris. I didn't even know what song was top of the hit parade in the UK.

At my recruitment interview I had asked to work at Heathrow. I had been posted to Dover. I had quickly realised that Dover East, where I was to toil, was not the same as Dover West. The East was characterised by modern glass-and-steel buildings, lifts, escalators, a multi-storey staff car park and subsidised canteen. As the Harbour Board expanded the terminal facilities by building further out into the harbour, the IOs found themselves working so far from the ships that they might just as well have been at an airport. Across the bay, at Dover West, the immigration office was a shack perched on top of the Dover Marine station, the sea crashed over the quay on stormy days, the trains rumbled below and alongside the office and if you wanted something to eat you went to the porters' canteen, known affectionately as 'Snotgobblers'. Dover West was a man's port. Dover East was for pansies.

For three weeks we had attended classes in Lunar House. Yes, I am afraid that was its name. It was a twelve storey office block in Croydon which had just been taken over by the Home Office, of which the Immigration Service was an arm. There, we listened to explanations on how to land students or businessmen and some of the more esoteric categories of passenger such as Japanese chicken-sexers and quail attendants. We followed the illustrations on the overhead projector. Then we tried it ourselves in role-play exercises where one trainee had to interview an instructor whilst everybody else watched and dreaded the moment when their turn would come.

We were shown a black and white film about security and told that homosexuals were a risk because they were vulnerable to seduction and blackmail. One was allowed to say things like that in those days. I was upset at the discrimination. Did this mean that, as a heterosexual, I was debarred by my proclivities from the opportunity of being seduced by a voluptuous Russian temptress? It did not seem fair.

Occasionally a representative of another department or organisation would come and talk to us. It made a change. Special Branch made it clear to us that the enemy was Ireland and the Soviet Bloc. Everybody was looking forward to Thelma. She was from MI5, or 'Box 500' as it was known to the initiated, and she was going to tell us all about spies and secrecy and how we could help the Security Service by keeping our eyes and ears open. Thelma was a horsey-looking woman of advanced years who spoke about 'gels' and 'fellers' and for fifty minutes was able to entertain us with anecdotes and opinions so circumstantial as to be utterly useless.

With the Home Office Immigration and Nationality Department situated within the building, opportunities were grasped for us to see how other sections functioned. The Traffic Index was mind-boggling. This was the bin into which all the landing cards from the ports around the United Kingdom were chucked. It was an airy room of a geometrical shape but I was unable to count the sides. In it were row upon row of card index filing cabinets and squadron upon squadron of white-haired ladies to service them. Here, we learned that some nationalities customarily used far fewer names than others but retained their width of choice by varying their spellings. This obliged the ladies to index them down to the last letter of the last name.

And nearby on a ground floor was the Public Enquiry Office. Foreigners who had already been admitted came to this office to ask to be allowed to stay longer. 'Applying for an extension' it was called. At eight thirty each morning when we arrived for our lessons the queue of applicants already stretched around the block like a multicoloured scarf. We sat in the cubicles with the clerical officers who took in the passports and forms and processed them. Mindful of the fact that as an immigration officer, albeit a probationer, I was a grade above a clerical officer, I picked out a passport and leafed through it with a professional air.

'Libya? He's probably an arms dealer,' I declared in a portentous voice.

'Oh has he been to Libya?' the girl asked.

'Well he comes from Libya,' I explained, closing the passport to show her the black cover with a golden tree printed on it. *'Passeport du Liban.'* I read.

'Oh, I thought that was the Lebanon. On account of the tree. It always looks like a Lebanese cedar to me.'

'Yes, confusing isn't it?' I tried to smile away my crass ignorance. Of course he was Lebanese. How would I ever become an immigration officer if I could make such an elementary mistake as that? I wondered

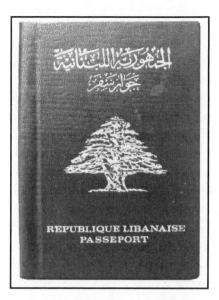

LEBANESE PASSPORT

Any fool can see
that the tree is
a cedar of
Lebanon.

whether I really wanted to become a civil servant, that most despised of parasites, rather than stay in the supposedly vibrant and efficient private sector. Could I make myself sufficiently petty-minded to fulfil the stereotype of the job?

I took my first pay cheque into the Croydon branch of Lloyds Bank and handed it to the cashier, indicating that I wished to withdraw five pounds.

'I shall have to phone your branch to see whether you have sufficient funds.'

'That's a cheque for one hundred and twenty-nine pounds. That will cover it.'

'But the cheque will not be cleared for five working days.'

'But it will be alright.'

'We cannot know that.'

'Don't be daft. It's signed by HM Treasury. Are you saying that you think their cheques will bounce?'

He telephoned my bank and debited my account the telephone charge of fifty pence because I refused to pay for the call on the basis that it was their call not mine. I knew I had enough money in my account. Several years later when they thought up the great idea of charging customers one pound every time they used the ATM I transferred my account to another enterprise, making sure that I withdrew fifty pence more money than I possessed. Yes, not only could I make myself sufficiently petty to become a civil servant, I was probably there already.

After the three weeks of cramming instructions, laws, regulations and rules, into our heads we were then sent out to ports for three weeks to try it all out. As I was to be posted to a seaport, I was mentored at an airport. It made sense. It gave me an insight into traffic that I would never see crossing the Channel.

Perry returns with the relevant volume of bound circulars from the safe. This tells us that Mr. Auf der Mauer had been previously found in possession of forty mandrax tablets at Heathrow and sent back to Switzerland. I have no idea what the tablets are but Perry says that they are a sort of stimulant and as such, are a controlled drug. Apparently you could do interesting things with them if you knew what to mix them with. I nod sagely and wonder where his knowledge comes from. He guides me through the unfamiliar forms, dictating what I should write.

'You have asked for leave to enter the United Kingdom for two weeks as a visitor but I am not satisfied that no more than a visit is intended. Furthermore, on a previous visit to the United Kingdom you were found in possession of a controlled drug, in the light of which I consider your exclusion to be conducive to the public good.' Perry looks at his watch. 'I think that ties him up nicely. Let's see if we can get him back on the same flight.' A quick turnaround. The 'bum's rush' as it is called. 'Sign that.' He throws a form across to me. 'Put your stamp there,' I crash my stamp down on the form. 'And there,' *Crash.* 'And there.' *Crash.* He grabs the phone. 'I'll get Security to pick him up.'

'I haven't refused him yet,' I observe. 'I haven't served the forms.'

'We'll do that when Security arrive. It's quicker.'

He is right. I officially refuse entry to the UK to Mr. Auf der Mauer whose response is one of disbelief and outrage.

'But I come for holiday. I have medicine for me.'

'Come along now. Get yer bag,' the security guard orders.

'But I...'

'When I say, "Come along" you move, sunshine. Now move.'

I am searching through the bundle of self-duplicated copies; forms that previously I have only handled in training exercises. 'I can't find the IS 87 to give to him,' I say to Perry. This is the form which notifies him of his right to take my decision to a court of appeal and tells him how to do it.

Perry ignores me. 'OK mate, take him away,' he says to the guard. I follow Perry back into the general office. He turns at the door and looks at me. 'You've got a lot to learn,' he says, and crumples up the appeal form and drops it into the nearest bin.

Obviously I had.

Now, whenever I smell aviation gasolene, I think of Terminal Three, Heathrow. Those three weeks of rainbow humanity telling me fantastic stories usually just when I wanted to go for a pee or eat my lunch. The IOs here knew so much about so many countries and peoples and religions. I, indeed, had a lot to learn. And one important maxim was that if you did not give a refused passenger his appeal form, then he did not appeal. It was wrong and I knew it but it was difficult not to collude. I was learning; this chap was supposed to be teaching me how to do the job. Well, if this was the way the job was done, I suppose that was how I should do it.

Perry made me write a report to ISHQ, pointing out that the passenger whom I had recognised on the suspect index had been landed at Luton airport several months earlier. I importantly showed it to another trainee who was on duty with me.

'You shitbag!' was her response. 'The Luton IO will get a file back from Estabs. for that. They'll give him a bollocking.'

'Well,' I said in justification, 'he should have looked him up in the book like I did.'

'Pompous git.' She scowled at me pityingly. 'Are you never going to make a mistake? You wait till you get a file back. You won't thank the bastard who reported you.'

Her reaction made me quite miserable. I sat at a spare table and immersed myself in the general noting file – a hotchpotch of informations and announcements, some of an official nature, others of parochial social importance only. I imagined that everybody around me was muttering about me but I cherished a childish conceit of my impact on the office; in truth, nobody knew who I was and even fewer cared.

The next day is an early start. In the northside carpark I crouch into the back of the bus shelter trying to evade the cutting wind and sousing rain. The shuttle bus looms up out of the dark and drives straight past me. I swear and edge out into the maelstrom so that the bus drivers can see me. The next bus does not even slow down. Why am I the only person waiting at this bus stop? I had driven down to this end of the car park because it had lots of empty spaces. I now realise why. In the mornings the buses pick up from the other end; in the evenings they pick up from my end. I gather my coat around me and trudge into the weather. Another crowded bus rattles past me before I get to a valid bus stop. I thought of the IOs who did this every day. Having to leave their car a mile from work in acres of car park and then take another twenty minutes to get into the office.

Apparently, after fourteen years at Terminal Three you could expect to qualify for a 'centre pass' which would authorise you to park just opposite the office.

The transatlantic flights start coming in from 6 o'clock onwards. The night shift are bleary-eyed from bed or poker or takeaway curry as they straggle out to the desks. The early shift is expected to take over any casework from them. If the night shift stop a suspect passenger they issue them with a detention form and hand the case over to a colleague so that they can go home to bed. Some of the headhunter IOs will stay on to keep their figures up. The more passengers you refuse, the higher you rise in esteem.

As I wander diffidently amongst the office furniture, trying to look as if I know what I am doing, an IO with his nose buried in the general noting file asks nobody in particular, 'Have you seen this?'

'What?'

'A Home Office directive about presents from the public and business contacts. We have to declare them and submit them for assessment and then we will be told whether we can accept them or not.'

'Oh.'

'That means the inspector will have to declare the pineapple that the station manager of Ghana Airways gave him last week. Ha!' He looks up at me to gauge my response. 'Oh, you're a trainee aren't you? Never mind.' I am dismissed.

Out on the desk, Perry is a little more solicitous of me and less of his crossword. 'No more excitement,' he warns. 'After this flight we can go for breakfast.' He runs a practised eye over the last few passengers in the queue. 'I'll see you in the general office.'

He wanders away. This is his way of giving me the confidence to work on my own. I stamp the passport of the blue rinse American, flick the landing card onto the pile and nod at the queue marshal. He points a man over to me. I watch him as he approaches. He is about thirty-five years old, wearing jeans and a blue denim jacket. His face is weatherbeaten and a red neckerchief is tied at his collar. His clothes look as if he has slept in them for more than just the time of the flight. When I take his Norwegian passport I notice that he has not shaved for several days. Quite frankly, he looks scruffy. I open his passport.

'How long are you staying?'

'I go to Holland.'

'Where have you come from?'

'Canada. Montreal.'

'What were you doing in Canada?' I am already suspicious for his passport bears only a Canadian embarkation stamp. So how did he get into Canada and how long has he been there?

'I do nothing in Canada. I am seaman. I lose ship. I come home.'

'You are Norwegian. Do you live in Holland?'

'No. I get ship there.'

'To Norway?'

He shrugs his shoulders. 'Norway, maybe. China, maybe.'

So what have I got here? An out of work Norwegian seaman coming to the UK to go to the Netherlands to look for another ship. How could I be sure that he would not take a ship from the UK? Would it matter if he did? All the role-play exercises concerning contract seamen to join ship's articles ran through my mind in ragged confusion. I start to sort out all the special seaman stamps from the box before me. It is then that I notice that his passport was issued in Canada. This explains why there is only an embarkation stamp but it also means that I have no way of knowing how long he had been there and whether he was in breach of his landing permission whilst there. But if he is a seaman, why isn't he travelling on his seaman's book?

'Where is your seaman's book?'

'Lost in the ship.'

'Why have you a passport issued in Canada? What happened to your previous passport?'

'Lost in the ship. All lost in the ship.'

I look around. Perry is nowhere to be seen. I fall back on the old favourites. 'Show me your ticket.' He burrows in a plastic carrier bag which, I now begin to suspect, had recently contained a quantity of in-flight duty free alcohol, and gives me a ticket. It was issued in Montreal and will take him to Amsterdam. So he will have to go across to Terminal Two for the KLM flight. I am stuck. 'Have you any baggage?' I ask. Perhaps a delve into his luggage will give me a clue.

In reply, he holds up the plastic bag. 'All my baggage.'

This was preposterous. You don't fly across the Atlantic with a bag of duty free booze and no clothes, even if you are a seaman.

'Where are your clothes?' He tugs at his shirt collar with his fingers. 'No, your other clothes?'

'All in ship.'

He left his clothes in the ship? He was not making sense. I have a sudden flash of inspiration. 'How much money have you got?'

'Money? Dollars?'

'Yes dollars, pounds or whatever.'

I notice that Perry is standing outside the office door and tapping his watch at me. The seaman lifts his plastic bag and upends it over my desk. A mass of screwed up paper balls rolls out. The seaman hiccoughs. I gaze at the variously coloured rubbish. I pick one at random and tentatively smooth it out on the desk. It is a Canadian five-dollar note. I take another. Ten US dollars.

'What are you doing?' Perry is at my elbow.

'Counting his money.' I straighten out another currency note. 'He's got no baggage, no clothes or anything. He's got a single ticket and he 'lost' his passport in the ship. Anything I ask for he says he lost in the ship.' Perry watches me in silence for a few seconds, then he takes the passport. 'He's a seaman,' I add.

'A seaman?' he repeats. 'Where is his seaman's book?'

'He says that he lost it in the ship.'

'A seaman?' he addresses the passenger. The man nods. 'Where is your ship?'

The man makes a plunging motion with his hand. 'Lost ship,' he says.

'Where are you going?'

'Amsterdam.'

'Roll him,' Perry instructs me. This means treat him like a tourist. The expression arises because to achieve the endorsement the IO has to roll his stamp forwards so that the tourist wording engraved on the flange above the main body of the stamp is also printed on the page.

'But he's got nothing—'

'Neither would you have if you had just been shipwrecked like him. Just send him on his way. He's had enough trouble this week.'

'Shipwrecked?' I blather. Passport 'lost in the ship.' The balls of screwed up paper suddenly make sense. They had been in the ocean. So had he, probably. And I was worried because he had not shaved.

By the end of my first week I was becoming hardened to some of the procedures. Taking passengers downstairs to have their baggage searched, we always let Customs do this so that they get blown up by the bombs or pricked by the syringes instead of us. If Customs find nothing of interest to us, then we take the passengers back upstairs and do their baggage again. I learn to count the baggage checks stapled to their tickets because crafty passengers, if they know that they have incriminating documents in one particular suitcase, simply fail to identify it and leave it rattling around the carousel to be collected later if they get through.

I was taught how to play the queue. Arriving passengers were herded into lines by garlands of rope looped on chromium stands. A British queue, a Commonwealth queue, one for the EEC, as we called it then, and one for 'aliens,' which was the Home Office term for all the others. Each queue was controlled by one or two marshals who handed out landing cards to those requiring them and then regulated the feed of passengers to the desks as they became free. I was about to land an American student who was coming for a trip into Europe when Perry suddenly butted in with some more questions. I sat back and listened. I must have missed something, but just as suddenly, Perry said, 'OK, roll him,' and then waved to the marshal for another passenger. 'I thought you could do with a Kuwaiti for a change,' he said. He had looked up the queue, identified his quarry and then purposefully prolonged my interview until the Kuwaiti was at the front and ripe for plucking.

The twenty-five year old Kuwaiti had flown in to go shopping. I looked at him, wondering whether he was taking the mickey.

'What are you coming to buy?'

'Clothes.' He shrugged. 'A watch perhaps.'

'How much money have you got?'

Another shrug. 'About twenty thousand pounds.'

Now I knew he was taking the piss. 'Show me.'

He shrugged again and pulled out a leather wallet containing a wadge of one-hundred pound traveller's cheques. Two hundred of them. He was going to spend seven times my annual salary on a shopping trip.

'I thought you needed an education,' Perry explained afterwards.

During slack periods I read instructions. Did you know that the vehicles on the airside aprons must show an orange flashing light on the roof, not an orange rotating light? And it had been sanctioned from on high that IOs at Terminal Three could now wear a leather jacket in the place of the sports jacket or lounge suit if they wished.

One quiet spell I was sitting out on the desk. The arrivals hall was empty except for a Pakistani cleaner who was lethargically swinging an industrial floor polisher back and forth up at the far end. I was listening to Perry as he regaled me with outrageous tales of the activities of certain of his colleagues.

'Just a minute. Watch this,' he said.

He sidled over to the wall, leaned down and clicked off the switch for the floor polisher. Thirty yards away the cleaner stopped and looked at the machine. He tugged at the cable and Perry switched the plug on again.

Satisfied, the man continued his sweeping back and forth. Perry repeated the action, simulating a break in the cable near the machine by switching on and off when the operator moved the flex in a certain direction. We then sat there for ten minutes and watched the man polish the floor whilst holding a loop of the flex above his head in the belief that this was the only way that the machine would work. I didn't know what this proved but it was entertainment.

On another day I spent some time on the 'medical desk'. Immigrants coming to settle in the UK would be issued with a special visa which was usually an intricately engraved label which was stuck into their passport. They would have been accepted for settlement on the condition that they underwent a medical examination upon arrival. My job was mainly clerical. I checked that the person presenting the passport was the rightful holder and not some cousin or other impostor; I ascertained that their sponsor, that is, the person whom they were coming to live with, was in the airport to meet them. This was a useful double check upon the claimed relationship, and then I sent them along to see the Port Medical Inspector. The PMIs were general practitioner doctors who were paid to provide a twenty-four hour service at the port. Many of the immigrants were from the Indian sub continent – usually wives and children coming to join the father or husband who had been given permission to live here. Occasionally one would see an aged relative who qualified on the grounds that, as all the rest of the family was already here, there was nobody in their country to look after them. There was a gamut of different stamps and regulations to be applied and these differed between Commonwealth and alien passengers. I was out of my depth, utterly confused and very glad when my stint was over. And I am sure that I did it all wrong.

I had applied for the job of immigration officer after having seen an advertisement in the *Daily Mail.* One of the conditions of employment which appealed to my immature nature was the assertion, 'you may be required to drive a car'. Now that was a job with status! I was but a little disappointed after a few days at Dover East to discover that the port only possessed one official car for one hundred and fifty staff. It was a Mini Clubman estate complete with the imitation plastic wood decoration laid over the urine yellow paintwork. I only drove it once before it was sold and it was never replaced. My task on that occasion had been to deliver a passport to Heathrow as quickly as possible so that a refused passenger could be removed. I arrived at the airport in time, handed over the passport and then realised that I needed to fill up the tank in order to get back so I pulled into a busy filling station on the Bath Road. Try as I might, I could not remove the filler cap. Unlike on the saloon version, this filler cap did not stand proud of the rear wing, it skulked in a sort of niche carved in the bodywork as if designed to house a religious relic or icon. There was hardly any space around the cap for my fingers. I tried my right hand, I tried my left. I tried both hands. I tried wrapping a rag around it to give me more grip. I tried straight-armed. I tried bent-armed. The filler cap was as if welded to the pipe. It did not budge one millimetre. By this time the other customers had recognised me as a trouble maker and had reversed and manoeuvered their ways around me.

'Ya fillin' up or just dancin'?' the cashier's tinny voice barked at me over the tannoy.

'I can't get the petrol cap off.' I gave it a demonstrative wrench. The only result was a torn fingernail.

The aluminium door banged in its frame and the cashier waddled across the forecourt to me.

'It's not my car, you see,' I explained in mitigation.

She looked at me with absolutely no expression on her face at all, clasped a hand around the cap and wrenched it off with a flick of the wrist and placed it with exaggerated care on the roof of the car.

'And I'm not selling you more than six gallons,' she said as she walked away.

'Why not?'

'It's only got a six gallon tank.'

Terminal Three, I discover, have three cars. Perry is chatting to a colleague and breaks apart when he sees me. 'If you've got room why not take my sprog with you,' he suggests. 'It'll all be training for him.'

'If you like.' His mate holds out his hand to me. 'I'm Derek.' I never did learn his other name. 'We're doing a VIP embark. Chokky bikkies,' he adds.

This is obviously a coded expression for something that I am supposed to be aware of so I hide my ignorance with a knowing nod. On the way down the corridor we pick up the other two IOs who are doing the embarkation with us. One is carrying a buff folder.

'Which have you got?' Derek asks him.

'The Mini.' He shows him the front of the folder.

The title on the file is a car registration number. I deduce that in the folder are the papers for the vehicle and the journey sheet that has to be filled in every time that it is used. What I also notice is that somebody has written in bold red letters across the front cover, *'this car is dangerous and must not be driven.'* When I timorously draw this warning to Derek's attention he says, 'Oh that's been on there for ages.'

So all four of us invest the Mini. I am over six feet tall and Derek is built like a rugby forward and we are squeezed onto the back seat, sitting with our unyielding cases on our laps. They usefully fill the space that might otherwise have remained vacant between our stomachs and the backs of the front seats.

'Here, shove my case between you will you?' the driver says and another black official bag slithers over the back of the seats and falls into the only gap that remained between us. In 1974, seat belts were not fitted in the rear of cars. In our situation they would have been unnecessary – we could not have moved had we wanted to.

Off we go. I had assumed that we were going to the VIP suite at Heathrow but I was soon disabused of this with a derisory, 'oh that's just for posers. The real VIPs don't come anywhere near the terminal.' We were to embark a group of MPs who were taking a plane of the Queen's Flight to go to Paris. These operated from a small apron right over the other side of the field. In my ignorance of the layout of Heathrow, this seemed to be in the middle of nowhere. I suppose that was why it was safe – everybody could be seen approaching. Access was via another revelation – the cargo tunnel. Many people are familiar with the approach road to the airport from the M4 where it passes under the runway in a tunnel. I now learned that there was another tunnel to be found on the other side of the airport.

The Mini whines and smokes its way amongst the buses, taxis and lorries and we plunge into the sodium-lit gloom of the cargo tunnel. As we gather speed, the driver steers out towards the white line. A van coming in the opposite direction flashes its lights. He steers back and we nearly clip the barrier. Back we go again, this time crossing the centre line, then back to the wall, then back and half way into the opposite carriageway straight into the path of three thousand gallons of aviation spirit. The tanker blows its horn and puts its lights full up. Our driver yanks the wheel back and we see the wheel nuts on the tanker spinning past our ears.

'What did you do that for?' Derek asks. 'Christ!' he adds as we clip the kerb.

'It's the bloody car. The steering's all to cock.'

'Slow down then, try to get a hold on it.'

He brakes and the amplitude of our zigzags begins to diminish until we are travelling more or less where the driver points us. We are now doing only twenty miles per hour and until we leave the tunnel we, in the back seat, are terrifyingly aware of the front bumper of a very frustrated lorry as it bounces and lurches four feet behind our skulls.

When we climb out, Derek observes, 'The Mini is alright with two up, but as soon as you put anybody in the back seat it lifts the weight off the front wheels.'

'But it does say on the folder that the car is dangerous,' I point out.

'Yeah, perhaps that is the reason. The steering needs tightening up.'

I look over the roof where I can see the top of a small airliner. 'That looks like a Hawker Siddeley 748.'

Derek grins at me. 'That's what happens when you get paired up with Perry Humber – you start plane spotting.'

'Not really. I used to travel regularly with a cheapy airline called Skyways. They used them. They were noisy, rattly and slow.'

'Yeah well this is not a cheapy airline; it's the Queen's Flight.' I was aghast. Did the Queen really fly in crates like that? 'Come on, we've got work to do. Chokky bikkies.'

'Right. Chokky bikkies.'

I still did not know what, in this context, the colloquialism for 'chocolate biscuits' signified.

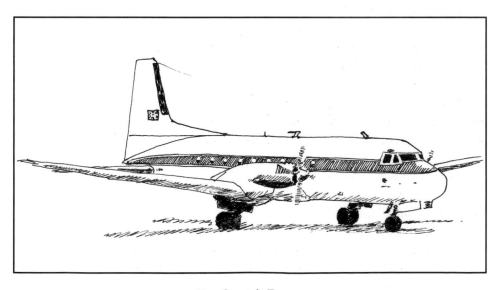

THE QUEEN'S FLIGHT
It was a Hawker Siddeley 748!

We followed the other two officers into the building. It looked like one of the original wartime huts that had then become the newly opened Heath Row Airport when it had been handed over by the RAF in 1946.

It was the typical prefabricated concrete construction with uniform windows running down both sides and huge concrete beams arching over to support the ceiling. This particular building had been divided half way along by the later addition of a pair of concertina doors. These were closed when we entered but we could hear the voices of a small congregation coming from the other side. We introduced ourselves to the customs and special branch officers and then sat back on the steel framed canvas chairs to wait.

After five minutes Derek decided that he had waited long enough and rapped on the doors. After some fumbling, they were opened by a young lady in a blue suit. Behind her, it was another world. No linoleum but plush blue carpet; not canvas and steel but upholstered armchairs. The group was even drinking percolated coffee.

'Immigration,' Derek said. 'Passport control.'

'Oh gosh! Yes. Well, this is the Foreign Secretary's party. They're going to Paris for the talks.' She tapped her clipboard importantly.

I was impressed. The Foreign Secretary. Wow! Derek nodded.

'Then they will all have their passports with them won't they?'

'Oh yes,' she grasped the offer. 'They all have their passports.' She smiled sweetly, assuming that to be the end of the conversation.

'Good,' said Derek. 'Then can I see them?'

'You want to see their passports?' She was nonplussed.

'I didn't come here to look at your pretty blue eyes, my dear, I am an immigration officer and we are here to embark those passengers.'

With this, she became brisk. She disappeared into the melé and returned with a dozen passports stacked in her hands. Derek picked up the top one and read out the name.

'Mr. Call-ag-han.' He pronounced the name as if he had never read it before. 'Which one is he.'

The girl was wide-eyed at his ignorance. 'That's the Foreign Secretary.'

'I know what he is, my dear, I want to know who he is. Which of this assembled crowd is Mr. Call-ag-han?'

'He's that one over there.' She half-turned and, hiding her finger under her nose, she pointed out the Foreign Secretary with her flicking eyes and jabbing digit.

I thought Derek was being a little unfair on the poor girl. She was only a PA or something. But Derek had not finished. 'I can't see his face. Can you get him to turn around please?'

This was too much for the PA. The thought of asking the Secretary of State for Foreign Affairs of Her Britannic Majesty's Government to turn around so that an IO could check his passport was beyond the pale.

'But he's the Foreign Secretary. Surely you know him?'

'Never met him,' Derek said and then raised his voice, 'Mr. Call-ag-han, could you turn this way please?' The PA crumpled into the concertina doors, hoping that they would eat her and the Right Hon. James Callaghan, MP, turned and waved at Derek. 'Thank you sir.'

The rest were easy.

And when they had all tramped up the steps and were safely on board, the significance of the phrase, 'chokky bikkies' was revealed to me. As the aircraft taxied away, in one body the customs officers, special branch and IOs turned and stampeded back into the building, through the concertina doors they raced and sharp right to the table where the percolator was still bubbling. Scrabbling hands fought over two plates. Derek turned, a chocolate digestive biscuit held daintily in his fingers.

'Chokky bikkies,' he said. 'It's what the job is all about.'

Well, they had not told me that on the training course.

I was to make another visit to the VIP terminal before my training at Heathrow was finished, in different company and for different passengers. HRH Princess Alexandra was due in on the Queen's Flight. We motored over, thankfully not in the deathtrap Mini, and stood outside the building whilst she disembarked from the plane. A green Austin 1800 drove up to the foot of the steps, she got in and was whisked away. As the car swept past the short line of officials who were trying not to look too deferential but were nevertheless standing almost to attention, Princess Alexandra turned and gave us a huge grin and a frantic wave. Caught unawares, we all waved back as if she was just our cousin going home and then we saw each other doing it and felt embarrassed.

But Heathrow had not finished my education. One sunny Saturday afternoon I drove in for a late shift which would finish at midnight. The traffic into the airport was unusually heavy and I supposed it to be because it was the weekend. Then we all stopped and did not move. Nobody was going anywhere. I eventually joined some others and pulled off the road and parked on the middle of the roundabout. There we waited. A bomb had just exploded in the multi-storey car park at Terminal One. The central area was now closed. We sat there in the gentle haze of falling kerosene and cooked in the afternoon heat. After a long delay, the traffic began to move once again and, an hour late, I made it to the staff car park, northside. Traffic had all been diverted around the perimeter road which was two lanes only and our shuttle bus was no exception.

We crawled and sweltered and swore. We were not allowed to alight because no pedestrians were permitted so we were trapped. Happily for the drivers who had arrived at the airport behind us, the act of diverting us around the scenic route now freed up the road to the centre. When I arrived on duty, the later shift had already been working for half an hour. I was sure that this sort of disturbance was not going to occur down at Dover. It had only been a small bomb and nobody had been hurt. The only effect I could distinguish was a scorch mark on the brickwork and the bizarre sight of a car park full of cars all with their boot lids raised, presumably by the shock of the explosion. I did not take the threat seriously. Bombs were for other people. Within a few months the IRA had killed two in a pub in Guildford, two more in a pub in Woolwich, twenty one with one hundred and twenty injured in Birmingham and finished off with a Christmas bombing campaign in London.

Perhaps some of what they told us at Lunar House had been important.

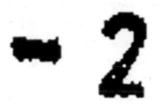

'Do you play football?'

I looked up from my file of General Instructions that I was updating. My inquisitor's eyes were brown and surmounted a big black bushy beard. That was practically all you could see of his face.

'No, sorry, I don't.'

'Squash? Tennis?'

'Nope. I don't do any sport at all.'

'What's the name of the other trainee? Does he play football?'

'Peter. And you can always ask him.'

He tapped the top of my table decisively and got up and went away. It seemed that whilst the Home Office thought that it had posted me to Dover in order to stamp passports and generally operate the immigration control, the port was rather hoping that I had been sent there to supplement the football team, take part in the squash tournament or play bridge. This was the third interruption I had been subjected to that morning.

At the moment my days were taken up with 'getting my instructions up to date' and trying to find my way around my place of work. This latter was not as simple as it sounded. Most immigration offices have certain common ground in their appointments because of their common function: they all must provide an area in which IOs can examine passports and an office in which they can follow up any enquiries and maintain any ongoing cases. So far, so good, but the needs of the shipping companies, airlines and ports are not those of the Home Office. For the comfort of their passengers, the carrying companies desire the passport checkpoint to be as near the gangway or aircraft as possible. The port authorities have to move hordes of people quickly and so want to keep space unembrangled to allow smooth passage. The more people they can get through the port, the more money they make. The IOs usually want to walk the shortest distance from their cup of tea to the passenger. All these different needs and desires cannot mutually exist.

At Eastern Docks, Dover, the country's busiest twenty-four hour ferry port, the other ceaseless activity, after passenger handling, was construction. If the harbour board was not demolishing a building it was relaying a road or reclaiming some more of the seabed to extend the lorry parking area. It was obvious that if they continued their reclamation apace then soon there would be no need for ferries at all, you would merely drive across to Calais.

I joined the port when they had just abandoned the use of the upstairs coach examination hall. This was a shame since at that time the IO's desks had been about twenty feet from the door of the general office. The coaches did not drive upstairs of course, they remained at ground level and discharged their passengers who then clambered onto the escalator to whisk them up to the examination hall. All right in theory but the increase in traffic frequently led to times when the hall became full and the passengers found themselves trying to mark time backwards on a moving escalator as they queued to reach our desks.

Vehicles are a terrible complication to passenger handling. At Terminal Three, passengers could disembark from all destinations into any part of the terminal building but they would all end up walking down the final corridor and into the arrivals hall. It is not so easy if some are in motor cars, others in coaches and yet others driving forty-foot long articulated lorries. That kind of traffic does not mix well together. In 1974, eight thousand cars a day were passing through the port at busy periods. For reasons of safety and practicality the various categories needed to be segregated. Thus at Dover East there was a car arrivals point, represented by an enormous car park leading to three double-sided car kiosks, and a foot passenger arrivals hall. To one side of this the walking passengers were brought from the gangway by the buses belonging to the shipping companies and on the other side of the building the tour coaches unloaded their own group passengers. The two streams of humanity met in the hall, passed through the passport and customs control and then reboarded their coaches or buses to continue their journeys. Further seaward of this, built on reclaimed land was an edifice described as the 'freight control'. This was an office built high enough for the IO to see into the cabs of the arriving lorries without having to climb a ladder.

But tourists have to be checked going out of the country as well as going in and, as the port ran day and night, it was impossible to operate the system used in many other ferry ports where the same kiosks would be worked in one direction for the arrival and then in the other for the departure. At Dover East the traffic was non-stop, so they had to provide a duplicate set of control installations for embarking passengers.

To maintain some semblance of order the port was organised on a one-way system. All embarking traffic moved towards the ferries down the landward side of the port, skirting the foot of the famous white cliffs, and all arriving traffic passed down the seaward side. Through this arrangement, inevitably, was weaved an intricate network of port service roads for vehicles which were not travelling abroad but which nevertheless needed access to the port.

How this impinged upon the IO was that in order to get to the point at which he had to be working at any one time involved a mixed salad of corridors, staircases, zigzags and double-backs, covered walkways, sliding doors, chain-link fenced compounds, doors which had to be locked and unlocked and the odd busy road. Not quite the twenty-foot stroll from the cup of tea.

Somebody had agreed with the harbour board that as the traffic was continuous then there would be certain parts of the immigration controls which would always be manned: cars inwards and foot passengers inwards for example. Any such position was known as a 'fixed point' and the officer assigned to it had to sit there even if his colleagues had cleared off for a break.

To staff such an arrangement must have been a nightmare and was not palliated in any way by the travelling public's expectation that the maximum number of officers should be on duty when their particular ship docked. This was a demand strangely at odds with the same public's vigorous protestations about civil servants sitting around all day drinking tea. In their view we never had enough people on duty when the ships were in port and too many when they were not. What were we supposed to do with the staff during the lulls – put them in cryogenic storage? On the long timescale one could make a fairly accurate prediction of busy times and then staff the port accordingly. Known peaks were the last weekend before Christmas, Easter, the third week in July when the schools broke up and the second and third weeks of September when the foreign university students arrived. Added to these would be the odd wild cards such as the trendy post-Christmas rush of Range Rovers to the ski slopes.

On a daily basis we had a sailing schedule which gave the timetable of arrivals and departures. It was not an even flow throughout the twenty-four hours. The shipping companies wanted to catch the most custom and to do that you had to sail at the times that the public required. Everybody wanted to leave Dover at a time which would get them to the Continent in time for lunch but they wanted to arrive in the UK at half past one in the afternoon. Of course, knowing which ships were arriving from which ports at which times was all very useful but the schedule did not say how many passengers would be on board. That information would be passed to us by telephone some time before the expected arrival. And it could be fifteen passengers or fifteen hundred.

To accommodate all these variables it was necessary for the IOs to work a shift pattern. The rotation could not be regular as in a factory with three eight-hour shifts, each one handing over in timely fashion to its successor, because the density of the diurnal traffic was greater than the nocturnal. Additionally, the pattern had to provide coverage seven days a week, all year around.

So when I started at the port I was required to work shifts from a selection starting at 06.30, 07.30, 11.30, 13.30, 15.30, 18.00 or 19.00. If this were not enough, the shift changed daily; you did not do a week of one type of shift. It was almost as if the management did not want you to get too comfortable and just to ensure this, only two of those shifts had a meal break in them. What? That cannot be true. Oh yes it was. It had been agreed with the union that, when possible, the meal break would be provided as the last hour of the duty, giving the officer the choice of eating or going home. Probably the most destructive was the 06.30 start. Just reflect a while. You get up at about 05.30 in order to be at the office within an hour. How much breakfast can you eat at that time of the morning? You are then scheduled on continuous duty until 14.00. This means that you started work before most people have eaten breakfast and will finish after most people have eaten lunch and you will do so without a meal break.

Of course, it did not work like that. You tried to arrange within your shift to cover for people whilst they nipped up to the canteen and grabbed a quick snack, but there was absolutely no guarantee that you would get any food and many a time I finished a duty with acid swilling around an empty stomach. How I did not develop ulcers I cannot say.

This was the milieu I was dropped into when I began my initial three week's service under the eyes of a local mentor. His name was Bert and he was a neatly-dressed Liverpuddlean of twelve year's seniority. I was told that this put him in the field for promotion to chief immigration officer. It also made him liable to transfer to the airport. He diligently cultivated an apparent indifference to what I was doing but nevertheless always managed to step in just before I made the big mistake. Unless, of course, he had decided that I needed to commit the gaffe in order to learn how to clear it up. I was to learn over the years that I owed more than I realised to Bert. He was softly spoken and this, coupled with his dry sense of humour, could be devastatingly funny or sometimes just devastating.

On my very first day wielding a stamp he pointed out to me a chief immigration officer who was talking to a colleague two desks away.

'That CIO there is called Alan Cottage. He is well known.'

As the man was in obvious earshot I took up the cue to enquire as to the source of his celebrity.

'What is he well-known for?'

'Being a bastard.'

The arrow went home.

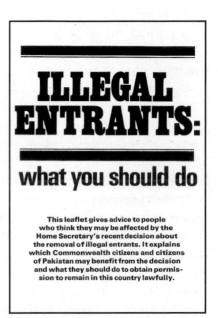

WHAT IS THE POINT OF ME BEING HERE?

This leaflet explained the Home Secretary's amnesty of 11 April 1974 which allowed certain illegal entrants to remain indefinitely in the UK. It even told some of those whom we had managed to find and remove from the UK that they could come back!

ILLEGAL ENTRANTS:

what you should do

This leaflet gives advice to people who think they may be affected by the Home Secretary's recent decision about the removal of illegal entrants. It explains which Commonwealth citizens and citizens of Pakistan may benefit from the decision and what they should do to obtain permission to remain in this country lawfully.

I don't really pay much attention to politics so I did not know whether it was a Conservative or a Labour Home Secretary who declared an amnesty for illegal immigrants on 11 April 1974, but it coincided almost to the day with my appointment as an immigration officer. I found it confusing to start off a new job by going backwards; the old lags were incandescent. Whose side was the Home Secretary on? The amnesty only covered a precise sector, to wit, those Commonwealth citizens or Pakistani nationals who had entered the UK illegally on or after 9 March 1968 and before 1 January 1973. Those who thought they qualified were invited by the leaflet to make themselves known by presenting themselves at their local immigration office with their passport and other proofs of residence.

As it turned out, the amnesty provided us with some interesting refusals. Some people who had overstayed their permission to stay turned up and happily gave us the proof of their misbehaviour before learning that they did not qualify for the amnesty. Others who had become illegal entrants either before or after the date tried to prove their eligibility by describing their journey across the Channel in an open boat. Some claimed to have crossed in only thirty minutes. We managed to torpedo false claims by asking the Meteorological Office what the weather was like in the Channel on the date they crossed and then comparing it to their account. But leaving these highlights aside, I think many IOs found it unsettling to believe that if things got tough then the government could just surrender in such a manner. Did it not throw into question their understanding of our purpose?

An incident which marked me during my mentorship was, without wishing to sound too pompous, a demonstration of the risks of being in the front line of the country's defence. Bert and I were squatting in our colleagues' kiosk, having a chat between ships. Under the bench was a rattling fan heater which was warming up the dust and blowing it out. Our kiosk in the other lane had no working heater and so was cold and empty. I was feeling cold and empty despite sitting in the full blast of the heater. When I started to shiver they realised that something was wrong and sent me home. I rang the doctor whose welcoming introduction was, 'Look, you can't just ring up doctors at any time of the night you know.'

Over the next three weeks my joints came up in the ugly stinging red blotches of prickly heat, I had pains in my chest and I turned yellow. The doctor took a blood sample and prescribed a peppermint concoction to ease my wind. The symptoms eventually dissipated and I collected my doctor's note allowing me to return to work. At the door I suddenly turned. 'Just a minute. This note says, 'Hepatitis B'.'

'Yes, that is what you had. Next patient please.'

One evening, Bert took me down to visit a ship. This was strictly unofficial and frowned upon by the inspectors, probably because they could not get away with it. Some of the CIOs knew ship's captains or, more usefully, pursers and when their ship was in the berth they might nip down for a quick bit of socialising which usually involved the consumption of alcohol at duty-free prices. In our case, it was curiosity. The French branch of Sealink had brought in their new ship, the m.v *Chartres*, and as it was the most modern vessel on the run, we wanted to see it.

We boarded via the vehicle ramp and I was struck by the courteous, almost subservient, attitude of the personnel. We were only British immigration officers but they treated us as if we had real power and importance and influence. It was quite a shock to the system. We never got that recognition in England. We shook hands with the purser and he took us on a tour of the vessel. I was worried that he might have mistaken us for an official visit of some sort but it was not so. The Continental attitude was to equate us with their police force and if we were in civvies, then we must be several grades up the ladder. The lasting impression I derived from this visit was of an interior decoration which seemed to have been moulded from buttercup yellow and pea green melamine. I wondered what sort of influence such a colour scheme might have upon tender stomachs in a force nine.

All the ferries operating out of Dover were known as 'ro-ro' ferries – roll on, roll off. This signified that you could drive on one end of the ship and out of the other. Astonishing as it may seem to modern minds, this has not always been the case. Leaving aside the early ferries where cars were lifted aboard on a crane, some had only stern doors so the vehicles had to either find some way to turn around inside the ship or reverse on to the ship in order to disembark forwards. With a ro-ro ship if you loaded through the stern you discharged through the bows. This dictated how you docked. If you berthed 'backwards' in Dover then you had to berth 'forwards' in Calais otherwise all the vehicles would be pointing in the wrong direction. The *Chartres* was the only ferry that always berthed bow first at Dover; all the others berthed stern first. I thought it might be dictated by the difficulties of navigating within the different ports but as at some point you have to reverse out of somewhere, I never understood what the difference was. It seemed to be six of one and half a dozen of the other.

The visiting of ships was a risky business, undertaken as it was in working time and hopefully when nothing was discharging. One CIO at Dover went down for a liquid breakfast one morning and was horrified to hear the purser making the sailing announcements. He hurried down to the car deck where his fears were confirmed. The ramp was up. The ferry was ready to sail.

'British Immigration,' he snapped smartly at the deck officer. 'Chief immigration officer. I need to go ashore. Just been visiting.'

'Sorry sir, the ramp is up. I need captain's orders to lower it. We shall be leaving in five minutes.'

The frantic CIO was calculating the double crossing time and working out in his head when he would again be in Dover. It did not look good. He would not be able to cover his absence for four hours.

'But you are leaving early,' he protested.

'We can leave up to fifteen minutes early if we wish. It's in regulations.'

'Look, I need to get off. It's important. I am one of Her Majesty's chief immigration officers.'

His pomposity normally served him well. It had no effect on the deck officer. At that moment another man appeared behind him.

'Why is the ramp up? I want to go ashore.'

'Sorry sir, as I have been explaining to this gentleman–'

'–I am a chief immigration officer.'

'Well I am the Sunblest man,' said the newcomer. 'And my van is on the quayside. If you don't let me off you'll get no bread tomorrow.'

Down went the ramp.

Then the great day came when I was on my own. I almost expected the other officers to realise and point me out but with the staggered pattern of shifts and permutations of annual leave I was completely unknown to three quarters of the eighty-five officer complement of the port at that time. The first time out on the desk all on your own is as frightening as driving solo after passing your driving test. What do I do? What is this? Where should I be? How do I land this passenger?

I braved my way through and tried not to make it too obvious when I had to unlock my case and refer to my forty chapters of General Instructions to find out how to land the wife of the domestic servant of an iron curtain diplomat not accredited to the Court of St James's or a Jewish Talmudical student coming for medical treatment. Thankfully, a large proportion of the traffic was innocuous: French and Belgian day trippers coming to strip the town of butter and wallpaper. The 1970s was a period when the pound was in decline and thus the prices in our shops were well below those across the Channel. The pillage was further fuelled by the ticket-pricing structure. The inequality of the traffic flows within the day meant that ferries carried more passengers towards the Continent in the mornings than they brought back so to fill up the ships on the return journeys the shipping companies adjusted the tariffs such that it became cheaper for a French or a Belgian to come to the UK than it was for a Briton to travel abroad. The microeconomics of it all did not bother me; the shoppers provided the necessary cannon fodder for me to familiarise myself with the mechanics of being one of Her Majesty's immigration officers.

A desktop can become a crowded environment when one has to make room on it for a large directory of naughty names, a metal-cased endorsing stamp on an inkpad, a tray of wooden-blocked rubber stamps of varying sizes, a stack of blank landing cards, a stack of completed landing cards, two stacks of different official forms and a pen. Somewhere on the table you need a space to lay the passport without rubbing your shirtcuffs in the inkpad or stamping your fingers. The latter was not such an uncommon occurrence since at that time we still endorsed French passports and these were bound as a blue plastic booklet. The spine was so tight that you needed to hold the passport open and flat with one hand whilst stamping in the space between your splayed fingers with the other. I found that if I achieved that task without impressing words onto my finger tips then I would discover ink smears on my shirt cuffs.

The Immigration Act requires the IO to give a written notice of the permission to enter to the passenger. To enable us to do this we were furnished with a selection of rubber stamps bearing the conditions which we desired to impose upon the passenger's stay. But now we were in the Common Market, some nationalities could travel here on their identity cards. An identity card has no pages. We could not stamp it. To solve this problem the Home Office invented the form IS120 – a folded sheet of paper written in six languages and provided with a space in which the IO could endorse his date stamp. They printed half a million. We had been using them for several months before a Danish passenger wrote in to the Home Office to ask why the Danish version of the text was entitled, '*Notice to all arse wipers*'?

Watching the other officers I noticed that there were as many different ways of using a landing stamp as there were wielders. Some grabbed it in a clenched fist, smacked it down on the passport and jerked it brutally forwards onto the flange to achieve the 'roll' whilst others ignored the wooden handle and held it elegantly by the metal body, placing it with precision and gentleness onto its target. I eventually adopted a mixture of the two by holding the metal base but hooking my index finger over the top of the handle to assist in effecting the roll. Now, as I write this, nearly four decades later, my right index finger is inevitably the one with the arthritic joint. All those years of crashing shocks onto the underneath of the knuckle has taken its toll.

However, what the future might hold for me was not part of my concern during the early days, for the present I was having problems with the clerical side of the job. The landing cards presented by the passengers had to be annotated correctly so that they could take their proper place up in the funnily shaped room at Traffic Index. As a sprog my cards had to be submitted via my team CIO whose job it was to check them and send them back to me if they were faulty. 'Where is the passport number?' he might demand. There is a limit to the number of times you can write,

'Regret not noted' and still expect a good staff report.

One day I was flicking my cards into the various pigeon holes when the sight of a pair of them gave me a sudden cold feeling in my stomach. I put them to the bottom of my handful and finished my sorting then I went and sat quietly in the corner. I laid the cards carefully on the table before me and inspected them. They were the record of the stamps that I had endorsed in the passports of a Spanish work permit holder and his French wife. I had landed the Spaniard in accordance with the permit for the requested twelve months with the condition that he register with the police. That was fine. His wife I had landed for twelve months with a condition prohibiting all employment, also with the police registration condition. This was just a trifle awkward in that, unlike Spain, she was in the Common Market as was the UK. The only permission I could grant her under those circumstances was to stay for six months as a visitor and instruct her to apply to the Home Office for an extension of her stay. She had a Treaty right to work in the UK. I had denied her that right. She could sue the Home Office. She could sue me.

Unable to think of a way out before laying my head on the block, at the end of my duty I lodged the cards safely in my locker with my equipment. At the start and finish of every duty thereafter I experienced a pang of panic and misery as the sight of the cards reminded me that I was no nearer finding a solution. I dared not submit them to my CIO, it would generate disciplinary procedures which would jeopardise my chance of passing my two year probation. If I somehow bypassed him and just put them in with the other cards then the clerk would send them up to Lunar House and they would have a record of my mistake. Then I would get the dreaded news, 'you've got a file back from HQ.' I thought of the wretched IO at Luton for whom I had ensured that he got a bollocking and I remembered the excoriating reaction of my trainee colleague at Terminal Three. The longer I delayed solving the problem the worse it would be. One morning, I could stand the strain no longer. I took the two cards into the lavatory, tore them up into minute pieces and flushed them away. Now the only evidence was the stamps in their passports. I got back to work and held my breath for a year.

When I look back on it now, I laugh, as you can when relieved of the pressures and stresses of the time. When training at Lunar House had I not seen an enormous room stuffed full of cards? Why on earth should I be scared that somebody would pick my particular card out of the millions and declare that I had used the wrong stamps? But I did not get off entirely scot free. Many months later I was accosted by a colleague whom

I knew to be younger and smarter than me. Unfortunately he knew it as well.

'Three-twenty. That's your stamp number isn't it?' You always dread an opening such as that. It can easily be the hors d'oeuvres to a menu of complaint. I nodded pleasantly. 'I just saw a very interesting endorsement on embarks.'

'Oh really?'

'Yes. A French lady, twelve months code three with police registration.'

By this time I was feeling considerably more confident in the job so I laughed. That caught him by surprise. 'With a Spanish husband on a work permit?' I asked.

'Yes. I've just seen them embarking. He's finished his job and they're going home now.'

'Well, no harm done then. Obviously a good landing.'

'She even went along to the Aliens Registration Office and got herself registered by the police.'

'They haven't got a clue have they?'

He shook his head as if trying to work out how the discussion had turned to this. 'I don't know how you got away with it,' he said.

Neither did I but I did not admit it.

In the early days the simple task of just being in the right place at the right time was difficult for me. Every duty within a shift was numbered and each duty was different. The geographical position of every IO was decreed for every hour within the duty. For example, although two IOs might both be scheduled an A duty and both start at 06.30, the IO allotted duty A1 might spend his first two hours working on cars inwards whilst his colleague on A2 might be on walkers inwards. Every hour on the hour, somewhere in the port, IOs would be changing places. It was like a timetabled version of musical chairs.

One evening I was sitting in a car kiosk with a colleague, gazing at the empty car park before me, aware that it would shortly be filling up with lines of cars for over to my right I could see the Zeebrugge ferry turning around prior to backing in to the berth to unload. We were chatting about the inconsequential things you do when you know that your conversation is likely to be interrupted at any moment and that the opportunity to continue it might not arise for a few weeks. He was a 'late' man. That is to say, he had started work at 15.30 and would go home at midnight. I was a 'night' man. I had started my duty at 19.30 and would not get away until 08.00 on the following day. The telephone rang. He picked it up. He looked across at me.

'Yeah, he's here.' He handed me the receiver. It was Greening, a CIO whom I vaguely knew worked across the bay at Dover West. What on earth could he want me for?

'You should have started an hour ago,' he snapped. 'Why aren't you here?'

I was dumbfounded. 'But I'm a Dover East IO. Are you sure you've got the right person?'

'Are you N12?'

I looked in my diary. That was the number of my duty. 'Yes.'

'Then you should be over here. We've been waiting for you. N12 starts at the West and works here until midnight and then goes across to the East.'

I had never heard of anything so daft in all my life.

'Apparently I'm supposed to be at the West,' I said as I began to pack my equipment back into my case.

'You'd better hurry up, the cars are just coming.'

I quickly stepped out of the door of the kiosk on my side and waved to the marshal to show him that I was closing my lane. He gave me a disgusted nod of his head. I could tell what he was thinking. 'Bloody civil servants sit around chatting and as soon as the work arrives then they clear off.'

I hurried up to the general office and locked away my Dover East stamps. Dover West would have to issue me with local stamps when I got there. I had never actually been to the immigration office at the Western Docks. I had passed through the port on several occasions as a passenger but when you are going on holiday you never really pay any attention to the port. You are too busy dragging baggage along platforms, searching for passports and tickets, looking for a luggage trolley and then worrying whether you will be standing up all the way to Calais.

I was not sure of the best route to get there. As I drove over unlit cobbles and swerved around the discarded articulated trailers that seemed to be littered everywhere I was painfully aware that I had already blotted my copy book by not turning up on time. If I got lost on the way there I would be a laughing stock – the two ports were less than two miles apart.

I managed to find a parking space by the white Victorian monolith of Southern House and tramped down the quay to the immigration office.

The next few hours were a blur of sensations, mostly unsettling. I was in the other world. This was railway architecture with bits bolted on, not the smooth glass and steel vision of the East. I found myself standing at a ridiculously small wooden desk which had no protective back. We were spread in a crescent around a tiled floor and the arriving passengers were let in to the arena like Christians at the amphitheatre by a grizzled man in an ill-fitting British Rail uniform.

I dealt with a Swedish student and then an American holidaymaker and was about to start interviewing a third passenger when the Swede reappeared at my desk.

'I need the card. You kept my card.' He pointed at his landing card.

'No I keep that card now.'

'But I need it to get out.'

'No you don't. I've stamped your passport. I keep the card.'

He did not seem convinced but he grumbled off. Some passengers have strange ideas, I decided. I was a little perturbed whilst I was talking to the Frenchman standing before me, to see, over his shoulder, the Swede and the American both queuing up to see me again. What was going on? As soon as I stamped the Frenchman the Swede was at me again.

'You must giff me the card. The man said so.'

I glanced at the British Rail scarecrow who was waving passengers across to the various desks as they became free. 'No you don't have it.'

'I've gotta have my card as well,' the American called over the Swede's shoulder.

I turned to the IO on the nearest desk to my left. 'What's going on? They're all asking for their landing cards back.'

He stamped a Canadian passport, slipped the landing card in it and handed the lot back to the passenger. 'You have to put the card back in the passport so that they can get out of the hall.' He pointed at a stream of exiting passengers. 'They have to surrender it to get out.'

'I'm glad nobody told me,' I said.

'You're supposed to know these things, thicko.'

At that moment I lurched forwards from a blow to my back. I half turned to find a large youth with a rucksack struggling through a door which I had not noticed in the partitioning behind me.

'So what's this then?' I asked my font of information. 'Where has he come from?'

'Thrown out of the British queue.'

I deduced from that response that the British control – the checking of British passports – was taking place out of sight on the other side of the partitions behind me. And on we stamped. I gradually accustomed myself to slotting the cards back into the passports and to the possibility of the odd reject flattening me across the desktop as he bounded unannounced through the door. I thought I was coping quite well until somebody presented me with a yellow landing card. All landing cards were white. He had got hold of an embarkation card.

'They've given you the wrong card,' I sighed. 'Fill that one in.'

Have you any idea how long it takes to fill in a landing card? If you are waiting, it takes ages. 'How long are you staying here?'

'I am Finnish.'

'I know that, I can tell from your passport. It says, "*Suomi Finland*" on the cover.' I am aware that irony is always lost on foreigners but I find it too tempting sometimes. 'How long are you staying here?'

'I stayed two months.'

'What will you do here?'

'I visit my girlfriend.'

'When do you go back to Finland?'

'I go now. I am Finnish.'

I know you are bloody Finnish. Something was not working in this conversation. I could see from his passport that he had been here before so he was unlikely to be much of a problem. Except that although I could see his UK landing stamp, I could not see when he had embarked. I leafed through his passport as he watched me. The more I searched, the more confused I became. Back to the front pages again and study that landing stamp. He had come in via this port two months earlier. I looked up and then glanced across at my Western colleagues. They were wielding their embarkation stamps and endorsing yellow embarkation cards like ones demented.

'Just a minute.' I leaned over to my colleague. 'Are we by any chance now doing an embarkation?'

'You Dover East IOs, you're really on the ball aren't you?' He banged his stamp down. 'Ostender. Sails in twenty minutes.'

I dared not admit that I had never embarked a passenger in my life. I had never had the chance at Terminal Three and at Dover East in the summer the embarkation control was manned by a special team which worked seasonally. I hauled my case up from the depths of my underdesk and then scrabbled in it to find my triangular embarkation stamp. I banged it down on his passport and handed it back. He had not been reassuring me of his nationality when he had insisted upon being Finnish. He had been telling me that his stay in England had come to an end.

Things were not progressing smoothly for me. An IO doing his two years of probation is assessed every six months. At the first interview my team CIO observed that I was having problems with the mechanical parts of the job – using the right stamps, putting the correct notes on the landing cards and sorting them correctly. It was true. At the twelve month interview my CIO highlighted the fact that I had had to write an appeal statement thirteen times before it had been approved. For the first year, every time a probationer IO refused entry to a passenger he had to write a complete appeal statement. This was a policy designed to give him expertise in this particular field. It was a drudge. The only workable format was the, 'I asked him... he told me...' layout. When it came to the section justifying the legality of his actions the IO was obliged to quote the relative paragraph of the immigration rules word for word. Ancient IOs would reminisce of the good old days when a couple of lines scrawled on a minute sheet pinned inside the file was sufficient. The apocryphal, *'No money, no tickets, no chance,'* was often quoted as the shortest refusal report ever submitted. It seemed that I was incapable of presenting an argument logically and chronologically and was prone to omitting the bits that others considered to be the most important. The next intake of trainees were already outshining me. I needed an opportunity to make my mark.

It was twenty to seven in the morning. I was on an early duty which put me on the desk at seven but I had gone down early to the fixed point on the embark control to relieve the night man so that he could go home. It was dead. The harbour board marshal was walking up and down outside the shed, swinging his arms about and shifting the ropes and poles into a straight line with his foot. Seagulls were wheeling about high above us. Out in the open, he was vulnerable; in my kiosk built inside the warehouse-like shed, I was safe. I was double wrapped. He removed his peaked cap and inspected the lining, then he replaced it. I viewed the pile of virgin embarkation cards and pondered whether to start building a card house. I had once managed to get to three storeys before being interrupted.

Activity. The marshal straightened, raised his arm and beckoned to a Morris Marina which was wandering down the road by the cliff. He spoke to the driver, checked that he had already filled in his embarkation card, and then pointed him over to my kiosk. I slid back the perspex window at the side of me and stuck out my arm, knowing that despite the enormous *'STOP'* which was painted on the road, the red traffic light burning by my left ear and the signboard bearing the slogan, *'Passport control'*, it was always a mystery to car drivers as to where they were supposed to go.

A blue passport came through the window. A few months earlier, the Turks had invaded the island of Cyprus. The result from our point of view was that we received various instructions from the Home Office on how to deal with the flood of Greek Cypriot refugees who were sure to stampede to the UK. Here I had a Greek Cypriot who was going home. How bizarre was that? And he was in the book. I looked again to make sure. Yes, it was him. I could tell from the entry that it was a security matter. I rang the bell and the marshal hurried over, glad of an interruption to his boredom.

'Can you just put him over there for a minute please?' I pointed to an empty lane in the shed.

'Yup, but he's on the Zeebrugge. That'll be loading shortly.'

'Thanks, I'll bear that in mind.' I picked up the internal phone and rang SB. 'I've got someone for you on car embarks.'

'Can you hang onto him? I'll send someone down.'

'I'll hang onto him for as long as I can, but that's limited, as you know.' Special Branch did know but were always willing to forget it and try to persuade us to use our powers under the Immigration Act to detain suspects for them to question. 'As far as I am concerned he is OK. He's not overstayed, his passport is in order, he's going the right way. I can't hold him.'

'I'll send someone down.'

There was usually an SB officer in attendance on embarks, looking over our shoulder and whispering in our ear. We had to make sure that we handed the passport back to the passenger and not to the police officer. It was the police officer's initiative to ask the passenger for his passport; not our job to turn him over to the fuzz. In the past, IOs had been rapped over the knuckles when detained police suspects had complained that they had been 'handed over to the police'. But there was no risk of that for me. There was no SB presence to be found.

At five to seven the marshal wandered over, waving his radio.

'They are closing the embarks for the Zeebrugge.' He nodded at the Morris Marina.

'OK,' I shrugged and handed him the Cypriot passport. 'Send him on his way.'

At seven o'clock I was relieved by the incoming officer and went up to the general office to dig out the suspect circular on my Cypriot. He was an EOKA-B terrorist bomber. I was utterly ignorant of the politics of the eastern Mediterranean but could vaguely remember a bloody campaign of terrorism and bombing in Cyprus when I was still at school, in which the British army seemed always to be the target. So why was a terrorist bomber going to Cyprus in the middle of a civil-war type conflict? I would never know and nor would Special Branch. The police officer tracked me down later in the day for a copy of the embark card. He said that he had managed to nip on to the ferry before sailing and had an announcement made to call the chap to the purser's office, but he had not materialised. I sympathised with him. There was not much more I could do. My moment of glory had escaped me once more.

I was still failing to generate that 'high quality casework' that my team leader expected of me. Refusing unemployed young Moroccan men who were coming to visit English girls whom they had met on holiday was not really anything to boast of. The Moroccans were not refused on some kind of racial purity grounds; it was simply that they were coming here to work. They nearly all carried their work references with them. The only amusement you derived was when you got to telephone some address in Cheltenham and ask the mother if she was awaiting the arrival of a Moroccan waiter who had intimated that he was going to stay with her daughter. The plum-in-the-mouth *mater familias* usually choked on the stone. I am sure many a young girl was given a stern talking-to about the advisability of handing out her address to holiday romancers. No, you didn't score many points for 'knocking off' Moroccan waiters.

Some of the veterans pretended to regret our joining the Common Market because now they had to land Italians who, under the Treaty, had the right to come here to look for work. In the old days the IO would simply search his baggage and refuse him for possessing a pair of black trousers and an alarm clock. The former were to be worn in the dining room, the latter allowed him to grab his afternoon nap before the evening's employment.

'Anybody with a green passport? Knock him off.' Casper would count them on his nicotine-stained fingers, 'Italy, Morocco, Tunisia, Algeria, Spain – all green passports you see. Stone cold knock-offs.'

'What about Belgium, Germany and Austria? They also have green passports.'

'Don't be facetious. Have some respect for your elders.'

One nationality which kept slipping through the net was the Iranian. The Immigration Service was the front line for trends. We saw them first. We noticed the variations in the traffic flows. By the time that the Home Office had seen them and had drawn up their charts and tabulations, it was too late. Why were all these young Iranians coming to England to learn English? We all knew that it was because they did not want to live in Iran. They had no right to settle in England but under the rules then in force, if they had enrolled for a course in English language at a recognised educational institution, had paid for the course, could support themselves without working, which they all could, and stated an intention of returning to their own country at the termination of their studies, which they all did, then there was nothing much we could do. This rankled with many of my colleagues who apparently wanted to alter the ethnic composition of the United Kingdom single handed. I was of the opinion that we should not be trying to do anything. The rules were there. If they operated within the rules and qualified for entry then so be it. There was no place in the procedure for our feelings and prejudices. It was not our fault if the government had brought in rules which were not producing the results that they desired. But I did not tell my colleagues of my belief. I moaned and vilified the Iranians as much as the next.

Madge was in the next kiosk to me. We were both waiting for the Sealink Calais to unload. Madge was one of the first female IOs to be appointed and the Immigration Service was one of the very last departments in the Civil Service to admit women. Despite the presence of the fairer sex, the Service was still blatantly and sometimes brutally, male. We were supposed to be all lads together. We were tough, we were men. We could take it. Unheated kiosks, smelly lorry drivers, stand-up toilets, we could cope with them all. The folklore was stuffed with incidents of IOs covering for colleagues who had been too drunk on duty to stand up or reports of wives enquiring about absent husbands and being told on the telephone that they had been sent to clear the Zagreb train when they were actually shacked up with their fancy bit.

With the arrival of the women, the men had to learn manners and try to join the human race. It is astonishing how primitive they were. Casper recounted how, in the early weeks, the IOs were sitting in the rest room between arrivals. Madge was knitting; the men were trying to converse without swearing and to watch the television without mentioning anybody's tits or arse. Eventually Madge went down to the general office to collect her case and as the door closed behind her, to a man, the IOs rocked in their chairs and let rip a symphony of farts which they had been bottling up.

Douglas made no concessions whatsoever. He was a hard-drinking Scot who had no place in his life for women. He ignored them utterly. He would not talk to them. He would not register their presence. He did not reply to their salutations. If a woman IO came and occupied the second place in his kiosk he would hold up his hand to the marshal to stop the traffic flow, pack up his kit and move to another kiosk.

The feminine invasion of some of the immigration offices in the older, unmodernised ports was sometimes delayed by the building modifications that were necessary to the accommodation: the ports had no ladies' toilets. I was outside all of this. Almost half the trainees on my course had been women; I had always worked in a mixed environment and liked it. Men on their own are stupid, boring and boorish. So I looked across the tarmac and waved to Madge. She waved back then she pushed back her window.

'What's on the Hengist?' she called.

'Forty-seven cars,' I shouted back. We were only twenty feet apart but the incessant roaring of lorry engines in the freight queue would drown out a voice at normal pitch.

'Any news on the Ostender?'

'About twenty minutes late.'

'Good.' She looked at her watch. 'I might get away before it.'

These were rash words as it turned out.

The marshal came out of his kiosk and walked towards the stop line before our controls. He had just received news over his radio that the cars were coming off. I tidied up my desk and opened my window. The first car was French with a 'sixty-two' at the end of the licence plate. Every *département* in France was identified by a number corresponding to its position in the alphabetical list. I knew that sixty-two was the Pas de Calais so he was a local from across the water. What was he doing coming over in the early evening – the shops would be shut? He was British, resident in Calais, coming to visit some friends. The next car was a white Renault with sixty-nine as the last two figures. That meant that it was probably an Avis rental car. They always purchased white cars and had registered this year's fleet of vehicles in Lyon. The *préfet* of the *département* of the Rhone had obviously given them a good discount on the regional portion of the national road tax. Next year Avis would court another *préfet*. The following two cars were British and full of day trippers. And so it went on. Forty-seven cars, that would be about twenty-three each. It should have been about twelve each but two of our colleagues had not returned from the pub. It was not their meal break but as they were drinking with the CIO, they were immune from censure. Madge and I were the two idiots.

A Mercedes coupé. It had a miniature black licence plate on the front bumper – that indicated that it was Italian. The orange letters 'NA' told me that it came from Naples. You've got to be rich to drive a Mercedes in Naples. The driver was alone. He handed me his Italian passport in a

waft of expensive after shave and then straightened his silk tie and sat
looking through the windscreen. I always found it intimidating when the
passenger behaved as if our business had been completed with the action
of handing over the passport. As if I were being put in my place. If I could
feel that, was I really in the correct job? On the back seat was a leather
grip. At that moment I noticed that Madge had also got a Mercedes and
the last car in the queue was also a Merc. And it was registered in Naples.

'How long are you staying here?'

'One, two weeks.'

'Where do you go?' He did not understand. 'Address? *Indrizzo?*' I tried
my approximation of Italian. He made a mime of writing so I handed him
a blank landing card and a stationery office pen. He laboriously copied
out an address from a piece of paper. I gazed about as I waited. The
marshal was pulling faces at me. I glanced across at Madge's Mercedes.
There was a hole in the door where the lock should have been. The
driver handed back the card and pen. He was visiting somebody on a farm
near Rayleigh, Essex.

'Friend? Family?' I waved the card at him.

'Si,' was his ambiguous reply.

I closed my window and phoned across to Madge. 'Madge did you know
that the door lock on your Mercedes has been drilled out?'

'How can you tell? Is that important?'

'Have a look at the driver's door on my car will you? Has it got a hole
where the lock should be?'

She stood up and peered across. 'Yes.'

'Is your car registered in Naples?'

'I don't know.'

'Has it got *NA* in orange on the license plate?'

She walked to the back of the kiosk. The telephone fell from the desk
and cut me off. She gave me a pantomime nod as she reassembled her
phone. I pushed open my window.

'Are you two together?' I pointed at Madge's car. '*Amigo?*' I tried.
He shook his head. Have you got the papers for the car?' He could not
understand me again. '*Papier. Machina.*'

'*Ah si, si,*' he handed me a paper from his wallet. I unfolded it. It was
his driving licence.

'*Machina.*' I pointed at the car and waved his licence.

'*Ah si.*' He delved into the glove compartment and pulled out a sheaf
of papers.

I put them on my desk and closed the window. The marshal was twiddling his hat around his fingers, trying to guess which kiosk would be free first for the last car. I phoned Madge again.

'What do you think?' she said. 'I'm fairly happy with mine.'

'Does yours say he is travelling with mine?'

'I haven't asked him.' She turned and spoke to her driver. 'No, he isn't.'

'A bit strange. Three Mercs, all registered in Naples–'

'–Three Mercs?'

I pointed through my window to the last car. 'My driver has the insurance papers in his own name but the car registration document in a different name. He took ages to fill in the landing card – he's not an educated person. He's not a Mercedes driver, he's just dressed up like one. He's not in the book.' I was still on probation so I still had to look everybody up. Madge was an established IO, she could use her discretion.

'What do you think they are then?' she asked.

'I wonder if they've nicked them.'

'But they look the part. Look at their clothes. Oh rats!' she added. 'Mine's in the book.'

I pressed the bell and the marshal raised his eyes heavenward. I filled in and stamped the detention form and handed it to the marshal.

'Just follow that gentleman there,' I said to my Italian. Whilst the marshal led the car over to the compound, I waved the third Mercedes forwards. His door locks were intact but he spoke no English at all. I did not waste my breath. I stamped the form and waved him to follow his mate. Even if he would deny later that he had never set eyes on him before.

We were still working on them forty-five minutes later when the CIO turned up. In order to refuse entry to a passenger an IO must refer his case to a CIO who must authorise the decision. I was slowly beginning to learn that you did not tell the CIO everything in one go. If you did, then he would ask you for some piece of information that you had not acquired and send you back with a flea in your ear and a 'tut' to obtain it. The technique was to present a good case for refusal by divulging all the necessary information, for and against, but retaining some 'extras' so that when cross examined by the CIO, you could satisfy his obscure line of reasoning. Josh Edwards was the CIO – an angelic face topped with a shock of white hair like a blob of whipped cream. A right old woman.

'What is this address in Essex?' he asked.

'It's a farm. SB reckon it is probably a fence for stolen cars. They nick them in Italy, stick them on Motorail in case anybody is looking for them and bring them to England to sell them.'

'And they say that they do not know each other?' he said.

'That's what they say.'

'Can we disprove it?'

'No.'

'Well then—'

'—But they are all three from the same town in Sicily, they are all driving expensive cars to which they do not have the correct papers and two of which have had their door locks drilled out. They all three came on the same Motorail train from Narbonne. You can see the stickers on their windscreens and their ferry tickets issued in Calais have consecutive numbers. On the weight of probabilities, I would say that they were lying.'

'And mine was previously deported from the UK for larceny,' Madge added.

Josh was a one for the ladies. He was particularly attentive to the new, young trainees with their innocent eyes and short skirts. Madge was a different kettle of fish. Nobody messed with Madge. She was almost an honorary man.

'Right,' he said. 'Knock them off.'

Two weeks later I received a letter of commendation from one of the two inspectors for having identified a difficult case after such a short experience of the job. Madge, bless her, had truthfully admitted that she had not noticed the door locks and was not familiar with Italian registration plates.

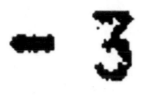

The IOs were divided up into teams, each supervised by a CIO. We did not work in teams as Customs did; working the same shifts in a predictable pattern. The pattern of shifts for IOs was as individual as the number of people performing them. The officers who were on the same early shift with you yesterday, might now be on days off, annual leave, or one of the other duties starting earlier or later in the day. So whilst you might see them again, either your duty would finish before theirs or vice versa. A similar but less complex system of duties applied to the CIOs. Putting the two together meant that the chances of being on duty with your team CIO were fairly slight. And he was the chap who wrote your annual report.

The annual staff report was confidential. In retrospect, the degree of confidentiality was bizarre: the subject of the report was not allowed to see it but at the time we accepted this denial as a matter of fact. When the principle of 'disclosure' was introduced it manifested itself in the CIO hiding the report in a folder on the desk and reading you the bits that you requested. You had to believe that he was reading what was written. By and large I considered that it would have been outside the competence of the CIOs to have extemporised convincingly so they probably were reading what was written down. But they might not have read all of it. We accepted that the management needed to be able to say things about us that we could not know, otherwise how could they manage us? The pertinent criticism, that what was not disclosed was not open to challenge, for some reason always got brushed aside.

To overcome the difficulty of writing a report on a member of staff whom they might have seen on only a few occasions during the reporting period, the CIOs would get together and pool their knowledge, gossip, prejudices, anecdotes and hatreds about the individuals and then go away and write their reports.

What they were marking was performance and promotability. Performance was assessed under the headings of: 'work activity', 'management', 'working relationships,' 'application of knowledge' and 'communication'. As an IO was the lowest grade in the Service, albeit equivalent to the executive officer grade in the mainstream Civil Service, he never had any staff below him so his performance in the 'management' field was usually marked as *'not tested.'* The grading in all these areas was made by ticking a box on a one to five scale. One was 'outstanding,' two: 'significantly above requirements', three: 'fully met the normal requirements of the grade,' four: 'not fully up to requirements, some improvement necessary' and five: 'unacceptable'. If you got a box five you also got a trip to Estabs. in London where they gave you a bollocking and discussed your future.

The promotion potential in the various avenues open to us was assessed under four headings: 'not fitted', 'likely to become fitted in the next two years', 'fitted' and 'exceptionally fitted'. The standard assessment of an IO who was doing his job and keeping his nose clean was that he fully met the requirements of the grade but was not fitted for promotion – 'box three, not fitted.' On my first annual report I had been marked 'box four' which I decided was acceptable to me because I had only just started the job and could hardly be expected to do everything correctly first time.

Ranked above the CIOs were the two inspectors. John was clipped in speech and incisive in manner; Dennis was unctuous in speech and confrontational in conversation. It was as if he were setting you up for the kill every time he spoke to you. I had learned from interviewing passengers that for an efficient use of your time you had to think carefully about how you phrased your questions. If, for example, you suspected that the passenger did not have a ticket to return to his home country, you could ask, 'Do you have a return ticket?' He might answer yes or no but either way you would not have actually found out what you needed to know. What you should have asked is, 'When you leave the United Kingdom which country do you intend to travel to?' and then establish whether he had the necessary tickets. With Dennis, he was always testing us in the same manner. Madge recounted a conversation she had with him in which the following exchange took place:

'Which newspaper do you read?'

'I read the *Telegraph*,' Madge had replied.

'Every day?'

'Yes, every day that it is published.'

'All of it?'

'All except the sports and business pages.'

'Did you see that article today about the detention of minors?'

'No, I didn't.'

'I thought you said that you took the *Telegraph*.'

'I did.'

'And that you read it all but the sports and business pages.'

'Yes I did.'

'But you did not read the article about the detention of minors?'

'No, not yet. My newspaper is delivered to my home and it arrived after I had left for work today so I will be able to read it when I get home.'

'I see.'

And once, on my day off, I was unable to avoid meeting Dennis in the lower ground floor of Debenhams.

'What are you doing here?' he said. From anybody else, this enquiry I would have judged to have been impertinent but with Dennis, it was normal.

'Oh just looking around,' I tried to be as non-engaging as I could. He was not my favourite interlocutor. 'I rarely come in to Debenhams.' I decided to turn the tables on him. 'What are you doing?'

'I'm looking for the garden tools section but I haven't seen it yet.'

'Oh.'

'Do you know where it is?'

'It's over there at the other side of the staircase.' I was glad of an opportunity to get rid of him.

'I thought you said that you didn't come in very often?'

'No, I don't.'

'But you know where the garden tools are.'

I looked at him for a second, wondering whether he could ever have a conversation with a person without trying to double check their story.

'Perhaps I'm more observant than you.'

So I was pleased that my eighteen month interview was with John. He sat me down in his office and put on his serious face.

'I've got your eighteen month probation report here,' he said gravely. I was still aglow from my success with the Italian car thieves so I grinned at him. 'It's not very good.' He frowned at me. I blinked. How could it not be good? After a letter of commendation? But he was still talking. 'If you don't buck up your ideas we might have to extend your probation for another six months. That's all.' He dismissed me.

I sat in the rest room with a hollow feeling in my stomach. I picked up the discarded newspaper from the chair at the side of me and turned to the 'situations vacant' page. Perhaps I should find something else to do in my life.

The next day was a challenge. I was the 'O-man.' Not the oriental sultanate but the immigration officer who had to run the casework office for the morning – the 'office man.'

The procedure for refusing entry to a passenger passed through several well-defined stages. First the passenger was interviewed on the desk by the IO. The Immigration Service always used the word, 'interview'; the Press generally used the word, 'interrogate' because it unfailingly conjured up bright lights, the rubber truncheon and a Gestapo dentist. During the interview the passenger might be taken through to the customs hall to have his baggage searched. When the IO had got all his facts together then he referred his case to the CIO who either authorised refusal or instructed him to land him. To refuse the passenger, the IO had to serve forms which stated clearly the reason for the refusal and what was to happen to the passenger. The stage after refusal was 'removal'.

A straightforward refusal would be removed on the ship upon which he had arrived or another of the same company's, to be carried at their expense. This was a requirement of law. If the ship was not sailing in the immediate future then the refused passenger would be taken to the harbour board police station and there detained until the ship was in dock and ready to receive him. The police would then take him down and hand him over to the purser. They were then supposed to wait at the shore end of the ramp to ensure that he did not just walk off again.

Sometimes it was not possible to refuse the passenger immediately because other enquiries needed to be made or it was impossible to remove him because he would not be acceptable to the country from which he had arrived. In these cases, the file was sent up to the casework office, his name and details were entered in chinagraph pencil on a plastic board screwed to the wall and he was either detained further or given temporary admission. It was the overseeing of these cases that was the task of the O-man. Some of the cases had been ongoing for months; one or two for several years.

I was dreading the duty. I really did not know what I was doing. It took me several years to realise that nobody else did either. They all just muddled along, doing as little as possible and marking files for action on another day when they had made sure that they would not be on duty. I checked the stamping-on book to see how many IOs had turned up for duty and glanced into the casework office as I walked to the CIO's office. I could already see two pink files waiting for me on the desk. They would be cases that had arrived during the night and required continuing action through the day. There was one CIO in the office – he was the night CIO, bleary eyed and drooping. I caught him tipping a thimble of whisky into his tea.

'Morning Gerry. We've got five early men in and three not in yet.'

'Are the night men away?'

Down the other end of the corridor came the sound of the office door banging followed by the characteristic explosion of IO's cases being slammed onto table tops.

'That sounds like them coming up now.' They would have been the last officers to be relieved from their fixed points and now had to dump their landing cards and lock away their official equipment, stamps and such like, before signing off.

'Oh, Customs got two Dutchmen for drugs. We've withdrawn leave to enter. They are due in court today. The files are on your desk.'

'OK, I'll go and have a look at them.'

BOOKMARK

A control coupon issued to passengers travelling on the Belgian Marine Sealink service from Ostend to Dover.

R M T - R T M

CONTROLEBILJET - BILLET DE CONTROLE
CONTROL COUPON - KONTROLLABSCHNITT

Te bewaren gedurende gans de overvaart.
Te vertonen op elk verzoek.
A conserver pendant toute la durée de la traversée.
A produire à toute réquisition.
To be retained during the whole sea crossing and must be produced if required by an official.
Während der ganzen Überfahrt aufzubewahren.
Bei jeder Kontrolle vorzuzeigen.

OOSTENDE { DOVER / FOLKESTONE

AML 1 2 3

Picking up the threads of a case from a file is more challenging than trying to solve an Agatha Christie mystery. We were not really taught 'file etiquette'. A standard procedure for the handling of files is in force throughout the Civil Service and some of it had filtered through to that last bastion of individualism – the Immigration Service. Some of it, but not all and few were the officers who felt themselves bound by it.

A file, once opened, should have two sides to it, left and right, in imitation of an open book. On the left side are attached the minute sheets which record the chronological action and on the right side are affixed the various letters, forms etc which are referred to in the minutes. A minute sheet is a blank piece of paper with a left hand margin. Any action taken must be recorded. A typical entry might be: *'Wrote letter as within to sols. asking for pax new address.'* It would then be signed and dated and usually timed, by the instigator. The 'letter as within' refers to the copy of the letter which is retained on the right hand side of the file. The 'pax' is the passenger; 'sols' are his solicitors. New documents and new minute sheets are always placed on top of their predecessors so that when the file is opened in the middle such that both piles are flat, then what falls under the eye is the latest action taken on the left and the most recent document attached on the right. So the further down the pile you dig, the further back into the story you progress. The only exceptions to this rule are the passenger's personal possessions such as passports and tickets. These should be placed in a marked envelope and should rise through the file to be readily available on top when it becomes necessary to return them.

I knew none of this. I learned it some years later when I was involved in clearing the arrears work of the Immigration and Nationality Department. Reading a properly constructed file was an eye-opener to me, even if some of the rules seemed petty. One file had been sent back down to the executive officer unactioned by the higher executive officer because the former, whilst requesting the latter's observations, had not affixed a new blank minute sheet on the left hand side of the file to receive the said deliberations. I thought it nitpicking but realised that it was inefficient to pay the higher echelons in the decision-making chain to perform clerical tasks; there were clerical assistants who were paid to do those.

I sat at my desk and looked at the pink files. I opened the first one. A half completed summary sheet, once deciphered, told a story of two Dutchmen in a car being landed by the IO and then stopped by Customs who had found drugs in the vehicle. The IO had cancelled the landing stamp in the passport, thus revoking their permission to enter. I flicked through the papers for the passport. I burrowed in the rear pocket of the file. No passport. That was the first bit of bad news. We always felt powerless without a passport to stamp. I read the other file. It was the same story with a different name. The file did not indicate where the passengers and their passports were located but if they had been refused permission to enter, then the next step was to remove them and for that, I needed both. I phoned Customs.

'You stopped a couple of Dutch nationals this morning for drugs. Can you tell me where they are and where the passports are?'

'Just a minute. Are they Van Leesen and Gerrits?'

'Yes.'

'I think they will be up before Dover magistrates this morning.'

'Will they get bail?'

'Shouldn't think so. It's a custodial offence.'

'Have you still got their passports?'

'I don't know. I'm not the officer dealing. It's all up at St John's Road.'

'I'll check with them, then.' But I forgot to ask him for the telephone number and was too embarrassed to ring back so it took me another couple of phone calls to obscure departments of the Waterguard before I ascertained that the passengers were definitely to be charged this morning.

Well that seems to be all under control. I suppose I had better look at the diary to see what is due up today. *'Adyoku – review; Benini IS 96 expires today; De Witte – prison review EDR.'* I turned to the rack and pulled out the files. Adyoku's file was about two inches thick. That, paradoxically, was usually good news. If a file was that thick then the case had been running for a considerable time, probably years and so was unlikely to be solved in a hurry or to require any drastic action on it today. I flipped it open. The last minute read, *'await reply from sols.'* I looked on the right side of the file. No new letter had been attached. Mrs. Adyoku and the two children could remain in their council house a little while longer. We were not going to get rid of her today. Although we had served notice of removal on her three times in the last eighteen months, each time she had submitted a doctor's note to say that she was too unwell to travel. In reality, we were not going to get rid of her ever. She had overstayed her permission to enter by five years and managed to give birth to two children here. I recognised the firm of solicitors. They were the right ones for her, they knew all the answers. We might just as well give her British nationality now. I picked her passport out of the envelope and studied the smiling face of the young lady. If she had come to my desk and said that she was staying for a month to visit her cousin would I have stamped her in? Probably. Almost certainly. I could learn nothing from such analysis. I packed the file away again. I would get around to it later.

Benini, his IS 96 expires today. This is the form giving him temporary admission to the United Kingdom. He is an Ethiopian who had been studying here for the last three years but two days ago had returned from a trip to Paris and fallen foul of the IO at Dover who had discovered that he had never passed an examination in three years and had been working full time in a burger bar in Shepherd's Bush. This was very naughty. He had been refused entry, his passport was on the file, and been given permission to go to London to collect all his belongings before being removed on a ship to Calais. Townsend Thoresen who had brought him over from Calais must have been sitting there with their fingers crossed because if it all went wrong and we ended up having to order his removal via Heathrow, direct to Ethiopia, then Townsends would have to foot the bill. This would not be a good financial return on a twenty-five pound ferry ticket. I scrabbled amongst the jumble of papers in the file and eventually found his IS 96. He was due back here at Dover East at four o'clock this afternoon. Fine. I would be at home by then. I put the file back in the rack. This was easy.

De Witte, prison review EDR – 'earliest date of release.' De Witte, a South African, had been convicted of importing cocaine and was doing three years in Canterbury prison. We needed to know his earliest date of release because this did not necessarily concur with the simple calculation of adding three years to his date of conviction. In some cases, time spent in custody before the trial count towards the sentence and sometimes prisoners could be let out early on parole. The problem for us was that although he was physically in the country, he was not so in legal terms. He was at the stage of having been refused permission to enter and was now awaiting removal. In his case, he was waiting three years. When the Prison Service released him, even on parole, our task was to serve a detention order on the prison so that they could hold him there whilst we made arrangements for his removal to South Africa, courtesy of Belgian Marine. I phoned up Canterbury prison.

'Discipline Office.'

'Immigration Dover East here. Can you give me the EDR on prisoner De Witte?' I gave his prison number.

'No. He's not here,' the man said after a pause.

'What do you mean he's not there? Where is he?'

'Dunno. He left about four months ago.'

'Left? What, you mean, released?' I began to panic.

'Oh, I shouldn't think so. Probably been transferred.'

'Do you know where to?'

'I'll find out and ring you back.'

I put the phone down and considered whether I ought to tell the CIO that we had lost track of a detainee. No, we had not really lost track of him, the search was ongoing. The Prison Service would know where he was. I hoped. I hoped he was still in their custody somewhere. I pinned a note on the file reminding me to ring them in an hour if I had not heard from them. I looked at the clock – time for breakfast. Oh, I must put the two Dutchmen up on the board. I squeaked the chinagraph pen across the plastic and then put a note on my desk, *'back in ten minutes.'* That should cover me.

The scheduled meal break for this duty was at two in the afternoon but I was hungry. The canteen was what you would expect it to be: stainless steel counter, orange partition, formica topped tables, black plastic chairs. And a queue. I had got in just behind Customs. There were eight lads in the queue before me and they all wanted the full English. I ordered my 'egg on fried bread, one sausage' and sat down with a cup of what they called coffee. 'Don't worry about the white frothy bits on top,' the cashier reassured me, 'he's just used the steamer to do the scrambled egg. It won't hurt you.'

On a table near the window four Townsend Thoresen hostesses were sitting in their turquoise uniforms, also despatching copious plateloads of food. Below the window, the lorries rumbled by, occasionally vibrating the metal window frames as they gunned their motors in changing gear. 'Egg on toast, one sausage,' the cashier called out. That was quick. I collected my plate and tore into the food. I should have been back in the office ten minutes ago. From the counter on the other side of the partition came the rough protesting voice of an irate building worker. I could see the top of his hard hat above the screen.

'Come on love, where's me grub? I've been waiting fifteen minutes.'

'What did you order?'

'Egg on toast, one sausage.'

'Well cook says you've had it. It's gone.'

I froze and looked into my plate. I had ordered egg on fried bread not toast. I was eating toast. I glanced quickly about the canteen. The customs officers who had been in front of me in the queue were still waiting for their breakfasts to be cooked. I was eating somebody else's breakfast.

'Well I haven't bloody had it.'

'There's no need to swear.'

I bolted the last mouthful and made for the exit. Eructating violently I turned at the door to catch a glimpse of my victim. Tattoos, dirty fluorescent waistcoat and big orange boots. I did not hang about.

I could hear the phone ringing when I opened the office door.

'Immigration Dover East.'

'Who am I speaking to please?'

I thought, if I don't reply you'll be speaking to yourself but instead I gave my name. It was a firm of solicitors. It had to be. Only they would ask for your name before you had said anything. He started a complicated enquiry about husbands and how they could qualify for entry under the immigration rules.

'I cannot give you any undertaking with regard to a particular case over the phone. Each case is decided upon it merits by the immigration officer at the point of arrival,' I explained

'You are an immigration officer aren't you?'

'Yes I am.'

'Well I am asking you. If my client comes over from Calais with his wife, will you let him in?'

'I cannot say. I have not got your client before me.'

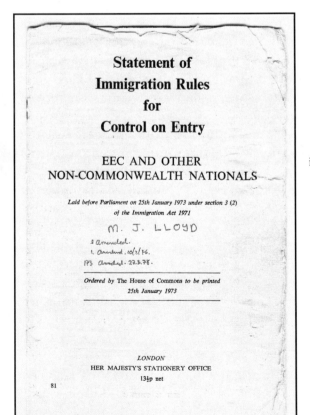

The
Immigration Act
is what the public thinks we do.

The
Statement of Immigration Rules
is what Parliament wants us to do.

The
Home Secretary's General Instructions to the Immigration Officer
is what the Home Secretary tells us to do.

The
Immigration Officer's Discretion
is what we actually do.

'But you might deport him?'

'No, an immigration officer does not deport, that is for the Home Secretary to do.'

'So you won't send him back?'

'I did not say that. I said that we would not deport him. Deportation is the removal of somebody who is already in the United Kingdom. What we do at the port is to refuse leave to enter and remove. What is the reason for your client wanting to come here?'

'Well, just to visit his wife's parents.'

'And what nationality is she?'

'She is Turkish. She is resident here.'

'And what nationality is her husband?'

'He is Turkish as well.'

'And where does he live?'

'They both live in Turkey.'

'But her parents live here? And you said that she is resident here?'

'Yes but she lives in Turkey.'

'If he is coming here purely for a holiday then I can see no problem–'

'So he will be allowed in then?'

'–no problem provided he can convince the immigration officer upon arrival of the reason for his visit.'

'But if he wanted to live here, he can can't he? He's allowed to because his wife is resident.'

I thought we would get around to that eventually. He was a solicitor, he had my name, he wanted me to say that his client could come here to live. I leafed through my already tattered copy of the *Statement of Immigration Rules for Control on Entry*, price $13^1/_2$p from the HMSO. I was thinking madly. Did he have the right to settle here? I suppose he did. We usually stamped the passports of the foreign wives of British men with a permit to stay forever. I found the paragraph on husbands and began to read it to him.

'A passenger has no claim to settlement in right of his wife unless she is settled in the United Kingdom–'

'–Which she is.'

'–And,' I continued, 'has been granted a current entry clearance issued because the Secretary of State is satisfied that there are special considerations, whether of a family nature or otherwise, which render exclusion undesirable.'

'So can he get his entry clearance from the Home Office?'

'Yes. No. Um. He must get his entry clearance before he arrives otherwise he will not be allowed in.'

'But he can come in as a visitor and then ask the Home Office.'

'In order to do that, surely he would be lying to the immigration officer at the port if he said he was coming for a holiday but really intended to ask permission to stay here?'

'Are you saying that my client is dishonest? Are you judging him already?'

'I have explained to you sir, that I can give you no assurances as to the success of your client getting in to this country, it is dependent upon the immigration officer who interviews him upon arrival.'

'Why is it that wives can come in to settle but men cannot? That does not seem fair does it?'

'I don't know what the thinking behind the policy is, sir.'

'But you are treating women differently from men. Surely that's discrimination, isn't it?'

Yes it is, but I must not admit it.

'Err... it looks like it.'

'So you are saying that the Home Office policy is discriminatory.'

I was getting worried now. He was pressing me too hard for comfort. I did not really know my ground. I had not realised that husbands were not allowed in like wives. Well, I had, but it had not sunk in.

'I am not saying that sir. I cannot comment on the policy, I am just here to implement it.'

'It does not sound to me as if you know how to.'

'Is there anything else I can help you with sir?'

'No that's all. Fat lot of use.' *Click.*

My hand was shaking as I replaced the receiver. The experience of being put on the spot and grilled as if I were an expert I found to be quite frightening. I walked through to the CIO's office to see if I could scrounge a cup of tea. Morrison was there. He was tall with a receding hairline. He spoke in a supercilious Scottish drawl. I told him about the phone call.

'Mnyees,' he slurred, 'I expect he was tape recording you. We will soon see if you made a fool of yourself. It will be on the front page of the Guardian.' That did not settle me one little bit. 'Now what about these two Dutch smugglers? Where are we with them?'

'Customs have got them. They are due in court today.'

'Have they been refused?'

'Yes, they were landed first but when the drugs were discovered, the stamp was cancelled.'

'And they were refused?'

'Well, leave to enter was withdrawn.'

'And what was it replaced with?'

'Ah, yes, I see what you are getting at. If we don't refuse them within twenty-four hours of withdrawal of the previous permission, then they get indefinite leave to enter.'

'Exactly. So you need to refuse them as soon as possible. When was leave withdrawn?'

'I don't know. It'll be on the file.'

'And we have the passports?'

'Um... not yet. I'm still trying to get them.'

'Refuse them on non-conducive grounds. You have asked for leave to enter, blah, blah, blah, but you have been found in possession of blah blah blah, and in the light of this your exclusion is conducive to the public good.'

'Right.' I knew I had not performed very well in Morrison's eyes.

'And you'll need to go to court and oppose bail.'

'Right.'

'Hop along then.'

Oh Christ, I've got to go to court. I've never been to court. We don't have any training for it. We are not prosecuting officers, we were told, we are investigating officers. That is why we do not have to caution passengers before we interview them.

Back in the casework office, the pink files were still sitting on my desk but now they were not a cuddly pink, they were more a sort of blushing embarrassed pink. I should have thought earlier about refusing the smugglers. I caught sight of a dark grey lounge suit in the general office.

'Dave,' I called to him, 'Can you help me a minute?' I was not proud. Dave Stonewell was a calm, unruffled senior IO whom I knew would advise me. I explained the situation with the Dutch. 'How do I oppose bail? Do I have to go in the witness box?'

He was horrified. 'No, don't do that. Magistrates' court starts at ten thirty. Get there a bit early, you can usually park around the back, and see the clerk of the court. Get an estimate from him of when they will be up before the beak. See the customs chappie as well if you can. Then sit in the public gallery and watch. When the Dutchmen are dealt with, if an application for bail is made, Customs will oppose it and add that there is an immigration officer in court. If the magistrate asks you what you will do if they are released on bail, you say that you will serve a detention order on them, take them into immigration custody and proceed with their removal from the United Kingdom.'

'Right.' I was taking notes as fast as I could. 'What if they grant bail?'

'You capitulate. You give them temporary admission to the same terms as their bail. Don't forget to take stuff with you. You will need to take detention forms and temporary admission forms. You can fill them in and stamp them up ready just in case.'

'There's only one problem. We haven't refused them yet. Leave to enter was withdrawn but they were not then refused.'

'When did they arrive?'

'Two twenty this morning.'

'That's alright. As long as we refuse them before two twenty tomorrow morning we will be OK.' He looked at the clock. 'You'd better look sharpish.'

Dover Magistrates' Court was housed in an enormous, mediaeval looking stone building. My footfalls echoed on the stone flags as I self consciously made my way up the grand chamber to the knot of people assembled at the top end. Some had battered brown leather cases and looked like solicitors, some were members of the public, one wore a black gown and turned out to be the clerk of the court. I found the customs officer and introduced myself. We confirmed the procedure we were going to follow. I asked the clerk where the cases were to be heard and when. He pointed me to court number two. I went in and bagged myself a seat.

At half past ten we started. Or at least, I think we did because I could not hear a word of what was going on. I was not far from the front but of course the actors in the play were not there for the audience, they could interact their drama by simply talking to each other, and this is what they did. Any remnants of their deliberations that might escape, immediately soared upwards to the high ceiling or wrapped themselves in the curtains. I watched avidly as people came in and out from various doors, papers were passed back and forth and various assumed villains rose from a well in the floor and then descended like a cinema organ. Occasionally the end of a scene was marked by a snap of the gavel but all in all, it was a most unsatisfactory performance. And it was dragging so. At twelve o'clock the court adjourned and I realised that I would need to phone the office to get somebody to take over because I finished my duty at two.

Out in the flagged chamber I collared the customs officer and asked him if he knew where the nearest telephone call box was.

'There are a couple outside the hospital. Are you still here then?'

'Yes,' I grimaced, 'It looks as if I shall have to get a colleague to take over.'

'I didn't think there was much left. Just a few drunk and disorderlies.'

I looked at him, not understanding. Hoping, that I had not understood.

'What about the two Dutchmen?'

'Gerrits and Van Leesen?' I nodded. 'Remanded in custody for a week.'

'Oh, that's what I thought,' I lied. 'You haven't got their passports by any chance have you?'

He looked in his papers. 'No, they'll be back in the office.'

'OK. I'll be off then.'

Well what an efficient officer I was. The two Dutchmen could have been released and I would not have known. I had been completely unaware of what was going on in the court. Back at the office I noted the file and telephoned Customs who promised to walk the passports around to me. This implied that they were in the building. Possibly in the office next door.

At one o'clock my relief turned up. It was Gerald. I had nothing in common with him. He played football and drank beer. He was one of the lads and I was beginning to realise that I would never be such. He crashed his case down onto my desk, knocking my fountain pen to the floor.

'I'm your relief but don't get excited. I'm going to the canteen. I haven't had my lunch yet.'

'Neither have I,' I said to his disappearing back. The irony made no mark whatsoever. He came back at a quarter to two.

'Right what's happening? You should have done it all by now.'

I pulled out a stack of pink files. He scowled. I picked off the top one.

'This chap, De Witte, we're waiting for Canterbury prison to ring back to tell us where he is.'

'Don't they know?'

'They're finding out.' He grunted. 'This one, Benini, Ethiopian, he's on temporary admission. He is due back this afternoon with his baggage. For removal to Calais via Townsends.'

'Have you served the removal papers on Townsends?'

'Not yet.'

'Why not? What have you been doing all morning?'

'I thought we could wait to see if the passenger turns up first of all. There is no point in serving papers if he absconds from TA.' I thudded the two inch thick file onto the desk.

'Adyoku,' he said. 'I know her. What's the action?'

'Waiting for a letter from the solicitor.'

'Waste of time.'

'And these two clowns, Van Leesen and Gerrits, were caught with drugs in the night. Dover magistrates this morning. Remanded in custody for a week.'

'Did you give an IS91 to the police?'

'What for?'

'To put them both in dual detention, idiot. If the court suddenly decides to grant bail the police will have to release them.'

'Well you can do that this afternoon.'

'There's tennis on the telly at three o'clock. I shan't be spending much time down here.'

'And they also need refusing.'

'What? Why haven't you refused them?'

'Not my fault guv. Their leave to enter was withdrawn but they were not refused. We don't have the passports but Customs will bring them to us this afternoon. I've sketched out the refusal formula.'

'Big deal.'

The door bell rang.

'I'll get it,' I offered generously. 'That's probably Customs now.' It was. I handed the two black booklets to him. 'Have a nice time.'

I had survived a casework duty.

But I knew that it had been a close-run thing.

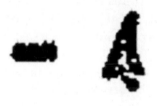

'What does this old geyser want?' Steven pushes his glasses up his nose and slides back his window as the silver-haired man makes his way down the line of cars towards us.

I sit and gaze at the acre of immobile cars and caravans sweltering on the hot tarmac before us: ten lanes, stretching right back as far as the port control tower, a dribble of vehicles being bled from the pack by the marshal as each kiosk becomes clear. I cannot deal with the next car in my line until the one I have just finished has moved forward, and it cannot advance because the cars before it are congealed in a solid mass in the buffer park for Customs. Over to my right two lines of coaches edge slowly forwards in fits and starts between the piles of rubble and the plastic cones, unloading their passengers into a queue which is shuffling towards both entrances of the foot passenger hall. To my left, the road by the cliff is a stationary line of lorries trying to embark; the centre of Dover town has ground to a halt from the tailback. Kent police are somewhere up the A2 near Lydden, trying to ease the problem by pulling lorries which are approaching Dover off the road and into a temporary park. And now, just as I open my window to talk to the next car which has managed to squeeze alongside, the hovercraft sitting on the pad decides to test all four engines at full power. I take the German passports, wave their owners to wait and close the window again. The sheet of perspex takes up the resonance of the propellers and buzzes in the frame of the guichet. I wait. The Germans wait. There is nothing we can do. Nobody could hold a conversation in that noise except by sign language.

A sudden howl of sound from my left indicates that Steven has opened the window on his side of the kiosk.

'What's the hold up? Why aren't we moving?' the silver-haired man thrusts his head into the kiosk to bellow. Steven silently points to the stationary mass of vehicles behind us. 'Absolutely ridiculous. Pointless exercise. Why don't you just wave us through?' he continues. Veins are standing out on his forehead. Steven again wordlessly indicates the traffic jam. 'Well, what's holding it up? Why aren't they moving?'

With a fading whistle the hovercraft engines die.

'They are held up by Customs sir.'

'Well what's the hold up at Customs? Why don't they work faster?'

'I can't answer that sir, you would have to ask them that.'

'I will.'

'Just a minute, sir.' Steven's voice is harsh and arresting. 'Do you have your passport with you?'

'What? No, of course not. It's in the car.'

'Well you can't go through here without a passport sir. You'll have to go and get it.'

'Bloody ridiculous.'

'That is why we are here. It is called passport control.'

'Don't try to be funny with me sonny. No wonder Lord Lucan got out.'

'His car was found at Newhaven, not Dover. Could you stand aside please sir, you are holding up the queue.' He beckons the next car forward.

'Right. I want your name.'

'Dennis Stephens, sir. Stephens with a 'ph' in the middle.' Steven shoots me a sideways glance to shut me up. I up shut. I rather relish Dennis getting a complaint. The man stomps back towards his car.

'Are Customs on a go-slow?' I call across the kiosk.

'Not particularly,' Steven replies. *'Vee langer blybenzee?'* he says to his Germans.

'And could you open the boot please?' I ask mine. They are two German girls in their mid twenties.

'We have nothing to declare.'

'This is not Customs. It is an immigration check.'

I push back my chair, stretch my legs and open the kiosk door. The car is a Volkswagen Beetle. She opens the boot which is at the front, of course. It shelters just a couple of small suitcases. She closes it again.

'And behind the back seat please?'

'Please?'

'Can I see in the storage space behind the back seat please?' Two months earlier, two Germans had been caught each trying to smuggle in a Pakistani in this storage space. They had been refused entry, the Pakistanis were currently in prison awaiting removal and the two hire cars, one lime green and the other bright orange, were sitting in our compound.

'That is just the engine,' she says. 'Look.'

'No, I don't mean there.' I point into the car. 'Pull the back seat forward please.'

'It doesn't move.' She is tall, with wispy fair hair, blue eyes and tight jeans. Her companion has brown hair and brown eyes but her knuckles are white on the steering wheel and she is staring fixedly through the windscreen. The omens are not good.

'There is a storage space behind the back seat and there is a tab at the side of the cushion which you can pull to release it.'

'I don't know. This is not our car.'

She tips the front seat forward and half climbs in. Jimmy in the next kiosk along makes a mime of licking his lips as he watches her bum wriggle from side to side. She pulls the top of the seat. It does not move. She backs out again. Jimmy holds up both thumbs to me. I know there is a space there and so do many West Germans because it had been one of the favourite ploys used for people-smuggling out of East Berlin.

'Where is the tab that you pull?'

She is looking worried now. 'It is not my car. It is borrowed to me.'

I feel around the seat back. The release tab has been doubled back and pushed out of sight. I unfold it and yank the seat forwards.

'Oh!' she says. 'What is that?' It is patently obvious what it is – a case of a dozen bottles of German white wine. 'It is not my car,' she repeats.

'OK, thank you.' I hand her the passports. 'You can go.'

'We can go?' She is disbelieving.

'Yes. Don't forget to tell Customs about the wine.'

Back in the kiosk I pick up the phone. 'Immigration here, cars inwards. Blue Beetle, registered in Bonn, two young German girls. They've got a case of wine behind the back seat. They might forget to tell you.'

'OK, got that.'

I am thinking that it will be a good vintage by the time they get through Customs. My two hours are nearly up. In an effort to keep us alive for a little longer the Immigration Service limits us to a maximum of two hour stints on cars because of the carbon monoxide poisoning. They recognise that we cannot avoid breathing it. My head is throbbing, my throat is dry and thick. I could do with a drink but I can see that my next point is walkers inwards and over there the end of the queue has only just crept inside the door so the IOs over there are working flat out like us.

The next car is a red MG Midget with a green licence plate bearing orange figures and a 'CD' in the middle. The last number is forty-five. French diplomatic plates identify the countries alphabetically and forty-five is *Grande Bretagne*. With a *K* in the middle it would be the British Consulate in Paris but the CD means that it is the British Embassy.

The driver is a young lady, she looks like a clerk. She has bought a left hand drive car, tax free in the UK and exported it to France where, at the end of her three year tour of duty, she will sell it at a tidy profit. For the moment, however, that steering wheel is on the wrong side of the car. Had the marshal noticed he would have sent her to Steven on the left side of the kiosk but as it is she has got me and although I lean far out of the window, I cannot reach her passport.

'Just a mo.' She pulls the gear lever into neutral and yanks on the hand-brake. Still holding the passport up in the air towards me, she twists around and slides across. The handbrake lever takes hold of the hem of her short skirt. I try, by my actions, to stop her but she keeps going. Just as I lunge forward and snatch the passport she gives a little squeak as cold metal touches naughty bare flesh. I studiously examine the passport to give her time to tug down her skirt which had ended up around the top of her thighs like a piece of string.

'I'll drop it on the passenger seat.' I smile brightly.

She blushes furiously and nods.

One of the perks of the job, I suppose.

The cars are rippling in the heat haze like a giant mirage. They are now taking as long to travel from the ship to the roundabout outside the docks as they did to cross the Channel. They squat there in lines whilst seagulls the size of turkeys beg for food and then crap half a pint of corrosive yogurt over their paintwork. Although the drivers can see that they might be there for forty or fifty minutes they keep their engines running, just in case. The air is still. The fumes just sit there, waiting to be inhaled.

'We must be doing the Ostender now,' I say to Steven as I take a Belgian i.d. card through the window.

Somebody in the car park blows his horn.

'So those on the far side will be the *Chartres.*' More motor horns sound. 'Oh we're getting the horn chorus now.' He turns to the driver at the side of him, 'I'm sure that'll make the port bigger.' The driver purses his lips, raises his eyebrows and says nothing.

The marshal pulls a white landing card from under the windscreen wiper of the next car in the queue, waves it forward and smartly snaps the rope across the lane behind it, closing off the last three cars. The baulked drivers look upset as he now starts to lead cars off from the lane to the left of them. It seems unfair to an uninformed observer but it is in fact, justice. The white landing card had been slipped under the windscreen wiper by the other marshal as he had fed the cars in at the top end of the lane. It indicated to his colleague that this was the last car in the line.

The opportunists waiting in other lanes see one line of cars moving and nip across the back of the lines to race down and join the tail, thus hoping to jump the queue. They can never work out why they fail.

'This is daft,' I say. 'I'm going to close down and go across to walkers. I'm not waiting for my relief.'

'I've got another hour.'

I wave to the marshal to close my lane and then I leave the kiosk and check the two cars in my queue. They are both British. I indicate to the marshal that they have been cleared and then return to the kiosk to pack up my stuff. As I clear my desk I find an embarkation card which had been folded so as to stand up like a notice. On it, SB have written the name of a person whom they want us to point out to them if we see them. I have only just found the card amongst all the paper trash that was hanging around.

'Did you know SB are looking for him?' I ask Steven.

He reads the card. 'Oh that's ancient. Last week I think. Where did you find it?'

'Amongst all these British Tourist Authority leaflets.'

I read the card and grin. The name of the suspect they were looking for was 'Saleh Saleh'. Underneath it, some wag had written, *'pride of our Ali.'*

On the trek over to the walkers' control I meet an IO coming the other way. 'What's it like?' I ask.

'Wall to wall South Americans. The Poisoned Dwarf is running around snapping at everybody's ankles.'

This is a reference to Alan Cottage, the CIO whom my mentor had pointed out to me as a 'bastard'. One of his problems was that he thought he was smaller than every other being on the planet and so had to go in for the attack with no preliminaries. I decide to defuse him.

'Sorry I'm early,' I say as I bang my case down on the table in the small watch room. Cottage opens his mouth to speak. 'It's jammed solid on cars so I came over here.'

'Go and help Trevor on blue X.'

Blue X was the fixed point on walkers inwards. The duties on the chart in the general office were distinguished by coloured lines across graph paper as they logged the various positions in which each IO was supposed to be at every hour. Black was the car inwards control and blue was the walkers or foot passengers inwards control. In practice they were referred to as the 'blue control' and the 'black control'. The latter nomination occasionally provoked raised eyebrows from liberal, do-gooding eaves-droppers. If you were at the X point, then you were the IO who was fixed and had to stay at his post, even when nobody was actually passing through the control. Blue X was the British desk. It was situated at the extreme right of a line of a dozen desks, alongside the window. Through this window blue X could see the funnels of the ships as they berthed, the signal at the end of the eastern arm which controlled entry to the port for the ships and he could check the traffic going down the port exit road. When a coach had unloaded its passengers into the hall, the driver then moved the coach forwards to this window which was provided with a guichet to allow blue X to examine his passport. After this, he continued to the baggage conveyors where Customs had the suitcases unloaded for the passengers to collect before walking through their red or green lanes. The coach would then drive through the port exit gate which was manned by the Dover Harbour Board Police and thence to the pick-up point where it would wait for its customers to reappear.

Trevor is the bearded IO who, on my first day back from training, had asked me if I played football. He is now facing a double line of British holidaymakers shuffling past his left elbow. He is clearing passengers at the rate of about one every two seconds but just as the tail of the queue struggles inside the door, the next coach unloads and another fifty passengers tag on the end.

I jump onto the podium of the vacant desk to his left and call, 'Come down this side as well.'

We plough through those Brits as fast as we can. I have developed a technique where I take the passport with my outstretched hand before the passenger has quite reached my desk, check it whilst keeping pace with the movement of the queue and then hand it back by putting it in my other hand and stretching my arm out as far as I can behind me, obliging the owner to move forwards to collect it. At the same time I have thrust my other arm out before my desk to collect the next document. In this way the queue never stops moving except for the occasional, 'what do you want here love? Passport?' as the handbag is heaved up onto the desk, the reading specs are levered onto the nose and the queue shunts into her backside.

Eight of the other ten desks are manned. This is summer and we have the full complement of staff available. Trevor turns away from his queue to deal with a coach driver at the window.

'OK, come over here,' I call to his line. They merge with mine whilst Trevor interviews the Spanish coach driver. I cannot tell one voice from the other, it is like overhearing a couple of Spaniards chatting in a bar. He is absolutely fluent.

A schoolboy in neat grey flannels and a blazer attracts my interest.

He seems out of place amongst this lot. I open his passport. 'David Albert Charles, Viscount Linley'. I look up sharply and, sure enough, behind him in the queue stands a man who looks like a retired army officer in civvies. I return the passport and the boy shoots off towards Customs like a rocket. The minder's face registers alarm. I nod him quickly through without a check. He acknowledges my favour with relief. It wouldn't do for him to lose a member of the royal family.

Trevor stamps the coach driver's passport and turns back to the hall. 'Next please,' he calls and the line surges forwards. We can see the end of the queue but it is only temporary. We now have a backlog of coaches waiting to unload at the baggage conveyors and no more vehicles can move forwards until they have done so. The line of coaches stretches back as far as the port control tower, we will soon have them queuing to get out of the ferries. We have achieved on the blue control the inertia that I had just left on the black control.

'OK, move across and do some of these Argentinians,' Cottage instructs me.

I wave the few remaining Brits. in my queue over to Trevor's and hop across the gap to the next desk. I arrange my book and stamps and then nod at the marshal. He points a middle-aged couple at me – Argentine passports with stiff blue covers, thin grey printing inside, black and white photographs where the definition has been washed out by over exposure.

'Kwanto tiempo akee?' I have not studied Spanish but by dint of hearing those who had I have inevitably picked up some useful phrases.

' *Tres dies,*' the man says.

I look at the landing cards. His profession is *'abogado'* and they are going to the Royal National Hotel. They usually are on these tours; lawyers, doctors, architects. I suppose that it is only the professional classes in South America who can afford to make a three week trip to Europe. They usually fly from South America to Spain and there they pick up a tour coach provided by a Spanish agent. They then go for an excursion around Europe, ending up in Spain for the return flight.

'What's the story?' I call to the IO on my left.

'Three days London, organised tour, home via Madrid, courier has all the tickets,' he says without looking up.

'That's a bit risky. I hope he doesn't lose them.'

Bang, bang, bang, go the stamps down the line and six more Argentines entered Britain. After three quarters of an hour we began to see the orange carpet tiles appear. It is a welcome sight.

A lull. I sit in the watch room in a low chair with my head resting on the cool wall behind me. I close my eyes and will my headache to disperse.

'Did you hear about that Yank on nights?' somebody says. 'Refused, not genuine visitor and removed on the *Hengist* so what does the prick do? He jumps overboard and swims ashore. Naturally nobody notices a dripping wet man squelching around the docks. He can't find his way out so he tries to climb the cliff.'

'He should have just walked down the exit road. The DHB police would have ignored him.'

'He got about twenty feet up and then fell.'

'Where is he now?'

'Kent and Canterbury hospital.'

'I hope he's on an IS91. He'll abscond as soon as he can walk.'

'We ought to refuse him again whilst he hasn't got a leg to stand on, ha, ha.'

'Is that the best you can do?'

'Oh Paul, you're a cricketer aren't you?' I say as I search in my case. 'Have you heard of an Australian called Ian Chappell?'

'Stop taking the piss.'

'Oh, I thought you might know him.' I read from the landing card. 'He put *'professional cricketer'* down on his landing card.'

'Eh? Of course I bloody know him. He's the captain of the Australian test team. Has he been through?'

I flick the card across to him. 'There was about a dozen of them, all Australian, all cricketers.'

By this time Paul is out of his chair and rummaging through my landing cards. 'Do you mean to say that you landed the Australian test team?' He is breathless.

'Well, if that's who they were. I don't know anything about cricket.'

The others laugh at the exasperation caused by my unworldliness.

'Have you ever considered that when they built this lot they held the plans the wrong way around?' somebody says.

'What do you mean?'

'Well, they stuck all the admin offices on the cliff side of the port, where all the windows have a beautiful view of a vertical chalk cliff face fifty feet away and then they built the multi-storey car park so that it has a panoramic vista over the Channel to Calais. Where's the sense in that?'

'You can always go and sit in your car in your meal break if you feel deprived.'

'Did you see that at Terminal Three they had a Nigerian 'working holidaymaker' the other day?' We all laugh. 'No, I'm serious.'

'There is no such thing as a Nigerian working holidaymaker.'

'Why not? He qualified. He was between 18 and 30 and only intended to take employment incidental to his holiday, like it says in the rules.'

'Yeah but the IO has to be convinced that he intends to leave at the end of his stay and nobody from Nigeria would.'

'Do you think the Aussies and Kiwis do? They are all shagging in Earl's Court. They don't go back either.'

'Yeah but they are from the Old Commonwealth.'

'You mean they are white.'

'Exactly.'

A buzzer sounds.

'We're off again. That'll be the Zeebrugge.'

We grab our stamps and books and file out to the desks. I have another hour to do on blue and then I am scheduled to finish up on black for the last two hours of my duty, but it does not work out like that.

We clear the foot passenger bus with no difficulty and whilst we are dealing with several coach loads of Germans going to London I become aware that the hall is becoming quieter. We still have forty people in the queue but they are not making any noise. A group leader comes forward and speaks to Trevor who has by now been relieved from his blue X point and is landing foreigners alongside us.

CZECH COACH

'Just a minute marshal, hold them all there,' he calls and the marshal grabs a man by the elbow and pulls him gently back into the line but not before I have identified the small grey-green passport in his hand. Czechoslovak. It is a Czech tour group. To confirm my analysis I glance through the window and there sits a modern Czech coach which looks thirty years old compared to the styling of Western European vehicles. This is the time of the Iron Curtain and it is still very much in place. It takes about three minutes to land a straightforward Czech. Before we can stamp their passports we have to make sure that they have at least six months validity on them so that they will be allowed to return by their own authorities, and we have to decipher the pink exit visas issued to them in Prague to see how many days they are valid for and then find their exit stamp so that we knew what day they crossed the frontier out of Czechoslovakia and then calculate how many days remained of their permission to be absent from the country. If we get this wrong, the Home Office insists, then we might get stuck with Czechs in this country who are no longer acceptable back home. And we believe this tripe. Or pretend to. But Trevor is waving his arms about and, following the directions of the leader, the group assembles themselves in four lines of ten.

'Trade test,' Trevor waves a sheet in his hand. 'Czech choir on work permit to sing at the Albert Hall. Land for seven days code three.' I look to the marshal but he has no passengers to hand out.

Then they begin to sing. I do not know to this day what they sang. It only lasts a few minutes but if any of us harbour doubts that this is a choir, then those doubts are dispelled. The harmonized voices rise and fall, float above the hissing of the air conditioning, the roaring of the lorries and the crashing of the trailers. The few Brits. who had been hurrying through stop and listen. Half the German group who had not yet cleared Customs straggle back and stand, blocking the baggage reclaim. As the last sibilant syllable slides silkily away, applause, genuine, spontaneous applause rings from all corners of the passenger hall.

'Right lads,' Trevor says as he jumps back onto his desk, 'Buckle to and let's get them landed.'

We landed those Czechs in record time. I had not encountered this interview technique before and, needless to say, the management frowned upon it and it was later proscribed as 'unprofessional' but for that day I was grateful to Trevor for making it all so easy for us and thankful to the choir for the sheer uplift that they gave to everybody working on that hot and crowded duty.

I never made it back to cars. At the back of the choir stood an American man in his early twenties and I got him.

'How long are you staying in the UK sir?' I opened his passport and checked his name in the book. Why do Americans have such bizarre names? Ludovic Dungel Frontman – did I want to know the history behind that label?

'I dunno. Two weeks, maybe three.'

'And what do you come here to do?'

'Oh I'm gonna look around. Visit.'

'Who will you be visiting? Do you have any family or friends here?'

I nurtured this erroneous linguistic bias that you only visited people not places. It always tripped me up.

'No, I'm just looking around. London. Windsor Castle.'

'Where have you come from?'

'Aah, Iddly.'

I knew this to be the country which had Rome as its capital.

'And just now you came from which port?'

'Calais, France.'

As opposed to Calais, Washington County, US of A.

'I see. How long were you in Italy for?'

'Couple of months.'

'And what were you doing there?'

'Vacation. Looking around.'

'You flew into Rome from the USA?' I knew that from the stamps in his passport but it is always safe to confirm it.

'Yup.'

'When you leave the UK where will you go to?'

'Back home. Back to the States.'

'How will you travel there?'

'Pan-Am.'

'Do you have a ticket?'

'Not yet.'

'How much money have you got with you?'

'About a hundred dollars.'

The figures were beginning to not add up. A hundred dollars was not enough to provide the passenger with food, travel and hotels for a two to three week stay in the UK and purchase a plane ticket back to the States. I have kept the best bit till last because it should not really matter, but it always has an influence: his physical appearance. His black hair was shoulder length, he wore mascara and eye liner and his finger nails were two inches long and painted red. Not a traditional American tourist then. Having accumulated some information it was now time for me to test it.

'How are you going to pay for yourself in England for two to three weeks and get back to the USA with only one hundred dollars?'

'Oh, I can get more from my folks. They can wire me.'

'Is that what you did in Italy?'

'Yeah. Well, no, I didn't have to. I had enough money then. I guess I sort of spent it since.'

Did I envy him? Just bumming around Europe for a few months and then telephoning home when he needed more money? No, I did not envy him. Neither was I certain that I believed him.

'Do you live in the United States?'

'Sure.'

'What do you do there?'

'I'm a sort of a songwriter for a band. You know.'

I thought he was a bit presumptuous of my knowledge.

'Why did you go to Italy?'

'I wanted to see Rome, the ruins and the museums and stuff.' He tried a disarming grin. 'Get inspiration.'

'Have you got any baggage with you?'

'It's on the bus.'

'Well it will have been unloaded by now. We'll go and get it.'

The baggage hall was empty of people. The carousels were frozen in place, a few disparate lumps of baggage stranded like counters on a giant ludo board. Ludovic Dungel Frontman grabbed a luggage trolley and loaded onto it a backpack and a large, silver, rectangular trunk which carried on its flank the word *'Queen'* tastefully realised in strips of black insulating tape. I pointed to the customs notices explaining the red and the green channels.

'Do you have anything to declare to Customs?'

'No sir.'

'Choose which channel you wish to go down.'

He walked down the green lane. A young preventative officer was standing behind the bench and picking his nails.

'I am still interviewing this passenger. Would you like to look in his baggage?'

The officer nodded. 'Anything special?' he asked, meaning, did I have an idea what I was looking for? I did not. I shook my head.

The silver trunk contained several sets of trousers and bolero-like jackets made in a shiny, silver lamé. One had sequins sewn on it. The more he delved into it, the more I became convinced that this was a costume box. Nobody would wear clothes like that in the street. Not even Ludovic Dungel Frontman with his eye shadow and painted finger nails. Or perhaps he would?

'What do you use these clothes for?' I asked.

'Well those are my costumes, like, for the band, you know.'

'Do you need costumes to be a songwriter?'

'Not to be a songwriter, no, but I sing as well.'

'With the band?'

'Yeah, with the band.'

'Do you normally bring your costumes on holiday with you?'

'Aah no, no, you see... er...' He scratched his head. 'I had a bust up with the band. They weren't paying me what they owed, so I walked out.'

But if he had had an argument with the band, why did he then get on a plane to Rome with his costumes? Or...

'When did you have this disagreement?'

'A couple of weeks ago.'

'When you were in Italy?'

'Yeah.'

'Where is the band now?'

'They are still in Italy.'

'Why?'

'They've got some more shows to do.'

The customs officer closed the trunk and nodded to me again. I thanked him and led my passenger back into the passenger hall. I filled out an IS81, a detention form, stamped it and handed it to him.

'This form is to tell you that I have not finished my examination of you but will be resuming it later. Just sit down there.'

'Is there a problem?'

That question always flummoxed me. Of course there was a bloody problem or I would have stamped his passport ages ago but I am not going to tell him of my suspicions yet to prevent him making up a good story that I cannot break down.

'I need to speak to another officer. Just sit there.'

He sat down, dragged an ash tray towards him and lit up a cigarette. I went into the watch room for a think. Two IOs were sitting there waiting for the next rush of passengers. I picked up the phone and dialled one of the car kiosks.

'Black.'

'Have you got a CIO over there?' I asked.

'Not unless you call Bill Ventian a CIO.'

'Can you tell Grandma that I've picked up a case on walkers and so he will be one short on cars?'

'Yeah, I'll do that. It'll worry him for hours.'

Bill Ventian, whether we liked it or not, was a CIO. He worried like an old lady, thus his nickname.

'Whatcha got?' Len Copse blew a cloud of foul pipe smoke up into the fug at the ceiling.

'Yank for a three week visit with no tickets and a hundred dollars.' I flicked the passport across to him. IOs always wanted to see the passport. It told the story in the way that they could understand.

'What was he doing in Italy?'

'Says he was on holiday but he was singing with his band.' A thought occurred to me. 'Do you know a band called 'Queen'?'

Len Copse shook his head. I looked enquiringly at the other IO.

'The Queen?' he said.

'It was just a thought. He's got 'Queen' written on his trunk.'

'Never heard of them. It's probably him who's the queen.'

'You can knock him off anyway,' Len opined.

When CIO Bill Ventian came over from cars, he agreed but a CIO's job is always to ask questions to which you have no answers. It justifies their existence.

'Have you seen his money?'

'Yes,' I lied. 'A hundred dollars.' I should have asked to count it. He might have had more. He might have had none.

'Why doesn't he go home via Rome?'

I had no idea. 'Says he wants to visit London and Windsor.'

Ventian stood up and looked through the watchroom window into the passenger hall where Ludovic Dungel Frontman was pacing back and forth flicking cigarette ash into the ashtray at each passage.

'Good Lord, is that him? He's a raving poofter, look at him.'

'It might just be part of his act.'

'We don't want that sort here. Knock him off.'

'Can I go now?' he asked.

'Well, yes and no. I have refused you entry to the United Kingdom and have directed your removal to Calais on the next service which will be in about three hours' time.' I gave him the official papers. 'You have the right to take this decision to appeal but only once you have left the United Kingdom. This form tells you how to do it.' I handed him a form that my mentor at Heathrow had carefully avoided giving to my first refusal.

Mr. Ludovic Dungel Frontman was outraged. He stood up and waved the papers at me. 'I can't accept that. I can't accept that. No, no.'

For a moment I had no response to give him. It had not occurred to me that somebody would not be able to accept my actions but then I realised that he was purposefully expressing his outrage in a manner which implied that I was offering him an option. These bloody Yanks get too much self-assertiveness training at school.

'You are not required to either accept or reject it sir. I have done it.'

'But why aren't you letting me in? You can't just stop me.'

'Well, I can, actually. That is what I have just done.'

'I can't accept that.'

'If you think that my decision is wrong then you can take it to appeal. I have explained how.'

'Why have you refused me?'

'Because I do not believe you are telling me the truth about your visit. You told me that you were on vacation in Italy but you were really singing in a band on a programme of bookings in the country. You then tell me that you are coming here for a tourist visit but you have all the necessary costumes with you to enable you to sing here.'

'Oh I can't accept that. Call the American ambassador.'

'You will be able to do that from the police station whilst you are waiting to be removed to Calais.'

'Police station?' He was appalled. 'Am I a criminal? I demand you contact the American ambassador.' He pulled out a photocopy of his passport. 'You can't do this to me. This is what it says in my passport, *"I the undersigned Secretary of State of The United States of America request all whom it may concern to permit the citizen of the United States named herein to pass without delay or hindrance and in case of need to give said citizen all lawful aid and protection."* The Secretary of State says that you have to pass me without delay or hindrance.' He tapped the paper in emphasis. 'Without delay or hindrance.'

I felt like telling this jumped-up jerk that the Secretary of State did not even know that he existed and that if he tried to get any succour from his embassy they would give him short shrift. They were fed up with destitute Americans expecting their peregrinations in Europe to be financed by the American taxpayer but I said nothing. He could discover that for himself.

I knew that some IOs got a buzz from refusing entry to a passenger. I suppose all IOs did. I felt good about having done my job and earned my salary – the Home Office was not paying me to wave to returning British holidaymakers – but I did not experience the almost sexual satisfaction that some IOs seemed to display when they knew that they had upset somebody's intentions, destroyed their plans, curtailed their liberty or wrecked their hopes of a new life in the West. I was a softie.

This refusal would give a positive lift to my end-of-probation interview which was due in a fortnight. Since inspector John had told me to pull my socks up I had encountered some luck. The duff passengers had almost thrown themselves under my stamp; a Moroccan youth coming for two weeks whose only bag contained of a pair of underpants, a leather jacket, five oranges and his school leaving certificates; an unemployed Greek Cypriot coming to visit his uncle in Stoke Newington who made the mistake of telling me on the telephone that the lad would work in his fish and chip shop and a Malaysian girl who said she was studying here but who was unknown to the college she had claimed to have been attending for the previous nine months. They were not very 'inspired' refusals but they were all grist to the mill.

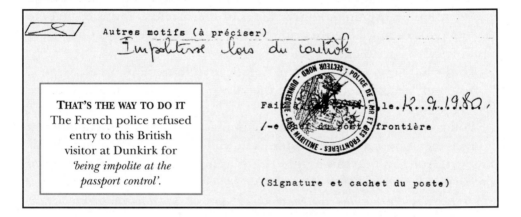

Autres motifs (à préciser)

Impolitesse lors du contrôle

THAT'S THE WAY TO DO IT
The French police refused
entry to this British
visitor at Dunkirk for
'*being impolite at the
passport control*'.

Fai...........le. 12..9..1980,
/-e............frontière

(Signature et cachet du poste)

All had been going well, and then I had had that incident with Dennis. It was about nine in the morning and I was thinking more of the breakfast that I was not now going to be able to snatch than the queue of French day trippers before me. Five of us were on the control. There should have been six but one had sidled off for an illicit breakfast, expecting us to cover for him. These French day trippers were of no interest to us. The process was mechanical. 'How long are you staying here?' whilst you look them up in the book. When they say, 'one day shopping' you stamp the passport and let them through. Then the marshal sends you another one. It was a stamping exercise, nothing more.

A man came up to my desk and handed me his French passport. I looked at the name and said, 'How long are you staying here?'

'One day, Marks and Spencers.'

I stamped his passport and returned it to him. Before the marshal could send me another passenger, Dennis had shot around from behind my desk and stood before me.

'Good morning Mr. Stephens.' I tried to be relaxed about what was obviously going to be one of his unpleasant cross examinations in guise of conversation.

'Are you off probation now then?' he asked obtusely. It was one of his favourite sarcastic tricks. It misled you and belittled you in one operation.

'Not yet. Another two weeks I think.'

'I see. I see. Are you aware of the instruction that all IOs on probation must look up every passenger in the book?'

'Yes Mr. Stephens.'

'I did not see you look up the last passenger.'

'No you didn't.' He waited for me to inculpate myself. 'I didn't.'

'Despite the instruction? I see. And why do you choose to ignore the instructions?'

'I didn't need to look him up in the book Mr. Stephens because he is not in it.'

He immediately saw the possibility that I had laid a trap for him. It was almost certain that if he looked for the name in the book, it would not be there and thus he would prove me right.

'The instruction is that all IOs on probation must look up every passenger in the suspect index. You are aware of that?'

'Yes Mr. Stephens, but I did not look him up because I know he is not in the book.'

I sensed that my dogged insistence was getting on his nerves. For once, I did not care.

'Hand me the landing card.' He was now clipped and stern. My head was on the block and he was letting me know it. And he was enjoying it. I gave the landing card to him. He read it. 'Give me your book.' I handed the volume over the top of the desk to him. 'It is quite possible that I will not find his name in the book, heaven help you if I do, but that does not absolve you from the obligation to obey instructions.' He started to turn the pages. He was ham fisted. Most IOs would have found the name and stamped the passport by now.

'I did not look him up in the book Mr. Stephens because he is not there.' Before he found the correct page, I continued, 'the only man with that surname whom you will find in the book has the Christian name of Patrick, not Jean, was born on 25th April 1945 and is German.'

He paused to look at me. Something in the assured way that I made the pronouncement unsettled him. He found the name and checked it against the landing card.

'Patrick,' I repeated. 'Twenty fifth of April, 1945, German, not likely to qualify for leave to enter.'

His eyes flicked from the card to the book to my face. He was thinking rapidly. How had I done it? Ah ha, he thought, the previous passenger must have had the same surname.

'Give me your cards.' I raised my eyebrows in a dangerous show of insolence as I surrendered my small stack of stamped landing cards to him. He stood there and checked every single one for an identical surname. There was not one. 'Are these all your cards?' I nodded. He stared at me for a moment. 'Hmm,' he grunted, snapped my book shut on the top of my desk and strode off.

He never worked out how I had done it. Could I have memorised the equivalent of a telephone directory? He could hardly believe that. Dennis never mentioned the matter again. Despite his unerring ability to wrong foot IOs, me included, I came to suspect as the years passed that he was never quite sure that he had got my measure. This hesitancy in his dealings with me might have been of use had I known how to exploit it. By the time that a stratagem had occurred to me, I did not care a toss.

So how had I carried off the trick? When I had been appointed as an immigration officer the first thing that I had done had been to look up the names of all my friends in the suspect index. One of them had the same name as an entry in the book and I had remembered it. Simple, really. Too simple for Dennis' tortured brain.

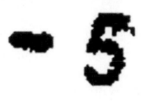

Tuesday was Iron Curtain day and I was on the freight control. In this outpost I was isolated from the rest of my colleagues by the port exit road. My place of work was the high-level control booth designed so that the IO could peer into the cabs of lorries. The drivers had to climb down from their lorries and stomp up the steps to queue in the miniature waiting room. I sat behind a sturdy locked door flanked on each side by a pair of forward facing guichets like at a bank so that I could check passports. If a jam built up then sometimes the CIO would send over another IO to assist. He sat at the other guichet and it was protocol that he should be permitted to moan about his bad luck and missed breakfast. The scheduled IO had no right to complain, he was supposed to be there.

Behind me is a door which leads to the back office. This houses a safe, a table and chair, a typewriter and a camp bed for the IO who gets to do the night duty. And a bottom drawer full of pornographic magazines. The freight control was a man's world. It stank of sour sweat and dirt, fuggy diesel fumes and acrid stale cigarette smoke. Any IO led into the office blindfolded would instantly know where he was. That morning the Civil Service Commission had sent me a letter begrudgingly accepting me as an 'established' civil servant. I had passed my probation. I was safe. Now, they could not get rid of me. Except for treason. My reward was the freight control on a Tuesday morning.

The Czech nationalised road transport company ran a fleet of Skoda lorries. They were painted a pastel shade of either pale blue or pale green with the logo of a winged 'CSAD' stencilled on the door. The trucks were all rigids with a drawbar trailer. This was presumably to make them more manoeuvrable in the snows of Central Europe; they could not jacknife as would an articulated lorry. Every rig was manned by a driver and co-driver. It was often suggested that one was there to make sure that the other did not defect but I did not believe that. I was pretty sure that they knew that they were well off with a job in a state-run concern and in any case, they would not have been allowed to travel abroad unless they had some family that the authorities could hold hostage in Czechoslovakia.

On Monday morning they set out from home and on Tuesday morning, they arrived at Dover, two to a lorry, three minutes each passport if you are quick.

I could see the fawn funnel of the Ostend boat jutting above the tangle of gantries and lighting pylons. It was in the berth. I perused the four sheets of the shipping manifest that the messenger had just shoved under the door. It gave the registration number, length and weight of each truck, the name of the customer, an indication of the load and the name of the local agent or importer. The Ostender was unloading seventeen lorries and by my deductions, eleven of those were either Czech or Hungarian. That meant twenty two Iron Curtain passports to check and stamp. There would be no breakfast for me today. Out in the harbour the Sealink ship was turning around ready to come astern into the berth. That would bring me the Spanish oranges, French glass, Italian olive oil and assorted loads of groupage. The traffic that the ships carried to Dover tended to divide along lines of geographical provenance; ships from Ostend and Zeebrugge brought the Scandinavian, German and Central European lorries and the Calais and Boulogne ferries attracted the Mediterranean customers.

The trucks roar towards me in two parallel lines. They stop under the canopy with a sneeze and a curtsey. The first few drivers are British. There are two types of British lorry drivers: old men in boiler suits and silvering hair and young cowboys in wooden clogs and jeans. The former are polite, reserved and respectful; the latter are boisterous and confrontational. One of the SB officers once told me that six out of ten British lorry drivers had a criminal record. It sounded an awful lot to me. If that were the case why was it so rare for us to see an SB officer sitting alongside us on freight? Could it be that it was unglamorous, smelly and unproductive?

The first driver in slaps two British passports down on the counter.

'Where's your mate?' I ask.

He goes to the window and raps on it to attract his mate's attention. He cannot possibly hear him above the noise of diesel engines.

'Oh for Christ's sake,' he mutters. Just as he reaches the door I call him back.

'It's all right. He's appeared now.' I check his face against the photo in the passport. 'Bloody hell, I can see why he was hiding.'

'I'll tell him that,' the driver laughs and scoops up the passports. 'Do your passport, clear Customs and I'll meet you in Hammond's,' he says to a younger driver whom he passes in the doorway.

I wave the newcomer forward. 'Just the one?' I ask him. He nods. 'No hitchhikers? No passengers?'

'No, just me.'

I stamp his form and return his passport. As he leaves to follow his mentor two squat men in check shirts come in. Was it only me who found amusement in the observation that Czechs were often dressed in checks? Probably. As I take their passports a second Czech rig pulls up on the other side of the kiosk. Looking down the waiting area and through the end windows I can see two more trundling up. Those two Brits. were lucky to have got in front of this lot and not behind.

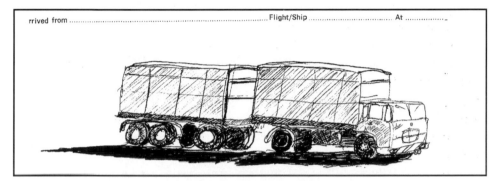

rrived from .... Flight/Ship .... At ...._

THE VIEW FROM MY DESK
On the freight control at Dover East.

I still find Czech passports challenging; trying to work out when they left their own country, how many days' exit visa they were given and consequently how long they can stay here. We rarely gave them permission to stay for more than one month. I flick through the early pages, searching for the exit visa stamp which would tell me how many *'napigs'* (days) they had been given. I can find three old ones but nothing current. I turn the passport around on the counter to show the driver.

'Doloshka?' I ask. He looks nonplussed. His mate leans over his shoulder to also study the passport. *'Vichestovakia Doloshka?'* I suggest.

This hits the target. He fumbles a leather wallet from his back pocket and pulls out a small paper. This was news to me. The Czechs were now issuing exit permits as separate documents rather than as stamps in passports. I trudge through the check shirts and the Skodas nudge slowly forwards. As I clear the few Brits. and a Dutchman who were stuck at the end, the lorries from the *Chartres* start to line up. The Dutch lorry full of flowers and a British tanker full of pvc granules are still alongside my kiosk, unable to move forwards until the lorries in front have cleared Customs. It seems that wherever we work in this port, the harbour board never provides enough buffer space between the customs and the immigration check points. It does not take much to choke the port to a standstill.

Eventually they move forwards and the marshal waves on the trucks which have just arrived from Calais on the *Chartres*. First to arrive are a long-nosed Volvo tanker full of wine and a pair of Renaults carrying sheets of plate glass from the works at Arques; further down the line I can see some refrigerated trailers pulled by Pegasos – they will be fruit from Spain. In idle moments when stuck for a whole duty on the freight control I study the cargoes on the lorries and challenge myself to achieve a goal in my imagination. I might decide to prepare myself a meal – today's would have consisted of green salads, tomatoes, peaches and donkey meat; the last being imported direct from Turkey to put into pet food. Another day I might start with the chipboard from Austria and see if I could gather enough relevant components to build something.

I am distracted by the sight of a tall, blonde woman in a flowing summer dress who is stepping down from the cab of the lorry alongside me. Hitch-hikers I have to send over to the walkers control. Members of the driver's family we allow to stay with him – they are often on the same passport. Sometimes you have to tussle with a lorry driver who tries to kid you that the twenty-one year old Canadian girl with the backpack is his wife. I can understand their disappointment but rules is rules and in any case, if I spent time interviewing the hitch-hiker it would hold up all the other lorries in the queue so common sense has to prevail. But this woman is not a passenger, she is the driver. She wobbles into the kiosk in a pair of shoes which would have been more appropriate to an evening at the opera rather than a truck cab.

'*Bonjour.*' She greets me in a husky voice and lays down a wallet containing two French i.d. cards. On the left is the man's, on the right, the woman's. I gaze through the window to check the man's face against the photograph.

'Where is he?' I ask.

'It's me,' she replies. 'They are both me.' She taps the man's card. 'That is my old card and that is my new card except that the government will not re-issue the card in a different sex so this is provided by the Association.'

I turn the card over and see that it is a facsimile of a French national identity card but provided by the French Association of Transsexuals. Well why not? I stamp her form and she/he climbs back into the lorry, happily acknowledging the whistle from another driver. Oh we do see life in today's Immigration Service.

Many British haulage firms use foreign-manufactured lorries such as Volvo, Mercedes and Scania. Some enterprises, notably in the Midlands, doggedly use Seddon, Foden and Leyland for Continental work but they are not properly suited because of the design of the cabs. For many years the Continental truck manufacturers had been building cabs with a rear compartment furnished with bunks and, in some cases, elementary cooking and washing facilities. This enabled the lorry driver to use his truck as a hotel and save money and time. British truck builders did not provide such amenities in their designs for the good reason that under the transport law in Britain, a lorry driver could only spend a certain number of hours per day in his lorry and then had to physically leave it to sleep. This policy supported two flourishing trades – that of the lorry drivers' bed and breakfast and that of the thief who would steal the load or the lorry whilst the driver was snug in his bed. When the law was changed, many of the transport guest houses fell on hard times, not something that saddened me much. I remember when I was at college, returning home to my digs unexpectedly in the daytime to find a lorry driver in my bed. The landlady was letting out the students' beds to overnight truck drivers in the daytime whilst we were improving our minds in academia. For the British truck manufacturers, the change in the law meant that now they could design a Continental truck cab but of course by then it was too late – the competition was too well established. Leyland was bankrupt so to give it a fillip it was merged with the other bankrupt truck manufacturer in Europe, the Dutch DAF, and they went down the pan together. Although I studied a bit of economics at college, I could not understand the logic of that policy. I wonder how the economists rationalised it.

The sleeper cab provides a hiding place in which naughty lorry drivers can secrete illegal immigrants or, more likely, half dressed hitch hikers so if the curtains are drawn across I ask them to pull them right back. After a couple of Pakistanis had been found in a truck coming through Harwich we were instructed to search all the cabs and the freight control was double manned to prevent delays.

Next time you see one of these juggernauts at a motorway service station, go and stand at the side of it and ascertain how many steps you have to climb to achieve ingress. It is very often three or four and they are vertical like a ladder, not graded as a staircase. How many times does a lorry driver climb into his cab in a day's work? I do not know, but not fifty times in one hour, I am certain. The practicality of carrying out the instruction to search the cabs was doubtful and the policy was clearly not popular, especially with skirted ladies, and so inevitably it was paraphrased by the IOs on duty. Eventually a special freight search squad was established and they were issued with fetching blue boiler suits. I did not volunteer for that particular empire.

I stamp another clearance form and a lorry load of fruit pieces to put into yogurt comes in from Germany. The next lorry is a British registered horse transport.

'Who have you got in the back?' I ask.

'A couple of grooms with the horses.'

'Can you send them in please? The grooms that is, not the horses.'

'They're trying to calm the horses.'

He looks at me. I look at him. 'I can wait. I'll get the marshal to send the other trucks around you.'

That persuades him and he storms out. I do not like having to flex theoretical muscle, it is not my style. I am not really a civil servant, or at least, not the stereotypical depiction of the petty minded bureaucrat. I just want a quiet but interesting life. The two grooms are both young ladies, one is Swiss, the other Austrian. They answer my questions quite openly and agree that they have both been working here in the stables for at least ten months. This is against the law because they have not applied for work permits. I am sure we have enough indigenous girls who are obsessed with horses who could do their job but that is not my decision, it is that of the Department of Employment. I give them permission to stay for one month with no employment possible and tell them to apply to the Home Office if they wish to stay longer or work. If I were a head hunter I would refuse them, but I am not. I fill the slack times between subsequent arrivals during my duty in composing the report on them which I will send to the

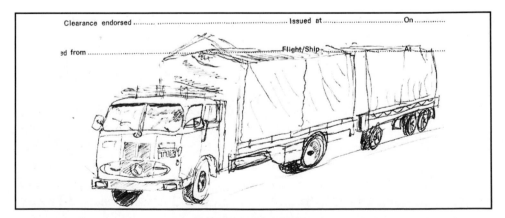

Clearance endorsed .... Issued at ....On ....

...d from .... Flight/Ship .... At ....

The view from my desk
On the freight control at Dover East.

Home Office so that it will be sitting there ready when their letters arrive. When I later recount the incident to a colleague he feigns astonishment that they had managed to transport the horses across France without their being eaten.

I am sitting and gazing, without seeing, at the view through my window. A customs officer walks across from the coach control and turns down the freight lane to get to his post. He looks at me as he wanders through. I look at him. He has blue eyes and fair hair. So what?

Once, when I was frantically examining British passports on the walkers control, the face of one of the passengers suddenly lit up with recognition.

'Hello Martin,' he said. 'Fancy seeing you here.'

As usual, I had absolutely no idea who he was. I have gone through life being recognised by people whom I do not know. They know I cannot remember names of faces so they pick on me.

I quickly opened his passport and scanned the name.

'Hello Bernard. How are you?'

He had been for a week's coach holiday. We parted, the best of friends with the small proviso that I still did not know how he knew me nor where we had met. That night, I had a brainwave. I phoned my brother.

'Do I know a person called Bernard Chapman?' I asked

'Of course you do.'

'How?'

'You remember when I was at college?'

'Yes.'

'And you came and stayed for the night in the halls of residence?'

'Yes.'

'Bernard lent you his electric razor.'

He had seen me for five minutes, five years earlier. What a memory for names and faces! He should have been doing my job.

The customs officer wanders back. He still has blue eyes and fair hair. He turns, climbs the steps and enters the office. I rise to meet him.

'Didn't you used to work for Paris Travel Service?' he says.

'Yes and didn't you used to work for Skyways?'

We both grin, but my grin was broader. I have actually recognised somebody and remembered who they were. The next hour passes quickly and pleasantly as we reminisce about our various meetings and common acquaintances in Paris and London and remark ruefully how bizarre that we should end up working fifty yards apart.

The last truck of the day is a small rigid with a tilt laced over the back. I recognise the name of the firm. It is a small enterprise which specialises in transporting vehicles discreetly. I always ask what they have on board. Once, the driver had lifted the rear flap to show me a German police Ford Taunus, all decked out in its insignia, stripes and lights. It had been sent over so that a British police force could assess the model's usefulness on their particular manor.

The lorry driver is British. 'What are you carrying?' I ask.

'A Lagonda.'

'But they are made in Britain at Newport Pagnell.'

'That's where I'm going. It's broken down.'

'But Aston Martin have only just released the Lagonda. It's a brand new model, it should not break down. What's wrong with it?' I hand him back his passport.

'The engine's blown up.'

At that time, I had been told that an Aston Martin engine was built by the individual technician who then signed his name on it and serviced it personally when it was returned to the works. It would be a black mark for him.

'How do you blow up a Lagonda engine?' I ask.

'Dead easy if you're a sheik. You go to Newport Pagnell to collect the car from the works and then you drive it down to Dover. When you get off the ferry at Calais you lock the automatic gear shift into first and tear off down the autoroute at one hundred and fifty miles an hour.'

'Blimey, that wouldn't do it much good. How far did he get?'

'Switzerland.'

One of the IOs remarked that when he first joined the Service he was afraid of being a square peg in a round hole but then he discovered that the entire workforce was composed of square pegs. Only two of the IOs in our office had joined directly from school – and somehow they seemed just a little bit naive. Everybody else had qualified in the University of Life and had done something else first; teacher, sailing boats, bank manager, army, navy, air force, computers, physical training instructor, accountant, cabinet-maker, radio technician, plumber, builder, and all other manner of activity. If we needed some insight into the esoteric side of a passenger's story, we could usually source it from somewhere in the office. Many had travelled in what were then, unfashionable places. 'This passenger claims that he drove through Iran in seven days. Is that feasible?' We would have an IO who could tell us. 'This fellow says he repairs televisions in Mauritius.

Do they have television there?' Somebody would know.

The wit of my colleagues I often found rewarding and so eclectic. Jokes and puns would be made and understood in several languages. During dull times between ship arrivals, the conversations in the rest room would naturally cover all the normal subjects like football and women but then somebody would complain that Spanish television was rubbish now that Franco had gone, it was all late night porn and variety shows. This would start off two or three officers discussing the various regions and peoples of the Iberian peninsula. Before joining the Immigration Service, one officer might have spent a year in Madrid as a language assistant; another worked illegally in a bar for two years; another had gone as far as to marry a Spanish girl and bring her home. Their knowledge of the country and language was the sort of asset that could hardly be valued.

When I started at Dover East, there were about eighty five IOs stationed there and only two did not speak a foreign language. I was one of the few who only spoke one language, French in my case. Most officers spoke French and German or French and Spanish. We had some with fluent Portuguese and Italian. We had a Greek native speaker and several with a smattering of Arabic. Russian, Serbo Croat, Hungarian, Swedish could all be found somewhere in our midst. Some of the brainy students collected languages like trophies; able to speak and write four or five with ease. I think the record was a chap who was qualified in eleven languages. Not that it did him much financial good for although the Home Office paid us a language allowance based upon the languages for which we had passed the relevant examinations, it capped the total amount of money that could be paid to an individual so those who mastered more than five were doing it for the fun, not for the money.

To make sure that the Home Office was not wasting its money, it made IOs pass an examination in the language every five years. My first exam took place in an upstairs room at Ashford library. Having finished the translations I then had to do a half hour oral.

The examiner was about ten years older than me and wore corduroy trousers and a green sports jacket.

'Here is a text I would like you to read aloud and then answer some questions on it. Take your time to read it through to yourself and when you are ready, read it aloud.' He pushed a photocopied magazine article across the desk at me.

I glanced at the article. It was from the news magazine *Le Point*. I could see no particular challenge in it so I started reading aloud straight away. This startled the examiner and he stared as I read it through at normal speed without a fault.

'Well,' he said in French, 'you obviously understood all of that. There is little point in me asking questions to test your comprehension.'

This was a dangerous misprision on his part; it is possible to read a foreign language text whose meaning is obscured from you but still sound fluent by using your knowledge of sentence construction and general grammar. However, we chatted away in French for about ten minutes and it became obvious that my accent was better than his and my everyday vocabulary was greater.

'Why are you working in the Immigration Service?' he asked. 'You could be up at Kent University as a lecturer like me.'

'Why would I want to? I've got a real job.'

He marked me ninety percent which I thought was a bit mean.

By the time that the next exam came around, five years later, the running of the language examinations had been farmed out by the Civil Service Commission to an independent organisation. It was grandly announced that for every oral examination we would be interviewed by a native speaker. I duly conversed with the little crinkled man about Paris and immigrants and food but was a little disturbed firstly by his lingering accent and secondly by mistakes that he made. For example, he began the word *'psychologique'* without pronouncing the initial 'p' as a Frenchman would have done and he had to correct himself. I deduced from this that he had been living too long in England.

'How long have you lived here?' I asked.

'Over thirty years.'

'But you are not French are you?'

'No, I'm Belgian.' This foxed me because his slight accent sounded to me more towards Swiss than Belgian. 'Why do you ask?'

'Because you have an accent. French is not your mother tongue is it?'

He shrugged. 'Well, I come from a part of Belgium where we speak German.'

'So German is your mother tongue then?'

'Yes.'

So much for being examined by a native speaker.

He marked me down to eighty-seven per cent.

The learning of languages became pivotal in my first attempt to alleviate the boredom of winter. I was sitting in the general office and reading the notices on the file during my 'down time'. The awaited ECO postings had just been announced. In most parts of the globe, the Foreign Office issued the visas at their consulates on behalf of the Home Office but in some countries, notably the Indian sub-continent and certain countries in West Africa, they requested assistance from the Immigration Service because of the density of the traffic and then IOs were selected and attached to the Foreign Office for periods ranging from three months to three years.

Apart from the fun of living the life of a diplomat and getting a suntan, an ECO posting looked good on your annual report. In some cases, the successful fulfilment of a long term posting could be the trigger for the IO being considered suitable for promotion and called to a CIO board upon his return. The other significant inducement to apply was the money. If you were posted overseas for a period of less than six months then you were entitled to a day subsistence allowance which varied according to the country. This was paid on top of your salary and was substantial. You could expect to return to the UK with a surfeit of three or four month's salary even after having enjoyed your social life to the full. The long term posting was the real money-spinner. You moved out of your house and rented it out for three years, pocketing the rent because accommodation in your overseas post was found for you. Your family accompanied you, to be educated at an international school at public expense and your wife was usually able to obtain a clerical post in the consulate, earning tax-free local currency. Although you might be sweltering in Lagos or sweating in Bombay, you had been transferred to the Foreign Office in London, so, of course, your salary was automatically augmented by the Inner London Weighting Allowance but having been posted abroad to an area which attracted an overseas allowance this had to be added to your salary. And so it went on.

At this time no Commonwealth citizen needed a visa to come to the UK for a holiday but they did if they wanted to settle in the country. The system required them to attend at the British High Commission in their native country and answer the questions and provide all the relevant documentary evidence at that point. If they qualified, the entry clearance officer (ECO) endorsed their passport with the permission. Because the citizens of these countries did not require visas ordinarily, the visas were called 'entry certificates'. That is the way you do it. Armed with this stamp or sticker in their passport, the immigrants usually flew into Heathrow, Terminal Three, where on my training course I had dealt with them on the settlement desk. I had not known what I was doing then and I doubted that I would know now what to do if I met a passenger brandishing a 'settlement EC' but given their customary provenance, it was unlikely that they would come to Dover East upon their first arrival. We do not have any cross Channel ferries from Nigeria or Bangladesh.

I read the list. Most of the postings had gone to IOs from Heathrow, a few were scattered as largesse amongst the insignificant ports such as Dover or Folkestone. Wally was sitting at the next table, updating his suspect index. He was a small, quiet chap, quite self contained. He did not mix socially with anybody in the office. He was not unfriendly; he just did his job and then went home. With his neat black hair, clear complexion and duffle bag, he looked like a schoolboy trainspotter which was quite appropriate for he once divulged to me that he had spotted every steam locomotive running on British Railways and showed me his Loco Shed book to confirm it. He and his turquoise cardigan never seemed to get older in all the time that I knew him and when he retired I almost felt like challenging him over his age.

'I see that Mike Jenkins has got Lagos,' I said.

'He's welcome to it.'

'He'll make pots of money.'

'But he won't come back here.' This was news to me. 'You are taken off the strength when you get long term ECO. When he's finished they'll send him to Terminal Three.'

'Ah,' I said, remembering the northside car park in the rain and the hour-long commute. Down in Kent, you could afford to live on the doorstep it you wanted to. Few officers lived more than a thirty minute drive away. 'Have you ever done ECO Wally?'

He put down his pen and put his hands together on the desk before him. This was not always a good sign because he could be a bit of a bore sometimes.

'I did four months in Ankara.'

'Why did you apply for Turkey?'

'I didn't. I was sitting here one day and the inspector walked in. "Headquarters are on the phone. They are looking for a volunteer in an emergency for ECO Ankara, short term," he said. I was the only IO in the office, the others were all down the pub so I got it. They sent me out three weeks later.'

'Good fun?'

'I came home early with dysentery.' He gave a boyish smile. 'Not my finest hour.'

I left him to his updating and turned to the next notice. I had a feeling that I was looking through these notices for a way out. I did not want to spend another drab, cold, drawn-out winter in the building site that was Dover Eastern Docks. There was no point in my applying for an overseas posting; I was far too inexperienced to qualify. The IO who had been given Lagos had at least nine years seniority.

I read the next notice. What about this? Winter language courses: two courses, one in oral Urdu, one in Turkish, twelve IOs on each course to be chosen from the entire country. They ran from late September to mid-December when all IOs were called back to their ports to deal with the holiday rush and then started again in January running through to the end of March. And the courses were run in London so I would get travelling expenses. What were the chances that I would be chosen? I had no idea but it was worth a try.

At that moment CIO Bill Ventian stuck his head out of the ops. room. 'Can one of you go down and help the temps on embarks? There's a queue building up.'

'I'll go. Wally is still doing his book.' I closed my case and locked it and made for the door. 'Do you want me on walkers or cars?'

'Oh go where the queue is longest. No, go to walkers, I can just see three P&O buses on their way down.'

Into the surreal gloom of the old arrivals hall, now partitioned into offices and leased by the harbour board to various agencies; a lofty-ceilinged space fitted with a zigzag of white partitions. I often felt like a mouse wandering around some laboratory maze although the mouse probably understood the value of his peregrinations more than I did of mine.

Embarks was a mirror image of inwards. We were now on the cliff side of the port. Tucked along the foot of the cliff was the port services road; next came the lanes used by freight. The drivers stopped their lorries just at the entrance to the building and then walked in to show their documents to the IO. On the other side of the central building ran the car lanes which were also used by the buses transporting the foot passengers to the ships. In the summer, the embarkation control was run by the team of 'summer temporary immigration officers' – STIOs for short. They had been picked from another world. Elderly, dignified gentlemen who were now retired but in their working lives they had been colonial governors, tea planters, bank managers, lieutenant colonels or police inspectors. Dressed in lounge suits and speaking a beautifully enunciated English of the 1920s, they brought a gentlemanly aura of calm and status quo to the hectic madhouse that was the embarkation control at Dover East in the summer. Essentially, the examining of travellers leaving the United Kingdom was a clerical job. In the vast majority of cases, the government did not actually care who was leaving, as long as they went. Britain was full.

Every embarking passenger left a bit more breathing room for the others. The real job was done on the seaward side of the port where the IOs turned back those whom the government did not want in the country. On embarks, the very small sample of people they were interested in were passengers who had been admitted on restricted conditions and needed to be checked to ensure that they were leaving within their time limit and others who might be of interest to the police. The latter were dealt with by the time-tested method of the Special Branch officer in attendance writing their suspect's name on a blank embarkation card and propping it up under the overhang on the IO's desk so that it stayed before his eyes but was hidden from those of the public.

I clattered down the steps at the end of the building and glanced into the customs hall where the officers had already removed the doors from a camper van. I weaved my way through the vehicles queuing to pass through Customs, around the end of the chain link fence and through the lines of cars and caravans proceeding to the embarkation control. The slowly moving queue of cars stretched back towards the road entrance to the port, its end was out of sight behind the No1 Control Building. Three robust double deck buses of the, 'I once roamed the streets of Huddersfield', variety but now painted the pale blue of P&O Ferries were crawling towards the kiosks. They were stuffed full of day trippers for the *m.v. Lion* sailing to Boulogne. Wednesday was market day in Boulogne.

'Morning Herbert,' I said to a short man with silver hair and sporting a rather dapper waistcoat and chain. I slid my case into the footwell of his desk. 'I'll nip out and do the coaches on board.'

'That would be most generous.'

As a proper IO I could use my discretion to clear the passengers on board the coach, a procedure which saved an awful lot of time and fuss. I could see that the coaches were Wally Arnolds and Shearings. They sported various destination boards advertising itineraries in Europe. There would be nobody under fifty years old on the coach, and that included the driver. I jumped up the steps to the first coach. *'Rimini, seven days,'* was written on the card propped up in the window.

'How many have you got?' I asked the courier.

'Thirty- seven.'

'All British?'

'Yes.'

'Have they all got their passports?'

'Yes.'

'Can you hold up all your passports please ladies and gentlemen?'

A stirring runs down the coach and hands carrying blue booklets waver towards the luggage racks. 'What about the Irish chap half way down on the off side?' I say to the courier. I can see his green passport from where I am standing.

'Eh?'

I wriggle down the aisle and glance quickly through his passport. He has lived in Bolton for fifty-three years. I have no intention of stamping his passport nor of looking inside any of the others. Some of them may have expired but frankly, does it matter? They are on a package tour for heaven's sake.

'OK driver, off you go.' I jump down to the apron and wait for the next coach to pull forwards. The STIOs would have had to make everybody get off and check every passport. They would have done the job properly.

I suspect that this obligation to stick to the rules riled them sometimes when they could see that a more pragmatic approach would benefit everybody but they foiled the anger and discontent of the complaining travellers with their unfailing dignity and politeness. And some of the public could be quite unpleasant. One lady in particular made a terrific fuss one day at being asked to alight from the coach like the other passengers in order to show her passport. She stood in the queue and lambasted her husband whose crime had apparently been to acquiesce to the STIO's request instead of fighting for her rights. She announced loud and large that she was not the class of person who should be expected to kowtow to petty-minded officials; ignorant upstarts who had no manners and even less intelligence and could only find menial employment stamping passports. By the time that she reached the front of the queue everybody in the hall knew of her opinion. The petty-minded ignorant upstart with no manners and less intelligence was a discreet gentleman in a sober lounge suit and impeccably impartial manners who had recently retired from a merchant bank. Fanny Cradock slapped her passport down onto the desk.

'Don't you stand up for a lady?' she screeched.

Handing back her passport and remaining seated the STIO replied with a stolid politeness, 'Without fail madam.'

The rebuff was unrecognised by the ex-TV chef but was not lost on the audience.

Back in the office I had some clerical work to do – to submit my resignation from the trade union. I had never wanted to join in the first place but on the first week of our training course we had been given an address by the union rep. who, whilst outlining the various benefits had added the unsubtle rider that if we did not join, the union would make sure that we did not pass our probation. This muscular bullying was one of the aspects of unionism that repelled me, along with the lies and other coercions that they generally practised but I had no intention of fighting them, not whilst I was in a vulnerable position. I needed to pass my probation and whether or not I believed that the union was capable or willing to torpedo my chances, I did not need the extra worry so I joined up with the intention of resigning the moment that I was confirmed as an established civil servant. My resignation caused the membership in the port to fall below the magical 100% and I was cornered by a posse of union reps. The CIO was the most offensive.

'You've resigned from the union. Why?'

'I never wanted to join it in the first place. I don't need it.'

'You'll be turning down the latest pay rise that we negotiated for our members then?'

'No. I'm not one of your members.'

'So you're not entitled to the pay rise then. You'll be paying the money to a charity? We'll accept that.'

'Why should a union that I don't belong to dictate where I should spend my money?'

'It's money we're giving you.'

'The union is not my employer. The Home Office is. They decide what to pay me.'

'Only because we have struggled and negotiated on your behalf.'

'More fool you. I am not in your union. You have negotiated on behalf of your members, not for me. '

'So you should not get the pay rise.'

'You had better tell the Home Office that. They might be interested in your argument.'

'Well perhaps we might. We might just do that.'

'When the union becomes my employer then you will be able to dictate to me. If the Home Office decides to pay me the same amount as a union member that decision is theirs to make. They are surely aware that they get more for their money from me. They ought to pay me more than union members. Perhaps I will suggest it to them.'

'More?'

'Yes. I do everything that a union member does but additionally I don't go on strike so they know at least that they have one reliable officer at Dover East.'

'I think you are despicable. Despicable.'

Maybe he did, but it was not me who got my face slapped when I tried to grope a young female IO to whom I was giving a lift in my car. Nor did I eventually get promoted to inspector.

Another union man, an IO this time, bearded me on embarks to point out that the union was negotiating to make the Immigration Service a closed shop so I would either have to join or be dismissed. I told him that I would become a Sikh because they could object on religious grounds. The IS did not become a closed shop, I did not become a Sikh and he went on to become the director of the Immigration Service.

Most of my colleagues did not know that I was no longer in the union and upon being appraised of my heinous crime, generally expressed a complete uninterest in the intelligence. Those who decided that it did matter would make a point of walking out of a car kiosk when I came in and installing themselves in another one. I derived much sport from choosing my kiosks with innocent care so that protesters were obliged to pack up and trudge through the wind and rain to go elsewhere. Those who decided to not speak to me merely left me more space in which I could talk to myself, something which I can do volubly and incessantly and which generally produced the same effect.

It did not matter to me that I somehow seemed to receive a heavier dealing of the more unloved duties; this was one area where the union could flex its muscle locally since the duty chart was composed weekly by a team of IOs appointed for this service, and they were all union officials of some sort. On the day that the union did eventually call a strike these duty-compiling officers allocated me an office duty to make sure that I was not scheduled to land passengers and thus not in a position to be able to diminish the dislocation that they wished to create. Needless to say, I was unable to swap this duty with any other officer, even though they would probably not be coming in to work. Some union members decided that they nevertheless had a duty to the public and turned up for work. The others discovered that putting me on the duty where I monitored the switchboard of the entire port was a tactical blunder. When officers phoned up to ask what was happening I told them that everybody had come in to work and the port was functioning normally. Those who asked to talk to a union rep. found themselves shunted up a dead line and eventually cut off. The immigration control was effected with no delay to the public and by employing only a third of the normal complement of officers. Had the union been trying to prove something, their only success was to suggest that Dover East was overmanned by 200%. However, all that was in the future. For the moment I sealed the letter and dropped it in the bin for the outgoing post.

Then my eye fell upon the notice about those language courses. Did I want to spend another storm-torn winter, trudging between kiosk and office in the dark and wet, squelching over the sewage-impregnated carpet tiles in the passenger hall and hearing the monotonous *tap, tap, tap* of water dripping through the leaking roof onto the desktops after every heavy fall of rain? Did I need to get up at five in the morning and skitter on ice-covered roads in order to see my first passenger five hours later? Trying to wield a stamp whilst dressed in overcoat and scarf and shivering to the core in draughty embarkation halls had never been mentioned in the recruitment ads. I took a sheet of paper and submitted my name as a candidate for consideration on the oral Urdu course. It was a long shot, but I thought it was worth it. We would see.

Inspector John poked his head into the general office from the corridor. 'Can't one of you chaps stop that racket?'

We raised our heads from the books we were updating, drew a communal sigh and then looked at each other accusingly.

'You're nearest,' somebody said to Douglas.

'Ah'm not a skivvy for the management,' he growled.

I put the cap on my pen and stood up. The telex machine had been buzzing for about five minutes and the red light was flashing forlornly. I sat down at the keyboard and smacked the 'send reply' key. The buzzing stopped and I tapped out an acknowledgment. It was a telex from Box 500 which was the cover address for MI5. They had sent us the details of some suspect passengers that they wished us to look out for. I tore the paper from the machine and took it to the photocopier to make some notices to put on the files from which we were updating our books.

'Anything important?' an IO asked.

'If you are that curious why didn't you come and deal with it?' I didn't wait for an answer because I knew that he would say that he did not know how to work the machine. 'It's just Box wanting us to look out for some Arabs.'

'Oh that makes a change.'

It didn't and we all knew it.

The telex machine was one of the proud representatives of technology in our office; the other was the photocopying machine. Many IOs could not type and so they handwrote their reports which were then sent to the typist. I was fairly proficient with a typewriter, having taught myself to touch-type whilst studying at college. My prowess with the telex machine came from my having made a nuisance of myself with the telex operator at the air terminal where I used to spend a lot of my time in a previous employment. The teleprinter at Dover East was used mainly to receive various notifications from Box or ISHQ – the Immigration Service Headquarters. This was the department situated at Lunar House in Croydon. Occasionally we actually initiated a telex. When a passenger holding a visa was detained pending a decision on whether to admit or refuse him, we needed to contact the consulate abroad which had issued the visa to check whether he had told them the same tale that he was now telling us. The telex allowed us to leap time zones in the sense that we sent the telex enquiry as soon as was practicable knowing that whatever the time of day or night that it was received at the other end, our message would sit on their machine until they dealt with it. We never perpetrated such bad manners as putting the buzzer on at their end to ask them to acknowledge receipt.

Whenever I was asked to send a telex I never did it 'live'; I always recorded it first on the punched paper tape and then, when I had received the answerback message, I started the tape. The advantage of this procedure from the recipient's point of view was that the message took less time to receive as it was transmitted at top speed, thus liberating their machine for the next message which might be on its way. The advantage from the sender's point of view was that if for some reason the link failed and the message did not get through, then it was a simple operation to repeat the message by redialling and feeding the tape back into the machine, obviating the need to re-type everything. Always assuming, of course, that you had not destroyed the tape.

We were forbidden to contact certain of the overseas posts directly and had to send our telex via the Diplomatic Wireless Service, presumably so that it could be classified and encoded. This could add forty-eight hours to the waiting time.

The photocopier was moulded in that beige plastic which got browner with age as it absorbed the nicotine from the pipes and cigarettes of the IOs. It printed a grey version of the document you wanted to copy, onto a sheet of speckled grey paper. Copying photographs was a pointless operation; they were interpreted as blotches of grey and paler grey and bore little useful information. A document written in blue ink it would reproduce provided that it had viewed it through a sheet of red celluloid which you had laid on the platen first. All these procedures we accepted without grumble in order to be in the forefront of technology.

Once, in the middle of a night duty, I had needed to refer to some instructions. The photocopied sheets were contained in a box file which had been left on top of a night storage radiator; another technological marvel of the time. I pulled them out and could easily see that they had been classified as *'confidential'* because our clerical officer had stamped this warning at the top and bottom of each photocopied sheet in red ink. Indeed, this was the only information the sheets could convey for, apart from this warning, they were entirely blank. The photocopy ink had faded to nothing.

I had heard rumours that over at Dover West they had acquired what they called a 'facsimile transmitting machine' which, in the space of forty-five minutes, would transmit a photograph down a telephone line and I remember that it was once used to trap a Greek who had inserted his own photograph into a British passport. The image of the original photograph pinned to the passport application form was sent down from the passport office via the facsimile machine and proved the forgery.

But putting technology aside, it was about time that I caught my very own loony. Many IOs have to deal with a loony at some stage in their career. Some nutters one could class as simply eccentric; others are stark staring bonkers but very few turn out to be dangerous. The procedure for getting rid of such persons was to call in the Port Medical Inspector who would examine the passenger and then issue a 'Port 30' which was a form indicating that in his medical opinion the subject should be certified under the mental health act. Once he had done that, we could refuse entry to the passenger on the grounds that his exclusion was 'conducive to the public good.' Since I had been at the port I had come across several nutters belonging to other IOs. One chap answered every question with the single French word, 'baromètre'. This somewhat stultified the IO's examination. We never got to the bottom of his fixation with things meteorological. Perhaps he just liked the sound of the word. I rather like the word 'equipollent' for a similar reason. It rolls around the tongue lovingly. In fact, the more I was exposed to those persons who were featherlight in the mental faculties the more I became convinced that theirs was a rather nice world. They often appeared to be quite happy and contented with what was happening to them in their version of reality.

Sometimes the IO was able to prevent them from bringing, what we would consider to be disaster, crashing down upon their heads. Trevor, the IO who had tried to press-gang me into the football team when I had arrived at Dover East had recently dealt with an American man of about thirty years who had arrived as a foot passenger from Calais. When Trevor had asked him how much money he possessed, he had said six hundred dollars but when Trevor asked to see it he said that he had thrown it away because it was dirty. Where had he thrown it? Oh in a bin somewhere. Which bin? Where I got off the bus. Trevor looked through the window at the wire rubbish bin bolted to the stanchion outside. That bin? Possibly, all these bins look the same. He went outside and, sure enough, nestling in the bottom of the wire rubbish basket was a bundle of notes to the value of six hundred dollars.

Sometimes the nutters gave themselves away immediately; sometimes they started off with rational replies which when tested became more and more fanciful until the examination wallowed into the surreal. The phrase which summed up the most common deviation was, 'royalty complex.' The number of individuals encountered each year who were coming to visit the Queen was astonishing. As soon as a passenger mentioned the Queen, in a social context rather than a touristic, alarm bells would ring in your brain. Was Her Majesty expecting you? Do you have an invitation? They usually avoided the latter by pointing out that Her Maj would be sending a coach and horses to Charing Cross to meet them from the train. One man was coming to marry the Queen.

'I thought she was already married,' the IO observed in a neutral tone.

'Oh I don't think that will be a problem.'

'The Duke of Edinburgh might not agree with you.'

'Oh he has said it's OK.'

There were seemingly no limits to their imagination. Almost without exception the people with a royalty fixation came from countries which had no royal family of their own. Quite a high proportion of these were French which was ironic considering that if they had not chopped off so many heads during the Revolution then they could have stayed at home and fantasised about their own royalty.

Although they always appeared calm and respectful, because of their obviously unstable nature one could never be sure that they were safe and it was made clear to us that if any one of these nutters actually got through to Buckingham Palace and made a nuisance of themselves then we would be to blame. In order to refuse entry to a nutter you still had to interview them as if they were normal in order to provide information to justify your eventual decision. Their irrational replies usually fulfilled this need admirably.

One little man, I think he was Belgian, declared that he was coming to England to see the Queen. Many tourists do but he meant to actually knock on the door of Buckingham Palace and ask if Her Majesty could come out to play. Even after he had been refused entry by the IO he did not really comprehend what was going on. At that time there was operating in Folkestone an organisation known as the UKIAS. It was a voluntary organisation set up by a worthy lady to aid immigrants who had been refused entry at the Channel ports. We often would ring them when we were refusing a person who had no money or other means of looking after themselves and they would come and offer assistance. In this particular incident, the UKIAS volunteer was actually the wife of the IO dealing with the case. A charming lady with sleek black hair, sober dress and a string of pearls. Her husband took her into the interview room to meet the passenger. The Belgian immediately rose wide-eyed from his chair and knelt piously at her feet.

'Your majesty,' he gasped.

After that, it was all plain sailing. No matter what was said to him to correct his mistaken assumption he was convinced that he had met the Queen and went home a happy Belgian with an incredible tale to tell. It did make us wonder whether such a procedure should have been adopted country-wide. The Home Office could have held on a small retainer a select group of impersonators ready to attend the ports at any time of night and day for a fee. It would have saved them thousands of pounds. The IO's wife was not so pleased. She was a good twenty years younger than the monarch for whom she had been mistaken.

Sometimes, a bona fide, compos mentis, homo sapiens would come out with a tale so bizarre that the IO would be reaching for the Port 30 whilst looking around wildly to make sure that he was not being left alone with the passenger. One day at Heathrow a Swiss man came up to the IO's desk.

'How long are you staying here?'

'Three days.'

'And what are you coming to do here?'

'I am going to fight the battle of Waterloo.'

Short pause whilst IO mentally revises his knowledge of nineteenth century European history. Deduction: this man is a nutter.

'And you think you can do it in three days?'

'I normally do it in two.'

'I see.' That was a lie. 'And you fight this battle on your own?'

'Oh no, I have an army.'

IO looks along the other desks for evidence of a platoon of Swiss infantry. Finds none. 'I don't see your army.'

'No. Would you like to see it?'

'It would help.'

Swiss man puts attaché case on desk top and opens it to reveal an array of neatly packed miniature soldiers. 'We have a war-gaming convention every year,' he explains to the relieved IO, 'the Battle of Waterloo is the highlight.'

'Which side are you on?'

'Oh I am Napoleon this year.'

'So you'll lose then?'

'No. Whenever we fight the Battle of Waterloo, Napoleon always wins. He was by far the best tactician but he was just unlucky on the day.'

Well that gives us food for thought, doesn't it?

OOSTENDE DOVER **Jetfoil** **P&O** European Ferries

Oostende · Dover **168004** os

Inschepingskaart · Hoofddek · Niet Rokers
(Zie ommezijde voor belangrijke mededeling)

Carte d'embarquement · Pont Principal · Non Fumeurs
(Avis important au verso)

Einschiffungskarte · Hauptdeck · Nicht Raucher
(Wichtige Mitteilung auf der Rückseite)

Boarding Card · Maindeck · Non Smoking
(For important notice, see back)

RMT/RTM-BRB

BOOKMARK

Embarkation card for the P&O Jetfoil service to Ostend, Belgium from Dover.

The three-to-midnight men have gone home. They went at a quarter to eleven when the boozing contingent of the night shift returned from the pub. It is all very immoral and corrupt. Some officers are paid to work until midnight but have not; some others are drinking beer when they should be stamping passports. It goes on all the time and many officers are party to it and because it has such a widespread following, the participants are never penalised. You cannot be disciplined for drinking in the pub when you should have been on duty in the port if you have taken the precaution of ensuring that the man standing next to you at the bar is your equally guilty CIO. The people who were punished were the colleagues who remained on duty to do the work whilst the others were skiving. I suffered in silence with the others.

By one o'clock in the morning the port has settled down to business. At midnight the P&O ship from Boulogne had brought a Cypriot minibus to the walkers control. Three passengers have been landed as returning residents, six are held up, three more have not yet been interviewed. I am on cars inwards for the Zeebrugge arrival which always brings a flurry of squaddies from the BFPO in Germany. They prefer the Zeebrugge sailing because Townsends give them discount. When you look in the boots of their cars they all contain a line of camouflage-green jerry cans full of duty-free petrol sufficient for their visit and return journey. Townsends would have a fit if they knew just how many mobile Molatov cocktails they were carrying below decks. Perhaps they know but turn a blind eye.

By the time that I get over to walkers the Cypriots have been allocated to IOs and I am elected to the fixed point, being the only free IO. I sit out on the desk and read an old newspaper that I find in the rubbish bin whilst my colleagues process the Cypriots. Outside the window is parked the battered, dark blue Ford Transit minibus. A man is standing in the enormous roofrack and lowering bundles to the ground for the customs officers to inspect. Further over I can see the lights of the lorries grinding through the freight control. Occasional pedestrians walk seawards down the port exit road. They are crew members and other workers starting their shifts. The minibus drives through to the baggage reclaim. The Cypriots have started to segregate. Nothing can be settled at this time of the night. You cannot ring up a sponsor at three in the morning. The Dover Harbour Board Land Rover turns up and the unfinished passengers are loaded into it for the short journey to the detention suite where they will be locked up until morning. The minibus and landed passengers will continue up to Stoke Newington without them.

I look at the perspective of orange carpet tiles, stained by the various breakages of duty-free liquor, which stretches out to the far wall of the hall. Up amongst the cream fibre ceiling tiles the fluorescent light tubes are polluted with Stationery Office rubber bands which bored IOs have flicked up persistently from their desks until, by impacting at just the correct angle, they drop down into the diffuser.

The Land Rover is back outside again. Why? I don't have any more Cypriots to give them. The Dover Harbour Board Police are not real police. Not according to us. They are just men in uniform. Even my plumber gave up pipes and joined their force with no problem.

The officer walks into the hall with a fair haired man of about forty years of age. He is wearing blue jeans, a red shirt and a loose, nondescript jacket which is closed by a zip fastener down the front.

'There you are sir, show your passport to the officer here. He will look after you.' He motions the man forwards. 'Found him in the Merry Dolphin,' he explains to me.

'OK thanks, I'll deal with him.'

The Merry Dolphin is the café which sits at the bottom of the port control tower like a faithful disciple crouched at the feet of the Messiah. It is open to the travelling public all night long but only those who are embarking can actually use it. Arriving foot passengers should have no opportunity to dally, they are whisked away to the passenger hall by the shuttle bus. This one has managed to get lost somehow.

'Can I see your passport please sir?'

'Parlez français?' he enquires.

I repeat my question in French and he pulls out a French passport. Its blue plastic cover is so grubby that the gold 'RF' emblem is black.

'How long are you staying here?'

'Where are we? What is this place?'

'This is Dover.'

'Dover?'

'Yes, Dover. Is that where you want to be?'

'I want to go to London.'

'Are you a foot passenger? No car?'

'No, I am on the train. Where is the train to London?'

'Well the last train to London has gone. The next one is at about six in the morning I think. Can I see your ticket?' He shows me a Paris-London rail single ticket which means that he obviously did not arrive on the *m.v Lion* from Boulogne, he would have travelled on one of the Sealink ships for they carry the rail passengers. 'When did your ship arrive in Dover?' I begin to look on my sailing schedule. He shrugs. 'Was it at about ten twenty?'

'Perhaps. I don't have a watch.'

'The policeman found you in the café. Why did you go in there?'

'For the same reason as everyone.'

'Which ship did you arrive on? Do you know?' He purses his lips and shakes his head. 'OK, never mind. So how long are you going to stay in London?'

'Well, that depends. I'm coming for a job.'

This was quite in order. As a national of an EC country he could work here.

'Are you looking for a job or do you have one to go to?'

'No, no, I've got a job.'

'What job?'

'Chauffeur.'

'Driving what? Lorries? Buses? Cars?' The job title in French could cover all three.

'Driving a private car.'

'Not a taxi then?'

'How could I drive a taxi here? I don't know my way about. I would get lost.'

'But you wouldn't get lost driving a private car?'

'That's different.'

'How much money have you got with you?'

'Not much.'

'How much.'

'Not very much.'

'Can you show me how much?'

He looks at me with his pale blue eyes, calm under bushy blond eyebrows. 'Yes.'

I wait. He looks at me. I wait some more.

'Well go on then, show me how much money you have with you.' He puts his hand into the pocket of his jeans and pulls out a bundle of notes. I count them and hand them back. 'You are right. It's not very much. Thirty-five francs will not last long.'

'I had more but I bought coffee on the ship. Anyway, I shall get paid so I will be all right.'

'When do you start work?'

'I don't know yet. I need to see my employer first.'

'Who is your employer?'

'Lady Hollinger.'

'And she wants you to be her chauffeur.'

'Yes. She's got a big Rolls Royce.'

'Do you have a letter from her about your job.'

'What would it say?'

'Well, a letter stating when you start and what your duties will be and how much you will be paid.'

'That's not decided yet. Lady Hollinger will tell me.'

'Does she know you are coming?'

'Of course, she asked me to come.'

'Where does she live?'

'London.'

'Where in London?'

'Oh Brunswick... Brunsheim... Something beginning with a B.'

'Can't you remember her address?'

'No.'

'And you have not got it written down? As on a letter for example?'

'No.'

'How will you find Lady Hollinger? Is she meeting you at the station?'

'No. Lady Hollinger is a lady. She would not do things like that.'

'So how will you find her?'

'I will go to London and look.'

I sniff discreetly. I cannot smell drink on him. The possibility that he might be a nutter has still not occurred to me. But shortly it will.

'You said that Lady Hollinger asked you to be her chauffeur didn't you?'

'Yes she asked me.'

'When?'

'About two months ago.'

'Did she write you a letter?'

'No.'

'On the telephone?'

'No, she asked me in my house.'

'Oh, she came to–' I look in the passport, '–Asnieres, did she? Was she visiting you?'

'She comes in the evening.'

'Which evening did she come?'

'She comes lots of evenings.'

'To your house? She talks to you there? Does she visit France often?'

'I don't know.'

'But she came to your house?'

'No.' He looks at me with a puzzled frown. I wonder why it is he who is puzzled.

'You said that she asked you to be her chauffeur when she was in your house.'

'Yes. I saw her on the television.'

'What programme was she on? Why was she on the television?'

'That was when she told me that she wanted me to be her chauffeur.'

'Lady Hollinger told you, on your television, that she wanted to employ you?' He nods, satisfied. It makes sense to him. It does not make sense to me. Perhaps I am misunderstanding his French. This is unlikely, given my facility in that language. Try again on a different tack.

'What is your present job?'

'I don't have one at the moment.'

'What did you used to do?'

'Lorry driver. Tankers.'

'When did you stop doing that?'

'Oh... last year some time. I can't really remember.'

'And what have you done since?'

'Nothing really. I was in hospital.'

'What was wrong with you?'

'Something wrong with my tripes.' He rubs his stomach to endorse his explanation.

'How long were you in hospital?'

'Two, three months.'

And still the alarm bells were not ringing in my head. It just showed how naive I was.

'But you are cured now?'

'Oh yes, completely cured. The doctor said so.'

'Good. Now this job with Lady Hollinger... I am still not clear as to how she engaged you and how you are going to find her.'

He turns those pale blue eyes on me in empty wonder. 'I watch the television in the evenings until late. I watch until it finishes, that's usually at about half past eleven. The TV presenter says goodnight and then I switch off the set.'

'Yes I understand that.'

'Then Lady Hollinger comes on.'

'She has a programme at the end of normal transmissions?'

'I don't know. The screen lights up and she is there. She talks to me.'

'Is she on everybody's television?'

'I don't know. How can I know that? I only watch my television.'

'So she comes on to your television at the end of the normal programmes.'

'Yes.'

'But I thought you said that you switched off your television at the end of the programmes?'

'Yes I do. Why would I keep it on? There is nothing else to see.'

'Except Lady Hollinger,' I suggest.

He looks at me for an instant as if measuring up whether he can trust me with the next revelation.

'She comes on when the set is switched off. I can unplug it and still she comes on. The screen lights up and there she is, in my *salon*.'

By this time, I am beginning to realise what I am dealing with.

'How does she come on if the set is switched off?'

'I don't know, I have never asked her.'

'And she talks to you?'

'Yes.'

'And you talk to her?'

'Of course, it is only polite.'

'Does she come on every night?'

'Most nights.'

'And one of these nights she asked you to be her chauffeur?'

'That's right.' He seems relieved that at last I have understood.

I stamp an IS81 and hand it to him.

'This is a form to say that I have not finished talking to you but will continue our conversation in a little while. Please sit down over there whilst I make a telephone call.'

'You are ringing Lady Hollinger?'

'Do you have her number?'

'No.'

'Well, I'll see what I can do.'

He sits down on the seat by the table full of blank landing cards and I retreat into the back office to think. He is an EC national so I cannot easily refuse him entry for having little means of support since he is allowed to work here and already claims to have employment to go to.

Now, you know and I know that the man is a screaming nutter but if the matter went to appeal the facts would speak for themselves – he is an EC national with an offer of employment. Although, I suppose, he has no means of proving the existence of that offer. I wonder if Lady Hollinger exists other than in his imagination? She might be a character in a French television serial. I pick up the phone and dial the general office. It rings and rings. I try the rest room. A voice answers. It is Willie. He was one of the officers who went to the pub before midnight to get tanked up sufficiently to get them through the night. I'm never going to be 'one of the lads' like him. He treated me as a sprog for the first ten years of my appointment.

'Rest room.'

'Willie, have we got a copy of *Burke's Peerage* in the general office?'

'I've got yesterday's *Daily Mail* and a ski holiday brochure.'

'I'm on blue X and I've got a hold up. I can't leave so can you go down to the general office and see if we've got a copy of *Burke's Peerage*?'

'Phone the CIO. He's already down there.' The line goes dead.

Thanks Willie, that's really helpful. I phone the CIO's office. His voice is slow and awakening from sleep. All that could have been done on the Cypriots has been done; there were no ships due in for an hour and three quarters so he has taken the opportunity to get his head down.

'Ken, I've got a case down on walkers.'

'Shall I come down?' He docs not sound enthusiastic.

'No, not yet. He's a nutter. At least, I think he is. Have we got a copy of *Burke's Peerage* in the office? He says he's coming to visit Lady Hollinger.'

'Sounds like a champagne family. Hang on, I'll have a look.' I stand in the interview room and look through the clear glass at the top of the window to make sure that my passenger has not wandered off. He is sitting calmly, turning the detention form over and over in his hands. Ken comes back to the phone. 'No, we've got *Who's Who* and *The Statesman's Year Book* for 1970.'

'Can you have a look in *Who's Who* for a Lady Hollinger?'

'I'll ring you back.'

I go out to my detainee. 'Have you got any baggage?'

'No.'

'No extra clothes?'

'Lady Hollinger will have a uniform for me.'

I decide to take him into the interview room where we can talk sitting down. I install him across the table to me. I need to get some background for the Port Medical Inspector.

'Tell me about your hospital stay.'

'What about it?'

'What was wrong with you?'

'It was my stomach.' He pats his stomach again.

'What treatment did the doctors give you?'

'Medicine. Every day.'

'And how long were you in hospital?'

'I can't remember exactly. One month, two months.'

He fumbles vaguely in his jacket pocket as if he might find the answer there. He draws out his hand. It's holding a knife. Christ, he's got a knife. It has a short stubby blade and the handle has string wound around it. He jiggles it about in his hand with the blade pointing at me whilst he settles into a comfortable grip. What do I do now? I am alone in an interview room in an empty building at three in the morning with a lunatic holding a knife. I do not have training to deal with this. None of us has. And of course, there are no panic buttons to press to call assistance – that is for cissies. I do not know what I can do so I do the obvious. I ignore it.

'You must have been very ill to have to stay there that long.'

'Yes I was. The doctor said I was. A lot of the time I was resting.' He is still jiggling the knife. He searches in his other pocket and eventually pulls out a pipe. He starts to scour the knife around the inside of the bowl. He looks up at me. 'I worried you didn't I?' He indicates the knife, now safely stabbed up to the hilt in the pipe.

'No, not particularly,' I lie and then decide to add a surreal touch. 'Lots of people smoke.' He continues to grind his knife in a miniature act of disembowelling and looks at me steadily as he does so. He knows I am lying. 'Where was the hospital you went to?' He tells me the name. It means nothing to me. I was hoping it might have 'psychiatric hospital' in the title. 'When you were discharged did the doctor give you a paper to say that you were cured?' Perhaps he will have some document to say what sort of nutter they thought he was.

'Probably.'

There is a movement outside and then Ken, the CIO, pokes his head around the door. 'Nothing in *Who's Who*. Do you want to give me the story?' I nod and stand up. 'I've just got to talk to my chief,' I explain to my aspiring chauffeur.

Five minutes later Ken is fully appraised and agrees with me.

'He's as nutty as a fruit cake. Get the PMI in to examine him and when he has issued the Port 30, knock him off, "exclusion conducive to the public good".'

Half an hour later the Ostender is unloading and the desks are busy. I get a call from the DHB police station to say that Dr. Kelly has arrived, will I come and collect him? I explain to my Frenchman that I have somebody who is coming to see him to make sure that he is fit and well. He nods and puffs at his pipe.

The DHB police station is a low brick building tucked under the cliff at the entrance to the docks. I walk back upstairs through the empty former baggage hall and out across the bridge which takes me down to a discreet but unguarded door which leads into the back of the departure lounge. The blinds of the NatWest bank are securely fixed. I wave to the Townsend hostess at her counter. The Sealink desk is unmanned – they are all sitting in the back room as are the P&O hostesses. A few passengers are stretched out on the seats trying to catch some sleep. Not much is happening at four in the morning.

The PMIs are local doctors who have agreed to run a rota for being available as and when needed at the ports. I had not had anything to do with them directly since I had started at Dover East. Dr. Kelly is a short Irishman with a broad accent. I never can tell from accents which part of Ireland the speakers come from and as one lot are regularly blowing us up and I don't know which lot, I keep quiet. Dr. Kelly makes up for my taciturnity.

'Now, oill be takin' yer down in me car. You just sit yourself there and tell me where we're aiming for.' I point him down the port services road. To get to the walkers inwards control we have to make our way down one side of the port, wriggle a route across the middle, and then aim for the exit and Bob's your uncle. 'Oi knew it. Oi knew it,' he says, as he pulls up at a red light. 'Dere's a little man in dat tower up dere and he's looking down at us.' He points at the port control tower. 'As soon as he sees Dr. Kelly coming along he pushes dat button and the loight goes red. It happens every time. I know he does it. As soon as he sees me. He says. 'dat's Dr. Kelly's car dat is and I'm going to stop him' and he pushes that little button and the light goes red.'

'It's green now.'

'So it is, so it is.'

'We have to go down to the left now, behind that marshal's kiosk.'

'To be sure we have but I'm tinking it'll be quicker dis way.'

I brace my feet against the floor and hold the door as he passes the *'no entry'* sign and trundles down between a line of plastic cones. Any minute now I expect a forty foot articulated lorry to meet us head on.

'We are actually going the wrong way down a one-way route. Perhaps you should cut through here.' I suggest in an outwardly calm manner which utterly belies my inner feelings.

'Down here, you're saying?'

'No, no, no,' I don't quite scream, 'the next one. By that lighting pylon.'

My Frenchman does not let me down. He answers the doctor's questions with a candour spiced with that twirl of unreality guaranteed to convince any medical man that he should be in a straitjacket. I take Dr. Kelly into our back office to complete the business.

'Dey always say, have yer noticed, that they have been ill in the stomach?'

'Um...' I was distracted by the doctor arranging the carbon paper in his pad. 'You've put the carbon paper in upside down doctor.'

'It's never the head, dey say, always down here.' He pats his paunch as he sits down at the table. 'Now what was his name?'

I pass the file across to him so that he can copy the name. 'I think you have put the carbon in the wrong way around.'

'Now you'll be wanting to send him back soon, will yer not?' He copies the name onto his Port 30. 'No, he's not really safe here on his own like dat. He could get up to all kinds of mischief.' He tears the form from the pad and looks at it bemused. 'Now will you look at dat? It's all written on the back the wrong way around.'

'Yes I did–'

'–some more of dat upside down carbon paper.' He crumples up the carbon paper and throws it in the bin. 'I had some loike dat over at Dover West only last week.' He takes another sheet of carbon and fortuitously inserts it the correct way.

I serve the forms on the Frenchman. He accepts them gravely and shakes my hand and thanks me. The DHB policeman takes him away to await the next Calais departure.

'So that was your first nutter was it?' the CIO says.

I watch the departing back of the PMI.

'I think it was my first two nutters.'

But people coming to marry the Queen or fight the battle of Waterloo was the safe madness. The dangerous madness we were reminded of constantly. A notice pinned by the office door so that all would see it on their way out reminded us daily of the 'state of alert' that currently obtained. We kept a wary eye for abandoned baggage. The year had started with the bomb at Oxford Circus tube station followed in the next month by a bomb at Cannon Street station. We were told how to take a call from a terrorist announcing that a bomb had been planted. 'Note down everything that is said. Every turn of phrase if possible. Does the speaker have an accent?'

'You're supposed to notice whether they say, "bastards"' Douglas, the office misogynist observed. 'That's the password used by the IRA.'

'I didn't know that,' I admitted.

'You're not supposed to. It's to filter out the hoaxes.' He returned to his volume of David Copperfield then, struck by a thought, he put it down again. 'If we had a bomb here the women would be too embarrassed to repeat the word, "bastards" and so it would get treated like a hoax and we would all be blown sky high.' He picked up his book again. 'The bastards,' he muttered. Nobody knew whether he meant the terrorists or the women.

We were issued with our own copies of the Prevention of Terrorism Act which I read. Whatever the extra powers we might have been given under this act it seemed to me that the Home Office did not want us to exercise them; we were to leave it to the police. This suited me. Whilst the SB officer tackled the gunman I would be cowering on the floor under my desk. The way I saw it was that they were paid to get shot at, we were paid to be shouted at.

The battleground as far as SB were concerned was the embarkation control. An officer would often stand behind the IO, looking over his shoulder at the passport and then questioning the passenger further. We could take a detached interest in most of what they did on embarks because we had no power to stop anybody from leaving the country unless the Home Secretary decreed it personally as he did in the case of the staff of the Chinese Embassy in retaliation for when their government detained a UK national in Pekin and prevented him from leaving. The IOs at Heathrow were given a new duty, the 'Ping Pong duty', where they roamed through the transit lounge and challenged any Chinese-looking person to produce their passport.

Half of the police cases discovered on embarks at Dover East were initiated by one SB officer called Northwood. He spoke with a broad Irish accent, had a bushy beard and an aggressive, almost cocksure manner. He treated IOs as a joke: knowing nothing, capable of less. He was not an easy person to like but that did not matter to him. One day I was checking the British passports of the occupants of a Rolls Royce. There were four men in the car. In their passports, under the title *'occupation'*, two had *'scrap metal merchant'*, one, *'company director'* and the fourth, *'police inspector'*.

Northwood growled in my ear. 'I hate a bent copper.'

He took the passports from my hand, I didn't argue with Northwood, and directed the car across the shed to wait for him. The men were grinning smugly. They were still there when I was relieved. I learned later that, having found nothing amiss and goaded by the police inspector's patronising smile, Northwood had ordered them to open the bonnet. Strapped underneath was a sawn-off shotgun.

One winter evening I was embarking the cars for the Ostender. Northwood was standing in front of my desk, gazing through the windows before which the cars stopped. A dirty white Volkswagen Beetle pulled up and the German driver gave me his passport. As I took it I noticed Northwood stiffen. He strode out of the office, wrenched open the passenger door and thrust his hand inside. He straightened up and walked back to the office. I assumed that he had found nothing. I could not see the German whom he was dragging backwards along the concrete by his hair, his heels scrabbling madly, his arms flailing.

'Found this little joker hiding on the floor,' he explained pleasantly to me and then barked at the German. 'Get your passport out.'

What had been a silly attempt to save money on a ferry ticket turned out to be a frightening experience for both the driver and the stowaway. I had no doubts that they would not try that trick again.

Northwood was not a sociable person. Where other SB officers would stand at your desk in the dead time between arrivals or departures and bore you with inane comment, Northwood would wander about, sucking through his teeth and making remarks like, 'You wouldn't know what to do if you did find an illegal immigrant would you? Dover East is just a dinky port.'

No, Northwood did not go out of his way to make himself pleasant so I should have been more careful one day when he suddenly indulged me. I had pointed out a British day tripper to him that they had been looking for. Northwood had walked back to the office with me and Julie, the female IO who was down on relief for a month from Heathrow. He took us into the SB office, which seemed to be a corridor full of filing cabinets, and showed us the German World War 2 spring cosh which Customs had found amongst other weaponry in the suspect's belongings.

'It's got the "SD" engraved on the handle,' he said.

'Ah yes, that was the German Secret Service wasn't it?'

'Nice little weapon.' He smacked it down into the palm of his hand and Julie gave a little jump. He was showing the girl how tough he was before the wishy-washy Civil Service pen pusher that I was.

'We had better get back to the office and unload our cards,' I said to Julie. I did not really know her, in fact, I had only worked alongside her for an hour. 'We must have a ton between us.'

We left to cross to our office opposite. Northwood called out after her.

'So when do I get to fuck you or do I have to queue up behind the other IOs?'

If it were possible for two people to freeze and yet continue to walk, then we did. I was embarrassed and humiliated to have put a relief IO in that position but I could not have known that he would react like that. Julie said nothing. Indeed we both ignored it completely. I wondered whether this charming chat-up line had ever worked for him.

The cancelling of the Channel tunnel at the beginning of the previous year had fired the port authorities of Dover, Folkestone, Calais and Boulogne to release the funds necessary for the modernisation which would be required to cope with the increasing traffic. Already Dover was dealing with one million cars per annum and nine million passengers and now that it was certain that none of the future traffic would be creamed off by the tunnel, alteration works were steaming ahead. The hovercraft were abandoning the East to inhabit a brand new terminal for them which was being built alongside Western Docks. The land freed up in the East would allow a realignment of the roads in the port and the potential for more land reclamation. Two new berths were being built to accommodate the larger ferries which were on the stocks. Since the 1960s, Dover East had been stretching seawards. The current foot passenger hall was built half on reclaimed land, the trace of the original sea wall could be found in a line of extra heavy kerbstones running parallel to the shore... and right down the middle of the hall. When the roof leaked and the workmen lifted the carpet tiles to dry them off, I saw a longitudinal crack in the concrete floor which corresponded with the alignment of the old sea wall. Was this why the roof was leaking, I wondered? Were the walls moving apart?

Out in the harbour, dredgers and cranes were clanking away, preparing for the caissons to be dropped at the first stage of reclaiming more acres from the sea. Once this was achieved the harbour board would use it for a lorry park. In fact, it seemed that all of East Kent was becoming a lorry park. Whichever road you drove along, come dusk, you would find foreign lorries manoeuvring onto any slab of hardstanding that they could find to park up for the night. Lay-bys, the hatching on slip roads, cycle lanes and any verge wide enough to accept three quarters of a juggernaut would be forced into service. Foliage and shrubs would be crushed to grass would be reduced to earth would be pulped into mud to be sucked away by their tyres. The hollows scooped out alongside the highway would fill up with water, a brown muddy slurry, and prevent any grass from re-establishing itself. The trucks were eroding the corners of every junction in the county. If the turning was not wide enough then they would drive over the bollards. After all, what resistance could a few metres of plastic give to forty tons? I saw an articulated lorry trying to make an illegal turn at Dover Priory station one day. His rear axle hugged the curve of the six foot high brick wall so, rather than reverse and try to negotiate the turn anew, the driver simply revved his engine and a structure which had been built by the Victorians and survived two world wars was deftly toppled over. I just hoped that nobody had been standing on the other side of it.

What the trucks were not destroying, the drought was killing. I had never seen yellow grass verges in England. In the south of France it was commonplace but in England? This green and pleasant land? In the glass sided car kiosks, the IOs doggedly sat in temperatures of eighty degrees and searing light where the blinds were broken, awaiting the permission from the CIO that 'jackets may be removed'. The tarmac melted, the concrete dust hung in the air, the fumes made us nauseous and dizzy.

Inflation was roaring ahead. We had a temporary 'cost of living allowance' added to our salaries in an attempt to stave off the worst effects of the economic downturn. The pound was plunging. This attracted a phenomenal number of French and Belgian day trippers who arrived from eight in the morning and made their way straight into town to await the opening of the shops. After half past ten it was impossible to buy butter in Dover. Belgians would snap up hundreds of pounds worth of wall paper which, one had to assume, was more desirable than Belgian paper. In Marks and Spencers I noticed that the balance in the range of men's trouser sizes suddenly shifted towards the short-legged, big-bellied stature of our Continental cousins. On an average morning, six or seven hundred day trippers would swarm, locust-like through the town. The Dover shopkeepers had never had it so good.

There was a small brown envelope in my pigeon hole. It could be good news, although I could not think what, but it was more likely to be bad news. A summons to the inspector perhaps? A request to explain in writing some erroneous action? I could leave it till tomorrow. I took it to a quiet corner of the office and slit open the envelope. It was a list of names. *The following immigration officers have been selected for the winter round of Home Office language courses. Andrews N (Dover East), Brownley A (Birmingham Airport), Edgecombe, J. (Heathrow Three)...'*

What had this got to do with me? Was somebody pulling my leg? No. There was my name. I had been selected for the oral Urdu language course, presumably on the basis of my prowess in the only foreign language that I did speak.

Well now, that was interesting news.

7

This was my last duty before I went off on my language course. It was an office duty. I had a removal through Heathrow to organise and there was a North African-looking Frenchman to be interviewed in the DHB police station. He had been detained overnight for interview until a French speaker would be available this morning. Given that about fifty officers spoke French I found this arrangement suspicious. Did it really signify that there had been no French speaking officers on night duty? Doubtful.

The internal phone rang. I stood up and searched for the chinagraph pencil in order to write the message on the board.

'FE3 from Calais,' I repeated. The FE3 was the Townsend Thoresen ferry *Free Enterprise III*. 'ETA ten fifteen at point alpha.' Point alpha was an imaginary spot in the Channel about ten minutes steaming from the berth. I once convinced a Heathrow IO on relief that this was the bit of the sea where the ships, turning day after day on the same spot to approach the port entrance, had worn the sea thin. 'Two hundred and fifty seven passengers, eighty-nine NB.' That meant, "non-British". 'One hundred and seventy-nine walkers, thirty-eight cars, one coach and seven freight.'

I put the pencil back in the pot and sat down. The message display was a large white notice board on which a tabulation had been drawn in black felt tip pen and then covered with clear plastic so that we could write in the entries in the appropriate boxes and rub them out when dealt with. The same system was used for persons detained temporarily. Eventually we needed a second board for those on long term detention.

Back to the removal via Heathrow. This Nigerian had been detained eight months earlier when Customs had found drugs on him. At the time of his first detention we had notified Sealink of their obligation to remove him at the end of his sentence but the French authorities had been making themselves awkward and would not now accept him back to Calais so he had to be flown back to Lagos. Removal of a Dover passenger by air was not a common occurrence and I was wallowing in a sheaf of forms which were necessary to ensure that the operation proceeded smoothly.

For some reason unknown to me, we had telephoned a local travel agent and got them to buy an air ticket to Lagos in the passenger's name and send the bill to Sealink. I now had to issue a form to the Prison Service to release the man into the custody of Securicor and a form authorising Securicor to detain him whilst they transported him to the airport. Prior to this, of course, I needed to arrange with Securicor to go and collect him from prison in time to get him to the airport. Although the man had now served his sentence and was entitled to release, the Prison Service were prevented from letting him out by the order we had served on them to detain him pending his removal from the country.

I had been at my desk since seven o'clock and it was now nine thirty. The casework CIO should be sitting opposite me at this hour. The fact that he was not did not bother me unduly. I had nothing that needed referring to him for his authority or opinion and as I was floundering around in my own ignorance I preferred to do it unobserved. I tried ringing Securicor but the line was engaged so I closed the file, scrawled, *'gone for breakfast'* on a scrap of paper which I left in the middle of my desk, and went to the canteen.

When I got back the CIO was poring over the French detainee's file.

'You'd better drop what you're doing and interview this frog,' he said. 'What are you doing anyway?'

'Trying to arrange a removal through Heathrow.'

'When for?'

'Tomorrow. Blue Sky Travel should be dropping the tickets in today.'

He threw the Frenchman's file across to me. 'You speak French don't you?'

I gave him one of my looks so he went away to make himself a coffee. I opened the file, took out the French passport and turned to the photograph. The man had North African parentage which, given France's colonial history, was not unusual. He was in his early twenties. The passport had been issued four years earlier at L'Hay les Roses which I knew to be a suburb south of Paris on the road to Orly airport. I stared at the photograph, wondering what he wanted to do in the UK. The IO's notes were brief in the extreme. *Five days to see Big Ben. Single ticket, two hundred francs. Detain to await French speaker.'* So, what was the suspicion? He did not have enough money to provide for his visit and his return home so how would he get it? He could apply for work as an EC national if he wanted to or he could sign on for some kind of benefit from the DHSS. I had a feeling that there was a rule that a simple EC holidaymaker had no valid claim to benefits. A workseeker had different rights but this man had indicated that he was on holiday. Or so we believed. The language difficulty needed to be despatched before any of his utterings could really count.

'Sitting looking at the photo won't get you anywhere,' the CIO said as he sat down with his coffee cup.

I was not so sure. I peered more closely. 'This is a 'subbed' photo,' I said. The CIO put down his coffee cup and came across to have a look.

'Looks alright to me.'

'Look at that dry embossing.' I pointed to where the corner of the circular stamp had pressed out its design on the page and across the photograph. 'It's not the same radius circle.'

'Are you sure?'

'Well look at it. That curve there is a different curve to the one on the photograph.'

'Perhaps the photo has slipped.'

'It can't, it's held by two rivets and in any case, even if it had slipped it would not change the curve of the embossing stamp.'

'But it's a good impression on the photo.'

'Oh yes it is. It's been done by a proper stamp, not the blunt end of a dead biro like they usually do, but the embossing was done when the photograph was attached to a different document. I reckon he took the photo out of his proper passport, whatever that was.'

'Jolly good then. Off you go. I'll hold the fort.'

In the DHB police station two men are leaning on the counter, trying to convince the police officer to issue them with a dock pass so that they can take their van down to the berth to collect their tools from a ferry that they have been working on. The policeman looks up enquiringly as I enter. I indicate the side door with a glance and without losing the thread of his sentence, he slides his thumb under the counter and pushes the button. I hear the click of the electric latch releasing and I lean on the door and pass into the custody section. Sergeant Royle is sitting at a table, filling in what looks like an overtime form.

'Come to talk to our jungle bunny have you?'

Sergeant Royle is a man who does not let compassion, sympathy or justice interfere with the pragmatic manner in which he discharges his responsibility of 'banging up the illegals' in his detention suite. Any foreigner whose skin tint was not a scrubbed European pink was a 'jungle bunny' to sergeant Royle. Any detainee who made himself physically awkward to the police would inevitably sustain bruises from, 'tripping on the stairs' and when an IO went one day to interview the sandalled Jamaican who had spent the previous twenty-two hours strumming on his guitar he discovered that the instrument had now 'had an unfortunate accident' in the shape of a size eleven boot.

He unlocks the wooden door. It is solid apart from two circular peepholes the size of grapefruit which have been cut in it, one at head height and one at ankle height.

'Oi Abdul,' he yells up the stairs, 'you've got a visitor.'

Needless to say, the man's name is not Abdul. Sergeant Royle locks the door behind me. I am always surprised by this procedure given the layout of the accommodation. I have to climb a double flight of steep stairs. I am in an utterly defenceless position until I reach the floor above. The stairs arrive directly into a communal living area from each end of which a door leads off to the rooms fitted with bunks. When women are detained as well as men, then the DHB supply a matron to maintain decency. This area is furnished with a table and some chairs. Chairs which could be thrown down onto anybody coming up the stairs; stairs down which one could easily be pushed as there is no door to close them off. Should you try to escape attack by running down the stairs to the only exit then you would find yourself trapped against the locked door with your assailant standing above you. A bell push is provided to call the officer to unlock the door. I have sometimes waited two or three minutes, ringing and banging on the wood before release. But... what am I worrying about? I have never been attacked and I don't think anybody else has. By behaving as if it were not the done thing to offer up fisticuffs then it naturally remains not the thing done.

My detainee is the only inhabitant. He is sitting at the table, smoking a cigarette and looking at a magazine. At his elbow sits a plate with the remains of his breakfast congealing on it. He has not eaten the bacon.

'Monsieur Michel Charrier?' I say and then kick myself for reminding him of his identity.

'*Oui monsieur.*' He is very polite and willing to please.

I explain who I am and that I am going to ask him some questions so that we can decide how long he can stay in England. I know that I am not being honest with him – he is a stone cold knock-off because of the forged passport and will not be coming in at all – but he does not know that and in any case, I need to discover his claimed intentions in order to refuse him.

'Just fill in this card please.' I hand him a blank landing card such as he filled in when he arrived. But now I am watching him and he has to recall what his name is supposed to be, when and where he was born and what his signature looks like.

He takes his time but so do many people when presented with such cards. He hands it back to me, trying to appear confident and nonchalant. He has no need to worry. He has done his homework. He knows that he is called Michel Charrier, that he was born on 7 September 1954 at Rungis and he has obviously been practising the signature which, unfortunately, appears to be a simple 'M C' with a horizontal line through it. Anybody could write it after five minutes' application.

'You have no address in England?'

'No monsieur.'

'Where do you live in France?'

'Paris.'

'Where in Paris?'

'You want the address?'

'Yes please.'

He writes on the card an address in the Aubervilliers suburb of Paris. I make no comment but store the fact for later. It could be important.

'How long are you coming here for?'

'It's just a holiday.' He shrugs. 'Four or five days.' The tone of his voice is the characteristic wheedling of a North African speaking French.

'Have you been here before?'

'No monsieur.'

'Do you work in Paris?'

'I work in a stockroom. It's a big shop selling all kinds of things.'

'And you live in Aubervilliers?' I make a point of letting him see me looking at the address written in his passport.

'Ah, I do now. I moved about two years ago.'

'Where did you live before?'

'Haif les Roses.'

I do not react to his misreading of the name of the town but need him to repeat it, just to make sure.

'And where was this passport issued?'

'Same place – Haif les Roses.'

I can see how he has made the mistake. He is undoubtedly an Arab from Northern Africa. I think he looks more Moroccan than Tunisian or Algerian. French passports are issued at the local town hall. *'L'Hay les Roses'* has been written as the place of issue in the passport with punctilious correctness by the issuing clerk: he has included the diaeresis on the letter 'y'. This means that the name of the town could be mistakenly read as *'Haif les Roses'* should you be unfamiliar with the name and *'Haif'* makes more sense to an Arab than *'Hay'*.

'Where did you get this passport from?'

'From the town hall at Haif les Roses. I was living there at the time.'

'How long had you lived there?'

'Some years.'

'How many years?'

'Ten perhaps.'

'Is it a big place?'

'No, not big.'

'Where is it?'

'It's part of Paris.'

'Near Aubervilliers?'

'No, it's a different part of Paris.'

I know it is. Aubervilliers is directly north of the city, L'Hay les Roses, direct south. But he does not know that I know.

'Is it near a motorway?'

'No, not near. It's the suburbs.'

Oh yes it's the suburbs. And the A6 motorway slices straight through the middle of it.

'Which is your nearest airport?'

'I don't fly. I came by ferry.'

'If you wanted to fly, which would be your nearest airport?'

'I don't know. I don't fly.'

But you claim to have lived for ten years at L'Hay les Roses which, if I remember correctly, is about three miles from Orly Airport.

'This is not your passport.'

'It is my passport.'

'The only thing in this passport which is yours is the photograph.'

'No monsieur, you are mistaken.'

'You are not Michel Charrier. What is your real name and which country do you come from?'

'My name is Michel Charrier and I am French.'

'Your name is not Michel Charrier and you are a liar.'

'No monsieur.'

'You don't even know the correct name of the town you claim to have lived in for ten years.'

'Haif les Roses.'

'It's not Haif, it's Hay.'

'No monsieur, it's Haif.'

Oh for heaven's sake, I'm wasting my time now. I've got enough to refuse him.

'Ok. You'll remain detained for a little while longer then I will come back and tell you what we are going to do with you.'

'Will he need lunch?' Sergeant Royle asks.

I shake my head. 'He will be back in Calais for lunch, but he doesn't know it yet.'

Several days later we received a note from the French Police de l'Air et des Frontières informing us that he had maintained his claim to be a Frenchman until later that afternoon at which point he had suddenly confessed to being a Moroccan. His abrupt change of mind was almost certainly triggered by their interview technique which, I have been told, can be somewhat physical.

But now it is a quarter to two and my relief has just arrived.

'What have you left me?'

I pointed to the casework board. 'That one, Charrier, is being removed to Calais. The Nigerian–'

'–Oh yes, I know him.'

'Well he's being removed via Heathrow tomorrow.'

'That'll be the day.'

'Well, it's up to you. I've been busy with Charrier all morning so organising the Heathrow removal should fill your afternoon nicely.'

'I'll leave it for you to do tomorrow.'

'Not me, squire. I'll see you in six months. I'm off to learn Urdu.'

Going off to learn Urdu was not such a simple operation as it sounded. The classes were being held in London, Monday to Friday, so I had to work out how to get there and who was going to pay for it. Another IO from Dover East, Nigel Andrews, had been chosen for the same course and so I deferred to his knowledge when it came to investigating the arrangements.

'We'll need the TSR file,' he said.

This meant nothing to me. Or, more correctly, it raised images of an expensive aircraft project which had been scrapped by the government at great loss some years earlier: the TSR-2, tactical, strike and reconnaissance aircraft. Nigel hunted down the much thumbed, dog-eared cardboard file which bore the title, *'Travelling, Subsistence and Removals.'* It was the bible for anybody trying to get money out of the Department. It covered everything from being paid 2.8p per mile for riding your bicycle on official business to interest-free loans of many thousands of pounds given to the lucky persons whose relocation was deemed necessary for the exigences of the Service and were granted a crown transfer.

'Now look, we can get refunded for buying a monthly season ticket to Charing Cross,' he said.

'I should bloody well think so too.'

'But we don't qualify for the subsistence allowance above five hours because our classes only run from 10.00–13.00. That's three hours.'

'But we can claim travelling time can't we?'

'No, we are travelling within conditioned hours. It all falls within an eight hour day.'

After another forty-five minutes of wrangling with the rules we decided to wait until the first day in London and see what everybody else on the course was claiming. As it turned out, this was a wise move. As a group we agreed that we were all entitled to an hour's lunch, 13.00–14.00, and we unanimously decided that the three hours of compulsory private study could be best undertaken in London from 14.00–17.00. The total hours thus took us outside our conditioned hours and entitled us to twenty-two hours of overtime per week, eighty-eight per month. And of course, none of us stayed in town to do our homework; we did it on the train and, in my case, I was home by three in the afternoon. I suppose that we were deliberately defrauding the government but it was not looked upon as such by anybody in my acquaintance.

The venue for the class was number eighty-five, Whitehall which was a nondescript government building squeezed between Richmond Terrace and something bigger. The Cenotaph sat directly outside our front door. The building was a converted house and two rooms had been allocated to us on one of the upper floors. On the floor below a charmingly refined young lady sat with a crusty old buffer in a pair of rooms stuffed full of filing cabinets. They were an entire department within themselves and were something to do with military decorations. I worked to develop a useful acquaintanceship with the lady since she had a bottle of Stationery Office issue black fountain pen ink from which my Parker 61 could drink when it ran dry.

We felt quite at home with the familiar grey tables and steel framed chairs. Our first day was spent getting to know the teacher, Rashid Ashraf, and our fellow course members. The IOs came from various ports. One chap was coming down from Birmingham every day. Nigel and I were a bit miffed to discover that he spent less time travelling each day than we did coming up from Folkestone.

The rail service from the Kent coast was abysmal. Over the decades, British Rail had deliberately withheld investment in the Southern Region line to Dover and Folkestone because it was waiting for the government to give the go-ahead for the Channel tunnel, at which point it knew it would be given a hefty dollop of millions to update the line. The irony of real life was such that when the tunnel was eventually built, it was funded by private enterprise which built a brand new line which did not serve Folkestone or Dover and left us with the crap trains.

Rashid Ashraf was a part-time lecturer at the Polytechnic of Central London, at which we had to enrol in order to receive his tuition. He also worked on the BBC Urdu service at Bush House. As we were learning to only speak the language, we had to learn to write a phonetic alphabet in order to record the sounds on paper. Sitting around the room we had people who could speak French, Italian, German, Spanish, Greek and Turkish. Prior to coming on the course I had started to teach myself Portuguese. We, all of us, discovered that when pressed to find a word in Urdu, we slipped into another language with the inevitable result that half the people understood nevertheless. The teacher was utterly mystified.

Urdu is the main language spoken in Pakistan. It is closely related to Hindi; what distinguishes one from the other is that Urdu is spoken by Muslims and Hindi by Hindus. Thus Urdu is for Pakistanis and Hindi for Indians unless the latter are Muslim. Generalisations are always flawed and I am sure that this one is no exception.

Rashid started off by teaching us to introduce ourselves around the room. *'Ardarb arz hay.'* (Hello) *'Meera narm Lloyd Sahib hay.'* (My name is Mr. Lloyd.)

Whilst outside the class we used each other's Christian names, when speaking Urdu, we stuck to the formal address. I suspected later that Rashid had introduced this custom to avoid any embarrassment that he would feel as a Muslim in addressing the three ladies by their first names.

I am not a competitive creature but I noticed that I was among the slower learners on the course. They had been chosen because they were proven linguists. I was not. I just spoke good French. I discovered that my difficulty was that I learned visually. When the circumstances demanded that I recall vocabulary or a particular phrase, then, without realising, I read it from the image of the page which rested somewhere in my subconscious. Remembering sounds was not so easy although I always found that reproducing them was quite entertaining.

Once we had mastered the phonetic alphabet then we started on the learning proper. Urdu puts the verb at the end of the sentence and there is no definite or indefinite article. Thus the phrase, 'the book is on the table' is composed: 'book, table on, is' – *kitab, maze per, hay.*

With twelve enquiring minds to satisfy, Ashraf sahib would get diverted from his purpose by interruptions.

'Now we are learning the body. This is the hand. *Hart*.'

'I thought that was elephant,' Nigel said. 'You know, *Jungle Book?* Colonel Hart?'

'No, no, that was *hartee*. That means "elephant". The word for hand is *hart.*' Twelve students assiduously added the word for elephant to their vocabulary despite Ashraf Sahib's assurance that we would never see an elephant in Pakistan outside of a zoo. The language we were learning served the culture of the country. This was natural and obvious but did cause us to reflect from time to time. As an exercise, we often had to describe what we had done the previous day. One dog-owner wanted the Urdu phrase for, 'to take my dog for a walk.' Ashraf Sahib was nonplussed. *'koee concept nahing hay'* – we have no concept of that. In Pakistan, about the only interaction you have with a dog is to throw a stone at it.

At the end of the first week, our homework was to compose sentences from the verbs and nouns that we had learned so far. There is a mathematical limit to the number of permutations of 'book', 'table' and 'hand' that one can present but this was where our gleanings of extra vocabulary were to prove so useful.

'Arpkee chutree layjow, meeree hartee same khatee hang,' I pronounced at the end of the first week.

Ashraf Sahib knitted his brows. 'I understand what you say, Lloyd Sahib, but why do you say, "bring your umbrella, my elephant eats beans"?'

Any explanation that I could have given was drowned out by the explosion of laughter in the class. Ashraf Sahib grinned good naturedly, not understanding the joke, if indeed, there existed a joke.

But we had not finished with the vocabulary of the human body.

'So what is the name for the forearm?'

'That is the *"bazu"*,' Ashraf Sahib said, pointing to his upper arm. 'It means "wing".'

'No, that is the upper arm. This is the forearm.' The inquirer ran his finger up and down his forearm.

'Ah that is the *hart.*'

'But that means "hand".'

'Yes, the hand goes from here,' he touched his palm, 'to here.' He touched the inside of his elbow.

'So you have no word for forearm?'

'No. *Koee concept nahing hay.*'

An interesting paradox. In Pakistan they have no way to distinguish between the hand and the forearm but they have a word specifically for a 'man with no nose.'

I may have found the learning arduous but I liked the regular hours. An early morning train up to Charing Cross, a smart walk down Whitehall, a quick cup of tea at Barclay's café, an establishment which inevitably became known as 'Barclay Sahib's', and then pound up the stairs to the classroom for a ten o'clock start. If I made sharp at the end of the lesson and caught the 13.30 home, I could be in my garden by a quarter to four. And I could do this everyday. I realised, rather naively, that a regular working routine was not something special; it was what most people enjoyed.

And then there was the incident of Nicoll Sahib and the cockroach. Returning to the class from a quick break at Barclay Sahib's establishment he began to unwrap the chocolate bar that he had purchased. Impressed lovingly into the fold of the foil paper seal lay a large dead cockroach. An opportunity to widen our vocabulary, thought I. What actually happened was that he telephoned the environmental health people and they closed down the café whilst it was cleaned from top to bottom. When he reopened, Nigel and I jigged in through the door in a short conger singing, *'La Cucuraca'*. Not very subtle.

One day in February we poked our head outside the door at tea break and Nigel noticed a man holding a placard and standing outside the Home Office building opposite us. By now the class was able to talk a kind of dog-translation pidgin Urdu which everybody could understand except the teacher. In recounting his previous evening's entertainment, for example, Nigel had just introduced the concept of the *meety cheezing art budgy kay baha* which you consumed after your dinner. Rashid had been mystified. 'You are saying, "sweet things later than eight o'clock," Andrews Sahib?'

We all knew that he was talking about After Eight Mints. It was obvious wasn't it?

'Let's go and see what that chap over there is protesting about,' Nigel suggested.

'We've only got five minutes.'

'It won't take long.'

As we crossed the road the writing on the placard began to make sense to me. This was definitely something we did not ought to get mixed up in but Nigel was not to be swerved.

'Hallo mate, what's your problem?' he said.

'Will you sign our petition? The Home Secretary is trying to deport these two Americans on the grounds of–'

'–Mark Hosenball and Philip Agee?'I said.

'Oh you know about them?'

I should think that we did. They had been the subject of several notifications to immigration officers from the Home Secretary for the last few months.

'Spies, aren't they?' Nigel said with a grin on his face.

'No, certainly not.'

'But Philip Agee was in the CIA.'

'That doesn't make him a spy. Anyway, the Home Secretary is wrong to deport them. He is only doing it under pressure from the Americans who want to get them to court.' The man flicked his hair across his forehead with the back of his hand.

'I thought they were being deported on the grounds that they are a threat to the security of this country?' I proffered.

'That's what the Home Secretary claims but they have done nothing wrong.'

'Apart from remaining in breach of their landing conditions,' Nigel said.

'But you don't get deported for that.' He flicked his hair again.

'You do,' I assured him.

'Lend us your pen then.' Nigel signed the petition. 'Go on,' he said, and handed the pen to me. 'It's justice.'

Oh well, why not? I signed below him.

'Thank you gentlemen, I always enjoy–'

'Sorry we must go back to work now,' I apologised.

'Oh you work–?'

'Over there,' I said.

'We are immigration officers,' Nigel added.

You could have driven a bus down the man's throat.

The months wore on. We learned that when Ashraf Sahib was talking about 'wobbles' he meant vowels and that there are about fifteen different words for brown. As we immersed ourselves deeper in the language and lore of the sub-continent, my conviction grew that I would need to go to Pakistan to see and speak to these people. The language we were learning was BBC Urdu. Any passenger arriving at our port and speaking that grade of the language would be educated and monied. They would not be seen as an immigration problem. It made me realise that the immigration rules were not colour-biassed; they were class-biassed. It did not matter what colour your skin was. If you spoke Oxford English and had money you could come in; if you were poor and inarticulate, you could not.

I knew that I would stand no chance of passing the exam unless I went to Pakistan and saw and heard why the people said what they did. The Home Office gave me two weeks extra leave and £30 towards the £400 needed for the air fare. I purchased my ticket three months in advance on the condition that I could not subsequently change my booking. On the day, British Airways were unable to supply an aeroplane for me despite having had so much notice so, twelve hours later I was put on a PIA flight. Losing twelve hours from four weeks was not so much a concern for me as was arriving at Karachi at three in the morning instead of three in the afternoon. I had intended to find a hotel upon arrival. As I answered the polite questions of the Pakistani immigration officer I realised that I was a stone cold knock-off. 'Coming for a month's holiday, knows nobody here and has no accommodation booked.' I could already see it on the refusal file. He stamped my passport and let me in.

The lady at the tourist desk in the airport lowered her eyes and flashed her eyelashes in a most becoming manner as she explained to me that it was difficult to book a hotel at that time of the morning but she thought she knew of one which would take me because it 'stayed open all night.' Indeed it did. It was a brothel. But the slamming of doors in the corridor did not stop me from sleeping.

With a rucksack which I had borrowed from Pete Bates, the customs officer whom I had previously met in Paris, my plan was to spend the month travelling by bus and train up the country from Karachi as far north as the Khyber Pass and then spend my last twenty-four hours in the first class air conditioned railcar service returning to Karachi to fly out. It did not quite work out like that. I arrived in time for the elections. President Bhutto was fighting to stay in power. The rallies of the Pakistan Peoples' Party were causing unrest throughout the land and as I wriggled my way up the map, martial law was being declared behind me, effectively cutting off my retreat step by step. By the time I reached Rawalpindi there was shooting in the streets and all the shops and banks were barricaded shut. This was unfortunate for an idiot like me who, in a fit of patriotism, had insisted on taking sterling travellers' cheques with him.

5 curfew violators shot dead

KARACHI, April 22: The Commissioner, Karachi Division, in consultation with the Military Administrator has issued the following Press Note here today:

Some instances of hooliganism and violation of curfew occurred in Liaquatabad, Nazimabad, Golimar and some other parts of Karachi. At few places the army and law enforcing agencies had to open fire as a result of which 13 persons were injured and five were shot

Martial Law in Karachi, Lahore and Hyderabad

The Federal Government on Thursday imposed Martial Law in Karachi Division, Hyderabad District and Lahore District with immediate effect.

A Press note issued by the Federal Government said that the Provincial Governments of Sind and Punjab have placed these areas for enforcement of law and maintenance of public order.

It said the Federal Government exercising its constitu-

DECISIVE ACTION
Leading article on Page 4

tional powers, has directed the Armed Forces of Pakistan to act in aid of civil power.

NOT THE BEST TIME TO VISIT PAKISTAN
The *Pakistan Times* which I read at breakfast in Lahore on 23 April 1977.

However, I never felt threatened personally, on the contrary, the crowd would often wave me away from any trouble that was brewing. The natural hospitality of the people was quite humbling – they would invite me in to their homes to meet their family and talk. It was a great education for me.

After an unpleasant incident in Karachi I decided to introduce a stratagem of mild deceit to work for the benefit of both parties. I had been invited to the house of the lady who worked in the railway information office. I had been introduced to various parents, aunts and outer reaches of extended family. The younger, more timid ones had peeked at me from behind a curtain and then the son of the house came in. He worked in Saudi Arabia and was back home on leave. Up to that time I had never concealed that I worked as an immigration officer. He came straight up to me and started talking. The women immediately fell silent.

'You tell me what questions I have to answer to get visa for England. You give me the good answers. You write them down so that I get good visa for England.'

There are no set questions or 'good answers'. I explained to him how the system worked and as I did so I could see from the corner of my eye how uncomfortable his sister felt at this interrogation. She was educated and spoke good clear Urdu. It had been a pleasure conversing with her and she had made the effort to make herself clear to me so that I could learn. He just wanted to get to England.

After that, when asked about my job I would say that I worked for the tax office and had been sent to Pakistan to learn the language so that we could make sure that Pakistanis paid the correct tax. It worked a treat.

After a month in Pakistan I was sufficiently confident in my very limited prowess in the language to be able to make a telephone call to a railway ticket office to enquire about train times and when eavesdropping on conversations I could not understand what they were saying but I knew what they were talking about. I had made considerable progress and enjoyed the forced education that I had been subjected to.

I had great fun talking to street traders and shopkeepers who would not believe that a European would speak any approximation of their language. I had no idea how to bargain for a purchase although the following exchange between me and an orange seller would seem to argue against my modesty.

'*Yeh kitnee paysay hein?*' I said to the lad. (How much are they?)

'*Panch rupei.*' (Five rupees).

I looked at his scales which bore a pound weight and a kilo weight.

'*Ek pound ya ek kilo?*' (For a pound or a kilo?)

'*Panch rupei pound, panch rupei kilo*' (Five rupees a pound. Five rupees a kilo.)

'*Ek kilo deejeeay.*' (Give me a kilo please.)

I paid my five rupees and walked away convinced that I had probably still paid twice what anybody else would have paid for the oranges. But it was all good fun.

However, those Pakistanis who were unaccustomed to intercourse with foreigners showed me a deference which I found quite uncomfortable. When I tried to queue for stamps at the post office, for example, the people before me in the queue all waved me forwards and the counter clerk also beckoned me to the front. I protested but it was not of any use. It felt very colonial to me.

I had some fun with the upper echelons of officialdom. I had booked a ticket on the railcar from Lahore to Rawalpindi and the clerk had written down the departure time for me: 09.00. When I presented myself at the station I was told that I had missed it because it had departed on schedule at 07.30. When I asked for a refund, he would only refund the ticket price and not the seat reservation fee. I was not having that. I argued as best I could but he would not budge. In truth he was probably bound by regulations formulated at the time of the Raj. In the middle of the town I had remarked an enormous pink stone building which seemed to be about the size of our Houses of Parliament. It was the headquarters of the

Pakistan Western Railway Company. I repaired there and effected a quick reconnaissance. It was pierced by a central corridor running from one end of the building to the other and both entrances were guarded by doorkeepers who stood with their rifles aslope. Nothing ventured, nothing gained. I marched up the steps to be met at the top with crossed rifles. I waved them aside and, astonishingly, the doorkeepers stepped back and saluted me. Emboldened by this early success I penetrated the gloomy interior. I was the only white person in there. As I walked briskly down the corridor, trying to look as if I knew where I was going, my eyes rapidly scanned the little wooden sign boards which projected above occasional doors. *'PWD'* – that would be the permanent way department. *'Telegraphs'* – that would be signalling. Ah, *'Company President'* – that would do.

I entered an ante room. Before the secretary could look up from his desk I had opened the polished wooden door marked *'boardroom'* and gone in. There, standing with his back to me, I found a distinguished gentleman in his sixties, with greying hair and dressed in an immaculate white pyjama suit. He was holding a pencil horizontally between two hands in the pose of somebody reflecting seriously. He turned at my entrance, expecting to see his secretary.

'Ap President hain?' I asked. (Are you the President?)

His jaw fell open, the pencil clattered to the boardroom table where it rolled noisily down the warped wood and he uttered a faint, 'yes'.

'Acha. Bayteeay.' (Good. Please sit down.) I pulled out a chair for him. He did not so much sit down as land in the chair as his legs folded beneath him. I explained my problem in polite Urdu and he took me personally to the office and obtained a full refund for me. We parted the best of friends.

I never did get on to the first class air conditioned railcar. The country was completely closed by the time that I returned from the Friday steam train journey up the Khyber Pass. The only guaranteed route southwards was by plane. I took an internal flight from Islamabad to Karachi and slept in the airport whilst waiting for my VC 10 to take me back to the UK.

Three weeks after returning home I managed to scrape through the Urdu language exam with the minimum qualifying marks. My monthly allowance now increased from £7 for French, to £12.25 to include oral Urdu. Over the following five years I was to use it twice, meaning that I was paid about £90 per minute for speaking it.

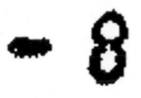

My first night duty back at Dover East was a shock to the system. For nearly half a year I had worked regular hours on my language course followed by a month's leave in Pakistan. Three o'clock in the morning was an hour at which every sensible person should be abed. I was in awe of my colleagues who could come in to work at six or seven in the evening, go down the pub for a couple of hours and then toil through the night with apparent ease. Did their legs and arms not hurt? Did not the fluorescent lights give them eye ache and the incessant hissing and droning from the air conditioning, headache? Perhaps the alcohol acted as a stimulant and anaesthetic all in one.

It is my meal break. At three in the morning. What do you want to eat at three in the morning? I am sitting up in the general office and trying to write up a report on a passenger that I have just refused. I always do my paperwork as quickly as I can because I do not like it hanging around and, just as important, you never know when you are going to pick up another refusal. I am tired and am having difficulty thinking straight. I wonder whether I should abandon my report writing until my next duty. I could just stick the file in my pigeon hole. I look down at the minute sheet before me. There is a spider on it. No, it's not a spider, it's a tight wiggly knot of black ink lines. I puzzle at it. How did that get there? It takes me some seconds to realise that I must have fallen asleep in the chair with my fountain pen in my hand and resting on the paper where I had paused in my composition. As I had breathed in and out, my hand had moved minutely on the paper, sketching out a black spider.

I put the cap on my pen and close the file. It is pointless to continue. Four more hours before I finish. Three, if I'm lucky.

Driving out of Dover after my duty, my head is thick with fatigue and my eyelids are dry and crackling. At half past six in the morning there is little traffic on the road to Folkestone. I drive carefully knowing that I am very tired and will have slow reactions. When I reach the three-lane section at Capel, a car appears at the mouth of a side street, waiting to join my main road. I watch it warily. It stays where it is whilst I drive past. I look in my mirror to see whether it turns to follow me but it goes in the opposite direction, down towards Dover. The road unfurls like a television screen; white hatching, bollards, road islands, kerbstones. It is dreamlike in its unreality. When I reach the bend by the general store I realise what is wrong. I have just driven two hundred yards whilst watching the road reeling out behind me in the rear view mirror instead of looking through the windscreen at the road ahead. I jerk myself back to reality and wind down the window. The cold air hits me in the face like a bucket of water.

Lying in bed as the world gets up to go to work I finally close my eyes to oblivion. My eyeballs flick and jerk under my eyelids, my knees sting, my hips are aching, my head is hot. I concentrate on peace and tranquillity and nothing at all. I am going... I am going... Asleep at last.

I awaken just after midday as usual. I try to get back to sleep but it never works. I get up and mope about in a dressing gown. I am completely washed up, without a thought or initiative in my thick, aching head. At about ten o'clock that night, when everybody wants to wind down, I pick up. I have energy and ideas.

Across the other side of Dover harbour, great works are afoot. A dredger is bringing shiploads of sand from the Goodwin Sands off Deal and spreading it on the foreshore at the side of the Prince of Wales Pier. The surplus is dumped on Dover beach where it becomes a favourite hunting ground for the metal detecting fraternity who dig up coins from ancient shipwrecks. British Rail are promising and then not promising that they will or will not lay a rail link to the new hoverport which is being built there. Seaspeed has sent its SRN-4 hovercraft *Princess Anne* back to Saunders Roe, or the British Hovercraft Corporation as it is now called, to have it stretched to increase its passenger carrying capacity. The French are building two brand new giant hovercraft to put into service in time for the opening of the new hoverport. Why should all this bother me? Not because, by moving the hovercraft from Dover East, the harbour board will furnish themselves with more acres to park lorries on. Something far more important. The hovercraft are not allowed to fly at night because of the noise they create. If they do not fly at night then there will be no night duties. I resolve to apply to transfer to the new Dover Hoverport as soon as the list goes up.

When we go into the CIO's office at Dover East to look at the duty lists, knots of CIOs move apart or stop talking and cover up papers. It is that time of the year again – annual staff report time. I have managed to reach the level of *'box three, not fitted'* which means that I am doing the job satisfactorily and am not ready for promotion.

'Your refusal rate is down this year,' my team leader said to me. 'Only nine. The port average is thirteen.'

I must have felt a little high-spirited at the time for I contradicted him.

'That's above average then, isn't it?'

'How can it be above average?'

'Well if thirteen is the annual average, and I got nine in six months then that is equivalent to eighteen per annum, which is well above the port average.'

My team leader was obviously confused.

'But why are you only counting for six months?'

'Because in this reporting year I spent the six months in Whitehall learning Urdu.'

'Oh did you?'

'You don't get much chance to refuse passengers on a language course.'

And that was my team leader who had not noticed that I had been absent from the port for six months. Oh yes, we had reason to admire the empathy and diligence with which the management operated the Immigration Service staff reporting system.

SEALINK FERRY *M.V. ST GERMAIN* IN FERRY DOCK, DOVER WEST.

In the rest room we have lots of new faces. We are having two intakes of recruit IOs per year. A cadence that I presume is dictated by the need to implement the Immigration Act 1971 which was the law enacted to slide us seamlessly into the Common Market. I now think of myself as a hardened established IO but am astonished at the confidence of these newcomers. They claim to assimilate the new immigration rules instantly and assess passengers with deadly accuracy. I feel they have a certain arrogance about them but their stance impresses the management. One new IO snaps my head off when I offer some advice.

'Piss off. I'm not a kid.'

I grin vacuously as the words wound. This lot were so sure of themselves that they steamed past me in the following five years to mop up all the plum relief postings and special duties that were offered. I just did not figure. I did not have that special belief that I was more important than the Immigration Service. Silly me.

'Bloody Spain is applying to join the EC.' Brian looked around the rest room in disgust. 'We'll have every wop waiter from Benidorm queuing up to come in.'

'Don't blame me, I voted against our joining in the first place,' I said.

'But they won't let them work for the first five years or so, will they?' another said.

'And how do you propose to stop them, once they are in?' Brian said.

'We could tell them that if they work here then they are being very naughty,' I suggested.

'Yeah, that's just about what this government would do. And then they would put them on the Benefit and give them a council house while they wait. I never got anything like that when I was in Spain.'

'How long were you in Spain for?' I asked.

'A couple of years.'

'What were you doing?'

'Teaching English in the mornings, lazing around on the beach in the afternoons and boozing in the bars at night. It was tough.'

'Was this the year abroad for your degree?'

'Nah, it was after my degree. I wanted a bit of sun so I just took the train to Spain and did what everybody else was doing.'

'Working illegally?'

'Yeah, everybody did it. The Spaniards didn't mind. They all wanted to learn English.'

'So that they could come over here and work illegally. It's your fault.'

A red-eyed Scot called Andrew lifted his feet from the chair opposite him.

'What did you drink in Spain, pal?' he asked.

I opted out of the conversation at this point. Andrew had been transferred on 'disciplinary' from Heathrow earlier this month. It was his second disciplinary transfer in three years. He had an uncontrollable affinity for alcohol. To put it more accurately, he was a drunkard. Like many alcoholics he could hide his incapacity exceedingly well. The passengers rarely knew that he was stoned out of his mind whilst he was talking to them. He had only been at the port for two weeks and already on a night duty I had been sent down to the foot passenger control to man the blue X desk because he had gone missing. Nobody could find him. When the passengers had started to stream through, from the sniggering observations I could hear them making behind my desk, I realised that they had discovered where he was and there, in the darkened back office behind me, he lay stretched out on the table, comatose and in full view of the public.

For the first six months of a disciplinary transfer, the miscreant is paid a subsistence allowance above his salary to cover the extra costs of his displacement. You can imagine where this money goes. One of my colleagues opined that the system was purposefully designed in this Machiavellian way to throw the victim into a state of uncertainty and wealth; a combination which would inevitably lead him to commit such a monumental offence that the Immigration Service would be able to sack him. What usually happened was that the miscreant was retired early on medical grounds and then drank himself to death on his pension.

'I blame Freddie Laker for the drop in our refusal rate.' Trevor picked a biscuit crumb from his beard. 'Have you tried refusing a penniless Yank lately?' We shook our heads. 'The buggers can get back to the States for ninety-nine dollars on Skytrain. All they need is their bus fare to Heathrow and a sleeping bag and we are scuppered.'

'You could always bring that up at annual report time,' I said. 'Ask your team leader to take into account the influence of the latest developments in mass market air travel and how they impinge upon the socio-economic behaviour of passengers arriving at Dover East. Always presuming that your team leader knows who you are, of course.'

'Bill Ventian is my team leader. He doesn't even know who he is.'

The buzzer sounded. From the window I could see the cars just coming down the ramp from the Calais arrival. I grabbed my case and made for the door; down the stairs and along the covered walkway towards the car kiosks. Suddenly an imperious voice hailed me from the customs compound.

'Could you hurry along please? The cars are coming off.'

It was Dennis. He must have come down the stairs which led from behind the CIO's office and down through the customs hall. A lorry thundered along the dock road. I stopped and cupped my hand to my ear.

'Sorry?' I called back.

'Could – you – hurry?'

'Pardon?'

'Could – you – run?' he shouted.   Could I run? Was that a general enquiry of my athleticism or was he giving me an order?

'What was that again?' I pressed nearer to the chain link fence in an apparent effort to hear him.

'I said, "can you hurry to the control?"' he bellowed. 'The cars will be here in a moment.'

I put on a puzzled face and looked back in the direction that I had come and then pointed in the direction that I had been walking.

'Well that is where I was going before you stopped me,' I called back.

He waved his hand irritably to dismiss me. I walked briskly towards the car kiosks, adding a hop and a skip every now and then to show him that I was hurrying.

I shared the car kiosk with Rob. He was from Yorkshire. He had a cadaverous face and dark stubble and his deep Northern voice and outward insouciance reminded me of the singer Jake Thackray. Once the ship had been cleared we stayed on chatting. Prior to joining the Service he had worked for a short time in a Sheffield steel works. Nobody stuck the job for long, the gang was always gaining and losing members. They were paid to load scrap into the blast furnace. Old engine blocks were dumped by crane in a barrow. You grabbed the barrow and you ran as fast as you could up a makeshift ramp and tipped the blocks into the furnace loader. If you ran out of momentum before the top, you yelled a warning and then jumped out of the way and hoped that nothing dropped on top of you. 'Of course,' he said wryly, 'they didn't bugger about with cissy things like armoured shoes or hard hats.'

I liked Rob but he was a man disturbed by something. He was beset with a restlessness. I remember him saying to me once, 'My wife is so boring. I told her the other day. "You are so boring."' I was not surprised when his marriage foundered. He became vegetarian at one point and extolled the advantages of it, adding that he would always have a steak and kidney pie if he felt he needed a boost. My favourite image of Rob was of his sitting in a car kiosk with his feet on the desk, smoking a fag and drinking from a can of Newcastle Brown Ale as he waved the cars through. What style! He did not care a hoot. Eventually he just stopped coming in to work. Nobody really knew where he went or what happened to him. His coat gathered dust on the coat rack in the general office for three years until I pointed it out to the admin staff and then that too just disappeared.

'Can I read your *Telegraph*?' I asked.

'Help yourself.' He put his feet up on the desk and lit a cigarette.

Latterly I had been surprised to find myself looking at the 'situations vacant' pages of the papers and measuring up my chances. I showed him the page of boxed-out job announcements.

'When I joined the Service three years ago, with my qualifications I could have applied for any number of the jobs advertised on these pages. Now I can't even find a job in the small ads that I would be qualified for.'

'Once you join the IS you are lost to the employment market. It's a dead end. What marketable skills have you developed here? – How to be nasty to foreigners. And what in-service training have you ever had? Eh?'

'I had a one day forgery course last month.'

'Big deal. So you can tell a forged passport when you see one. What use is that in the outside world?'

'I could apply for this job,' I said. 'They want Administrative Officers in Brussels for the EEC; two 'A' levels, fluency in two EEC languages and a degree or equivalent qualification.'

'What is the point of requiring 'A' levels if they are asking for a degree anyway? Do you know anybody who got a degree without 'A' levels?'

I did not. But I applied for the job and got invited to sit the entrance exam in London. But before I failed spectacularly at my only attempt to join the cohorts of the European Civil Service, I was involved in an incident at Dover whose triviality we would today find quite charming.

One afternoon, at about half past four I took a phone call from the police station in Dover town.

'We've got a chap here who wants to claim political asylum.'

Political asylum? In Dover? How could anybody claim PA in Dover?

'What nationality is he?'

'I dunno. Doesn't speak much English. It sounds as if he has been taught to say "political asylum".'

'Where has he come from?'

'Off a ship, I suppose.'

'Have you got his name?' The policeman laboriously spelled out a name in the phonetic alphabet. It had quite a few 'Whisky Zulus' in it. 'Sounds Polish to me. Ask him if he is Polish.'

'How do I do that?'

'Say, "Polski?"'

I could hear talking as the policeman turned away from the phone.

'That got him excited. He's nodding his head.'

'OK. I'll ring you back in a while.'

Political asylum? Ballet dancers applied for political asylum in London. Brilliant foreign scientists carrying secret plans defected at Heathrow in operations smoothly planned by MI6. What was a Pole defecting from in Dover? Before I told the CIO I consulted my General Instructions. Apparently the first action the IO should take was to tell the Home Secretary whilst ensuring that he did not indicate any acceptance of the claim to the applicant. Well that sounded reasonable enough. Naturally I was not expected to talk to Merlyn Rees himself, I did it through the Immigration Service link with the Home Office.

I dialled ISHQ No answer. It was ten to five. They had all gone home. How was I supposed to contact the Home Secretary? I went into the CIO's office.

'Dover town police have just rung in. They've got a Pole there who's claiming political asylum.'

'Oh piss off.' He returned to his crossword.

'No, really. I'm not joking.'

He looked at me, patently disbelieving my assertion of sincerity. 'A Pole? Claiming PA?' I nodded. 'In Dover?' I nodded again. He was slowly coming around. He sighed. 'What does it say in GIs?'

'It says that we have to tell the Home Secretary. I've rung ISHQ but they've all gone home.'

'You'll have to ring the Duty Officer.' He studied my face again. 'You're not pulling my plonker are you?' I assured him that I was not. 'I'll get the number.' He consulted a circular pinned to the notice board.

I rang the number.

'Duty officer's phone,' a voice answered.

'Immigration Dover East here. We've got a Pole who wants to claim political asylum. It says in our instructions–'

'You need to talk to the Duty Officer.'

'I thought you were the Duty Officer.'

'No. This is the DO's phone. The DO is on his way home.'

'So how do I contact him?'

'You'll have to ring him at home.'

'What's the number?' I prepared a pen and paper.

'Haven't you got it?'

'I've only got this number.'

'I don't know whether I can give out his home phone number. I don't know who you are.'

'So how am I supposed to tell the Home Secretary?'

'I'll go and check and ring you back. Immigration Dover you said?'

'Immigration Dover East.' I gave him my name.

This Pole obviously did not speak much English. We would need an interpreter. Now who in the port speaks Polish? I looked at the duty list. We had one IO qualified in Polish and he was on annual leave. There was one officer over at the West. I rang them and they said that he was on his days off. I rang Folkestone. They had an officer who would be on nights tonight. If he turned in. He sometimes did not.

The man at ISHQ rang back, satisfied himself that I was who I said I was and gave me a telephone number. I rang it. A lady answered. Her husband usually came in at about seven, would I like to ring back after he had eaten his dinner, say a quarter to eight? I left her my name and number and asked if her husband could give me a ring when he got home.

I telephoned Dover police. 'How is he?' I asked.

'He's quiet. He's having a meal at the moment.' Lucky chap, I thought. 'What's happening?'

'We're doing what we have to at our end. I will get a Polish speaker to him as soon as I can.'

'So do we detain him?'

Do they detain him? I had no idea. What could they detain him for? If I said 'yes' they would lock him up on my authority without a backward glance, remarking how lucky we were to be able to detain people without charge.

'No, he's not detained. Not by the Immigration Service anyway.'

'So he can go if he wants to?'

'I'd rather he didn't until we have seen him. We need to check his passport to discover on what basis he is in England.'

'So you'll send somebody along to see him?'

'Yes. I'm looking for a Polish speaker at the moment. I'll give you a ring when they are on their way.'

I looked at the Polish name that I had written on the paper in front of me. If he had come in at Dover East as a passenger then he would have filled in a landing card. I went to the stack of pigeon holes and removed the bundle of conditional landing cards. There was a pretty selection of

Arabic and Iron Curtain nationals but nobody with my chap's name. There was not much more that I could do at that moment so I went to the canteen for a snack.

By the time that I came back the day CIO had been relieved by the early night CIO. I briefed him. He gave me the same sardonic look as his predecessor.

'I wonder if he has jumped ship?' I said as I gazed out over the Eastern Arm to where a an untidy grey freighter and a blue and white reefer were moored. 'Have those ships been visited?'

The CIO did not know so I went and looked in the register of ships visited. One was a Cypriot-registered vessel and two IOs had been on board that morning just after it had docked. The other ship had not been visited. The IOs would have been given a copy of the crew list. I searched their pigeon holes and found the sheet. My man did not figure on it. Back to square one.

At ten past seven I rang the Duty Officer at home. His wife said that he had not returned yet. I rang Folkestone and asked if their Polish speaker had turned in for work. Not yet. Then the police station rang.

'This chap is getting a bit agitated,' the policeman said.

'I hope to have a Polish speaker to him within half an hour,' I said, not knowing whether or not that was feasible.

'His passport says, 'Seaman's Passport' on the cover.'

'Ah, he is a scaman then. He must be off a ship.'

'I said he was off a ship ages ago.'

'Yeah, sorry, I mean he's not off a ferry. He must be crew from one of the freighters that are in the port at the moment. I'll see if we can find his details.'

I scratched my head. I knew not the first thing about the control of seamen in Dover. I had only ever done it once and the experience that had been etched in my memory had nothing to do with the processing of seamen.

I had gone down to the Eastern Arm with a small hairy Scot called Fergus. He looked like a garden gnome.

'Do you know what we are supposed to be doing?' I had asked him as we got out of the car.

'As much as you do. We go to the captain, he gives us a beer and we sit down with the crew list and look intelligent.'

'But we don't interview anybody do we?' I remembered this from my training course. 'If we interview them then we have to land them or refuse them and that gets complicated.'

'All we do is look at the crew list and check the occasional seaman's book. The captain will have collected them together for us. If we are satisfied that they are all regular professional seamen then we tell the captain that they can have shore leave.'

'How do you know whether they are professional?' I kept a wary eye on a pallet load of oranges that had been fished out of the hold by a crane and was now swinging towards us.

'Training and experience.'

'What about supernumeraries?'

'Just hope that there aren't any. Those we would have to see and talk to.'

'I'll follow you.' I pointed to the gangway.

It was a walkway the width of one person. It had transverse wooden slats fixed on it to give some sort of purchase for feet although I thought that they were more likely to trip us up. To stop us from falling off, every few yards an iron pole had been welded to the edge of the gangway and through this the three parallel ropes were looped. I was not convinced that a rope at ankle, knee and hip height would be sufficient to prevent me from hurtling into the briny: I am over six feet tall. Little Fergus would have no worries at all.

There was no safety net under the gangway. When later I enquired about this I was told that although it is a standing regulation in Board of Trade ports that all gangways must be protected with a net to catch persons falling, Dover was a port incorporated under Royal Charter and so could do what it liked.

We stepped down onto the deck and asked a man in a greasy tee shirt to take us to the captain. He made some guttural noises and pointed down a companionway. That is what you are supposed to call the staircases in ships. We found the captain, Fergus got his beer, we checked the list. I had to believe that he knew what he was doing. I had no idea what we were supposed to be looking for in seamen's books but I went through the actions. After a pleasant hour chatting to the Waterguard rummage crew we decided that we had skived off for long enough and it was time to get back to work. Easier said than done.

'We seem to have gone up in the world,' I remarked from the height of the deck. With the joint action of the emptying of the hold and the rising of the tide we now found ourselves about thirty feet above the quayside.

Carrying our official cases, we made our way to the head of the gangway. It was almost vertical like a ladder. The comforting iron uprights were jutting out horizontally. Fergus peered over the edge. Black water sloshed back and forth in the gap below us. He tried reaching out for the rope. It was too far away.

'Give me your case,' I said.

He did, but it did not help. Fergus was frightened.

'We can't go down there.' He squatted on the deck and gingerly draped a leg over the side hoping to contact with the gangway. 'It's nowhere near us. Tell them to put the ship back down again.'

'They can't put it down, you twit. They've taken all the stuff out of the hold and the tide has come in. That's why it's gone up.'

'We can't get off.'

'Well we can't wait another ten hours for low tide.'

'We can't get off.'

'Let me have a try.' I put my official case on the deck and dropped a leg over the side, feeling for the first slat on the gangway. I found it and brought my other leg over and lowered myself off the deck. Now I was half lying but I had one hand on the bottom of the first iron stake. The ankle-height rope was level with my cheek. 'Right, hand me my case over. I'll go down and then come back up for you.' I took my case and by dint of wedging it on the rung which was always above me, I crawled backwards down to the quayside. The problem now was that I needed to dump my case to go up and help Fergus but I could not just leave it on the wharf – it had classified material in it.

'Fergus, can you chuck the car keys down so that I can lock up my case?' His white face appeared at the top of the gangway. 'No, better not, they might go in the gap. I'll come up and get them.'

I stolidly climbed back up the quasi-ladder, jumping my case up the slats in front of me. I stowed the keys safely in my pocket and then climbed back down again. With the case securely locked in the car I climbed back up to Fergus, the words of Gerard Hoffnung, 'meanwhile the barrel...' facetiously repeating themselves in my mind.

'You'll have to do it the same way that I did. Bring your case down above you.'

'I donna like this.' His Scottish accent became more intense. 'I donna like this at all.'

'It's not exactly a picnic for me, Fergus,' I called from my perch. 'Come on, put your leg over the side.' He dangled a tentative leg. It was about six inches too short. 'Come lower.'

'I can't. I can't let go.'

I reached up and guided his ankle.

'Lower yourself slowly and I will put your foot on the rung.'

'It's too far.' He was beginning to panic.

'Fergus, I am not going to hang here all day. Either you put your foot on the rung and I help you down or you sort yourself out.' His foot waggled slightly lower. 'Another two inches, as the actress said to the bishop.' Success. His shoe wedged firmly on the ridge. 'Right, keep your case above you and bring your other foot down to the rung below and with your free hand you will find the iron upright on the gangway.' He lurched downwards and I descended a rung at the same time, smacking his foot onto the tread above me. 'Now bring your case over the edge and onto the top rung.'

'I can't lift it over the ridge.'

'Give it a tug,' I said, noting the nautical flavour of the suggestion but wisely deciding not to share it with Fergus.

'It won't go.'

'Look, I can't get past you to help. You'll just have to sort of jump up a bit and lift hard but try not to knock me off the plank.'

'Christ!' I heard him mutter as the case suddenly vaulted over the gunwales and onto the top rung.

'Right,' I said gaily, 'down we go.'

After that, it was easy.

It seemed that my contact with Fergus would often lurch into drama. A year or two later we were walking along a London street to the Albert Hall to hear St. Saens' Organ Concerto. We were talking four abreast which would have been rather selfish behaviour on a crowded pavement but it was unobstructed. Well, not quite. Suddenly we realised that we were only three. There was a Fergus-shaped gap in the conversation. We stopped and looked back. He was standing utterly stunned before the scaffolding pole that we three had missed because it had not been on our track. It was like a gag in a Tom and Jerry cartoon. The bruise came up like a plum.

But Fergus was another one of those souls in torment. He eventually transferred to Heathrow and then, he too, just stopped coming in to work. He disappeared. Some say he went back to Scotland. I don't know.

The phone rang. It was Folkestone. The Polish speaker was on his way. I rang the police station.

'He's gone,' the officer said.

'Who's gone?'

'The Pole.'

'Gone? Gone where?'

'He didn't say. He got fed up and went. You said we couldn't hold him.'

'No, that's right. Thanks.' I did not know what else to say. I reported developments to the CIO. He had not really believed in the Pole in the first place. When I got back to the office the phone was ringing.

'Immigration Dover East,' I said.

'Home Office duty officer here. You've been trying to contact me.'

'Yes. We had a Pole who wanted to claim PA but he appears to have changed his mind.'

'Oh well, that's settled then. Good evening.'

By the time I left the Immigration Service, there were 450,000 people awaiting decisions on their asylum applications in the UK.

I am not a political animal. The whole business bores me to tears. I was amused and vindicated to discover when learning Urdu that to call a person 'a politician' in Pakistan was an insult. I rarely vote. Why should I? It only confirms the politicians' belief in their own importance. And despite what they say, it is not a secret ballot. Last time I visited a polling station I objected to the man writing the serial number of my slip against my name in the voters' list.

'Why are you doing that?' I asked.

'We have to. It's regulations.'

'But this is supposed to be a secret ballot.'

'It is. You go behind that screen, mark your paper and put it in the box. Nobody will see what you write.'

'But you have linked my slip to my name on the list. Anybody, once the box is opened, can trace it back to me and know what I voted.'

'It's a secret ballot,' he insisted.

A history professor acquaintance of mine was saddened and upset to hear me propound that there was no point in voting because you could not change anything.

'Do you really believe that?' she asked.

'Of course.'

'That's terrible. Can't you see that you have the mandate? You can change the country if you all vote for the change.'

'No we can't. You've been brainwashed. The only result of everybody voting is that a politician will be elected. The way to change the country is for nobody to vote and then we would have no politicians. This country runs by itself, despite whichever government is in power.'

'But what about Parliament?'

'I think it is a superb institution. What an intelligent idea to lock up all the politicians in a big building in London. They would be dangerous if we let them run around in the streets.'

You can see from the above how immature and uninformed is my grasp of current affairs and constitutional history. So what am I doing forging my route through the haranguing crowd to attend a meeting of the National Front in Folkestone?

The crush barriers are in place and a strong contingent of police are bouncing around in the crowd. I walk down the alley which they have cleared up to the steps of the town hall.

'Fascist!' an objector yells at me from the crowd.

I stop and turn. The nearest policeman looks nervous.

'Fascist?' I shout back. 'Me? I'm not even a Folkstonian.'

'It's Nazi propaganda.'

'I haven't heard what they have said yet. Have you?'

And that was the point. The National Front had long been vilified in the Press and they provided some exciting copy when they brought their anti-immigration and anti-colour beliefs to explain on their marches in Lewisham and Birmingham, along with a selection of blunt instruments to assist in the elucidation. Civil servants must be seen to be apolitical, which is daft – patently they are not. I suppose I could be the exception. I don't care about politics but I am curious about the National Front. Here we have a paradox. A genuinely apolitical civil servant, by attending an extreme right meeting, risks having himself branded as a virulent fascist. If, as if claimed widely in proper-thinking circles, the National Front are the enemy of civilisation then would it not be a good idea to get to know the enemy?

The town hall is a tired building. The white paint is peeling from the pillars of the portico, the window panes are dirty, the wooden stairs are worn and dusty. They lead me to the upper chamber which is a posh name for a large room with tall Victorian windows through which I can see the demonstrating mass outside. The space is laid out with seven or eight lines of dark wooden chairs of the type which were common in Baptist chapels, arranged with a central aisle. On the dais are two tables. The Union Flag is draped across the front of one; four people are sitting behind the other. The front rows of both blocks are occupied already. I choose a seat three rows from the front and near the aisle. I look around to assess the audience. We are about thirty. Half a dozen men are hanging around at the back of the hall near the top of the stairs. I recognise one of them and wave to him. He is embarrassed and cannot wave back. He is one of our SB officers. He will certainly report my presence.

The meeting is called to order and a thin man with a pencil moustache stands up. He welcomes us and is almost ecstatic at the 'strong support' of the people of Folkestone. The front row all clap loudly. Then he introduces a lady who looks like somebody's older sister and who is going to address us with her maiden speech so we are asked to be indulgent. The woman stands up clutching her address written in longhand on a sheaf of blue lined paper. She reads it word for word, pausing in mid sentence when she has to turn over. It seems to be the usual tosh about dedication to maintaining the Britishness of Britain. As she ploughs through the drivel in an utterly unconvincing conversational manner, I begin to hear mutterings coming from behind me to my left. A man starts to heckle her with various political challenges. She deals with these by waiting for him to finish, ignoring him completely and then reading on from the next word in the sentence.

She manages to finish although I doubt whether anybody at the back heard a word that she had uttered. She sits down and the front row clap enthusiastically again. A brash, loud man then jumps up and starts what he hopes we will think is an Oswald Moseley-style oration. It is not. The only link with Moseley is the black shirt that he is wearing. He seems to be saying that not enough people are being locked up and the National Front will be tough on crime and if the prisons are full then they will just build more prisons. The heckler, I now realise, is tipsy. Not dangerously drunk, just tanked up enough to give him some fire. He is being fed his heckles by a posse of five men in raincoats who are sitting around him. They are the Press from London. He is the secretary of the local Labour party whom they have been carefully entertaining in the pub prior to the meeting.

'The flag, the flag. It's an insult to our flag,' I hear somebody whisper.

The heckler stands up. 'It's an insult to our flag,' he shouts. 'I'll not let you use our flag for your ends.' He lurches to the front and pulls the Union Flag from the table. As one body, the front row stands up. The three men nearest to him turn, pick up their chairs and bring them down on top of him. I also stand up. I march directly to the door at the back and hold it open for the boots that I can hear running up the stairs. The uniformed police run in, I wink at the SB officer, and walk down into the street.

It's a rum do, politics.

Ordnance Survey maps were originally compiled for the British Army and publication was started at the beginning of the nineteenth century. Never before had Britain been so comprehensively surveyed. The maps are a delight of hatching and black lettering and carry at the bottom an indication of their military origins: *'Engraved at the Drawing Room at the Tower.'* The Tower being the Tower of London.

It was realised, however, that the maps would be as useful to an enemy as they would be to the British Army and so to foil the machinations of our foes the decision was taken to not mark upon the maps any military establishments. They were simply not engraved on the copper plate. Thus, if you consult sheet eighty-one of the first edition, on the eastern cliffs above Dover you will find an irregular area of white where nothing apparently exists. This would amuse rather than confuse an enemy arriving by sea because the mass of Dover Castle stands four hundred and sixty feet above sea level and the Norman keep itself is ninety feet tall. It can be seen from France but not on the map.

It was garrisoned until 1966 at which point it was handed over to English Heritage to serve the needs of the tourist. I am waiting at the traffic light which controls passage over the drawbridge but I am not a tourist. I am wintering at the 'Arrears Unit.' The numbers of passengers arriving at Dover naturally form into peaks and troughs depending upon the holiday seasons. It is a staffing nightmare. Inevitably we have too few staff in summer and too many in winter. The summer problem is addressed by accepting relief officers from other ports but in the winter we need to be given jobs to do. A staffing review in the 1960s suggested that IOs could be gainfully employed in their 'down time' by visiting pharmacies and checking the poisons registers. Thankfully, the Home Office had other ideas. Up at Lunar House in Croydon the caseworking executive officers are slowly submerging under the files of the people whom we have landed and who have applied for extensions to their stays. What more apposite a solution than to get IOs to shift some of the backlog in winter?

The light changes to green and I drive over the dry moat and under the portcullis into the inner curtain of the castle. The tall, rectangular keep that was built on the orders of William the Conqueror to stop anybody else from doing what he had just done, stands high on a bank to my left as I branch off on a road leading to the top of the White Cliffs of Dover. There stands the officers' mess. It is a two storey, Victorian-looking building of grey stone and flint and the Arrears Unit is housed within it. In our office at the western corner of the first floor, the metal window frames fit badly into the stone mullions and the cold wind rattles through but who cares? We have an unobstructed view over Dover harbour, across the Channel to the French coast. It is a wonder that we get any work done at all.

THE VIEW FROM MY OFFICE WINDOW.
It is a winter's morning and the eastern light is silhouetting the French coast on the horizon. The wind is lightly ruffling the surface of an otherwise calm English Channel and the first hovercraft arrival of the day is making its way to the eastern entrance of Dover port.

The work sent down from Croydon originates from the B3 Caseworking Division which deals only with Commonwealth citizens. The files of non-Commonwealth, or 'aliens' as they are termed, are processed in B1 division and this work is presumably considered too difficult for us. Either that or the division is so efficient that it has no backlog.

The files are delivered by van to the castle every week, twenty-five to a leather pouch. They are checked against the list to make sure that they are all present and then we help ourselves.

When the job was advertised on our general noting file, applicants were promised that Home Office 'flexitime' rules would apply and, as long as we worked our forty-two hours weekly, we would be permitted to attend the office for any eight hour period between 8am. and 8pm. What was not pointed out was that the drawbridge closed daily at 6pm.

Working with files instead of with living people was a challenge to all of our *modus operandii*. The first thing that an IO did when he sat down with a new file was to open the transit envelope laced inside, remove the passport and study the photograph. Then he would work through the passport reading the various visas and frontier stamps to learn the history. Only then would he apply his attention to the contents of the file. I noticed that Jeremy, the higher executive officer who had been sent down from Croydon to oversee the operation, would open the file and go straight to the last entry on the minute sheet and then check to see if there had been any new correspondence. He only looked at the passport if it needed stamping. For IOs at the port, the files were people. For EOs in the Home Office, people were files.

I park my car on the gravel and stomp in through the entrance.

'Morning David,' I say to the clerical assistant who sits in a cubbyhole at the bottom of the stairs. He is the general dogsbody. He looks up from a plastic Airfix kit that he is constructing on his table.

'Good morning.'

'Focke Wulfe 190?'

'Messerschmidt 109.'

I climb the stairs to our room. The IOs have segregated themselves according to empathy. Our room is the preferred workplace of the non-smokers and non-swearers.

'Morning all.' I welcome the three colleagues who are already at work. One is from my port, the other two are from Dover West. They had been strangers to me until we had met at the castle. I do not drink and I practise no sport and these are the two pastimes that will guarantee you an entrée into any immigration office in the kingdom. 'I see you've left me the draughty seat again.'

'There's three to choose from,' one of the Dover West IOs remarks.

'And they are all draughty.'

'A small dose of pneumonia never did anybody any harm. Bloody Dover East pansies, don't know they're born.'

'I deduce from that observation that if I should go down into the town for jam doughnuts this morning you would not be interested?'

'You can sit here,' he says quickly.

'Not until you've fumigated the chair.'

I dump my coat onto an empty chair and go and collect my first file. For the next two hours I decide whether a Malaysian can stay for another year to finish her nursing course (yes); if a seventy-eight year old Indian can have another six months as a visitor in his son's house in Southall (no, but he'll appeal and we'll never get rid of him) and I enquire why a Nigerian who has been studying computers for three years now wishes to learn English. (In order to prolong his stay forever.)

Handling the beige files week in and week out teaches me, little by little, how the Immigration and Nationality Department really works. If it is an exemplar of a Civil Service department then it becomes obvious to me that the Immigration Service runs differently from all the others. The lowest grade in the IND is the CA – the clerical assistant. The lowest grade in the Immigration Service is the IO which is graded equivalent to an EO (executive officer) but is paid more.

When a letter arrives at Lunar House from a person who wishes to stay longer it is opened by a CA in the Registry. They stamp on it the date that it was opened, which can be several days after it has arrived, and check that all that is stated to be enclosed with the letter is actually present. This they indicate by ticking in the text with a red pen. Thus the letter might read, *I wish to apply for an extension of stay as a student. I have enclosed my passport* (tick) *a letter from my college* (tick) *and a bank statement* (cross – *'not enclosed'*). The correspondence is then pinned together and sent for 'linking' which is the process by which the appropriate file is retrieved from its repository and the letter is attached to it or if no file exists, one is raised. It is then sent up to a CO (clerical officer) who minutes the file with a statement of what has arrived, e.g. 'application for extension as student.' In this case they would send out a stock letter asking the applicant to forward the missing bank statement and put the file by to wait for a reply. When the reply is received it passes through the same stages until it gets to the file which is then sent to the EO who considers the application.

If he can grant it he minutes the file, stating which stamp should be endorsed in the passport and then hands it back down to the CO. The CO stamps the passport and the file passes on to the CA who fills the envelope and sends the passport out in the mail. If the EO feels that he should refuse the application he minutes the reasons on the file and sends it up to the HEO for permission.

The procedure I have just described reads like the typical bureaucracy that is ridiculed in the Press and conspued by the public in general, but you know, it works. Thirty years later I find that I open official letters with a red pen in my hand and annotate them when necessary and it has served me well on the occasional brushes with Authority. Being able to state time and date and what was said or was not enclosed is a killer argument when in dispute with organisations whose employees feel they can address you, unbidden, by your Christian name but are unable to read or write English.

This hierarchy of administration did not exist at Dover Castle. We were the messenger who carried the files, the EO who made the decisions, the CO who stamped the passport and then the CA who mailed it out to the applicant. We also made our own tea and refilled our stationery cupboards. Such a lean operation could work well at Dover; it could not work at Lunar House because of the sheer quantity of applications received.

From an IO's point of view the work was rewarding because we dealt with the interesting people without having to work through all the chaff. Once when I was up at Lunar House an EO asked me what percentage of the passengers that we saw did we put 'on conditions' – stamping their passports such that they could apply later to the IND for an extension of stay.

'How many do you think?' I asked.

He sucked on his teeth and looked at the pile of files on his desk.

'It must be in the high sixties, low seventies.'

'You mean, seventy per cent?' He nodded. 'It's just under three per-cent,' I said.

'It can't be. Look at all those.' He pointed to the files.

'I'm afraid it is. You should come down to the port sometime and see for yourself. We spend an awful lot of time landing people in whom we have no interest at all.'

This distorted view of the composition of the passenger traffic also manifested itself when the IS began to receive recruits who were formerly EOs in caseworking sections. They treated every passenger as if they were a potential knock-off. They were still seeing files, they were not yet seeing people. Some never did.

We IOs were similarly corrupted by that proportion of a country's population which decided to travel. We subconsciously assessed an entire nation on the quality of its representatives that we saw. Thus all Iranians wanted to come to the UK to learn English, spend their money and date the girls. Cypriots came to weddings and stayed to run fish and chip shops. Turks wanted to buy a tractor with a pocket full of money which they gave back to the man who had lent it to them and then worked illegally in a kebab shop – we noted the numbers of the notes and saw the same £500 several times. Algerians were pickpockets. Moroccan women were prostitutes. Americans were either blue rinse and Samsonite and had no idea what country they were in or they were penniless world travellers who would work at anything clean to support themselves. The Japanese were all under thirty, had no compunction about lying to Westerners and would not go back to Japan on any account. West Indians would not look you in the eye unless they were lying and Russians always disguised their lies with a hearty laugh. Colombians were organised into shoplifting teams. Australians stayed for five years and got jobs driving overland buses to Nepal. Nigerians were drug smugglers and benefit fraudsters.

I remember one of my colleagues who learned Greek and then went to the country to practise his skill. He came back, utterly astonished. 'The Greeks are lovely people in their own country. They are kind, generous and thoughtful. The ones that come here are the grot.'

I was sure that the same observation applied to all nationalities of the world. Except to Israelis, of course. They are universally arrogant, hyper-sensitive and aggressive.

I suspect that the IOs working on files at Dover Castle made decisions more quickly than the EOs at IND. We were accustomed to assessing people and passing on as quickly as possible to keep the queue moving. At Lunar House, the discretion did not seem to be practised as readily. They felt that they had to have all evidence necessary before them in order to be certain that the person qualified for what he was requesting. This was inescapable. We could settle most suspicions immediately by putting a question to the person standing before us. You cannot do that to a file so all questions had to be listed in a letter and sent with a stamped addressed envelope for the reply. And the pressure to come to a decision was not felt in the same way: a pile of files on the desk does not shuffle and complain or faint or flatulate.

When we did not know what to do with a file we either looked in Instructions or slipped along to the HEO's office and asked his opinion. Jeremy had a vast knowledge of procedure and precedent in the IND but was no match for the guile of IOs. I developed a system of carefully choosing paragraph numbers from Instructions, which was a very thick file, and then quoting them if I needed to add credibility to my proposal on a case. This technique gave him the choice of agreeing with me and thus confirming that he knew Instructions off by heart, or losing face by asking me what the paragraph stated. I had great fun with this until my favourite, 'Oh I think it's a case of para 14.1.5. don't you?' thrown at him in my customary casual manner, prompted him to check up after I had left with his blessing.

'That paragraph you used...' He stood in the doorway, the file of Instructions open in his arms. 'You did say "14.1.5"?'

The other IOs looked up with interest.

'Yes that's right.' I grinned.

'You've used it several times.'

'Oh yes,' I agreed pleasantly. 'It's very adaptable.'

He peered into the file again, his eyebrows twisting themselves like anxious fingers. 'Do you know what it says?'

'Yup. It tells you where to park your car when visiting Lunar House.'

'Quite.'

'And the supplementary instruction I sometimes quote, tells you not to leave a carafe of water on a conference table on a sunny day because the jug acts like a magnifying glass and concentrates the sun's rays onto the paper and can cause a fire.'

'Fine. We know where we stand now then don't we?'

I had to agree but I turned my mind to inventing an automatic decision taker. We IOs suspected that when an EO did not know what to do with a file or was in a hurry, he would invent a reason to write, *'hold one month'* in the 'action' box on the front cover. This meant that the file was kept out of Registry on his desk whilst he frantically thought up a way of solving it or unloading it on to a colleague.

The next time that Jeremy poked his head around our door to discuss a case, one of the IOs rose from his chair and walked to the notice board. Pinned sturdily to it was a cardboard wheel with a pointer mounted over it. He flipped the wheel and waited whilst it spun to a halt. We studiously ignored him. He then returned to his file. Jeremy could not help noticing this activity from the corner of his eye and when he had finished his discussion, he made his way out of the office via the notice board. There he found my cardboard contraption labelled *'Patented File Decision Maker'*. The wheel was divided into six segments, each containing a suggestion for a file destination: *'Hold one month, new file covers please, translation requested, bottom of lift shaft, look for linking, check for embarks.'*

'Very ingenious,' he said. 'Very ingenious.' He stuck out his bottom lip. 'I sometimes wonder if that is how they do it already.'

Another activity that I introduced was that of bouncing passports off the ceiling. I am not particularly proud of this. By flipping the booklet skywards with just the right elan, you could get it to make a mark on the white plaster. Some countries' passports gave up their colours more readily than others. By the time we left we had lines of various shades of blue from Indian passports; pinky reds from Malaysian and Singaporean and a very rare green impression from a Nigerian.

But it was not all a hard slog. The last Thursday of the month was the luncheon day. A couple of IOs would volunteer to prepare a meal for all those in the luncheon club. They would be excused file work in the morning whilst they did the cooking and then all would sit down to eat and drink at lunchtime. Somebody was needed, however, to run the shop and my job, as a teetotaller, was to answer the phones so that the others could continue their revelry uninterrupted. Most of the calls were from EOs at IND who either wanted one of their files returned urgently or had something to tell us that needed marking on the file.

Answering the phone one Thursday with my usual, 'Immigration Dover Castle' prompted my interlocutor to enquire if we were really in a castle. I described it in lurid detail with its stone stairways, torture chambers and smoky oil lamps hanging on iron brackets. When he asked me to get one of his files I told him that it might take some time as I had to go down into the dungeons for the files and I thought that the keeper of the key was out feeding the ravens. The result was that my mystified colleagues noticed thereafter that requests for files were couched in most apologetic terms

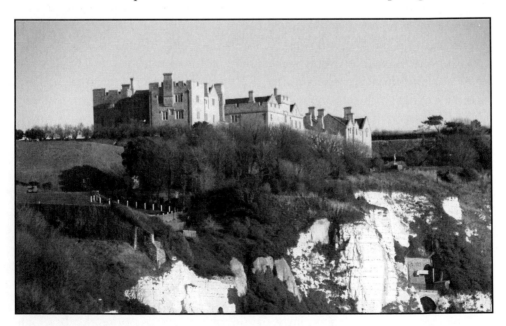

The Officers' Mess, Dover Castle
Perched on top of the White Cliffs of Dover.
There was nothing between us and France.

accompanied by exhortations to 'wrap up warm'.

One morning in May, we were studiously applying ourselves to our files probably because we had no view from the window that morning. The disadvantage of being on top of a cliff was that sometimes the cloud would come down and envelope our little building and that day, against the window sat clammy white cotton wool. It was so thick that we could not see the ground. As if in sympathy with the isolation, we worked with just the occasional *bonk* of a stamp breaking the cocooned silence.

'What was that?' I said.

'What?' a colleague replied.

'That noise. A sort of clinking noise.'

'You're hearing things.'

We returned to our files. I was dithering over the correct form of address for a Malaysian who had changed sex.

'There it goes again,' I said.

'I didn't hear anything.'

'Nor did I.'

'And I can hear voices,' I insisted.

'Oh that's always the start. First they hear the voices then they try to change the water to wine. You won't get my vote.'

We went back to work. I wondered whether 'it' was the appropriate term I should use to refer to the applicant on my file.

'There's something going on out there,' I said. 'I know there is.'

'Oh go back to sleep.'

Boom! The explosion was right outside my window. The frame rattled in its mullions. My heart jumped into my mouth.

'Christ!'

'Shit!'

One officer pushed back his chair and crawled under the desk. I leaped from my seat, uncaring of the paper snowstorm that resulted, and followed the rest of my colleagues in the panic stampede for the door. We had received no bomb warning although the state of alert was still high. How I wish I had paid more attention to the evacuation procedures. I heard a shout. It came from the thick cloud below my window.

Boom!

I stopped. The others did not. There was a certain logical pertinence to what I thought the man had shouted.

'Fire!'

Boom!

I tiptoed to the window. The firing of the third gun had cleared the fog

from around our building. On a concrete pad sat three green field guns
and an assortment of soldierly types.

'Fire!'

Boom!

'It's all right. You can come out now,' I called to the chap cowering
under the desk. 'They are on our side.'

'What the hell are they doing?'

'Firing a salute to somebody. It's not your birthday is it?'

Colleagues drifted back in again. I think that the situation could have
been handled better. If you are going to arrive under cover of fog, set up
three field guns and fire a twenty-one gun salute underneath somebody's
window then surely you could pop in and warn them? But then, thinking
about it, if I had been in charge of the platoon I could imagine myself
whispering to the chaps, 'keep it as quiet as you can lads, they don't know
we're here yet but they soon will.'

File succeeded file, the satchels emptied and refilled, the days passed.
I could see that the work would become a drudge if one were faced with
it day in, day out and had to commute to Croydon every morning but for
me, the novelty was refreshing and learning how the Immigration and
Nationality Department functioned was useful experience for me,
although I did not recognise it at the time.

One highlight of my stay at the castle was my day out to London. As a
result of my application, the selection board of the European Commission
had invited me to attend a venue in London to sit the entrance exam for
the next intake of administrators to work in Brussels. I had no idea what
the job entailed but often saw the European Civil Servants driving through
the port with their blue 'Euro' plates on their duty-free cars as they
exercised their right to their two annual free trips home and I had envied
them. It seemed to me that if there was a job with a load of freebies
attached to it, then I should be doing it instead of being stuck in a stinky
kiosk on a windswept quayside and having to argue and cajole to gain
possession of a bottle of stationery office issue black ink to feed my
fountain pen.

There must have been nearly a hundred of us waiting to sit the exam.
We milled around the vestibule nervously avoiding eye contact with each
other so it was all the more surprising when I was hailed by a colleague
from Folkestone port. I only knew him because I had seen him playing the
French horn in a silver band. We exchanged pleasantries. There was a
large contingent of Irish candidates and they were all arguing volubly with
the treasurer, affirming that, under the EEC selection procedure rules, they

had the right to claim a refund for the hotel room as well as the air fare because it would have been impractical to expect them to fly over on the morning of the exam. They were fluent and very insistent and I believe they deserved, all of them, to succeed to Brussels.

The morning's exam paper was general knowledge. We sat at our desks whilst five European civil servants, dressed in the latest Continental fashion, faffed about at the front of the room sorting out the question papers. They spoke to each other in enthusiastic French which was daft because we could all see that they were British, earnestly showing that they were European.

'Are there any French-speaking candidates here?' a smart young thing asked, in English.

I raised my hand, as did about ten other people. This surprised me. Only ten French-speaking candidates in a hundred? That was statistically very unlikely, unless of course the other French speakers could not speak English and thus had not understood the question.

'Oh there's some French speakers here,' she muttered in alarm to her collcagues, reverting to French to do so.

They scurried about and searched in their various designer leather bags and polycarbonate briefcases and eventually drew out some sheets. One of the team came to me and exchanged the question paper on my desk for another. Bizarre. I looked at it. It was printed in French. Now this was not fair. The rules stated that candidates were to be examined in their mother tongue. I raised my hand as did the several others who had been similarly served.

'Can I have a paper in English please?' I asked. I had realised, as they had not, that the question that she should have asked was, 'Is there any candidate whose mother tongue is French?'

At last we were ready to start. We had ninety minutes to answer one hundred multiple choice questions. The instructions divulged that the paper was to be marked by computer. I had never seen this before. On the right hand side of every sheet were five columns of black lozenges whose centres were blank except for a set of fine, truncated cross hairs. Each question had five possible answers. In order to indicate our choice of answer we had to put a vertical line in the lozenge of our choice. If we changed our mind then we were to ring the wrong choice and make another. That was the essence of what I understood but I was not sure that I had grasped it. Helpfully they had printed the first question as a completed example underneath the instructions. I studied this. I could not work out how they had made the choice or what I was supposed to do.

After a minute of valuable time I discreetly glanced across at the other tables. Everywhere candidates had turned over and were busily attacking the paper proper so I did the same.

It was a bit like a grown up eleven-plus exam. One group of questions required a knowledge of geometry, basic maths, percentages and fractions. When at school I had failed my O-level maths three times. The one example that I remember was the classic trick question which, naturally, tricked me. Imagine that the equator is a steel wire. One extra metre is inserted in the wire. By how much will the equator now stand proud of the surface of the Earth? The various answers ranged from a ludicrous thirty centimetres to the infinitesimally small figure whose magnitude I cannot now recall but which I naturally chose. As did anybody else who had forgotten all that they had been taught about pi.

Another group of questions demanded logical reasoning which I found enjoyable although I have no idea how I fared in them and yet another revolved around an understanding of language, which, given the performance of our invigilators so far, smacked of securing the stable door subsequent to the equine absquatulation.

At lunchtime the Irish went out and drank Guinness. I sat in a park and ate my sandwiches. As I thought through the administration of the examination, it occurred to me that, using a computer to mark the paper meant that they could programme it to pick out those people who could count but not explain their reasoning; those who could talk plausibly about impractical schemes and those who could reason without producing a workable application to their deductions. I submit this observation without comment.

After lunch, the examination took on a more 'applied' twist.

'You have been tasked to set up a staff college. Your budget for staff salaries is X thousand dollars. You are authorised to employ fifty staff. State how you will allocate this money. Academic staff must have a remuneration which is thirty-five percent above administrative staff. Administrative staff must have a remuneration which is twenty-five percent above the housekeeping staff.'

I gulped. Question two.

'Fifteen thousand dollars have been allocated to prizes for attainment. One gold cup, one silver cup, three bronze medals and ten certificates of merit will be awarded each year. The winner of the gold cup must have achieved a marking fifteen percent above silver. The silver...'

And so it went on. I was floundering. Did they mean me to state how many cleaning staff were in the fifty personnel? How many cleaners do you need anyway? And how much do you pay them? I had no idea. I felt like writing, *'why don't you contract it out to a specialist training company and get the job done properly?'* across the paper.

I gnawed my pen, I became despondent but I soldiered on. I have never been able to calculate percentages properly despite having passed the statistics paper in my HND in Business Studies. I qualify that claim by admitting that one of the answers I came to in class was that the predicted average weight of a baby to be born in 1980 would be two tons, thirteen hundredweight. It had taken my tutor some time to find the mistake. Midwives countrywide breathed a sigh of relief.

Five minutes to go and I had ground to a halt. I had given it all I had got. Whatever the quality of my contribution, I could do no more. Well, not strictly true, for here, on the back of the paper, I found the last question. Even when sitting the eleven-plus we had been told to always look at both sides of the paper.

I was not picked to administer Europe, which, I claim, is the reason it is in the state it is today. My colleague from Folkestone passed the selection procedure and started with the task of running the car pool in Brussels. The next time I met him he was in a bar in Dhaka, Bangladesh where he was trying to spend four and half million dollars of relief funds but failing miserably because the EEC would not allow him to pay the bribes that the Bangladeshi politicians demanded in order to authorise their departments to accept the money.

The last Thursday dinner had been eaten and the final load of satchels was sitting in the hallway awaiting the van. I had carefully dismantled the Patented File Decision Maker and presented it to Jeremy. He had wrapped it venerably in a transit envelope to take back to Lunar House.

By the end of March I was back at the port for an auspicious date. Auspicious, that is, for Kent Police; disastrous for the Metropolitan Police. For at the end of the month the Kent force were taking over the function of the Special Branch, which was staffed by the Metropolitan Police and had been allocated to passenger ports of the United Kingdom since World War 1. The Met. Police officers faced transfer back to London, having to sell houses in rural Kent to move into a city. Most of them were not pleased. Northwood had already departed; having found Dover a backwater, he had transferred to Northern Ireland. Kent Police were raring to go and showed enthusiasm in all their dealings with us, hoping that the IOs would give them the leads they needed to make their mark. It was unfortunate that their first tour of duty was April 1st.

For the IOs the changeover meant that we would lose the long chats about crime detection and policing in the metropolis that we had enjoyed during the hours of downtime, stuck in a kiosk, waiting for a ship to dock. Most of the stories that they told were entertaining, some may have been true, but I doubt it. As a cyclist, I remember raising disbelieving eyebrows when an officer had recounted how he had pedalled a Sturmey-Archer geared bicycle down Bluebell Hill at forty miles per hour but fortuitously, such overt displays of incredulity never discouraged them from pushing on to achievements superlative. If they had really done all that they recounted why, one could ask, were they stuck in Dover and not running Scotland Yard?

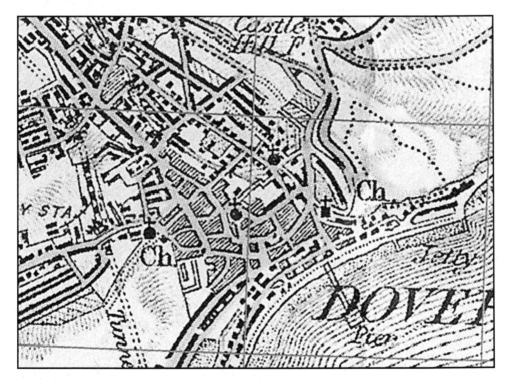

THE MISSING CASTLE
Dover Castle was purposefully omitted from the early Ordnance Survey maps so that invading foreigners would not know that it was there. The blank space on the cliffs above the word 'Dover' is where it stands, as suggested by the nearby *Castle Hill Farm*.

When I was at college I used to often hitchhike on the M1 between Sheffield and Hemel Hempstead. The stories the lorry drivers told me were incredible: transporting live warheads for guided missiles with a police escort front and back; kidnapping Prince Philip at a student rag week by hiring a limousine and swooping up a minute earlier than the official car; picking up a mayday signal on their radio and relaying it to the coastguard, oh they had me enthralled. It was not until years later that I began to question their veracity. It was the same with Special Branch. I wanted to believe their stories and so I indulged the raconteur. It helped pass the time.

An IO dealing with foreigners on a daily basis cannot help being sensitive to language and I found it fascinating to listen to the police radio conversations. When an SB officer saw what he considered to be an interesting or suspect passenger or vehicle he would radio the details from our kiosk to the collator in his nearby office and the collator would spin the 'fish fryer'. This was a large rotating drum of index cards which held all the information they had amassed. This was at a time when computers were still the size of a wardrobe and cost hundreds of thousands of pounds. The police officers used coded language which enabled them to discreetly describe the gender and ethnicity of their target. The phonetic alphabet was sometimes truncated almost in the manner of cockney slang where the original meaning is several translations distant. 'I think I'll foxtrot now,' would indicate an intention to depart. 'Foxtrot' was short for 'foxtrot oscar', the phonetic identifiers for the letters F and O, which in turn represented the initial letters of two words of a well known slang combination indicating movement.

And they were inveterate donors of soubriquets. They had a woman officer who was known as 'the Olympic torch' because she never went out and an officer called 'Duracell' because he had a ginger top and went on and on and on. One rather bumptious soul they called, 'Two Shits'.

'Why do you call him "Two Shits"?' I asked.

'He's a pain in the arse. If I say that I went to Cyprus for a week then he'll say that he rented a villa there for a month; if I tell him that I've just won ten quid on the horses, then he'll have won a hundred. He always has to go one better. No matter what it is, he always reckons to have done better than you. So if you say, 'I've just been for a shit,' he will say, 'that's nothing, I've just been for two shits."

As it transpired, the changeover made little difference to us. We still had a plain clothes officer lurking around behind us, tapping our foot or coughing discreetly and they could tell whoppers just like the Met., so nothing was lost. And they rose in our esteem when, seeing Dennis leaving the Christmas party, they radioed to one of their colleagues and had him breathalysed on the way home. He got banned for a year.

There is a God.

The staffing list for Dover hoverport had been published and my name was absent from it. The IS had drawn upon staff from all around the country but that is not to say that nobody from Dover East was transferred there: an officer junior to me got the appointment because she had just married an IO who also served at Dover East and the IS decided that their policy was to not allow married couples to serve in the same port, but to sweeten the pill, or turn the knife in the wound, whichever you choose, they posted me to Dover hoverport on three month's relief to help run the port whilst they filled the places I had applied for. It's a good job I have a sense of humour.

Dover East was a large port. Dover hoverport was a small one. In a large port, there are so many IOs producing work that a large support staff is required. In a small port, you actually learn more about the job because you have to undertake many of the smaller jobs such as sending statistical returns to the Home Office or negotiating with the landlords over the television licence. When I arrived at the hoverport they gave me the responsibility for the photocopier. They had noted my interest in the process of reproduction, I suppose.

The terminal building at Dover hoverport was a two storey, brick-built affair with a flat roof. It stretched from one side of the plot to the other, filling the gap between the Prince of Wales Pier and the entrance to Wellington Dock. On the landward side lay the necessary approach road, coach sweep and car parking. On the seaward side were acres of unobstructed concrete which slid gently into the water – the pad. The terminal building was arranged in the conventional manner; passengers embarked through one channel and landed through another. On the floor above, a corridor ran the length of the building to serve the offices. The immigration office was at the dead end over the tunnel used by the motor traffic disembarking. On the seaward side we looked over the flat roof of the passenger inwards hall to the pad, the harbour and beyond. On the landward side we looked over Wellington Dock to the Western Heights, Shakespeare Cliff and the seafront. And from the locker room at the end of the office, the windows let directly onto the passage which gave access to the Wellington Dock. It was a complete contrast to Dover East where our offices were now so far from the ships that we might just as well have been working at an airport. Here, the hovercraft rumbled up and gazed through our windows and it was not unusual to see ships pass within a few feet of the end of the building.

The arrangements for the control of passengers required some fine tuning. We could do nothing about the purple carpet and orange walls;

that was merely a matter of taste but the lighting on the foot passenger control was atrocious. The only daylight came from the floor to ceiling glass doors through which the passengers entered from the pad. The ceiling lights were of a type that needed five minutes to come to full brilliance. It was all very cosy and soothing. But from our point of view, we were looking down a brick tunnel with a purple floor towards the only source of daylight. Standing in this flare was the mass of silhouetted humanity called passengers. They could see us beautifully; we could just see black blobs. We made urgent representations to Seaspeed and they installed a line of fluorescent tubes in the ceiling behind us. Brilliant. Now we had black blobs in front of us and three shadows of our heads which converged onto our desks as we tried to read the passport. The only recompense us chaps discovered for having to stare into the flood of light at the end of the hall was that as the Seaspeed hostesses stepped through the doorway their summer uniforms became transparent.

Out on cars, the problem was different. It appeared to me that the designers had originally intended to lead the disembarking cars from the hovercraft straight to the three double kiosks that they had built at the side of the pad for the use of the Immigration Service. The kiosks having been erected, Somebody Important must have said, 'what precautions are there in place to stop a manoeuvring hovercraft from rolling over a line of waiting cars?' Oh bum! So they built a ten-foot high concrete blast wall which curved along the edge of the pad and they directed the cars to queue on the other side of it. The landward end of this wall abutted to the front of the first kiosk, leaving the left side unusable because it was on the wrong side of the wall. The lane at the far side of the third kiosk was equally redundant because it led straight into a brick wall. This left four lanes available to three kiosks but because the blast wall had encroached upon the queuing area so much, one of the lanes presented such a sharp turn that it could only be used by small vehicles. The buffer zone between the passport control and the customs search area was the length of about four cars and was two lanes wide. The hovercraft could carry sixty cars. Once the first eight were waiting at Customs, we were held up. If the marshal directed a car and caravan to the left hand lane, it blocked three lanes until it was cleared.

I am sure all ports have teething troubles. I bet the ancient Greeks had similar problems at Piraeus. We had no complaints, however, about the appointments of the general office. All the windows were double glazed with the nine-inch gap for effective sound insulation – an important factor when you have four of the world's largest propellers spinning a hundred yards away and we had been provided with our very own kitchen, complete with cooker, bain marie and hot water urn. It was also nice to inhabit a space that nobody had yet degraded. It was not chipped cream-painted wood and soiled linoleum; we had hardwood doors and carpets.

From the operational point of view I discovered the luxury of being allocated a desk for me and nobody else. Surely everybody in the Civil Service, even the lowliest clerical assistant, had a desk? But not us IOs. It would have been impossible to provide space for one hundred and twenty desks at Dover East, but here, at Dover Hoverport, we were given individual desks arranged around the office and they all had views either to seaward or landward. I was like a child with a new toy. I could put my belongings in the drawers and when I came back they would still be there. I could leave a file open on the desk and it would remain untouched. We even had our own stationery cupboard and, shock horror, it was not run by an admin grade but was the responsibility of one of the IOs. This meant that he could order fountain pen ink for me.

The customers who were attracted to the hovercraft tended to be the monied section of society. The hovercraft fitted their image of needing to be somewhere more quickly than anybody else and the premium fares filtered out *hoi-polloi* so that they felt comfortable amongst their own. Even the marques of cars arriving were representative. Nearly every flight would have a Rolls, an Aston Martin or a Bentley on it. The Ford Escort and Austin Allegro were rarely present. Within the first month of operation the French air traffic controllers went on strike and airline passengers across Europe converged upon Dover. They provided a useful mass to test out the infrastructure.

A small port is human. It is at the scale of man. I found myself chatting not only to SB and Customs but also to the cleaners, the ground hostesses, the shop assistants, the check-in personnel and the operations office which handled the movements of hovercraft. It was a different world and a different job. I liked it and when my three months were up, I tried to dig in my heels. Even the hoverport CIOs wanted me to stay there but to no avail; Dover East could not survive without such an experienced officer.

Yer what?

The buzzer had sounded and I was late down to the foot control. After clearing the previous ship I had nipped back up to the general office to get my suspect index up to date. As I crossed the redundant coach lanes, CIO John Jacques barked at me from the doorway of the foot passenger hall. Jacques was as tall as I was. He had a florid face which was not improved by the intimidating scowl twisted onto it. He stood there, feet planted well apart in a Henry VIII stance and fumed at me like a colonel taking a parade of incompetent rookies.

'Come on Lloyd, hurry up. We've got queues waiting. Where have you been?'

'In the general office doing my book.'

'Well you should be down here landing passengers.'

'Oh,' I said, raising my eyebrows at the innocent discovery of my purpose on this planet.

'Er, Mr. Lloyd,' he snapped. I stopped. 'I don't want any of your cheek. When a CIO tells you to go to the control your job is to obey, pronto. Now get to work.'

I never have anything to say when somebody shouts at me. I just fume and quake inside. To help me retain some semblance of sang-froid I dilated my nostrils in a pulsing rhythm at him whilst he bollocked me. I don't think he noticed.

The hall was full of a Colombian tour group. They had flown to Madrid and picked up a coach there to 'do' Europe. We were accustomed to landing groups of Brazilian professionals: architects, doctors and lawyers but these Colombian tour groups were a new thing and a bit of a mystery to us. The passengers did not even live in the capital Bogota, they all came from a town upcountry called Medellin. We had never heard of it. We did not know it was the crime and drugs capital of Colombia

My first passenger was a middle aged lady with a teenaged daughter. She was short and had a beehive hairstyle that had been in fashion in the 1960s. The occupation on her landing card was *'housewife'* which was exactly what she looked like. How could a Colombian housewife afford a trip to Europe? The wonders of cheap air travel never ceased to amaze me. After a few questions and a check of her funds and return ticket I stamped her passport. She must have been nervous because she kissed my hand in gratitude. Funny people.

Once the hall was clear, Jacques came to mete out my real punishment. He stood in front of my desk and in a 'hail fellow well met' tone of voice he bored me rigid for thirty minutes with his reminiscences of army life in North Africa. I could hardly imagine this pompous, self important gas bag serving as a private in the army. With all the contacts that he claimed to enjoy he must have joined at field marshal level at the very least. I grinned sycophantically and gave monosyllabic responses which were as pointless as they were ignored since all that was demanded of me was to supply an audience.

We did have a real soldier on our roll. Mac was in the Territorial Army and was an expert on the deployment of PIATs which, for the uninitiated, are Personnel Infantry Anti Tank weapons. Recently he had been absent from the port because he had been called up for NATO manoeuvres in Europe. He was a likeable, chatty and enthusiastic chap in his fifties. His one disadvantage was that he carried with him a cloud of halitosis that could fell an ox. It was a wonder NATO did not employ him just to breathe on the Russians. When warming up to a subject he would trap you in a corridor and exhale and expectorate his enthusiasm over you till you wilted or fainted. But I did not hear anybody say a bad word about him. Mac was a law unto himself but still within the law. When he was served with a parking ticket he elected to go to crown court. Knowing that his house backed onto that particular seat of justice he was able to sit in the shade of his summer garden until he heard his name called and then slip through the gate to arrive fresh and cool in a stuffy overheated courtroom. His defence was quite simple. He had consulted the published local orders and had noted that the prohibition on parking was authorised to extend thirty metres from the junction. He had measured the length of the double yellow lines and photographed them. They were forty metres long, so his car had been parked on the ten metres which were not authorised. The case was dismissed.

But one did sometimes have cause to question his reason. I remember interviewing a passenger whilst at the far end of the hall Mac had held up an Italian. The discussion became more and more heated, with rising voices and thumping of desks until a red-faced Mac leaned over the desk, blasted the poor meridional with a bolt of halitosis and roared, 'We were shooting better Italians than you in the war.' Everybody in the hall heard every word and he did not care.

Was this why he was called up to Estabs one day? I don't know, but a visit to Estabs or the Establishment Division of the Home Office was equivalent to being summoned to the headmaster's office. A passenger had probably made a complaint against him and, let's face it, it could probably have been justified. Indeed it was astonishing that he received so few complaints. The Immigration Service decided that this time they would hound poor Mac. They always like to have a dog to whip. Yes he was a liability but he was doing the job with a fervour and dedication that was barely evident in many of his colleagues.

He went in to the interview to be faced by an assistant chief inspector and an inspector in charge of investigating complaints. They laid out the case before him and asked him if he had any observations to make.

Mac leaned towards them. Doubtless his accusers retreated by an equivalent distance.

'Yes,' he said clearly. 'I'm the only person sitting around this table who has not got a police record.'

And he was right.

One day, Mac went home, had a heart attack and died. It was standing room only at his funeral.

John Jacques was still spouting his drivel. I looked at my watch, put the cap on my pen, flipped the lid over my ink pad and stood up. He took the hint and wandered off. Pompous old fart.

Up in the rest room, IOs were putting the world to rights.

'Never mind the IRA, it's these animal rights loonies that will be the new terrorists.'

'Don't be daft, they are not blowing up pubs.'

'Not yet. They will do. Cruelty to animals is more repugnant to the British than cruelty to humans. If they had put dogs, cats and horses into the front line in the First World War instead of soldiers the fighting would have been over in a few weeks. The country would never have stood for it. If we are killing humans, who cares? But animals? Whoah, you've got problems there.'

'No, they're just trendy liberals with pretty coloured ribbons in their hair.'

'You wait. You'll see. They'll get organised and then they will be worse than the IRA.'

'Talking of fighting, have you seen this new instruction about pointing out mercenary soldiers to SB?'

'How do you recognise a mercenary? Do they wear those belts full of bullets draped across their shoulders? And where are they going anyway?'

'Rhodesia. Young men in small groups being accompanied abroad by sun-tanned army looking types must be asked of their eventual destination and if they say Rhodesia, or if we suspect it is, then we must tell SB.'

'If they are there.'

'And what will they do? We have no power to stop Brits from leaving unless the Home Secretary signs a specific order against them.'

'Leave it all to SB.'

'Oh then we are in safe hands then.'

'I shan't be bothered by all this trivia.' Willie flicked his cigarette ash into the ashtray. It missed. 'I'm putting in for Adelaide House. That's where the real work is done. After entry – that's the future.'

'Yeah and the overtime. They claim about twenty hours a week.'

'How can they do that?' I asked.

'Well when they raid a restaurant and pull illegals out of the kitchen then they have to deal with them whatever time it is. You can't hand the case over to the morning shift. By the time they have interviewed them and taken them back and searched their rooms and banged them up in the local nick they have overrun their duty by two or three hours.'

'Lucky buggers.'

I looked at Willie sitting sideways on his chair so that he could watch the telly whilst keeping an eye on the ships from the window. He would probably flourish at Adelaide House. He already had a London accent and a leather jacket; what more do you need? He was also having an affair with a female IO at Dover but I did not learn that bit until he had transferred.

Adelaide House was our central London office. It dealt with the occasional ship arriving in the Port of London but most of its work was called 'after entry'. Under the Immigration Act, which was the law giving us the powers to do our job, rules were published in the form of Statutory Instruments. Anybody could buy these from the Stationery Office. They were more specific than the law and dealt with each category of passenger individually. We had two sets of rules that we used at the port: HC79 which dealt with the control of arriving Commonwealth nationals, and HC81 which did the same for EEC and other non-Commonwealth nationals. Every time that we refused entry to a passenger, we had to be able to quote the paragraph of the rules under which we had refused them. There were two other statutory instruments that IOs at the port were issued with but never looked at: HC80 and HC82 and these laid down the rules for dealing with passengers after they had been admitted. Thus the 'after entry' idea.

On the ground this translated as finding people who had overstayed their permission to enter or who had entered illegally or who had taken forbidden employment. Once apprehended, we then tried to remove them. It meant issuing detention orders to the Metropolitan Police, not to the Noddy police that we had at the docks; it meant visiting prisons to interview detainees; it involved attendance in court. The Adelaide House IOs went out knocking on people's doors and detaining them. I found the thought of all this quite frightening, probably because I knew nothing about our powers in that area. You wouldn't catch me knocking on doors in London. Willie would be in is element.

'Why is Len always in the casework office now?'
'Oh, haven't you heard? Dennis did a spot check on his SI. He hadn't put a name in it for six months.'
'That is just asking for trouble,' I said. 'Some people have a death wish.'
'I suppose your book is up to date then, Mr. Arselicker?'
I just pulled a face and looked away. My book is always up to date. We are issued with a Suspect Index full of names. Three or four times a week circulars are issued to enable us to add to or subtract from the book. The SI is an essential tool for our job. What is the point of not keeping it up to date? Once, I actually picked up somebody whose name I had written in the book just ten minutes earlier. Yes, copying a list of names, dates of birth and codes is a drudge but we do get paid for it. Early on I bought myself a mechanical drawing pen and filled it with Indian ink. This enabled me to write neatly and accurately in the small spaces provided and the density of the ink made the text legible whatever poor lighting we were working under. And the lighting was generally poor throughout. I could also use it to make quirky sketches on the backs of landing cards whilst I was waiting for ships.

If I were honest with myself I probably admired the IOs who had the guts or stupidity to stick up two fingers at the regulations. How did they keep up to date with the amendments to our General Instructions? The answer was: they did not but they managed to bluff the CIOs into believing that they knew it all and as they probably now knew more than the CIOs, then they got away with it. I did not have that courage. I fastidiously updated my instructions. The Immigration Officers' Circulars which were issued on an occasional basis as needed, I indexed by subject and stored them in date order. My copy of the Immigration Act 1971 had divers flaps and tickets pasted to its pages but hinged so that I could read the original paragraph underneath the amendment. When we came to be issued with new Immigration Rules to replace our beloved HC 79 and 81, I sat down and read the old and the new side by side, comparing the differences and identifying the innovations. I suppose it never occurred to the IS that they could run training courses to explain the changes. In industry we would have been given in-service training, probably at some swish hotel. What we got was the booklet of rules stuffed into our pigeon hole sometimes as much as a week before we were due to introduce them.

It sounds presumptuous on my part, but I worried about this lack of guidance. But we steamed on through the year. The drudge of the summer holiday traffic was lightened by the Victorian politeness of the STIOs. I heard one remark to another as they watched the Wimbledon women's singles on the television, 'That young lady has a nicely turned ankle.' The fact that you could see her legs up to her bum was irrelevant, it was the ankle that was the erogenous zone for them. And of course we had the Heathrow IOs who came in three-week streams through the summer to provide us with relief. It was often comic relief, albeit of a rather spiteful humour.

As I knew from my short spell at Heathrow Terminal Three, not much happened there between midnight and half past five in the morning but the IOs were still scheduled for night duties. When they arrived for relief at Dover East, their first duty would usually be a night duty so they would travel down during the day, expecting to be able to sleep for five hours during the night. Oh the rude awakening!

'Where's the best place for laying out my sleeping bag?' was a not uncommon question. It was a treat to watch their eyebrows knit in consternation as they copied down their hourly positions from the duty chart. 'So, this two hour spell on walkers at one o'clock, is that the best time for shuteye?'

'Not if you want to live. The Boulogne comes in at a quarter to one, the Zeebrugge at one twenty and an Ostender at two fifteen. That'll keep you going until three. Then you are on cars.'

'So there is a break then?'

'Not likely. At three o'clock you will still be doing the cars from the Ostender. And Ostend traffic is messy.'

'So when is my meal break?'

'Midnight till one. The canteen closes at eleven.'

Oh we did enjoy ourselves. But we did have to thank the Heathrow IOs for educating us in the current fashions. It was astonishing how parochial we were down in Kent. We were still wearing flared trousers and kipper ties when the Heathrow IOs were already in leather jackets.

In August an El Al crew bus was attacked in Mayfair by Palestinians throwing hand grenades and spraying sub machine guns. An air hostess in the coach was killed as was one of the attackers. As the UK government had steadfastly refused to allow the Israeli security guards to carry firearms in the UK I wondered who had shot the terrorist? At Dover we suddenly had pretend SB officers with bulges in their sports jackets hanging around the embarks controls. They made me nervous. I don't like firearms, especially in the hands of amateurs.

If looking out for Arabs was not sufficient, a few weeks later we had the Bulgarian broadcaster George Markov killed on the steps of Broadcasting House by an assassin wielding a poison capsule-firing umbrella and suddenly all Bulgarians were assassins. In the midst of this the Vietnamese refugees started to fly into London and the more subtle Iranians escaped the troubles in their country by enrolling in English courses in language schools that had blossomed along the south coast from Ramsgate to Brighton.

Sitting in a car kiosk, swathed in the autumn fog which was rolling off the Channel, Roger and I were doubly isolated from all these troubles. We could still hear the staccato chattering of a pneumatic drill out to seawards. Roger was senior to me as an IO but contemporary in age. We seemed to hit it off. Perhaps we both could see the ridiculous side of the job which nevertheless did not stop us from applying ourselves to the practical manner of performing it. Indeed, when you reflect upon it, it made the whole operation even more ridiculous. Roger also had an agile mind which he was not scared of exercising.

As we sat there, our visibility restricted to a few yards of dripping tarmac and a soggy seagull, I was trying to convince him that the noise that we could hear was the Harbour Board who, under cover of the fog, were piercing a perforated line through the concrete apron so that they could break off the entire port and float it across to Calais. To his credit, Roger was not phased by this suggestion and we discussed the practicalities of maintaining the telephone lines and the effects on the legal side of the control of passports.

From out of the gloom loomed the shadowy shape of a penguin – a harbour board marshal. They were called penguins because they wore a dark uniform with a white cap. He pulled the rope aside and a line of cars nudged through the mist towards our kiosk. We turned away to our windows and slid the perspex panes aside.

'How long are you staying here, Titanic?' Roger said to a Frenchman.

I was momentarily distracted but not so the visitor who answered his enquiry without demur.

'How long are you staying in the United Kingdom?' I asked my Frenchman and then pointing to the boot of his car, 'Could you open your iceberg please?'

The man got out of his car and opened the boot. There was nobody hiding in it. Without discussing it further, Roger and I landed the entire complement of passengers by throwing absurd word associations to each other across the kiosk. It became more and more surreal.

'Pineapple...'

'... hand grenade.'

'Chelsea...

'...fruit bun.'

'Washing machine...'

'...clothes peg.'

When the forty odd cars had disappeared into the whiteness of the customs control behind us, we rocked about the kiosk in hysteria. It was painfully obvious that it did not matter what we said to these people, they knew what we were going to ask. I asked a Belgian to open his Salvation Army soup kitchen whilst pointing to the back of his car and he opened the boot for me. I told an Italian to switch off his trombone and he cut the motor, as I desired.

We split up at the end of the hour and went off to our next positions. The fog had now stopped all ships from entering or leaving the berths so we were twiddling our thumbs. The fog cleared ten minutes before the end of our duty and I phoned Roger from the freight control to tell him that I had just succeeded with 100% gobbledegook. I had said to a Frenchman, 'Hooligan spray tinplate earwig' and he had replied, 'five days.'

Roger's voice sounded a little subdued. The first foot passengers to materialise from the fog and wander through the door to his desk had been two French officers of the Police de l'Air et des Frontières and he had wondered if Dover port really had been floated across the Channel.

Roger and I had got to know each other through the Dover East Christmas revue. This was a satirical show which was cobbled together by various members of the IS staff who fancied airing their thespian talents. It was a ramble through songs and sketches which poked fun at everybody and everything to do with the job. My involvement had started in my first year. Trevor, the IO who had tried to get me engaged in the sporting activities of the port had told me to have a go at the revue. I had no idea what the format was so I wrote a couple of sketches and parodied songs. Trevor had suggested that I take the mickey out of an observation by some bigwig whom I had never heard of who had compared the immigration control to the restrictions on entry to a posh restaurant. I sat down one day and conjured up a scene in which a couple order from a menu composed entirely of the wordings of the conditional landing stamps that we endorsed in passports. It was quite esoteric and, it transpired, very funny. The character of the maitre d' was played by our Turkish Cypriot IO, Alper Mehmet, in the costume of a Dover Harbour Board marshal. He was pretending to be an Italian but whenever he said the words, 'a coach-a party' it always sounded like, 'a cold chapatee'. After the show, in the new year without fail at least one member of the cast was transferred to another port. Alper finished his career as Her Britannic Majesty's Ambassador to Iceland.

Roger and I eventually joined resources and wrote an entire show together, a grown up pantomime loosely based on Snow White. Needless to say, none of the seven dwarfs was under six feet tall. We hired a local village hall and sold tickets at fifty pence each. We never had any left over, possibly because we also got somebody in to run a bar. The IS training unit had a burgeoning film department and they managed each year to claim a training day to come and professionally film the show which they did using two cameras, a mixing table and a recording system which at that time was known as 'pneumatic video'. From this they were able to transfer the image to VHS with minimal loss of quality. Viewing those tapes now it is quite an eye-opener to recognise the talent that lurked beneath some of the more quiet and reserved IOs.

The immigration officers at Heathrow also staged a Christmas revue which on one occasion hit the headlines in the newspapers when the Hounslow Community Relations Council objected to the title, *Whittington Singh.* They demanded the right to be able to attend a dress rehearsal and vet the script because the title was 'offensive'. I thought it was a lot of fuss over nothing especially considering that the show was a private affair, not open to the public. However the organisers decided to postpone the show until after Christmas when it was held without conflict in the hall at the Intelligence Unit. The Heathrow show had been a spoof pantomime. In the same year, for our revue I wrote a spoof Agatha Christie whodunnit which I wittily entitled, *Ten Little Sniggers.* The inspector at Dover East told me that I would have to change the title. I asked why.

'Well, it's really Ten Little... er... you know, isn't it?'

'Ten little what?'

'Well, "sniggers" is only um... You've just put an 'S' on the front.'

'Of what?'

'You know exactly what I mean.'

'How can I? Your argument is incomprehensible. Are you saying that the show is really called *Ten Little Niggers?*'

He blanched and clutched the desk. I thought he was going to have a heart attack.

'Well the assistant chief inspector has said that you must change it.'

'Is this the ACI who lives in a house called "Jagoes"?'

'Yes. So what?'

'Well that's only "dagoes" with the first letter changed isn't it?'

The argument rumbled on. It went to an assistant under secretary of state at the Home Office who decreed that the title should be changed. It wasn't and it was a bloody good show.

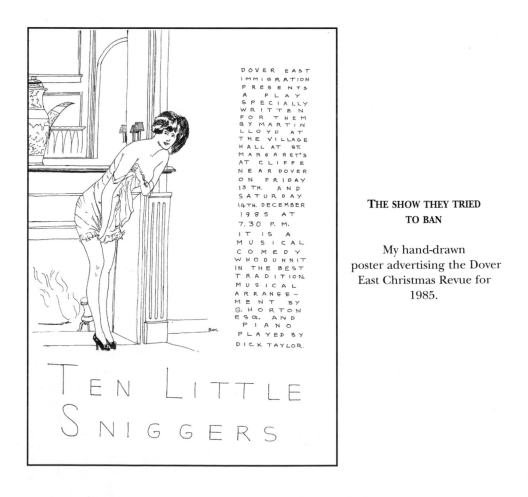

**THE SHOW THEY TRIED
TO BAN**

My hand-drawn
poster advertising the Dover
East Christmas Revue for
1985.

It is the last week in March. The Channel is grey and foam topped; the wind is rattling around the window frames and blustering enough to make it difficult for the ferries to dock. The ferries have grown in size since the time of the *Free Enterprise I* and the *Compiègne*. Now they look like floating blocks of flats and stand much higher above the breakwaters. They have little protection from the strong westerlies which persist in blowing them off the berth.

I had exploited the delay in arrivals to go down to the counter of the Westminster Bank in the booking hall and to cash a cheque as I was short of money. This service that the bank provided for port workers they did not publicise. It was very useful at a weekend. The ATM had not yet arrived at Dover East.

I wandered back along the top corridor whose linoleum floor was the colour of urine. In the rest room, the IOs were lounging about smoking, arguing, playing pool and watching television.

'Did you know that the petrol station at the dock exit has now got four star at 120p per gallon?' I said.

'I can remember when the *Evening Standard* ran one of those panic headlines forecasting that petrol would go up to fifty pence per gallon. We all laughed.'

'Talking of laugh, who are the happy chappies hanging around behind our controls?'

'Aaah,' said another, tapping the side of his nose. 'The need to know, old boy, need to know.'

'Oh are they nudge, nudge, wink, wink?'

'Yeah. Mac challenged one to show his i.d.'

'Good old Mac. He would.'

'Well, he said that anybody could put on a sports jacket and pretend to be from Box. We wouldn't know.'

'So did he show his i.d?'

'Yes. He said it looked like a crappier version of our warrant but done in red instead of blue. It was so naff he knew it had to be genuine.'

Our warrants were a piece of folded blue card bearing a gold crest. Inside, above a cyclostyled signature of the Home Secretary, a bald statement informed the reader that the holder of the card was an immigration officer. No further details. No photograph. The only use that I had managed to put it to was to get free passage across the toll bridge at Sandwich.

'So what are they doing here?'

'Got an operation on. Looking out for somebody.'

'We do that every day.'

'This one must be special.'

'Well I hope they don't start shooting. I am frightened of loud bangs.'

'How long are they here for?'

'All this week. They're staying at the Holiday Inn.'

'Poor dears.'

I sat in my smelly office on the freight control. The MI5 operative was lounging in the chair to one side, poring over the crossword. I had tried to engage him in conversation on several occasions but had failed. He was not going to chat to me; merely to sit in my office. He and his colleagues had been at the port now for four days but, interestingly, not four nights. They were all back in their hotel by eight o'clock. Presumably they knew that the suspect they were waiting for would not travel at night.

I tried again. 'So, do you often get out of the office?'

He looked up with irritation puckering his brow. He sighed and shook his head and returned to his newspaper. It was going to be a long duty. Did they really believe that their target would come in to Dover on a lorry? The whole set-up seemed half-baked to me. It had not occurred to me that, in the last week of March, you need to spend what is left of your budget otherwise it will get cut for next financial year. Half a dozen operatives in the Holiday Inn for a week should go some way towards solving that problem.

Thirty minutes before the end of my duty I had a brainwave. I called out, 'Thank you Mr. Edwards,' just as the last Czech lorry driver returned to his truck. *Crash!* The self locking door slammed behind him. The MI5 chap looked up vaguely from his paper.

'What did you say?'

'When?'

'To that last man.' He peered above the high window sill to see the jeaned posterior wriggling itself into a pale green Skoda truck.

'Oh I can't remember. I was just being polite. I think I said, "Thank you Mr. Edwards."'

'Oh for fuck's sake.' He leaped from his chair. 'That was him.' He grabbed the door handle. 'That was who I told you I was looking for.' He tugged frantically at the door.

'Just a minute,' I said, 'It's locked. We do that for security.'

'Get it open. Get it open.' He screamed.

I fumbled the key into the lock and snicked it open just as the lorry started up and roared off in a cloud of blue smoke towards Customs. He pushed past me and ran to the outside door and began pulling at the handle.

'Turn the yale latch,' I shouted to him.

He got the door open and discovered that there were five steep concrete steps immediately outside. Down these he tumbled, his tie flapping up around his ears and then he sprinted after the Czech lorry. I ambled to the back of my office and opened the door there so that I could watch his antics. Silly really, had he asked me he could have gone out of that door and intercepted the driver before he had driven away. He was now running alongside the truck and smacking the door with the flat of his hand. I returned to my seat and picked up his discarded newspaper. I tried to finish his crossword for him but he did not come back.

THE VIEW FROM MY DESK
A foreign TIR lorry baking in the sun at the freight control. Dover East.

Later that year I went straight from work to lunch at a friend's house. I sat in the chair. My head was thumping thick with carbon monoxide fumes and I felt nauseous. It was the usual feeling you got after a few hours working in the car booths.

'So,' my friend said as he sharpened his carving knife, 'tell me about Box 500 and how immigration officers have to point out suspects to MI5.' My jaw dropped to my knee. 'And what is all this in your instructions about Communist front organisations?'

I sat there with my mouth open. Box 500 was secret. We were not allowed to talk about it or even admit that it existed. He grinned at my obvious discomfiture and handed me that day's copy of *The Guardian*. They had obviously managed to get their hands on a copy of our instructions and had taken great glee in airing a selection of the secrets which were contained therein.

'Oh,' I said, when I had recovered some of my composure, 'you don't want to believe everything you read in the newspapers.'

His sardonic smile annoyed me. I, for once, was being more pompous than he.

I wondered how the *Guardian* had obtained their information. I recalled that on our training course we had been told that it was not worth trying to sell a copy of the suspect index or our General Instructions to the Russians because they probably already had a copy and if they didn't, they would just turn the vendor over to the police, assuming that he was an *agent provocateur.*

Anyway, we had enough on our plate to worry about. The firemen at Manchester Airport went on strike and all traffic was diverted elsewhere for two weeks. Astonishingly, some of the tour companies bussed their customers through Dover to catch cheap flights on the Continent. In Iran, the Shah had been toppled and the ayatollahs were in. Willie Whitelaw, our new Home Secretary, made it clear by his instructions to IOs that Margaret Thatcher was no great supporter of Muslim rule in Iran. Even the earthquake in Naples impacted upon Dover East, although not in a seismic manner. Throughout Great Britain owners of Land Rovers and caravans carefully watched over their property as gangs of thieves targeted them. On the embarks control at Dover, lorries transporting Land Rovers or caravans were pulled over for SB to check.

Another winter at Dover East and I should have been forging my future and planning my career. I wasn't. I was just sitting there stamping passports. I had been brought up to believe that if you worked hard for your employer then you would be suitably rewarded. I had not been told to fight my corner and make myself awkward; to do down my colleagues and exploit their weaknesses.

What did I want out of the job? I had not given it a thought, really. I would quite like to go abroad for a spell at HMG's expense – that would be fun, perhaps. I also had a possibly conceited idea that I would be an effective trainer. I had noticed that when a probationer IO was unsure about procedure he would wait and ask me the question rather than approach the hard nuts in the office with his enquiry. He did not want to be belittled by colleagues who were trying to hide their own ignorance with bluster and ridicule. He needed reassurance and the correct answer. I often used the conspiratorial, 'let's see if we can find an answer to this problem together' approach; encouraging them to think for themselves and discover the solution where it lay waiting for them. It seemed to work.

Although I was trained at Lunar House, some induction training was now undertaken at ports, probably in an effort to reduce costs. Locally, this meant that there was a band of trainers who worked at Dover West, inculcating the raw recruits with their wisdom. But I was a Dover East IO, so I had no opportunity to apply.

What other empires could I join? There was a seamen control team who specialised in visiting cargo ships. After my experience with Fergus I had no desire to clamber up and down ship's sides but I knew I was safe from that because there was no possibility that a teetotaller should be picked for the team. It would be recruiting a nun for a brothel.

Similarly the activities of the freight rummage team who were provided with snazzy boiler suits and purple enamel badges bearing the legend *'HM Immigration Service'* and then encouraged to clamber up, over, under and inside lorries to look for illegal immigrants did not attract me. Apart from the noise, dirt and smell there was a fairly good chance of being killed. I had already lost an acquaintance, Chris, who worked as a berth marshal for P&O. The unloading lorry had not bothered to drive around him. Many of the fatalities in the south east ports involved TIR lorries.

I missed out on the port security team. I was granted a half duty day with Paddy, an Irish IO, to check up on port security after a journalist had dressed himself in a pair of black trousers and a white shirt to impersonate the generic ship's steward and had walked into the port via the crew gate and then written a story about it. Having no pass he had negotiated the police control using the universally successful 'security nod'.

Paddy and I stood watching the DHB police waving cars through their gate at a hardly diminished speed on the basis that they 'knew the car'. I chatted to one of the officers who was on duty at the gate.

''Course the trouble here is that the security in this port is fucking non existent,' he divulged, allowing two cars to pass unchecked behind him as he spoke. The irony of the situation escaped him.

I wrote a summary of what we had both observed and made some recommendations and handed it to Paddy before I went off on leave. He gave it to the typist to make into a fine copy, signed his name at the bottom and forwarded it to the CIO. By the time I came back, Paddy was in the port security team. It did not really matter; I would never have had the panache, for example, of Rob, the Yorkshireman who didn't care a hoot for anything, and who was also co-opted to the team with Paddy. One day the CIO took them both on a walkabout to check the port defences. These were fairly rudimentary since on one side stretched twenty-five miles of sea and on the other, three-hundred-foot high cliffs. They studied the eight feet high chain link fence which surrounded the fuel depot.

'Right,' said the CIO, 'Rob, see if you can get over that.'

'Nah, that's too much effort,' he said. He dropped to the ground and crawled underneath and stood up on the other side. He held up the fence for them. 'Do you want to come through as well?'

No, I was not in the port security team. I did not disappear down to the Eastern Arm with the seamen control officers when a cargo ship was in dock. I was not allowed to train because I was in the wrong port and I was excluded from the team compiling the IO's duties because it was run by a mafia of trade union representatives.

So I sat there and stamped passports.

That is what an immigration officer is supposed to do, isn't it?

So you wouldn't catch me knocking on doors in London? Why, then, am I walking up the steps to the entrance of Adelaide House? Well, you can always change your mind, can't you? A friend offered me very cheap accommodation in Chelsea and the attraction of receiving the inner London subsistence rate for a month's relief was too much for my morals. Everybody can be bought.

We were discussing this topic in the rest room one day. What price to corrupt an IO? Would you accept money in exchange for endorsing your landing stamp in the passport of a non-qualifying passenger? Of course we would not. We were incorruptible. We were Her Majesty's immigration officers. As the discussion progressed it transpired that we would not accept money because we could not see anybody offering enough. When the hypothesis of one million pounds was proposed, most of us said yes, we would. With that sum you could stick up two fingers and disappear off to Spain for the rest of your life.

I then posed the question of working for the enemy. What would you do if the country were successfully invaded? I was thinking of the situation in occupied Europe during World War 2 where the workers who remained in their posts were often stigmatised as collaborators. If you were given the choice of remaining as an IO and implementing the new government's rules or taking off to the hills and joining the resistance, what would you do? Think of your family. By remaining in position you would continue to provide for them and you could square your conscience by pointing out that civil servants were supposed to be apolitical and their job was to serve the government of the day. If the enemy was now that government, it was not your fault.

Adelaide House was opened in 1924. It is an office block standing eight stories above King William Street at the City end of London Bridge. The previous Adelaide House had been the headquarters of the Pearl Assurance Company and when it was demolished in 1921 one of the arches of the old London Bridge was uncovered and removed to the London Museum.

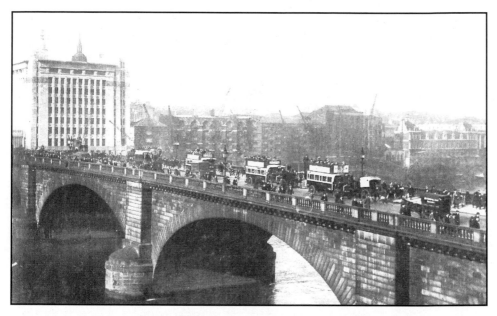

ADELAIDE HOUSE AND LONDON BRIDGE 1926
Adelaide House is the tall white building at the left of the photograph. Our offices were
at the right corner of the building, looking downriver towards Tower Bridge.

The Immigration Service rents an office on the third floor. There is a large general office in which all the IOs work, a couple of smaller offices for the inspector and CIOs and a public section which is in effect a broad corridor fitted out with skewed partitions to divide it up into interview booths.

Adelaide House is our London office. Heathrow is London Airport but if you disembark from a ship, plane or train in the the City of London your landing stamp will bear the word, *'London'*. Whilst I am here I shall be interviewing members of the public who have been invited to attend the office to settle their immigration status; I shall be investigating claims to stay longer by processing files sent down from Lunar House and I will be responding to requests from the Metropolitan and City police forces to examine persons whom they might have detained for transgressions various and whom they believe to be foreign. It was very unlikely that I would see any passengers. I would be doing 'after entry' work – about which I knew practically nothing.

I started my first duty on a Sunday afternoon. I spent the first hour waiting for my allocated officer to come in. He was going to show me the ropes. The CIO had given me two files to read which represented the two jobs that we had been assigned for that duty. I spent most of the time gazing out of the window, for the general office enjoyed a panoramic view down the Thames to HMS *Belfast* through Tower Bridge to the Pool of London beyond.

From one of the files I deduced that we were expected to visit an address in Dalston in response to a request from the entry clearance officer in Islamabad who had received an application from an elderly Pakistani woman to join her son as a dependant relative. We had to make sure that the accommodation was sufficient for her before he could issue the visa. I took an office volume of the London *A-Z* from the bookcase and searched for the address. I had no idea where Dalston was.

'Here you are Charlie, here's your oppo,' the CIO called to an elderly man who had just appeared in the doorway. He must have been near to retirement. He was small with silver hair which became visible when he removed his trilby. Nobody wore a trilby nowadays. He was dressed in a suit of a nondescript dark colour and his watery eyes peered at me through spectacle lenses as thick as beer glasses.

'How do you do?' He held out his hand. I shook it. 'We're on 'visits' today. Have you got the files?'

'Yes, I've just been reading them.'

'Good, good. We'll leave in about an hour.' Why the delay I thought? 'That'll give you time to familiarise yourself with the files.' Oh that's why. He started to fill his pipe. 'If you've got any problems, just come and ask. I'll be in there.' He pointed to a back office.

An hour later we were walking along Lower Thames Street past Billingsgate Market. Here the street was still paved with granite setts to better resist the wear from the fish porters' iron-wheeled barrows.

'The advantage of Billingsgate becomes apparent with time,' Charlie said. 'You see that pub over there?' I nodded. 'It opens at four in the morning. It has a special licence to serve the needs of the porters.'

'What time does it close?'

'I've never found out.'

As he pushed his hat firmly down on his head, Charlie explained that when he had joined the Immigration Branch, as it then was, an officer turning up for work without a hat would be sent home for being improperly dressed.

I followed him along the frontage of the magnificent Custom House and into their car park. This was where Adelaide House IOs were allowed to park their official cars.

'It's a blue Escort,' Charlie said, handing me the keys. 'You can drive.'

I had already driven up from Kent that morning. The journey in those days took two and a half hours. I did not really want to spend another couple of hours pottering around London on a Sunday afternoon.

'If you don't mind Charlie, I'd rather not. I drove up from Folkestone just this morning.'

'You'll have to,' he said, 'my eyes are too poor.'

Brilliant. I found the car. It was the Popular model of Ford Escort – the cheapest in the range with the black bumpers and rubbing strips. It was rancid with the stink of stale cigarettes.

'We get as many IOs as possible out on visits at the weekend,' Charlie explained as he pointed me up the road. 'You can drive around so much easier and you can park practically where you like on a Sunday.' He waved his arm again. 'Straight on past Liverpool Street Station then you're on your own.'

I looked at him. 'Don't you know where we are going?'

'You've read the files. You've got the address.'

'But I don't know where it is.'

'Neither do I.'

We were approaching a junction. 'Which way do I go here?'

'I've no idea old chap.'

I reached behind me and jiggered about in my bag till I felt the reassuring bulk of the office copy of the *A-Z*.

'It's somewhere in Dalston,' I said, handing it across to him and then quickly changing gear for the traffic lights. 'Get us to Dalston and we can look for it there.' He was still turning pages when we arrived at the next junction. I pulled into a bus stop and waited. The pages were still turning. 'Give the book to me,' I said. He handed it across. I turned to the index and looked up the address. 'Page sixty three,' I said and then jumped as a horn blasted behind me. How many buses do you think are running on a Sunday in the City? I had found one. 'Find the page. I've got to move there's a bus wanting to use the stop.'

'I shouldn't worry about buses old chap.'

My perspective on the situation was coloured, in more ways than one, by the expanse of throbbing red which filled my rear view mirror. And then of course I could not see around it to be able to pull out. I began to nudge out and nearly suffered a nose amputation by a large Austin. I reflected that had the two vehicles contacted, thanks to my language course I now knew the Urdu word to describe my car as 'having no nose'. That would have looked good on the insurance claim form. I joined the traffic stream. Charlie was still turning pages.

'Sixty three,' he said and looked up through the windscreen.

'So which way do I go?'

'Well it's... Probably it's...' He was still gazing through the screen as if the answer would be writ large before him. I realised then that he could not even read the map.

'Are you on page sixty three?'

'Yes.'

'Right, keep it open at that page.' I could see a space ahead where I could put two wheels up on the pavement. 'Where are we now?' I said as I pulled on the handbrake. 'According to the map we need to be in the Kingsland Road.'

'Haven't the foggiest, old chap, not the foggiest. Probably somewhere near Hackney.'

The bus whooshed past my right ear and rocked the car in its wash. I peered at the tangle of streets and roads on the map. This was daft. How was I supposed to know where I was? I lived in Kent. 'Hold on a minute. Didn't we go over the canal a little way back.'

'Did we old chap? Can't say that canals are really my line.'

This bloke was unreal.

'Yes, I'm sure we did. That means that we must be about here. Put your finger there, and keep it there. I'm turning right at the next junction.'

'As you wish.'

I cut across the taxis and locals who all knew where they were going, in order to reach the filter lane.

'Doesn't that sign say *Highbury*?' Charlie was proudly pointing at the only road sign he had ever managed to read. He was pointing with his map finger. I turned right and pulled in to the entrance to a cul de sac. 'By Jove, that was nifty. Are we there?'

'No, I just need to look at the map again.' He surrendered it to me with an indecent haste. After four more map stops I pulled up in the correct street.

'Better leave this to me,' Charlie suggested.

'I'll come with you.' I objected to the idea that I should be merely a chauffeur.

The door of the terraced house was opened by a Pakistani boy of about nine. 'Yeah, wodjer want?' he said and then turned and threw some Punjabi over his shoulder in reply to a shouted enquiry from within.

We were shown in to the front room which contained a sofa, two armchairs and a gas fire. I sat and drank the tea we were offered whilst Charlie interviewed the owner of the house who was the son of the old lady in Pakistan who had applied to live here. We were taken on a tour of the accommodation with Charlie taking notes as we went along. It seemed that once the grandmother had been admitted she would be sharing a room with her three grandchildren. As we moved about the house I could not suppress the feeling that there were more people in the building than we were seeing. I supposed that any of the women would be hidden but it was almost as if when we went into one room, characters would scurry down the corridor, vacating the next room on our round to occupy the previous room visited. It was all a bit like a Whitehall farce, for those of you who remember them.

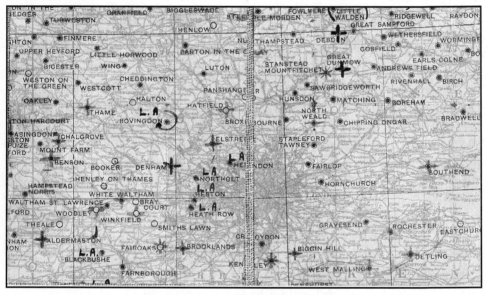

AIR STATIONS IN THE LONDON DISTRICT
A post World War 1 map which had been annotated to show which air stations (the early name for airports) were in the London District of the Immigration Branch.

Our second job was to visit a flat in Hackney but nobody answered the door so Charlie marked the file for a return visit and then he allowed me to navigate our way to the office on the basis that I had got us here so I would now know the way back. Astonishingly, I did. I slept well that night, despite the many questions that were spinning in my mind.

Working in an office overlooking the Thames was a distraction which I happily surrendered to. At Dover East, all we could see from the general office window was a white wall of chalk. Whilst ferreting around in cupboards for various telephone directories at Adelaide House I found a bound volume of *Instructions to the Immigration Officer* dated 1920. It was absolutely fascinating reading. One notice expounded upon a forged

British passport which had been discovered in the hands of a doubtful refugee. Europe was awash with millions of refugees after the Great War. The British passport which had been forged was the new design which had been introduced in 1915 and the notice conveyed a sense of official outrage that anybody would dare to try to forge this new passport rather than simply misuse the old double sheet design which had been in service for the previous seventy years and examples of which were still in circulation.

On another shelf I unearthed an old map which at some time must have been pinned up on the wall of the office and marked out to show the boundaries of the London district of the Immigration Branch. It was a very early Air Ministry map and the names of many of the 'air stations', as airports were originally called, were evocative of another era, a time utterly unknown to me: Heston, Hendon, Cricklewood, Hornchurch. Was I the only officer to feel this empathy with history? It seemed so.

The IOs at Adelaide House were living in the present and had no time for the past. Heathrow IOs considered themselves to be the cream of UK immigration control, working at the most important port in the world. Adelaide House IOs looked upon them as wet namby pambies who didn't know a wrong'un when they saw one. As I watched them strut about in their leather jackets and dark glasses, using Metspeak like, 'spinning a drum' instead of saying that they were searching a premises I could not suppress the observation that many of these IOs had come from Heathrow in the first place. At what point did their opinions and allegiance and indeed, language, suddenly change? Was it, as they crossed the Temple Bar into the City?

I spent a couple of duties in the office, clearing files and interviewing people. Working on one of the files I felt that I needed to check the validity of a birth certificate so I phoned Somerset House.

A Commonwealth citizen who was born in the UK has the right to live here. If such a Commonwealth passport holder walked down the British queue at passport control, in most ports, once the IO had read the place of birth on page two of his passport, he would allow him in just as easily as if he had presented a full British passport. This was exploited by some Nigerians who obtained Nigerian passports by presenting certificates in the Lagos passport office to prove they were born in the village of Ondo. Once the passport had been issued, they would carefully add an initial and terminal letter on page two so that the place of birth then read as *'London'*.

With the Immigration Act 1971 was created the concept of being 'patrial'. This strange word was dragged from an obscure corner of the

English language, dusted down and buffed up by the law writers and re-introduced into contemporary conversation. We now have 'patrial,' 'patriality,' 'non-patriality' and 'certificates of patriality'. If you were a Commonwealth citizen, you had to prove your patriality and to succeed at this, many applicants would submit their birth certificate. Sometimes a naughty person would submit the birth certificate of somebody whom he knew to be born in London, claiming to be him, in order to establish a false right to live here.

So I was phoning up the Registrar of Births to check the validity of the birth certificate which had been presented in support of this subject's claim to the right to live here. It showed a male baby of Nigerian name who had been born in Wandsworth. I had decided to check because the certificate was not the original but was a certified copy, which anybody can obtain from the registrar upon payment of a fee. The registrar explained how the process of applying for a copy certificate worked.

'First you look up the entry in the lists that we have here. They are ledgers and are arranged by date of birth and surname. You copy down the serial number of the entry and come back to the desk and then we call up the original certificate from which we make a copy.'

'So,' I deduced, 'If anything on this certificate that I have before me is different from the original that you have there, then it has been tampered with.'

'That is a fair deduction. Just hold on whilst I look up the initial entry.' Whilst he did that I watched a tug tow two lighters down towards Tower Bridge. Presently he returned. 'Yes, we've got sixteen ticks against that entry.'

'What does that mean?'

'It means that there have been sixteen requests for copy certificates of that entry. It must be popular.'

'Is that one person requesting sixteen copies?'

'No, it is sixteen separate requests over the last eighteen months. That was when we first started making ticks in the margin to record each request.'

I was quite thoughtful as I replaced the receiver. That revelation suggested that there could be sixteen impostors of the original entry and all claiming the right to live here. I tried to narrow down the identity of my subject by checking his national insurance number. We were not supposed to be able to access the DHSS computer in Bootle, it was a politically sensitive area for one government department to have access to the records of another. I was introduced to an expression: 'civil rights'.

We would be contravening those, whatever they were. It sounded daft to me and to most other IOs. Weren't we all on the same side? The inter-departmental protocol stated that we had to obtain the authority of an inspector in order to make a request for a DHSS check but the IOs at Adelaide House had found a telephone number which got results, no questions asked, so I used that. The DHSS confirmed the NI number as belonging to my chap so I asked if he knew how many other people of the same name and date of birth they had on their records? He could not say.

I next rang the subject's local Social Security office and spoke to an HEO there. They also were not allowed to give us specific information but I did manage to wheedle out of him that they had had administrative problems with my chap because the identity had been used by somebody else and they were having to pay out benefits to both applicants until they could identify which was the genuine and which the impostor. I felt it would be unnecessarily cruel on my part to suggest that they both could be impostors. I was becoming more and more enmired in this investigation and could see no way out so I put it aside to continue with on the morrow.

I slipped out to eat at a place on the corner of King William Street which served lunches to office workers. We sat four to a table and ate whatever was on the menu of small choices. I liked it because it was so unpretentious. You want food? We've got food. Eat it. The waitress who often served me was a foreign lady in her sixties whom I had heard speaking French with another customer. I often exchanged the odd French pleasantry with her, it lightened my day and seemed to please her. A proper Adelaide House IO would have asked to see her work permit.

After lunch I was due to interview a couple suspected of contracting a marriage of convenience. They had been invited to attend the office at 14.30. A 'marriage of convenience' situation arose when a person who was in breach of the immigration rules or who had exhausted all other avenues which would prolong his or her stay in the UK, gets married to a person settled here. The suspicion in the nasty mind of the Home Office is that they have done so purely to avoid having to leave. The IO has to try to prove that the marriage is a sham.

The case that I am to deal with is complicated because of the rules currently in force. A woman who is in the UK in a temporary capacity can marry a man who is settled here and immediately have any restrictions on her stay in the UK cancelled. This is not the case for a man. The relevant paragraph of the rules states that:

'If a man who was admitted as a visitor, student or fiancé, or in some other temporary capacity, marries a woman who is settled in the United Kingdom, he is not on that account to be granted an extension of stay or any variation of conditions to enable him to settle here unless refusal would be undesirable because of the degree of hardship which in the particular circumstances of the case, would be caused if the woman had to live outside the United Kingdom in order to be with her husband after marriage.'

To put it succinctly, the resident woman marrying a man who is here temporarily is expected to give up her residence and depart with her husband to his country.

The newly weds arrive early and sit in the waiting room. I have read the file so I know what to expect. Mr. Rezatollah is a 26 year old Iranian who came here four years ago to study English. His permission to enter required him to study for at least fifteen daytime hours per week and did not prohibit him from taking employment incidental to his stay here. The requirement to undertake daytime study suited Mr. Rezatollah admirably and he immediately got a job working evenings in the local burger bar. After four years and several extensions of his stay here, not only had he not yet passed an examination in English, he had not even sat one. By this time the suspicions of the Home Office had been aroused and it refused his latest application to stay longer and told him to leave. For the past few years, IOs at the ports had realised from the influx of such students that Iran was not a nice place to live in. Young Iranian males would do anything to stay out. Mr. Rezatollah, for his part, decided to get married.

Mrs. Marie Davidakis is resident in the United Kingdom and until her recent marriage to Mr. Rezatollah was a widow. She is Greek and is seventy-two years old. She has lived in London since 1938. I can see that I will have no success in submitting the argument that a seventy-two year old Greek lady should leave the country of her forty-two years' residence to live with her new husband in Iran. I suspect that such a suggestion would evoke a defence of 'undue hardship'. I shall have to try to knock down the marriage.

I interview them individually and alone and keep them separated so that they have no chance of conferring and agreeing what answers to give. If they have not worked out their story by now, it is too late.

Mrs. Davidakis is unusually tall for a Greek woman. She has grey hair which is whitening on the crown of her head and is wearing a thin knitted cardigan over a tweedish skirt. I am not at all surprised to discover that despite her decades of living in London, she speaks approximate English.

'When did you meet your husband, Mrs. Davidakis?'

'Now I am Mrs. Rezatollah,' she reminds me. 'I see 'im at a friend's house and we fall in love.'

'What is your friend's name?'

''E's called 'Arry. I know 'im a long time.'

'And when was this?'

'Christmas.'

Two months after he had been told to leave by the Home Office.

'And where did you get married?' I know already because the marriage certificate is on the file.

'At the council office. We do it there. It's all legal.'

'I'm sure it is. Was that the Registrar's Office?'

'Yes at the council office.'

'And where do you live now?'

'I still live where I do. Twenty-three, Adelphi Mansions.'

'And your husband lives with you there?'

'Yeah, 'e live there with me.'

'Is it a flat?'

'Yeah, ees a flat.'

'Is it high up?'

'Ees on the third floor.'

'How many rooms are there? Tell me about them.'

'Ees a two bedroom flat. I got a kitchen and a dining and a bathroom and a toilet and a hall.'

'Where are the bedrooms? Are they at the front or the back?'

'One bedroom at the front, one bedroom at the back.'

'Which bedroom do you sleep in?'

'The beeg one.'

'And is that at the front or the back?'

'Ees at the back.'

'And where does your husband sleep?'

'Ee sleep in big bedroom.'

'How many beds are in the room?'

'One bed. A beeg bed.'

'And you both sleep there?'

'Yeah, we sleep in the beeg bed.'

'Which side of the bed do you sleep on?' She pats the empty chair at the side of her. 'On the right side of the bed, then? Is that the side nearest the door?'

'Ees near the door.'

'So your husband sleeps on the left side of the bed?'

'Yeah, he sleep with me. We are in love.'

'What does he eat for breakfast?'

'I don't know.'

'Why don't you know?'

'He get up before me and go out.'

'Do you never eat breakfast together?'

'No. He go before I wake up.'

'Where does he go?'

'He go to work.'

It never occurs to me to question the propriety of my poking my nose into the sleeping arrangements of a married woman of seventy-two. I know the marriage is duff. It has to be doesn't it? A twenty-six year old man does not fall in love with a woman nearly half a century older than he; there must be another reason for his getting married and we all three know what it is. My task is to prove it.

Mr. Rezatollah is polite and helpful and respectful. He met his wife at the burger bar where he works. She came in regularly for snacks and they struck up a friendship which quickly blossomed into love. He lives with his wife at her house since he only had a bedsit. He describes the flat fairly accurately so it is obvious that he has done a serious reconnaissance. They sleep in the bedroom at the front of the flat, overlooking the main road. He sleeps on the left side of the bed but sometimes the right. They have breakfast together, she eats cornflakes with sugar. He drinks coffee. And so it goes on. I delve into the personal mundanities of their lives in an effort to scupper their marriage and get him kicked out of the country.

I call Mrs. Rezatollah back to settle the discrepancies.

'Your husband says that he sleeps on the left side of the bed. You said he sleeps on the right side.'

'Ee sleep here.' She pats the chair on her right. 'Sometime, 'e sleep here.' She pats the other side. 'Sometime I sleep here.' She pats the chair on her right again.

'Now the bedroom you sleep in is at the back of the flat, correct?'

'Ees at the back.'

'Your husband says that you both sleep in the bedroom at the front.'

'Ees the bedroom at the back.'

He had told me that it looked out over the main road.

'What do you see from the window of that bedroom?'

'Ees the main street.'

'So, the back of the flat looks out over the main street?'

'Yeah.'

'What is at the front of the flat?'

'Ees a bit with the dustbins in.'

'Your husband said that you have breakfast together and you eat cornflakes with sugar.'

'Yeah, thass right. This mornin I 'ave cornflakes.'

'So you had breakfast together this morning?'

'Yeah, 'e get up late.'

'You told me that he left for work before you got out of bed.'

'Yeah, but not today. 'E not go to work, we come 'ere. 'E don't eat breakfast, 'e drink coffee.'

'Your husband told me that he met you at the burger bar where he worked.'

'Yeah, 's true. 'E see me there.'

'You told me that you met him at your friend's house.'

'Yeah 's true. Arry. He run the burger bar. I know him twenty years.'

I sit them back together whilst I collect my wits. There is no further need to keep them separate. I am not clever enough, or dedicated enough to disprove the genuineness of their marriage within the parameters of the immigration rules. I return to them.

'I shall now write my report to the Home Office and they will contact you regarding their decision.' They thank me. 'Just before you go, I need to see your passport or identity documents.'

This is necessary to ensure that I have been interviewing the correct people. I should have checked before starting the interview but I forgot. What a crap IO I am!

Mr. Rezatollah shows me his Iranian passport with the horrible maroon plastic cover. I hate the feel of these things because the fine ridges in the plastic set my teeth on edge. It has the same effect on me that the scraping of finger nails down a blackboard does on others. The passport bears out his history to the letter.

'Do you have anything to show who you are Mrs. Rezatollah?'

She delves in her handbag and pulls out a blue book with a big gold cross on it. It is a Greek passport such that I have never seen before. She hands it across the table to me. It bears the photograph of a thirty year old woman and an immigration officer's stamp showing that she had landed at Harwich in 1938.

'This passport expired in 1942,' I say. 'Have you got a later one?'

'No. I go nowhere. I stay in London.'

'But you must have had a police registration certificate and stamps from the Alien's Office to show that you can live here. They would have been put in a later passport.'

'I got no other passport. My 'usband 'e do all the writing.'

'When did your husband die?'

'Nineteen fifty two.'

I go away to think again before I dismiss them. What questions can I ask her? She has overstayed her permission to enter the United Kingdom by forty years and nobody has realised. There is no way that the Home Office can get rid of her now – England is where she has lived for the most of her life. I send them away and then write my report for the Home Office. I would let them decide what to do. My prognosis is that Mr. Rezatollah will be allowed to stay. Once his conditions have been cancelled he will abandon his wife and not pay her the remainder of the sum they agreed for marrying him. She will get somebody to write to the Home Office for her in order to denounce him and the Home Office will write back and say that it is too late; he is in. Do I sound cynical?

H.O. Form I.S.58

To be retained in passport

CANCELLED FLIGHT

Further embarkation card (IS.29) not required

4016 Dd 8301743 25M 9/82 SP&D Gp 606

BOOKMARK

At Dover the random conversations in the general office would be along the lines of, 'I've just caught a Yank working without a work permit' or, 'did you hear about Sam finding a load of porn in the baggage of a German?' Up here in London I hear, 'Two o'clock in the morning it was, me and one cop went up the front path and Gerry, Bill and the other cop crept around to the back. We knocked on the front door and they caught two Banglas trying to climb over the garden fence at the back. They're banged up in the nick.'

I cannot extract such juicy snippets from my activities. It's not that I don't have a sufficiently acute sense of drama, it's the fault of the mundane quality of my material. 'I've just interviewed a seventy-two year

old Greek who overstayed by forty years,' would evince derisive laughter
and a bollocking for not locking her up. I decide that it would be good
tactics for me to admire their strutting and posing whilst keeping a low
profile myself. With luck they will never discover just how little I know.

I turn in for a duty starting at three o'clock on a Friday afternoon and
am immediately accosted by an IO in the tribal uniform of black leather
jacket, left open with the belt hanging loose and with dark spectacles
clipped onto the top pocket.
    'I'm Bill Norton. You're with me today. Where are you from?'
    'Dover East.'
    He does not quite wrinkle up his nose, but almost.
    'You're going to see the real life now, sunshine, like a big boy. No more
dinky ports.'
    I open my mouth to say, 'don't be such a supercilious prat,' and say,
'Thank you.'
    He nods. Fifteen love.
    'Have you got any work you can do for a bit?' he says.
    'I've got some collator's checks. Are we going out then?'
    'Yeah. We've got a couple of things on. I'll tell you about them later.'
He dismisses me. I resent this attitude in a supposed colleague, especially
one younger than me. At least when you are rebuffed by a colleague at
Dover it is by somebody nearly old enough to be your father.
    So presumably I don't need to know anything about the jobs in
advance, then? Is there nothing that I can prepare? I am thinking of my
first day with Charlie, wandering across the A-Z like a drunken fly. I do not
want a repetition of that fiasco.
    I take a volume of the London telephone directory down from the shelf
and look up the number of the police station that I am to ring. It is good
practice to learn what the police might already know about any address or
person living on their manor before you knock on the door. You don't
really want to be confronted by a sawn-off shotgun or a heroin filled
hypodermic.
    The London telephone system is awful. It's noisy, crackly and prone to
misdialling and interruptions. I discover that you cannot dial the police
station you desire; you call a central number and the police telephonist
checks that you are addressing your enquiry to the correct place before
putting you through. It makes sense and I am sure that it increases the
efficiency of the police but it is one more complication in what I thought
would be a straightforward two-way conversation.

The collator is a jolly sounding individual. I imagine him a bit like the Laughing Policeman of the popular song. I tell him the address that I am due to visit next week and he looks it up on his records and on the voter's list.

'Got nothing at one-eight-three. They had a domestic next door at one-eight-five about six months ago. One-eight-three goes down to a Subramanian.'

That's OK then. Subramanian is the name on my file.

'What was wrong with the domestic next door?'

'Usual story. Mister came home pissed and Missus wouldn't let him in. Mister starts shouting in the street. The neighbours complain. Mister throws a brick. Normal life.'

I am confused. I cannot work out where the domestic servant or au pair or whatever she was fits in. 'So where does the domestic come into all this?'

'What do you mean?'

'You said that they had a domestic next door.'

'Yeah, that is what I was just telling you. But we've got nothing on one-eight-three.'

'What kind of accommodation is it?'

'They're terraced, three storeys. Lots of our darky friends living in them.'

I thank him and mark the file, *'collator check – nothing of interest.'* It was not until about a week later that I learned that a 'domestic' was not a charwoman, it was a 'domestic disturbance'. Blindingly obvious when you know it.

By five o'clock I am twiddling my thumbs with impatience. Each time that I approach Bill Norton he waves his hand and assures me that he has 'just got this little job to do'. He is very busy popping in and out of the office. At half past five he suddenly appears at my elbow.

'Have you got us a car yet?' I look blankly at him.

'Did you want me to?'

'Yeah, get one of the Escorts, the Minis are clapped out.' He disappears off into another part of the building.

I go to the box file and sort through the ignition keys. I sign a Ford Escort out to myself and return to my desk with the vehicle log book and keys and I sit and wait.

At six o'clock Bill bursts into the office with two colleagues.

'Got the car?' I show him the keys. 'Come on then.'

I follow the noisy group down the stairs and into the vestibule where the security officer sits impassively behind a table. I have never seen him move since I have been here. He is like an ebony monolith. I wonder if he is real. I am tempted to go and pinch him. A few months later they checked his immigration status and he was pinched, as was the Ghanaian who had been employed by the agency to clean the office. Result: one dirty office. However, that is all in the future. The IOs are laughing and joking about people I have not met and events that I have not experienced. I trudge along behind them like a faithful manservant.

London is going home. Traffic is roaring over London Bridge and commuters are marching in line abreast towards London Bridge railway station. Heaven help you if you want to walk in the other direction.

'In here,' Bill says and pushes me into a pub. At this time of the evening it is catering for those who need 'a swift half' on their way home. The IOs make straight for the bar and order pints of beer. 'Well?' Bill looks expectantly at me.

'Oh, I don't want anything to drink thanks, I had a cup of tea before I left the office.'

'Pillock! This is a pub.'

'Yes, I am aware of that. We do have them in Kent.'

'So what do you want to drink?'

'Nothing thanks, I'm not thirsty.' He stares at me as if I am not making sense. 'I'm a teetotaller.'

'Bloody hell,' he says. 'We had one of those in the office before and he was a queer.'

'How do you know he was a queer?' the Scottish IO says.

'Oh come on, you only had to look at him. Flowered shirts? Streaks in his hair? That's not normal.' He leans on the bar and turns to me. 'So what's it like at Dover then? Cushy number I bet.'

'You from Dover?' the Scot says. I nod. 'Do you know Fergus?'

'Oh yes.'

'Last time I met Fergus we got absolutely rat-arsed. I mean, really rat-arsed. Went into his local for a game of darts and came out at closing time. Well, we were poured out, more like. Had to leave the car at the pub because we couldn't find it anyway. Spent half an hour looking for it, staggering around the car park, bumping into things. Tried to get into a Vauxhall but it wasn't his. Had to walk back to his house and when we got there, what do you think we saw?'

'His car?' I suggest.

'Too right. His bloody car parked outside his house. We hadn't taken it in the first place, we had walked to the pub. We were that legless we hadn't got a clue. Then he couldn't get the key into his door he was so pissed.'

'How frustrating.'

'His missus gave him hell.'

Fergus isn't married but I say nothing.

But Bill is not to be outdone. 'What about that time when Vince and Dave and me we all went to the Met. Police College for that forum? Eh? Remember that? It was a one night residential. They had Youngers on tap and after your fourth or fifth pint of that you don't care what you drink or who you drink with. We could hardly get upstairs. Christ you should have seen us all in the morning for the first lecture. God, we were a mess. Old Dave kept wincing every time they chucked a slide up on the screen and I had a tongue like sandpaper.' They bang their empty glasses down onto the bar and I pick up my case. 'Same again, landlord,' Bill says.

I put down my case. By seven o'clock my legs are aching from the ankles to the hips and they have drunk four pints each and talked non stop about the bloody good times they had enjoyed getting drunk elsewhere.

'You stick around us and you can learn something,' Bill assures me. 'Adelaide House IOs are experts at interviewing people. You don't get that down at the ports. We interview people every day.' His conceit nearly takes away my breath.

'How many people?' I say. 'Two? Three? We see hundreds in a day.'

'Yeah but you are just waving them through.'

'An IO at Dover deals with more people in a day than you deal with in a year. How can you be experts?' This arrogant git is getting on my wick.

He ignores my testiness.

'And we are experts at getting entry. Port IOs can never do it. They can never get in to the address. I could take you to an address in Brixton or Clapham and they would slam the door in your face. You've got to know how to get your foot in and rush them. You'd never get in. I know them.' He tapped his nose. 'I was out in Nairobi.'

'What were you doing out there?'

'We were sent out when the passport crisis blew up. We had to interview applicants for passports.'

'What? Adelaide House IOs?'

'Nah, this was the Passport Office. I was an EO there. We had a great time. I tell you, I was walking up the stairs in the Sheraton Hotel one day and as I turned the corner on the landing a brown hand came out from behind a curtain and stroked my balls. It was the bloody prostitutes.

They lived in little niches everywhere in the hotel. There was no bloody subtlety to it, just a grab at your tackle. Bloody hell.'

By a quarter to eight I am in considerable discomfort from shifting my weight from one leg to the other for nearly two hours. My ankles and knees are throbbing and I just want to go home.

'Don't you think we ought to get going?' I suggest.

'You're bloody keen.'

We leave the pub at eight o'clock. I have now been on duty for five hours and I have done nothing. The Scot disappears off on his job and Bill and I walk to the car. I know what is coming before he opens his mouth.

'You can drive.'

At least he knows his way around. He directs me to a police station in Lewisham where we pick up a constable to accompany us to the address. The family who live there are Cypriots and we want to interview the brother of the householder if he is still there. The technique is to use the police uniform to frighten them into inviting us in because, despite what the police are sometimes led to believe, an immigration officer has no 'right of entry'. If the householder does not want us to come in then we can do nothing about it. From listening to the braggings of the Adelaide House IOs I suspect that they just flash their warrants and shoulder their way in.

'Park on the double yellows and leave your flashers on,' the constable says. 'You'll be OK.'

'I hope so. It's my licence.'

The three of us unfold ourselves from the two-door saloon. Bill holds the file smartly under his armpit.

'That must be it, number twenty-three with the green door,' I say and before Bill can get his wits about him I pull the file out from under his arm and march up the path. 'So who do you want me to find for you to interview?' I am knocking on the door before they catch up with me.

A short man with crispy white hair opens the door.

'Hello,' I say pleasantly. 'I'm looking for Mr. Christodoulou.'

'That's me. Good evening,' he replies.

'Good evening sir. I am an immigration officer.' I show him my warrant, leaving it in his hand for him to study. 'This is my colleague Bill Norton and this gentleman here is a police officer.'

'Yes,' he says, agreeing with me. He hands me back my warrant.

'My colleague would like to talk to your brother Petros. Is he there?'

'Sure, he is here.' He shouts back up the passageway. 'Hey Petros.'

'May we come in then?'

'Sure, sure, come in, come in.' He beckons us in with welcoming sweeps of his arms.

I turn and hand the file to Bill. 'Piece of cake,' I say. 'Over to you.'

Fifteen all.

But the night was not finished. At ten o'clock we met up with three other IOs and raided an Indian restaurant. Most of the diners were finishing but all the kitchen workers were still there. There was no time for finesse. Straight in, grab the manager and push him into the kitchen. One policeman posted at the street door to prevent anybody from leaving, another around the back. We took away four Bengalis.

It is a bizarre fact that most Indian restaurants are run by natives of what is now Bangladesh and most of them come from one district of Bangladesh called Sylhet. We had a Sylheti interpreter with us but he was overworked and by midnight we had to acknowledge that we had done all that we could for that night and we sent them off down to the nick to be banged up.

Oh dear, I am already beginning to talk like an Adelaide House IO.

I crawled into bed at three in the morning.

One day I was sent out on my own. I had been minding my own business in the office, writing up a report when the CIO said, 'Brixton police have pulled a couple of South Americans. You'd better go down and see what they are.'

I looked at the car register. All the cars were out at that time so I went by tube. Brixton police station was like a fortress. It had girders set into the pavement to stop vehicles from being rammed into it and there were metal grilles fixed across all the windows.

The two men were Colombians. They were both in their late twenties. A police patrol had pulled them out of a bus queue because they 'looked foreign'. I interviewed them separately about how they came here and what they were doing in London. One was able to show me his passport which confirmed that he had come here four months earlier and been given permission to stay for six months by an IO at Heathrow. Whatever he told me now about what he was doing here was in practice, irrelevant, given that he was quite legal and within his time limit. Also, from the stamp in his passport I could know that no landing card had been submitted to Traffic Index at Lunar House so they would have no trace of him or of what he had said on arrival about his intentions here. He told me that he was studying English which was quite a boon because I could not speak Spanish and a short term student would have been landed as the stamp in his passport showed. Whatever suspicions I might have, I had no way of corroborating them.

His friend told a similar tale but did not have his passport on him so I issued him with a form requiring him to come to our office and present his passport and sent them both away. The police patrol who had brought them in seemed disappointed that I had not taken them outside to be shot. When I returned to the office the CIO quietly observed that I should have detained the one without the passport. He would not come in to the office with his passport as requested and even if he had given us his correct address for the form, he would not be there after tonight. We would not see him again. It made me look a bit of a fool.

'Did you leave enough fuel in the car for the next shift?' he added.

'What car? I didn't go by car, there wasn't one available.'

'How did you get to Brixton then?'

'Tube. Northern Line, change at Stockwell.'

'You went to Brixton by tube?' He was flabbergasted. 'On the Northern Line? Blimey!'

Possibly as some sort of recompense he took me to land the jetfoil passengers. The Boeing Jetfoil was a marine craft which worked up enough speed to lift its hull above the surface of the water on a pair of 'foils' or ski-type legs. This enabled it to travel at fifty to sixty mph over the water. The power came from a pair of water jet engines which were just what they sounded: instead of sucking in air and throwing it out the back to make the craft move forwards, they sucked in water and spat it from the stern. The shipping company, P&O, had introduced this service from the Belgian port of Ostend to the City of London. The craft crossed the Channel, skimmed up the Thames and disembarked its passengers at Tower Bridge Quay near St. Katharine's Dock.

'We'll only need two IOs to land it,' he assured me. 'Get your case and meet me and Sam downstairs.'

Sam was overweight and not very healthy-looking. His hair was black and lank and his complexion a bit pasty. We walked down to the Custom House car park. I was expecting at any minute to hear the usual, 'you can drive' epithet but it was not forthcoming.

'We don't need the car, it's not far,' said the CIO.

We strolled with the tourists along the promenade between the Tower of London and the river, we passed under the roadway of Tower Bridge and out onto Wapping High Street. The latter was an eye-opener to me. I had never seen a high street which consisted simply of an empty road between two continuous corrugated iron fences .

'That's where the jetfoil comes in.' The CIO waved at a white wood pier building. 'We're going to the waiting room.'

As one would expect, the waiting room turned out to be a pub ten minutes' walk down the road and whose garden led directly onto the river. We sat at benches and I drank a fruit juice whilst my colleagues downed a couple of beers. The ETA for the jetfoil was two o'clock. At a quarter to two, knowing that we were ten minutes walk from the pier, I opined that we ought to be making a move.

'No, it'll be late. No need to rush. The tide has turned and it had to come down off its foils to get through the Woolwich Barrier. It can't get up enough speed in the river to get onto them again so it has to paddle up on its diesels against the falling tide.'

I was not sure of the technical accuracy of this explanation but it sounded quite convincing. In any case, I reasoned that for once in my life I was drinking with the CIO so if something did go wrong I would be immersed in that same quality of immunity that had long been enjoyed by my colleagues at Dover. We drank and sunbathed.

'Is that not the jetfoil?' I asked half an hour later. I had never seen one but I had seen the posters advertising it.

The CIO glanced down the river to where what looked like a huge white launch was crawling upstream.

'Yeah, sup up,' he drained his glass as the jetfoil chugged past the end of the garden. We wandered casually out of the pub garden and back along Wapping High Street, overtaking the jetfoil as we did so.

'So it crosses the Channel at fifty miles per hour and then comes up the Thames at walking speed?' I observed.

'That's about it.'

I felt completely at home with the passengers. I don't know what sort of market research P&O had undertaken before starting the service but I felt that the weak spot in their service was the link with Ostend. City of London? Yes, good idea. Lots of people would like to arrive slap bang in the middle of the City, but from Ostend? Even with a rail link from Brussels it did not make it an attractive option.

The traffic was a mixture of bemused businessmen, who were probably wondering why on earth they had used this route and opportunist Belgian day trippers who had no doubt wangled a special ticket price out of the P&O agent in Ostend. Having landed the disembarking passengers with Sam and then embarked the departing passengers on my own, I packed up my case ready to return to the office.

'Hang on a minute,' the CIO said. 'Sam's got a hold up.'

I raised my eyebrows in surprise. With my years of experience of cross-Channel traffic I had immediately assessed this lot as harmless. What had a keen Adelaide House IO discovered that an experienced south coast one had ignored? It just went to show that one should avoid complacency. Perhaps Bill Norton had been right when he had said that I might learn something if I 'stuck around them'.

'What's the trouble Sam?' I asked.

'Belgian with a duff i.d. card.' He jerked his head in the direction of a middle-aged man who was sitting in the corner under the suspicious eyes of a P&O hostess.

'What's wrong with it?'

'It's reddy brown. Belgian i.d. cards are a greeney brown. You should know that.'

'True they are usually greeney brown. Except for the consular-issued cards.' I took it from him and turned it over to show him its place of issue. 'Consular-issued cards are exactly the colour of this card which was issued at the Belgian Consulate in Lille, France.'

'Is that so?'

'Yup. But don't tell your colleagues. Let's keep it our little secret shall we?'

In one of the desk drawers I found a long forgotten copy of the *Memorandum for the Guidance of Officers Newly Appointed to the Immigration Service*, issued by the Immigration Branch of the Home Office in 1955. It was an eye-opener. Apparently in the thirty-five years since its inception the Service had built up 'a reputation for courtesy, keenness, common sense and loyalty'. When identifying the traits to be found in the ideal immigration officer it stated that:

```
     A knowledge of languages is an obvious desideratum.  No
doubt the perfect Immigration Officer would possess not only the
wisdom of Solomon, the acumen of a Sherlock Holmes, the resource-
fulness of a Crichton, but also an all-embracing command of
foreign tongues.  If such an individual exists outside the pages
of fiction he has eluded the Civil Service Interview Board.
The Immigration Service endeavours therefore to build up teams
at the ports in which each member contributes his quota to the
common pool.  What should be aimed at is a sound knowledge of
more than one European language and in addition an understanding
of as many others as possible.
```

Difficult cases were summed up in one word – undesirable. *'Undesirable activities are of infinite variety. Different forms of turpitude are constantly being revealed.'* Some were listed:

```
A moral pervert.
A crook, share-pusher, card sharper, a trafficker in
drugs or women.
A merchant, financier, agent or representative whose
business does not appear to be genuine or sound.
A social "parasite" or one whose means of livelihood
is derived from an illegal, dishonest or doubtful
source.
```

I loved the language and the picture that it portrayed. It was a world never to return. A world in which, as Charlie had described, an officer turning up to work without his hat would be sent home for being improperly dressed. It was the world that Charlie was desperately trying to hang on to.

I was back with Charlie. That morning we had already turned up at an address which was a vacant plot in the middle of a street of semi-detached mansions. Like a gap in a row of teeth. It was overgrown with sizeable trees which suggested that this was not a recent demolition. Charlie rang back to the office to double check that he had got the correct number in the street and his colleague had said, 'Not number twenty-eight, Charlie? You didn't fall for that one did you?' Apparently it was not the first time that IOs had been sent to that address to look for people. My hands were clean. It had been Charlie's responsibility to do the collator's checks on the file. The police would have told him that he was on a wild goose chase.

Then we went to an address in Lewisham. We were to interview a Turk who had married an Irish woman and as one would expect, the marriage had come once he had finally exhausted all the other strategies to stay here.

The door was opened by a young lady who identified herself as Colleen O'Hara and was the new Mrs. Ozcan. She showed us in to the flat and we sat down. Charlie sat on the sofa opposite her and spread out his files at the side of him. I sat to one side. Mrs. Ozcan explained that her husband was at work but would be home that evening. Charlie assiduously wrote on his minute sheets and peered short sightedly at the waif sitting opposite him.

We were not aware at the time that Mr. Ozcan had chosen wisely, if one were to assume that he had married in order to settle in the UK, for Ireland has a special relationship within the immigration control setup. Jointly with the UK it forms the Common Travel Area which is why there is no passport check between the UK and Eire. Unknown to us IOs, the Home Office was automatically granting residence to husbands of Irish nationals because under EC law, the immigrant was not to be landed on terms less advantageous than his spouse and because of the Common Travel Area, Irish citizens could enter and leave the UK as they pleased. The Turkish community knew more about Home Office practice than we did.

But I was uneasy about interviewing the wife without the husband being present and in any case, what right had we to question her? She was Irish; she could live here unrestricted. My unease was not dispelled in any way by Mrs. Ozcan's pallor and behaviour. She was ginger haired with very pale skin made paler by the dark rings under her eyes. She was not the healthiest looking person I had seen that day. And she seemed to have some sort of nervous tick which made her twitch her head and flick her hands about. She was wearing a tee shirt and a white skirt which she was incessantly rearranging by lifting it from her lap with both hands and then allowing to drop onto her thighs.

Charlie sat opposite her, watery eyes peering at her through his beer bottle lenses and he doggedly put the questions to her in his arcanely polite manner. I had nothing to do but glance around the flat and listen to her replies to see if I could think of a line of questioning that Charlie had not followed. It was in allowing my eyes to wander that I noticed at her third or fourth skirt-flick that she was not wearing any pants. And there was Charlie sitting opposite, peering intently at her from four feet away, blind as a bat. We had to get out of there.

'I think we've got all we need now Charlie.'

'Just a couple more points to clear up old chap. Do you want to wait in the car?' He had no idea. That was the last thing to do.

'Well we really need to come back when Mr. Ozcan is here,' I said, but Charlie did not seem to take the hint. What could I do? I could hardly say, 'Charlie she's flashing her pussy at you, I think we should go,' could I?

At last he closed the file and we left Mrs. Ozcan to twitch and find her knickers. We climbed into the car.

'I'm glad we're out of there, Charlie, I didn't like that situation at all.'

'What was all the hurry old chap? I was enjoying myself. Didn't you notice the hussy wasn't wearing any drawers?'

The days passed quickly which they always seem to do when one encounters something new on every duty. My excursion into Brixton by tube earned me a bit of ribbing but I was above all that now. A tube train was quicker than a car and I did not have to park it.

Sometimes we were issued with radio pagers. Was there no limit to the technology that was available to this port? The pager was made of beige plastic and was the size of a spectacles case. When the office wished to contact the IO, it dialled a telephone number which set the pager bleeping. The IO then had to find a public telephone in order to call the office and ask them what they wanted.

I returned one day to find the CIO fuming because they had been trying to radiopage me to get me to do an additional interview at a police station close to where I was already working.

'We've been trying to contact you,' he accused. 'Didn't you get the bleep?'

'Oh I don't know.' I opened my leather bag and there was the brown spectacles case bleeping at me. 'Oh yes, it's bleeping now, look.' I held it up.

'You bleeding idiot, that is to tell you to phone in to the office.'

'Yes I know that but I checked it before I went in to the Underground and it was silent then.'

'You can't go by tube with a pager. They don't work underground.'

'Nobody told me that, but if that is the case then this thing could only have started bleeping when I came out of the tube station three minutes away. It would have taken me longer to find a working telephone kiosk than it would have to just continue walking to the office. So here I am.'

He stomped away, muttering, but he soon came back.

'Well you'll have to do this job instead then as Gerry is doing yours.' He thrust a paper file into my hand. 'Hackney police have got an operation planned, they want our help. Go and see what it is all about.'

I looked inside the file. It contained a single sheet letter telling me exactly what the CIO had said.

I showed my warrant to the officer at the front desk of the police station and he lifted up the flap and beckoned me through. He took me down a corridor, knocked on a door and then respectfully ushered me in. 'Ho ho' I thought, 'this office has got carpet on the floor.' Seated at the desk was a police officer of advanced years with all kinds of stripes and funny coloured little squares on his uniform. I was so bedazzled by the display that I did not register whether he was a superintendent or a chief superintendent but he was definitely somebody high up.

'Bring the team in Boden,' he said to my escort.

'Yes sir.' He bowed out.

I introduced myself and we shook hands. The next time I turned around there were about ten police officers standing in a horseshoe shape around the office. The boss man unrolled a large scale plan onto his desk and pinned down the corners with desktop knick-knacks.

'We've received an indication that there are illegal immigrants employed in this factory so we intend to raid it on a Friday afternoon when they are all collecting their pay.' I nodded at him to continue. 'So what plan have you come up with then Barry?'

An officer stepped past me and pointed out various spots on the plan.

'This is the main gate here, sir. We will have two patrol cars across the entrance and another down here at the back gate. The Bizzy Lizzy with five officers in will be parked on the corner of this street here, where it can see both exits. One motor bike patrol will divert the motor traffic on this street and we will have one other to be used as back up or liaison.'

'How many immigration officers do you think you will need?' the boss man said to me.

'How many people are we needed to check?'

'The workforce is about two hundred and sixty but you will only be picking out the black ones won't you?'

I stared at him for a second, not certain that I had heard correctly.

'So how do you envisage the checking work to be done? Will we have tables and chairs to work at?'

'Oh yes, we can find those from the canteen. We will set them up outside the pay office and when the employees turn up for their packets, you check their passports. No passport, no money.'

I was out of my depth here. Was this really the kind of operation that they undertook at Adelaide House? Holding an entire workforce to ransom until they could prove their immigration status?

'What about those who are not carrying their passports? There will be many.'

'We bang them up whilst you check on them.'

'What we would normally do in those circumstances would be to accompany the person back to their home to collect their passport.' I needed to find a way out of this situation without losing face. 'And what is the information that you are working on?'

'Denunciatory letter.' He pulled a scrap of lined paper from the file on his desk and showed it to me. 'It alleges that there are illegal immigrants working at the factory.'

'Who sent it?'

'It's anonymous of course.'

This was getting worse. 'Have you got a date in mind?'

'We can organise it for any Friday with two weeks' notice.'

'Fine,' I said, trying not to let my relief be too apparent. 'I'll go back to the office and put this in to the inspector and he can work out the staffing implications and get in touch with you.'

That seemed to satisfy him and the posse trooped out. I considered that I had wriggled out of that situation quite well. The questions were spinning around in my head as I drove back to the office. What about the British people in the factory? They could easily be black or brown but they would not carry their passports on them. And many of the immigrants also would have left their passports at home. How could we possibly accompany all those people back to their homes to check their passports? It just would not work and we were doing all this on the basis of an anonymous letter? The operation would cause a riot.

I put a factual report in to the inspector and prayed that I would be back in Dover before he made a decision upon it.

And then one Sunday morning I discovered that I was the only 'office duty' man. Everybody else had been scheduled on 'operations'. Well, that suited me. Few people phoned up with enquiries on a Sunday and I was quite content to be paid double time to watch the shipping on the river and read instructions dating from the 1920s. But I sensed a strange atmosphere in the office. As the IOs came in they were whisked into a back room by the CIOs. I was obviously excluded. I had to suppose that they were doing something too difficult for relief IOs to tackle.

I turned to the report that I was checking. I had made a visit with an Adelaide House IO to the home of a Pakistani family. It was the first time that I had been in a house where every bedroom door had a yale lock. There must have been seven families living there, except that they were not families. Only the men came to England, the women stayed at home. There were probably about twenty wage earners in the house which would explain how they could afford the large-screen colour television which occupied the corner of the communal downstairs room. I sat there with my oppo who displayed no desire to get on with the interview whilst the BBC was broadcasting the test match. Neither did the three Pakistani men who were also following the action with great interest. After half an hour I nudged my oppo and suggested that he started the interview. He managed to put his questions and the respondent managed to reply without either of them moving their eyes from the screen.

He needed also to see this man's brother whom we were told was sleeping off his night duty. During a lull in the test match we crept upstairs and one of the Pakistani men silently opened a bedroom door and pointed to a brown figure, lying fully dressed on the bed. He had his back to us but we were satisfied. Then I thought, hang on, how can we be satisfied with this? So I drew the passport from the file, pushed open the door and went in. Without waking him I walked around the bed to view the face, gentle in repose. I looked at the photograph. I looked at the face. I double checked. 'This isn't him,' I said. I showed the passport to the Pakistani. 'Where is this man?'

'Ah, he is working.'

'So he is your brother?'

'No, not my brother. He's the brother of Amjhad.' He pointed to the floor to indicate one of the cricket spectators below.

'You've just spent that last thirty minutes interviewing the wrong man,' I said gleefully to my oppo. 'The one you want is downstairs.'

He was equally gleeful. 'Good-oh. More cricket. Come on.'

The IOs filed out of the room and left the office in a phalanx. They were in high spirits. I did not see them returning for I had finished my duty by then so they never told me what they had been doing. It was all so very childish and cloak and dagger.

When it hit the papers, all hell was let loose. They had raided the Hotel Hilton in Park Lane and taken away thirty-five of their kitchen staff and chambermaids for questioning; thirty-one of whom proved to be in breach of their immigration conditions. The operation blew up into a storm. Questions were asked in the House of Commons. The trade unions accused the Immigration Service of conducting 'fishing operations' and having no specific intelligence. We were compared unfavourably with the Russian secret police. The management at ISHQ issued an order banning all operations which were not based on specific intelligence.

'Do they count tip-offs as specific intelligence?' I heard one IO ask another.

'Yeah, a tip-off is intelligence; denunciatory phone call, anonymous letter, they all count.'

'That's alright then. There's a phone box at the corner when we need it and letters can always be written with the left hand.'

I could not convince myself that he was joking.

The passenger traffic at London was slight. The jetfoil represented the greatest part. Occasionally a cruise ship would come in to Tilbury and a couple of IOs would be sent down to clear it or perhaps a cargo ship would declare a couple of supernumeraries on its manifest and the CIO would consider it prudent to have them checked. Once I had to go to Victoria railway station to land some passengers who had come in on the night train from Paris. This must have been one of the last arrivals of the through train service which used to be called the Golden Arrow. I duly turned up at the station and examined the few passengers who had wandered down the platform. Afterwards I chatted in the British Transport Police office whilst they made me a cup of tea. High on one wall was a bank of CCTV monitors showing grey stripey pictures of various parts of the station.

'Those two don't seem to be getting on very well,' I said, pointing to a couple of men on the screen.

The three officers turned their heads idly to the display as the taller of the two men socked the other one on the jaw and then began kicking him in the ribs as he lay on the ground.

'Oh Christ, always at tea time.'

Two officers grabbed their helmets and hurried out.

'Get it on the VCR,' the sergeant shouted and the remaining officer jumped to a video recorder and pushed the buttons.

In no time at all we could see the two policemen on our screen as they separated the men. I was more impressed by the existence of a video recorder in a police station. I did not have one at home.

'Can that be used as evidence?' I asked.

'Not yet. Only as supporting information. We usually show it to the offender and they cough anyway, which saves us the trouble.'

And then we had the siege of the Iranian Embassy. You've all read the story. You've all seen the television footage. I, along with many other law-abiding civilians had never heard of the SAS. We had no idea what it was: this super secret elite army unit. Very little had been written about it and the Press kept it in the background of the stories it ran. If you had asked the average person in the street what the letters, 'SAS' stood for, he would have said it was an airline that flew to Stockholm.

But now when I went in to police stations they were all abuzz. Every officer could regale me with tales of operations that they knew about or had taken part in and which had involved the SAS: they had attended anti-terrorist courses run by the SAS; they had run joint exercises with them. It was astonishing to my mind that so much had been going on behind our backs. One constable told me that the SAS had a hostage coach. This was a normal looking coach with a proper coach company name on the side and it was to be used for ferrying the gunmen and hostages to the airport, which is what they usually demanded. The modification to this vehicle was that at a press of a button the sides and roof blew off so that at a chosen spot en route, SAS marksmen could shoot the hijackers but leave the hostages intact. Hmmm. If you're going to make up a story you might as well make it a whopper.

The newspapers screamed abuse at foreigners, particularly Iranians and wanted to know what the Immigration Service was doing about it all. One of the articles bore the tag, *'Why is it that two thirds of the surface of the earth is covered with water and the other third by Iranian students?'*

Well, the siege was lifted in spectacular fashion. I missed it. I was in a train coming back to London. There was no television in my lodgings and I did not listen to the radio that night so I went to work on the following morning as the only person in the capital who did not know that the siege had ended. When I got back that night and mentioned it to my elderly landlord he mused, 'of course, that's what Mark in the house across the square does. He's in the SAS you know.'

I began to wonder who wasn't.

But my period of relief in London was coming to an end. I had enjoyed lots of it, hated some of it, been scared by bits of it and not understood most of it. I regretted not being able to check the passport of Sir Douglas Bader when he came in to Battersea Heliport. The CIO decided that we could not spare the staff so he was cleared by telex – an interesting modification to our working method that I had not encountered before.

I thank the IO who treated me to my first doner kebab when he stopped the car for lunch. Marvelling at the lump of compressed meat as it slowly rotated before the vertical grill I could not understand why their customers did not all die from salmonella poisoning.

I had not liked the way that the police officer had walked my hand-cuffed Jamaican who was dressed in his pyjamas and socks, on a zig-zag route through every puddle in the police station car park to take him back to his flat to get his passport. The man had enjoyed a quiet revenge as his damp feet had warmed up in the police car. And I shall always remember the occasion when an IO directed me to drive onto a track alongside a canal in order to solemnly point out to me a sign which read, *'National Coal Board Bow Locks.'*

But the mortifying scar that I shall carry to my grave is the memory of my bending down to place my case on the floor in a Ghanaian lady's flat prior to interviewing her and being ambushed by an explosive flatulation which caused a rather sweet WPC behind me to collapse in giggles and the interviewee to say, 'Ah beg your pardon?'

Living above the port in Folkestone not only gave me an accurate idea of how busy the immigration officers were at that office but also afforded me an uninterrupted view of Boulogne and the coast of France. Satellite television was to me, still unproven, so I had a high-gain UHF television aerial on my chimney pointing straight across the Channel and a multi-standard television which allowed me to watch French television as well as the UK stations.

This facility assumed a greater importance in April 1982, when Argentina invaded the Falklands Islands. Parenthetically, isn't it funny that all the while we were fighting it was called the 'Falklands Conflict' but as soon as it was over, we had not 'resolved a conflict,' but had 'won a war?' The importance of the French television was, that every time that the British TV reporters on the aircraft carrier 'counted them all out and counted them all back,' the French news gleefully beamed pictures of a wrecked Harrier jet near Port Stanley – a fact which my lesser-connected colleagues did not wish to believe.

What did you do in the war, Daddy? Well, on the lead up to the invasion, whilst various factions were spitting blood and feathers at each other on the international stage, I was single-handedly redrawing the map of the Argentine Republic. You see, on the outside back cover of the Argentine passport figured an outline map of their claimed territory which was executed in smart gold blocking. Naturally, it included the Falkland Islands. I discovered that if I dragged the outside edge of the little finger of my right hand into my inked stamp pad just before I closed and returned the passport, I could neatly black out the disputed islands, thus removing them from the Argentine empire.

Birmingham airport was constructed for Birmingham City Corporation and was ready for operations in 1939 just in time to be closed for the outbreak of war. The style of architecture is art deco but surely this fad was old hat by 1939?

I had found accommodation at the Erdington YMCA. Two other IOs from the south east had been given the same period of relief, Ockenden from Dover East and Darby from Dover West. I had decided that I really did not cherish the company of either for my three months in Birmingham so I was quite disappointed when they discovered where I had booked and managed to secure themselves rooms there also. I did succeed in convincing the hostel manager that it would be nice if they were lodged downstairs at the western end of the building whilst I was lodged upstairs at the eastern.

There was nothing wrong with Ockenden; he was just a bit wet. I had never worked with Darby but I had been warned not to lend him any money because his credit status was just below that of Mexico and he only repaid his debts by borrowing from another mug. Rather like Mexico, I suppose. Darby and I met on the first day in the queue for breakfast.

'What's for breakfast?' he asked.

'Cereals are over there and the ladies at the hatch are serving a fry-up.'

'Great. Can you lend me a fiver? I'm a bit short.'

'I don't see how my lending you a fiver will make you any taller,' I responded with my well known sharp wit.

'No, come on,' he held out his hand, 'I only need a fiver.'

'We're getting paid subsistence for three months. That comes to about nine hundred pounds.'

'Yeah, I know, I know. I just haven't got the cash at the moment.'

'And if I give it to you, then I won't have it.'

'It's only a fiver.'

'Exactly. It's not worth worrying about is it?' I said pleasantly. He relaxed. 'I'm certainly not worrying about it.'

It took him some seconds to realise that I was not handing over the money. His indignation was almost comic to experience.

The YMCA provided a shed in which I could store my bicycle. I had returned to cycling only a year previously, not having cycled since my schooldays. I had taken this decision as a result of an otherwise inconsequential remark made by a colleague at work. We were sitting in the on-call room at Dover East, waiting for a ship to unload when somebody had mentioned that Trevor, one of our really sporty members, was off sick for three weeks with a broken leg which he had acquired when playing football.

'You can easily tell who are the fitness freaks in the office,' I had said, 'because they are always off sick.'

'Yeah but you'll just keel over with a heart attack when you're forty,' the beer-drinking, cigarette-smoking footballer had responded.

That had set me thinking. It was true that I was taking no exercise at all. I sat in a car for the nine miles to work, sat at various desks breathing lungfuls of carbon monoxide, ate a big meal in the canteen if I had a chance and then drove home. I have always been slim and am one of those annoying people who can eat what they like without it affecting their shape but I realised that there was a risk that I would slowly decline. And it was true that I found sitting and standing and climbing stairs more painful than before. Perhaps all these aches in my joints were a signal that I was unfit?

So I bought a bicycle. The climb out of Folkestone from my house was a half a mile long and took me from sea level to an altitude of five hundred and fifty feet. The last quarter mile of the incline was at a gradient of one in seven. It took me two weeks of cycling to get up that hill to the top in one attempt and even then I had to stop and gasp back my breath before I could enjoy the gentle five mile descent towards Dover. But I stuck at it. To enable me to get to work at any time of night or day I bought waterproof clothing and a selection of cycling lights, none of which was particularly brilliant. I derived not only a physical benefit from exercising my body; there was a large mental component to the gain. It takes a certain strength of character and determination, although some would call it stupidity, to get up at five o'clock on a winter morning and leave the house at a quarter to six on a bicycle when the wind is blowing at force eight, it is pitch dark and raining and you know that the first mile of your journey is relentlessly uphill. Conversely, after a stressful day at work the continuous effort needed to drag that weary bicycle up the five mile incline to Folkestone acted as a purge to my mind. By the time I arrived home I was at peace with the silly and stupid world that I found myself living in. I had my argumentative, beer-drinking, cigarette smoker to thank for this improvement in my well-being. The irony of life is that as I wrote this chapter, he keeled over and died from a heart attack.

The route from the hostel to Birmingham Airport, although on busier roads than those to which I was accustomed, would present me with no topographical challenges at all. It was gently undulating. Some of the detritus on the road was more hazardous; in this workshop of the world it was not uncommon to find small bits of jagged scrap metal lounging on the tarmac to slash your tyres rather than the smashed beer glasses that lurked outside Dover pubs.

One of my first early duties, which at Birmingham started at 06.00, presented me with an unfamiliar peril – freezing fog. This was January in the Midlands. It was cold and clammy and uncomfortable to cycle in and when I wiped the mist from the lenses of my spectacles with the back of my glove I discovered instantly that it was not moisture, it was ice and both lenses had become opaque. With a nod of my head I managed to jerk my spectacles down my nose sufficiently to be able to peer over the top and see where the road led. For the remaining seven miles I cycled with my head tilted back and, by expelling my warm breath through my mouth and shaping my bottom lip so as to direct it upwards over my glasses, I managed to warm my spectacles sufficiently to prevent the fog from freezing on the lower crescent of the lenses.

Not surprisingly I arrived a few minutes late. I hurriedly dumped my bicycle in its accustomed spot in the ante-room. My route to the general office passed momentarily through the passenger hall and when I entered it the line of thirty or so businessmen who were queuing at the IO's desk all gasped like a football crowd at a missed penalty. It was not until later that my colleague explained the reason for their reaction. Not only had the fog been freezing on my spectacles but it had been freezing all over me. What had walked into the hall was a spectre covered from head to foot in sparkling white. By the time that I had reached the general office the

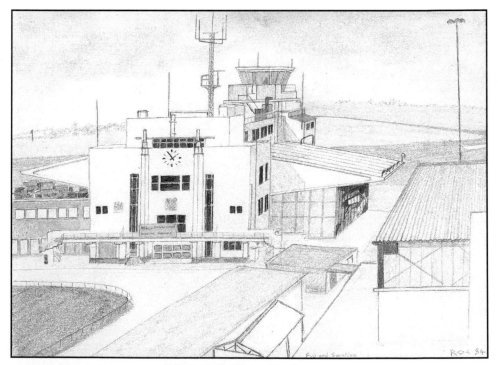

BIRMINGHAM MUNICIPAL AIRPORT
The immigration office is the two storey building to the left of the main terminus.
The weather was fog and sunshine.

rime had melted and the effect had disappeared.

The airport terminal was laid out on the classic and simple premise of 'airside' at the back of the building and 'landside' at the front. Our office on the first floor thus had windows which looked out over the car park in front of the terminal building and others that had a view directly onto the apron.

Although we relief staff had been sent to the port to assist them in conducting nationality enquiries at the Midland Enquiry Unit for the Home Office, we were scheduled a complete range of duties. My first duty was on passenger control and the flight I was waiting for was the KLM from Amsterdam. I had already been told not to expect any casework because it would be all Dutch businessmen coming to visit various industrial firms in the Midlands. Shortly after nine o'clock a Fokker Friendship alighted, rather than landed, on the runway and taxied towards us. It is a twin propeller aircraft and I watched in fascination as it wandered up to the building and began to try to poke its nose through my window. I could see the colour of the pilot's shirt.

'Shouldn't we go down?' I asked.

'Engines haven't stopped yet.'

I watched. The other IOs continued their individual occupations and manifested no interest in the arriving aircraft at all.

'The engines have stopped.' I gathered up my case.

'The steps aren't up yet.'

I put my case down. Every one of my subsequent terse commentaries on the progress of the morning flight from Amsterdam met with a suffocating uninterest. I could now see the passengers walking across the tarmac and into the passenger hall entrance below my window and still the IOs did not move. Eventually a buzzer sounded and they grabbed their stamps and books and made for the stairs.

The bell push for the buzzer which I had heard was in the passenger hall at the bottom of the stairs leading up to our office. It was the job of the first passenger in the queue to lean over the desk and press it in order to summon the IOs down to stamp the passports.

And they called Dover East a 'dinky port'!

I liked the cosy charm of Birmingham Airport. As with other small ports at which I worked, the staff of all the various authorities knew each other and pulled together. At Dover I did not know all the immigration staff let alone those of Customs, the harbour board, police and the ferry companies. The relaxed attitude at Birmingham permeated the passenger handling side of the operation. I was once on the embarks control when a ground hostess called through to hold the gate because she could, 'see Mr. Worthington out at the front just locking his car and he always takes this flight on a Thursday.' The late businessman was duly scolded as he hurried through to the waiting plane.

Occasionally I felt a little uneasy with the chumminess. I was alone in the office one morning when the cleaner came in, using her own key. That, for a start, surprised me but when, whilst waiting for the kettle to boil, she leafed through the confidential noting file commenting aloud upon various aspects of Home Office policy as they related to certain Arabs, I was distinctly worried. What about security? I mentioned this aspect obliquely to one of the local IOs and he remarked that she was no problem, she was just interested in current affairs. 'She's got three A levels' he added, as if in mitigation. As far as I was concerned surely this made her more of a risk? Why would a young woman with three A levels get herself a job which gave her a key entry to an immigration office and passive access to files within it? It was obvious from the reactions of my colleagues that I was making a fuss over nothing, so I probably was.

The nationality enquiries that we conducted for the Home Office were to help reduce a backlog of applications which had arisen when the British Nationality Act 1981 had come into force on 1 January 1983. The big change which came in with this Act was that now you could get your nationality from either one of your parents and not just from the father as under the 1948 Act. The House of Commons Home Affairs Committee had issued a report in 1983 criticising the Home Office for making a profit of over six million pounds from applications for British nationality so David Waddington, the Home Office minister, reduced the fees and set up an experimental interview centre at Birmingham Airport to try to reduce the eleven month queue for registration. For one person in particular he reduced it dramatically. The South African athlete Zola Budd wanted to take part in the Olympic Games to be held in Los Angeles but was banned because of the boycott on South Africa so she applied for a British passport and got it within seven days. Not from us at Birmingham, I might add.

The work was unchallenging. We were in the familiar territory of inviting people in for interview, reading their Home Office file, asking questions and then writing a recommendation on the file which was returned to the Home Office for action. It had a limited attraction in terms of entertainment but it was another skill to add to your CV. Not that I had one. There was little point. By now, after nine years in the Immigration Service I was unemployable except in a similar capacity within the Civil Service and the latter already knew what I had done and what the management thought of me. The answer to the last question, in case you are wondering, was 'not much'. I was just an IO, coasting along easily, inventing private procedures and techniques to make the effective and efficient discharge of my duty as painless as possible. And in that, I was pretty good, although I did not know it.

One day my early morning duty took me to Coventry (Baginton) airport to embark the passengers on the 07.30 Air Commuter flight to Paris Charles de Gaulle. This was a daily service provided by a company which flew a Vickers Vanguard in to Paris in the morning and out in the evening. The return fare was £111. I would have loved to have seen that four-engined turboprop aircraft skimming along the runway and then windmilling up to the terminal in Paris but I never did.

I collected the white Mini Metro, DYL 701 Y and set off down the A45 to Baginton. The little engine of the car was quite noisy at seventy mph but I discovered after ten minutes that if you shifted it into fourth gear, the noise dropped considerably. When several days later one of the IOs remarked that the Metro was 'using a lot of oil' I just nodded knowingly with the others and derided Sir Michael Edwardes.

I turned off the main road and up the track to the airport, ducking involuntarily as a plane skimmed overhead. I had not realised that the airport was so busy. I had been told that it was a tinpot organisation hanging on by its fingernails. The airport terminal was a collection of single storey huts which looked as if they had been left over from World War 2.

'Could you tell me where the immigration office is please?' I asked a lady sitting behind a counter drinking a cup of coffee.

'Are you Immigration?' I nodded. 'You share with Customs.' She waved her arm. 'Straight down the end of the corridor on the right.'

I followed her directions through a miniature customs examination hall and into a corridor. I knocked on the door. Gordon, the customs officer was a friendly chap. He invited me in, leased me a side of his desk and made me a cup of instant coffee.

'So what are you here for?' he said eventually.

'Air Commuter to Paris. Embarkation.'

He clinked his teaspoon on the side of his beaker and then lay it on the desk. 'It's gone. It went on time at seven o'clock.'

'Oh that's interesting,' I said. 'I thought the departure time was seven thirty.' He shook his head. 'It must have been that plane that I saw taking

THE VIEW FROM MY OFFICE WINDOW
Coventry (Baginton) Airport. The Air Commuter Vanguard is taxiing up to the customs
apron alongside which the avgas tanker is parked. It was into this space that British
Airways had to slot their three diverted aircraft.

off as I arrived. Anything of interest on it?' I asked casually.

'No, but you'll see all five of them again tonight at half past seven when they come back.'

'According to the timetable, the plane does a ten thirty arrival here.'

'No, they don't do that anymore. Nobody in France wants to come to Baginton. It stays on the tarmac at Charles de Gaulle and then comes back tonight.'

As I was not expected back in the office until eleven thirty we sat and chatted. He pointed out the customs apron outside the window which was a white box painted on the concrete. All aeroplanes carrying bonded goods had to be parked inside that square. Two private monoplanes were resting there. At the far side sat a Foden avgas tanker moulded into a beautifully rounded body and looking like an overindulged matron. I employed the word 'avgas' there just to prove to you that I had worked at an airport. It's short for 'aviation gasolene' and the word is only ever employed by posers like me wanting to show off.

'It would probably be a nice thing, Gordon, if the office were not made aware of my missing the embarkation this morning,' I suggested as I left.

'Mum's the word, old son.'

The passenger traffic at Birmingham had a completely different mix to that of Dover. The Midlands attracted foreign businessmen to the firms of the region and their British counterparts flew from Birmingham to reach the Continent. There was an important package holiday traffic – the equivalent of the coach traffic at Dover. I was hearing new destinations and then looking them up on the atlas when nobody was around. I did not know where Faro or Monastir was. Why should I?

The factories of the Midlands had attracted an immigrant workforce over the previous three decades and they too flew from Birmingham to visit family. I even succeeded on two or three occasions in making myself understood in Urdu much to the surprise of the passengers, my colleagues and above all, me.

Ockenden managed to score a first for Birmingham: he refused a passenger who had arrived on a Birmingham Executive flight. This company operated twin-engined executive jets to business centres usually in Germany or Switzerland. It used the Cessna Citation in which, one of the hostesses explained to me, the passenger cabin internal door, when opened, became the toilet door in the closed position and vice versa so if a passenger was in the toilet, nobody could leave the plane.

Ockenden's knock-off was a young Swiss engineer who had come to visit a company in Wolverhampton for training. Upon further enquiry Ockenden had realised that it was employment which had been dressed up as training. The man did not have a work permit and so he was refused. Birmingham Executive were quite excited about it. They had never had one of their passengers refused before. Even the fact that they were obliged to take him back to Geneva at their expense did not worry them. I was not long in discovering why.

I had accompanied a Birmingham IO down to the Securicor detention suite to serve refusal papers on two Pakistanis and the associated removal papers on British Airways. I handed the passenger's passport to the airline rep. so that it would be returned to the passenger upon his arrival abroad. I also served upon the rep. the form requiring British Airways to remove the passenger on the flight that we had arranged with them.

'Where is his ticket?' the BA rep. said.

'I gave it back to him along with his money and diary.'

'Well we need it.'

'Yeah,' said the Birmingham IO, 'you give the ticket to the carrying company,' and he raised his eyebrows at the rep. to show him what a dumbo I was.

'No you don't,' I said. 'The ticket is his property. He paid for it and he has an unused return coupon on it for which he can get refunded.'

'No, no, we use that coupon and amend it for his return flight.'

'No you don't,' I insisted. 'That is his property. Under the Immigration Act you, the carrier, are required to pay for his return flight.'

'No, that's not the arrangement we have at Birmingham,' the local IO said.

'Well, if you take that ticket from the passenger, you are stealing.'

They took it from him. I wonder if they still do at Birmingham.

When undertaking interviews for the Midlands Enquiry Unit we were usually scheduled a morning and an afternoon appointment in the same day. For this we were provided with the first floor of a separate office building which was about five minutes walk across the airport. I can remember the several occasions when the minutes dragged by as I waited for my interviewee to turn up. Sometimes there was a 'no-show'. When that happened I would tell no-one, stay where I was and use the time to catch up on other work.

One day a man brought his solicitor in to the interview with him. This was a recent innovation by the Home Office in its attempt to show that it was being 'firm but fair.' No IO liked a spectator at interview. This initiative proved to be the thin end of the wedge. By the time I left the Service it was possible that you would have at an interview, the interviewee, your interpreter, the interviewee's legal representative and their interpreter. Some of the cubicles could get quite crowded.

I extended a cool welcome to the solicitor who pomped and prissed about his being his client's legal representative and attending to protect his interests. They always say something like this to posture before their clients. In fact, they have no idea what they are doing nor what they can do and they spend their time making frantic notes of the questions asked so that they can appear knowledgeable when next trying to hook a client. I explained to the solicitor that he was there as an observer and was not to prompt or interrupt. If he wished to make a point he was to note it down and I would address it at the end.

'When you returned from Saudi Arabia why did you go to live in Dudley and not at the address from which you were writing to the Home Office?' was one question I put to my interviewee.

'Oh I can answer that for you,' says the solicitor. 'My client explained that—'

'Please be quiet. I am not interviewing you, I am interviewing your client.'

'I am trying to help you by answering the question,' his pompiness responded.

'You are not helping either me or your client by interrupting me. If you have something to say, you may say it at the end. I have already explained that to you. Was it not clear? If you interrupt again I shall terminate the interview.'

We continued. Three minutes later he rustles up a paper from the depths of his bag and pushes it onto the table.

'If you look at this you can see that–'

I stood up, walked to the door and opened it. 'Please wait outside until I have finished my interview,' I said pleasantly. I was trying to be firm but fair.

'This is ridiculous. How can you expect me to represent my client if I am not allowed to talk?'

'By listening and then asking questions at the end, as I have already explained to you.' I closed the door and sat down again. 'This is your last chance. One more interruption and I will close the interview and it will be re-scheduled for another day.'

THE VIEW FROM MY OFFICE WINDOW
Birmingham Airport in the snow. A Boeing 737 is taxiing towards the terminal.

He sat quietly and wrote furiously, not daring to ask me to talk more slowly so that he could record every word. He should have learned shorthand like I had. At the conclusion I asked him if he had any points he would like to clarify. He had not. I glanced across at his client who was plainly thinking, 'how much am I paying for this prat to mess up my interview?'

But rarely were interviews as entertaining as that.

For several days we had snow. I watched the runway clearing operations with great interest from my grandstand seat in the office. What I had previously viewed as rather tawdry countryside now assumed a clean, sparkling and theatrical allure. When the snow cleared I was attached to a local IO for 'ops' which was the same kind of after-entry work that I had already performed at Adelaide House several years before. This duty was not representative of my work at Birmingham but nevertheless instructive and worth recording

'Are you taking CYH 444 V down the Soho Road?' an IO asked me, seeing me with the log book. I nodded. 'You'll have fun then. You know that the registration number is on the police list of kerb crawlers don't you?' he laughed.

I didn't. Just as I had not known that there was an area of Birmingham called 'Soho'. For me, Soho was the night club and theatre district of London. For Brummies, Soho was a place to pick up the best Indian take-away or a tart. If you are an IO looking for an address, you drive slowly alongside the pavement and peer at house numbers, sometimes stopping to ask directions from locals and in this innocent discharge of their duties the Birmingham IOs had come to the notice of the local vice squad.

My oppo was a reticent chap called Mike. He was difficult to fathom. If you said something your words would appear to have no effect upon him. You would wonder whether or not he had heard you and then about thirty seconds later he would respond with a question or an observation. This behaviour made him appear a bit dolt-like. Perhaps he was. He had a habit of brushing his hand over his hair which was unfortunate because he appeared to have worn it thin on one side of his head.

We found the address with no difficulty and Mike spoke to a brown skinned man on the doorstep as the Friday night traffic roared by on the busy street.

'I want to talk to your brother, Amir,' he shouted at the man.

'Amir not here.'

I wondered if, when he did arrive, he would say, 'Amir', but I kept my musings to myself.

'Where is Amir?'

'He's working.'

'What work does he do?'

'Restaurant, restaurant.'

'What time does he finish?'

'Ten. Ten thirty.'

'Where does he work?'

'He work Greenland.'

Such an answer we both found stupefying.

'He works in Greenland? Very cold in Greenland.'

'Yeah, he work Greenland.'

'But he comes home tonight?'

'Yeah he finish ten, ten thirty.'

'How long has he worked in Greenland?'

The man thought for a moment. So did I.

'Four months.'

'Mike,' I said, 'I think "Greenland" is the name of the restaurant.' I was sure that I had seen a neon sign at the corner of the street.

'So he's been in Greenland since last year but he's coming home tonight?' Mike turned to me, 'We were lucky.'

'Ten, ten thirty.'

'What flight is he coming in on?'

The man looked at Mike.

'Mike,' I said.

'Which airport is he coming in to?' Mike continued.

'Airport?'

'He's coming back from Greenland tonight?'

'Yeah, ten, ten thirty.'

'He comes in to Birmingham?'

'Yeah, Birmingham.'

'When did he go to Greenland?'

'He go every day.'

'Mike, I think–'

'He can't go every day to Greenland.' Mike pulled a 'what a load of cobblers face' at me. 'How does he get there?'

'He walk.'

'To Greenland?'

'Yeah, he work Greenland.'

'I know he works in Greenland but he can't walk to Greenland can he?'

'Yeah he walk Greenland.' The man waved an arm down the street.

'Mike, I think you'll find that–'

'Do you know,' Mike said, 'I reckon that "Greenland" is the name of the restaurant that he works in. He can't go to Greenland every day, can he?'

'I think you are right. In fact, if you look down the street you can see the corner of a green neon sign. I noticed when I drove up that it said, *'Greenland'.*'

'That will be it then.'

We could not wait around until half past ten so Mike decided he would get the job re-scheduled for a morning visit. By now it was about eight o'clock so we ate a bag of chips and drove on to our second job.

I was navigating with the street plan on my knees and with its aid I skilfully directed Mike into the middle of an expanse of waste ground. My plan suggested that we were in a street of houses. The view through the windscreen said not. It showed a street, with a kerb either side and the correct name board and nothing else. Just scrub. We were in the middle of some gigantic Birmingham residential redevelopment. The acres on each side of us stretched empty out into the darkness. The line of the streets was marked by the few street lamps which glowed yellow in the desert. The houses had all been removed.

But Mike was not to be discouraged.

'What number are we looking for?' he said.

I looked at him and burst out laughing. 'It's two hundred and seventy-five but the street has been demolished, Mike. All the houses have gone.' I thought it wise to add the clarification in view of the difficulty that I had encountered trying to convince him about Greenland.

I had not forgotten the incident with Charlie at Adelaide House when we had been sent to an empty site which he should have known about. This was obviously the Midlands equivalent of it. But I was apparently not getting through to Mike. He put the car in gear and began to kerb crawl along the empty road. We came to a junction which boasted a street lamp and an abandoned fridge. We were in an enormous black hole whose rim we could just define from the distant twinkling lights of the metropolis of Birmingham around us.

'Which way do we go here?' he said.

I switched on the interior light and looked at the plan and then out at the blackness of nothing. I really could not believe that we were doing this.

'Well our road goes around to the right here.'

As he turned, our headlamps swept across the nothingness like the searchlights at Stalag Luft III.

'Two hundred and seventy-five, you said?' I nodded, not trusting myself to speak. 'Well it should be along here somewhere.' He put the lamps on main beam. 'It'll be in that lot.'

I looked. Against all reason, there, standing before us was a double line of back-to-back terraced houses, about thirty in all. They were a black block on a black plain. Half way down the row a solitary street lamp glowed in the night sky like the star over Bethlehem. He drove slowly down one side whilst we viewed the black holes where the front doors had stood and perused the bare roof timbers silhouetted against a growing moon. He turned across the end and continued up the other side of the terrace. He stopped the car.

'Two hundred and seventy-five.' He nodded at a front door. The only front door in the entire street. Possibly the only front door within a quarter of a mile.

'So what are we looking for here then Mike?'

'An overstayer, Akram Reza. We've had a denunciatory note that he is living here.'

'Right then.'

He lifted the metal knocker and rapped it hard. I half expected the door to fall inwards as it would in a slapstick film. The noise echoed around the roof, disturbing some roosting birds who shuffled and fluttered in the darkness. Was there not some famous poem about a chap knocking at a door and then shouting out something like, "tell them I came"? Well, just like the poem, nobody answered the door.

'We'll have to go around the back,' Mike said.

'Mike, the house is in darkness. The whole area is in darkness. We are the only two specimens of intelligent life within a mile.' I did not add, 'and I'm being generous including you in that category.'

I followed him to the end of the street from where we could gain access to the alley which ran between the backs of the houses.

'It's the seventh house down on the right,' I called forward to him as I stumbled in the pitch dark over fallen roof timbers and slithered and slid on chutes of slates. The moon glowed eerily on the white of a Belfast sink at my feet and sheened off scattered slates.

'Here we are then. This is it.'

'Akram Reza, here we come,' I muttered under my breath. The house was as black and abandoned at the back as it was at the front.

Mike knocked on the door and he tapped on the glass. We got no response even from the roosting birds. And then, when it was obviously all over and finished, I did a very silly thing.

'Mike,' I said, 'If you look up at the top floor window at the back of the house next door, you can just see the glow of a candle. I reckon there is somebody living there.'

He turned and hollered until the window opened and a dark face appeared.

'What's your name?' Mike called. 'I'm looking for Akram Reza.'

'No, no, name not Akram Reza.'

'What is your name then?'

'Name not Akram Reza.'

The window was pulled down again. It must have been freezing cold in that room.

'Oh well, he's obviously not here,' Mike said. 'You can never tell with denunciatories. Sometimes they are a waste of time.'

So we went back to the office.

It was my last fortnight of duties at Birmingham and we were drinking coffee and eating Jaffa cakes in the general office whilst waiting for something to happen. The local IOs were chatting. I was listening.

'Hey, hark at this. I heard a good one. You know Trish, the BMA hostess?'

'Is she the one with the big–?'

'–Yeah, that's the one. But she wants to sell it because that V-8 guzzles petrol.' I did not know the British Midland Airways hostess concerned but I continued to listen. 'A couple of weeks ago the ground staff were taken over to the new terminal to see how it was getting on and be shown what the facilities were like.'

'And?'

'Well as you can imagine, it's all swish and bright. No more rubber matting and chipboard. So the project engineer chappie takes them to the main hall and shows them the check-in desks which they were just installing and the conversation goes something like this.

'You've got twin desks with scales under the rolling carpets on each side,' he says proudly, 'You'll have height-adjustable, gas-lift chairs and this is where we fit your VDU in the middle of the desk where both employees can read it.' He is all very enthusiastic and then one of the girls pipes up.

'How do we get in?'

'What do you mean?'

'This is the front of the desk, right?'

'Yes.'

'So the passenger stands there. This is the carpet on the right for the baggage handling?'

'Yes and on the other side is your colleague with their baggage scales on their left.'

'Exactly. And behind us is the wall?'

'Yes.'

'So how do we get in? Do you expect us to clamber onto the scales like a suitcase and ride along the belt till we get to the desk, are you going to knock a hole in the wall behind us for a door or are you going to put us in the terminal first and then build the desks around us?"

We all laughed.

'What a cock-up! So what are they doing?'

'Apparently they're building a sort of gantry along the back with sets of steps leading down to each desk.'

'That'll look nice. They'll have to hurry, isn't it due to open next week?'

'Birmingham International' it was to be called. From our office we could just see the new terminal nearing completion over on the far side of the field. The new airport was to be West Midland's attempt to grab some of the business and tourism traffic away from Manchester and Heathrow. From now on, the civil aviation world would have to take Birmingham seriously.

In the meantime I soldiered on, conducting interviews, landing passengers and eating big breakfasts. My final attendance at Coventry (Baginton) airport turned into something of an event for me. Now that I had familiarised myself with the Air Commuter timetable I missed no more flights but I was intrigued by the other occasional aircraft which I saw on the apron. Who landed them?

Well the answer was that Baginton was a 'customs port', not open to commercial passenger traffic and so the occasional private passenger who did require immigration control would be examined by the customs officer on duty. He had a set of our stamps and instructions and discharged his duties as and when they were needed. However, we IOs were obliged to attend for the Air Commuter flights because the Home Office had agreed to authorise the airline to use this 'non-approved' airport for their scheduled timetable. It was the only commercial airline operating from Baginton. The likes of British Airways and KLM were not interested in Baginton because of the paucity of handling facilities and poor road access.

On the day in question, when I left the office at Birmingham to get the official car I could hardly see my way across to the car park because of the fog and my drive along the unfamiliar A45 tested my eyesight to the limits. I could only assume that the drivers who passed me at seventy mph were navigating with some kind of radar. Thankfully, the fog began to clear as I approached Baginton and I found the turning with no problem.

A young customs officer called Nick was on duty and confirmed that the Air Commuter flight was due out on time at 07.00 so we had a quick cup of coffee and embarked the flight. Several of the passengers said, 'see you tonight' to me as they left. The airfield was clear and the Viscount rattled down the runway and climbed towards the low cloud.

We sat in the office chatting about various aspects of the job and the advantages and disadvantages of living in the Midlands. I looked out onto the apron. 'That white plane there with the registration letter N', where does that come from?'

'The USA. It's a private charter.'

'Who chartered it?'

'Some businessmen.'

'Blimey, they must be loaded.' I stopped and listened. I looked at Nick and he looked at me. 'Was that the sound of jet retrothrusters I just heard?'

'It did rather sound like that didn't it? Perhaps somebody on the field is testing an engine.'

'Yes perhaps.'

I had volunteered to amend his immigration instructions for him so I set to work again with my scissors, glue and pen. I was fully engrossed in this task when he spoke again.

'Oh that's interesting.'

I followed his glance. The nose of a British Airways 727 was nudging past our window.

'What's that doing here?' I said.

'It's probably the aircraft we heard them testing.' We watched as it manoeuvred onto the customs apron and the steps were wheeled up to the cabin door. 'I think I'll take a look.'

I was not sure what he meant by that remark but he grabbed his jacket and cap and disappeared out of the office. Thirty seconds later I could see him running up the steps to the aircraft door. He waited until it was opened, had a short conversation and then skipped down the steps and back indoors.

'We've got some work to do,' he said. 'It's the BA from Dusseldorf diverted from Birmingham because of the fog.'

'It's lucky I'm here then.'

'Well now I come to think of it, Derek called up a few minutes ago when you were in the loo–'

'–Derek?'

'From the control tower. He asked if 'Immigration' were still on the field. I said you were. I bet he told BA and they decided to divert their plane here.'

The passengers were now descending the steps so we snatched up our stamps and hurried out to the examination hall. I was thinking of the contrast that would meet these passengers. I had never been to Dusseldorf airport but I felt certain that its decor was not painted cream woodwork and olive green linoleum.

The passengers were mostly businessmen and they took it all as a joke as they lined up at a single desk. There were eighty-five of them and it took me twenty minutes to land them. I was working at top speed. As the last grey suit disappeared towards the exit we both heard the rumble of jet engines as another plane landed. Nick looked at me.

'I think I'll give Derek a ring.'

Whilst he was dialling the tower, I glanced out of the window. There were now two British Airways planes on the tarmac. I signalled this discovery to Nick who was frantically nodding to me as he spoke to Derek. He put the phone down and picked up his cap.

'On the tarmac is the BA from Munich.' Even as he spoke the steps were being wheeled across from the Dusseldorf plane. 'And the Paris has just landed.'

'It's a good job they've only got one set of steps here,' I said as we made for the examination hall.

'Oh I think they could probably rustle up another set if they looked hard enough.'

By half past ten we were back in the office, enjoying a cup of coffee. Outside the three BA planes were slotted onto the customs apron, wings interlocked like an enormous red, white and blue jigsaw puzzle. They would fly them out empty to Birmingham as soon as the fog had cleared. My eye fell on the American charter plane.

'So these Americans...?' I began.

'What Americans?'

'The businessmen in the charter plane.'

'Oh they weren't Americans, they were Libyans.'

'Libyans?' I gulped, thinking, 'Libyans whom the Home Office have been telling us for the last two months to double check and point out to SB? Libyans like the assassins/students who were removed via Heathrow last week?' 'How many were they?'

'Seven or eight.'

'You haven't got their landing cards have you?' At least that would give us some names and addresses to work on.

'No, I just did a stats tally in the weekly return.'

I did not quite bury my head in my hands but I was near to it.

'Where were they going?'

'Only down the road to Alvis.'

I did not want to hear any more.

By the time that I got back to Birmingham the fog had cleared and the flights were coming in thick and fast.

'God, what a morning!' one of the IOs greeted me with. 'It's been absolute chaos. Flights cancelled and diverted, absolute mayhem.'

'It seems to be running all right now,' I remarked.

'God knows where the BA Paris got to. We're still waiting for it.'

'Oh I can tell you where it got to. The same place as the BA Dusseldorf and the BA Munich – Coventry. I've just landed them all on my own so I can't see what you are complaining about.'

'What? Coventry isn't an approved port. They are not allowed to land there. The diversion port for Birmingham is Manchester. You shouldn't have done that. They only went there because it was cheap. You should have refused.'

'You don't get much choice when the passengers are walking into your hall. I could hardly order them back on the plane and tell them to fly away again could I?'

'Oh, you shouldn't have done it. You shouldn't have done it. They'll try it again next time.'

'Well then you will have the opportunity to tell them to take off again and fly around in the fog until they run out of fuel, won't you?'

I went to call on SB. I told him about the Libyans at Coventry and suggested that he visit the customs officer and see if he could give any more information. I told him whom they were visiting.

'Alvis?' he said, 'They used to make big luxury cars didn't they? Our old doctor used to drive one. Great big silver thing.'

'Yes, that's right. They got taken over by Rover years ago.'

'So what do they do now?'

'Their latest model if I remember is the Stalwart. They manufacture armoured personnel carriers and other armoured vehicles. Those Libyans were arms dealers.'

'Ah,' he said.

Two weeks later WPC Yvonne Fletcher was murdered in London by a burst from a semi-automatic gun firing into the street from the Libyan Embassy.

And here I am at Birmingham International Airport in its first week of operation. It is, indeed, very swish. I have just completed an embarkation hour during which three businessmen missed their planes because the car park was so far away and they discovered that the boarding gate closed fifteen minutes before departure. Birmingham International was taking itself very seriously and not everybody was adapting quickly enough.

'OK, off you go, you're relieved.'

'Thanks Rob. Did you see the terminal on the television news last night?'

'Yes.'

'Did you see my bicycle? It was chained to the stanchion at the front of the terminal. I think I'll put a sticker on it, 'as seen on TV."

'Twit! The next inwards is the Faro at ten to six. You'll be on your own for that – the late duty doesn't start till seven.'

'That's OK, I think I'll manage.' The flight would be returning British holidaymakers.

MY SECURITY PASS – BIRMINGHAM INTERNATIONAL AIRPORT
Nobody ever spells my name correctly.

I walk across the concourse to the security gate which gives access to our offices. I shall only be at the new terminal for the next three days so I have not been issued with one of the plastic magnetic pass cards that open the doors automatically; I have a little cardboard tab which I show to the Securicor man. He nods me through.

I dump my gear in the empty office and pass back through the door to find something to eat before the next arrival. But there is no cosy canteen as existed at the old terminal. Now we are bright and plastic and take-away. I manage to find victuals of a sort and masticate whilst watching the holidaymakers and businessmen milling around the smart new terminal.

It's twenty minutes to six; time to get back. The Faro is due in ten minutes. I return to the security gate. Mr. Securicor is not there. He finishes at five thirty. The door is closed and I do not have a pass. I cannot get back to my office in order to land the flight. There must be another way around. Try the exit from the baggage claim.

I do. It has sliding glass doors which will open when somebody approaches them. But only if they approach them from the other side. They are one-way doors. I had not yet learned that if you wiggled your fingers into the minute gap where the doors met in the middle and then pulled them apart with all your might then they would open for you. Looking madly around for inspiration my eye catches the VDU display above the door. The flight from Faro has landed ten minutes early. The passengers are disembarking now. At the passport control they will be confronted by nothing more sinister than an empty desk. I hang around by the doors. The first passenger comes through and I shoot through in the opposite direction and fight my way up the stream like a salmon to its spawning grounds. I reach passport control. Returning holidaymakers are streaming both sides of the unoccupied desk. I jump up onto the stand and examine the last two passports.

Midland businessmen are not the only people having difficulty in adapting to the new, modern world of Birmingham International.

On my first duty back at Dover East I grab my case and make off through the mouse-maze of partitions towards the foot control. At the corner of the building I stop in amazement. The door has gone. Where are the stairs to take me down to the foot passenger hall? What has happened? For a few seconds I have the bizarre feeling that I am in a science fiction film and have slipped through one of those wormholes in time and entered a parallel world where all is nearly the same but not quite.

Running my hand along the wall where I think the door should be I can feel the freshly painted plaster covering the aperture. Whilst I was working in Birmingham the harbour board has bricked up the door and blocked off the stairs. Feeling rather stupid I retrace my steps and use the longer route through the customs car hall. Roger, the IO with whom I had formerly played word games in car kiosks, would have been amused by the surrealism of the situation but he is no longer here. He was posted to Kingston, Jamaica as an ECO and, having completed his three years, has now been transferred direct to Heathrow. I miss him.

The obstruction of the route was not an elaborate practical joke, it was the early phase of the rebuilding of the passenger control facilities in the port. We were to have a brand new foot passenger and coach control with new on-call offices and examination rooms and a doubling of the size of the staff multi-storey car park. It sounded magnificent. But we weren't there yet. The docks had become one amorphous building site. Routes were changed daily by shifting the cones and barriers, the coaches queued right back to the berth and the harbour board had to install portable toilets between the ships and our control point because the coaches were spending more time in the queue than they had to cross the Channel. The confusion in the public's mind was not helped by our pragmatic approach to clearing coaches which was to send IOs outside to check passports on board so that the passengers could remain in their seats. A grand idea, completely cancelled out by Customs' insistence that passengers should disembark to reclaim their luggage. The result was that the IOs appeared to be sitting doing nothing as the grumbling passengers filed through.

The first stage in the reconstruction was the pile driving which shook the building and shattered any attempt at conversation. This was a shame since satisfying the requirements of our job relied upon our ability to talk to people. We were forced to time our questions to alternate with the concussions.

'How long *crash* are you *crash* staying in *crash* the United *crash* Kingdom? *crash*.'

The unions complained about the noise and the damage that was likely to be caused to our ears so what did the Home Office do? They issued us with ear plugs. Problem solved. Now we could still hear the pile driver but not the answers to our questions. However the *pièce de résistance* was yet to be served. Sitting at my desk on the walkers control one day and interviewing an Argentinian man I was somewhat distracted to see a hole appearing in the end wall of the building behind him. Then a workman's face appeared. As I spoke to the tourist the builder continued to chip away at the concrete blocks until I had a window to the outside which gave me a view down the port to the berths. I continued my examination, he continued to demolish the building we were working in. When the hole was large enough, one of his mates drove a roaring diesel dumper truck through it into the hall and began to load up the rubble. You couldn't make it up, could you?

By this time, Inspector Dennis had been transferred to Adelaide House and replaced by Henry; someone described as 'the highest paid clerical officer in the Service'. He called me up from the control one day. Now what could I have done wrong?

'I've got these two plans here.' He indicated a couple of ammonia prints on his desk. 'It's the proposal for our accommodation in the new control building.'

'Yes,' I said, wondering what was coming next.

'The trouble is that one half of our accommodation appears on one plan and the other half on another.'

'As long as the builders don't construct it with a gap in the middle that should not be a problem.' I was known for my irreverent and flippant remarks which, I now take the opportunity to point out, were always based on a sound rationale. It was not my fault that I saw the slanted view.

'But the harbour board need to know how we want to arrange our accommodation and I can't do it on two halves of a plan. I understand that you can draw?' I nodded. 'What I want you to do is to draw those two halves of the plan, to scale, together on one sheet. Find some paper in the stationery cupboard and take the rest of your duty off.'

I took the two plans, folded them both down the common line of the join, butted them together and laid them on the photocopier and pressed the button. Two minutes later I was back, handing a bemused inspector five copies of the amalgamated plan.

'Oh that was clever. I didn't think of that,' he said. 'Now look at this. This is how I have laid out the on-call office.'

'What is this triangular area at the end of the corridor?'

'I have altered the plan there to make the secure accommodation for detainees. We'll put them in there while awaiting the DHB police to pick them up.'

'Oh it's very secure.' I immediately thought of the check-in desks at Birmingham International. 'What are you going to do, put the detainee in and build the room around him?' He looked at me, a perplexed frown on his face. 'You've omitted the door,' I explained. 'There is no access. The DHB will build it like that if you submit the plan, they won't mind.' And before he could think of asking me to redraw it, I whispered, 'Snopake.'

BOOKMARK
A P&O boarding pass in a resistant plasticised card which made a lovely bookmark.

Out in the big wide world the silicon revolution was taking place. Three years earlier the USA had issued its first edition machine-readable passport, known as an MRP. This designation provided much confusion in the Immigration Service which had just introduced a new way of writing reports which it had called the Modified Report Procedure, but we coped. The new passports would be read by machine. The militant groundswell began grumbling about the 'thin end of the wedge' and the Home Office's 'secret intention to do away with immigration officers.' I tried to point out that the MRP would eventually relieve us of our daily chore of writing foreign names in little lines in a book one day and then deleting them the next because now it would all be done by computer but some people just like to grumble.

It naturally turned out that we were both right. By linking the passport-reading computer to a system which could check names on the suspect index and by discounting the value of the human assessment of a passenger, then all that the Immigration Service would need in future would be machine operators. These could be of a lower educational achievement and thus paid less money.

The introduction of a newly designed passport to be used universally in machines world wide was only achieved after years of discussions across the globe. The idea was sold to the passengers with the promise that this would speed up passport control. It would if the country you were visiting possessed the machines for reading the passports. The first American passengers wielding MRPs started to arrive at Heathrow and elsewhere in early 1981. The first machine to read passports in the UK was installed at Heathrow in April 1983. Governments could see no sense in spending money in order to process foreigners more quickly. Once they were about to introduce their own MRPs then the machines magically appeared. It would seem that border control forces valued more the ability to check up on their own citizens than to check those of other countries. That should tell you the real reason why we now have electronic passports with micro chips and heaven knows what else in them. It is nothing to do with making your journey quicker.

One of the first 'successes' of the Terminal Three trial of a machine to read the MRPs was to identify Patsy Fagan, the well-known snooker player. What do you mean you have never heard of him? No, neither had I but the Immigration Service Suspect Index knew him. When his MRP was swiped through the reader it flagged up an outstanding warrant for his arrest. Ten years earlier he had been detained in the west end of London for allegedly trying to obtain ten pounds from a plain-clothes police officer as a payment to take him to see a pornographic film. He did not turn up for his trial so an arrest warrant was issued. Ten years later, on his way back from the All Irish Snooker Championships he suddenly finds himself in the cells overnight and up before the beak at the Old Bailey in the morning. It all fizzled out in the end but it was fun whilst it lasted.

At Dover East, the twentieth century was creeping in. We did not yet have machines to read passports but the inspectors' secretary now had an IBM golfball electric typewriter. Only she was allowed to use it and she locked it up when she went home. Several IOs who had started tinkering with the Sinclair ZX81 personal computers had now advanced onto Amstrads which came with their own monitors. The Sinclair computers you plugged in to the back of your television at home. You had to tune the set to a spare channel but spare channels were not easy to find on the television in Dover since we often picked up the French stations where in other parts of the country there existed gaps in the waveband.

We had no computers in the office but when our new accommodation was finished we were provided with a terminal which gave us access to the Intelligence Unit computer at Harmondsworth. This unit was staffed by IOs on secondment from Heathrow. It gathered and disseminated all forms of information relating to the operation of the immigration control. They had experts who would distribute photographs of the latest forgeries which they had detected and advise us of the trends in dishonesty. They also ran a large card index recording details of persons and organisations who had come to notice. It was this index which they had put onto a computer database. Formerly we would ring up the IU and give them the name that we were interested in and then listen to the planes taking off from Heathrow because the IO always left the phone receiver on the desk whilst he searched in the filing cabinets. The din was terrific for the IU was housed in the government buildings on Harmondsworth by-pass just opposite Heathrow airport.

Several agencies were tenants of the same site which, I believe, was at one time the Road Research Laboratory. From the Immigration side, apart from the IU, we also had a training unit and an appeals unit and later a detention management unit all based there. There was also a detention centre for housing people whom we were in the process of removing from the UK. Customs had a training presence and right at the back of the site, away from the road and prying eyes was a GPO telephone research unit. Did we suspect what kind of 'research' they were doing? The fences surrounding the unit were about fourteen feet high with cameras on the top and access was by a pass card only. I think we all knew who they really were and what they were really doing. I am sure they are still doing it.

Using the IU computer terminal at Dover East was my introduction to computers. I was a fairly competent typist but the electric keyboard seemed illogical to me. Why, when I tapped what I thought was the carriage return did the computer think that I was commanding it to send something somewhere? And why did I have to use the tab key to move from one line to the next? It was all very confusing and as I became more familiar with the dratted machines I was forced to accept that I had to conform to their illogical way of working because computers were too inflexible to conform to mine. I still bridle when on my word processor I have to 'enter edit mode' when I want to write something. I don't want to edit it, I want to write it. Editing is a different process altogether but I can only 'write' to a hard disk or a floppy. And not 'on' a disk but 'to' it.

Software and memory were pretty rudimentary in those days but the improvements progressed almost at the speed of light. I was chatting to an IO who had come to the Service directly after graduating in computer programming and he told me that by the time he had finished his course, it was out of date. He was unemployable. The kids at school were already programming faster than he was. The computers he had used nearly filled the room; now they sat on a desktop. But they were still slow by today's standards. I made the mistake one day of entering the name 'Singh' on the green screen to the IU. The computer took thirty minutes to call up all twelve hundred references.

The computerised suspect index was on its way. I was sitting in the car kiosk when Will, a newly arrived CIO from Heathrow, came in with the IT expert from the Home Office. On the desk were the two experimental computer terminals. The IO's task was now to type the name of the passenger into the computer and it would come up with any matches. The system was waiting to be commissioned; the IT chap had not yet seen the installation but was here to talk us through it.

Will leaned against the back wall of the kiosk and lit up a cigarette whilst the expert switched on the machine in front of me.

'Oh, you can't smoke in here,' the expert said. 'Not with computers. They can't cope with it.'

'Yer whaaaat?' he said. 'Yer joking aren't you?'

'No, no, not at all. They have to work in a clean air environment.'

Will continued to drag on his fag whilst he thought.

'What about carbon monoxide?' he asked.

I took up my cue. 'Every time I open this window the car exhaust fumes come in.'

'Oh we can't have that. We can't have that,' the man wailed.

'And fog?' Will proposed, looking at the glowing end of his cigarette.

'Yes, in winter we get salt-laden fog rolling in and what with the condensation dripping from the ceiling and the pipe smoke from colleagues it gets quite unpleasant in here.'

The IT expert was now white.

'Can I get a direct line on that phone?' he said.

And that was when they decided to give us car kiosks with pressurised ventilation to keep the fumes out. Humans were expendable, it didn't matter if we got headaches, bronchitis and cancer, we would still do the job but computers were fussy. They would not work if the environment did not suit them. They needed proper air. I suppose that is one thing we can thank computers for – making the environment more healthy for humans.

The chief inspector came down on a visit and any IO who could be spared was marshalled in to the general office to provide a rent-a-crowd audience for His Highness Pink Shirt. He outlined to us the various trends in the world of immigration control and baffled us by referring to immigration tribunal decisions by their case names, unwittingly giving birth to the expression, 'being Khawaja'd', to describe having had a legal point hammered into one. He also reviewed the operation of the Home Office computer system known as INDECS.

This acronym stood for, 'Immigration and Nationality Department Electronic Computer System' and in physical terms was represented by a bank of ICL 296 computers (do you remember ICL?) in Bootle which were the property of the DHSS and upon which the Home Office had bought some space. Running a software called 'Status' which allowed what was quaintly known as 'free text retrieval,' INDECS had been brought into service a couple of years earlier. Its goal was to get rid of the little old ladies in the funny shaped room in Croydon who sorted landing cards into filing cabinets. Now, all blank landing cards were supplied pre-printed with a unique number. If the passenger was of a category whose movements in and out needed to be checked, then the IO wrote the unique number in the passport alongside his stamp and the card was sent off to Traffic Index at ISHQ where the number and accompanying details were entered into the computer. When the person left, all the embarking IO had to do was to copy the number from the passport to the embarkation card which was then sent off to ISHQ to be matched with the computer record of the landing. It was probably intended to be the first step in a process which would eventually involve IOs at the ports making the data entries directly. It made sense, even if some of us could not quite grasp how the technical challenges would be overcome.

For some time I had been intrigued by the IOs' flawed process of self-assessment. We were employed to let in the people who should be in, as quickly as possible, and to keep out those who should not. It was not a black and white process, if one may use such an expression. There were people whose intentions one might doubt but about whom one could not gather sufficient information to refuse them entry. These passengers were landed on a restriction, generally known as 'one month, code three.'

Whilst limiting their stay to only a month it also prohibited them from working in any capacity. Having done this, the IO heard no more about them unless a file came back from ISHQ to say that they had overstayed or been prosecuted or committed some other misdemeanour. So, having had doubts about the passenger, the IO gives them one month code three, hears nothing more and concludes that his decision was correct. A passenger arriving subsequently with a similar story is thus treated in a similar fashion. Nothing went wrong last time, did it? Well, we don't know. Not everybody gets caught and it takes literally years for an overstayer notification to reach the IO. In that time the IO could have compounded the error many-fold. What was needed was for the IO to test his judgement as a continuous process. One could use the straightforward yardstick: 'did this person leave the UK within the time limit I gave them?' It would not be error-free but in the majority of cases it would give a good indication of how accurate the IO's assessment had been.

It occurred to me that now we had the INDECS system running, we had a means to check embarkation rapidly. Why not accord every IO the right to make a restricted number of checks on his own landings directly with the clerks at ISHQ? Rationing the number of checks per IO would avoid flooding the admin staff at ISHQ. The IO would rapidly see where he was going wrong and, usefully, might even identify trends earlier. It would be an economical and effective staff development tool.

So after His Highness Pink Shirt had waffled and it came to question time I decided to submit my proposal. Naturally I had to wait for the first question which was from an ambitious colleague just transferred down from Heathrow who was on first-name terms with Pink Shirt. He asked when the next CIO promotion board would be and then the second question was from another colleague just transferred down from Heathrow and also on first-name terms asking when the next CIO board after that would be. But I got there eventually. Pink Shirt listened to My Non-Entitiness spouting this ludicrous proposal and stated formally that he could see no benefit for the IO in checking his landings but he would certainly consider a scheme where the CIO would be able to check them in order to monitor the IO's performance. In other words, we will deny the IO a tool which he might use to hone his judgment; we will forge a weapon that we can deploy against him at annual staff report time for failing in this judgment. I suppose I was naive to expect any other reaction. The IS had never shown any intelligent, pro-active approach to staff development, why should it start now?

But why was I worrying about all this? What was the matter with me?

Was I taking the job seriously? I don't know the answer to any of those questions. Perhaps I could see a sense where others could only see nonsense. The one thing that I had not realised despite it being glaringly evident at Pink Shirt's question time was that I should have been looking after myself. Instead of thinking what I could do for the Service I should have been demanding favours from it.

What concerned me was that after ten years as an IO I still did not really know what I was doing and perhaps more frightening was that nobody seemed to notice. Brash colleagues would snap off quick answers to the CIO with such a show of confidence that they would be believed without question. I would squirm uncomfortably in my ignorance and then go and look up the answer afterwards. The smart-talking IOs were usually wrong and yet they did not have that reputation.

By frequently swapping off my night duties I had ended up doing a great deal of casework office duties – these being the least attractive to most IOs – and so I concentrated on trying to make my job easier by studying and trying to understand the official instructions. As I absorbed more and more of the published guidance I realised two things; one, it was written in an appallingly dense and sometimes ambiguous style and two, the reason why IOs did not like doing casework office duties was because, like me, they too, did not know what they were doing. They did not have a clue but they succeeded in brushing off their ignorance with bravado. I decided that I would try to help them to do the job properly and that would make my task easier; I would not be spending three quarters of my time correcting cock-ups and fulfilling omissions.

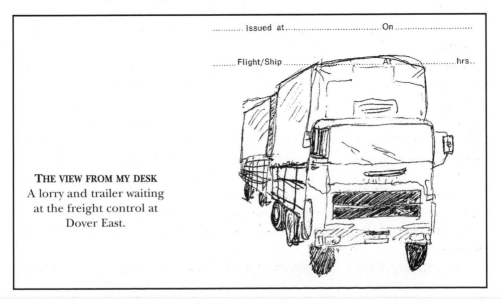

THE VIEW FROM MY DESK
A lorry and trailer waiting at the freight control at Dover East.

I drew up for myself a set of instructions in clear language explaining how to do casework. I inserted related information where it was needed. For example, in the section dealing with the issuing of removal directions I added the telephone numbers of the various carrying companies who operated from Dover, listing which routes they served, and which vessels they used. It was a trivial addition but its usefulness was great – especially for the relief staff from other ports who would not have this information in their heads or know where to find it. I went further. When a sixteen page instruction was issued by ISHQ on how to deal with persons coming for settlement I read it carefully, worked out the key questions that I had to ask myself in order to obey the instructions and then drew a flow chart on one side of paper. So, if it could be presented clearly on one side of paper why was not the instruction originally issued in this manner?

Don't ask me guv, I only work here.

So here I am on a Saturday afternoon relaxing into another casework duty. Will is the casework CIO. He became my team leader a few weeks after the incident in the car kiosk with the IT expert from the Home Office. The first thing he did was to throw my annual staff report across the desk to me and tell me to read it and give it back in a couple of days. I was flabbergasted. I had rarely held my staff report in my hand and had never been allowed unrestricted access to it. Good heavens we could not permit that – I might read it. When I explained to him that this was not the local practice he was as shocked as I was.

'What a load of bollocks,' he said with Liverpudlian succinctness. 'All Heathrow IOs see their reports.'

Today, when he had come on duty he had listened to my resumé of what was happening and then disappeared into the CIO's office.

'You're a senior IO. You know what you're doing. Just call me if you need me.'

'OK Will.'

'Tea or coffee?'

'Erm... tea please, thank you.' This is the first time a CIO has made me a cup of tea. He has a lot to learn about real life on the south coast.

We also have another new inspector, Geoff. He too has transferred down from the airport. His scrubbed pink face is usually wearing a genial smile; he is approachable and treats the IOs as if they are knowledgeable adults. I am deep in a file when he wanders in to see what the casework board looks like.

'What is happening to Mantelli?' he asks.

'I'm reading the file at the moment Geoff. As soon as I know, I will tell you. The last I remembered was that we were trying to get the Jamaican High Commission to document him so that we could remove him.' Had my colleagues minuted the file correctly I would have been able to open it and know in a matter of seconds what the state of play was.

'What's this *Casework Guide?*' He picks up my folder.

'It's what I refer to so that I don't make too many cock-ups.'

He flips through it, smiling at the cartoons. He taps the flow chart.

'Where did this come from?'

'I did it. It's easier to understand than the official instructions and you still get to the correct action.'

'Well I don't know half of this,' he smiles. 'I think I'll go and read it so that I don't make too many cock-ups.' He takes it with him.

'Bring it back won't you?'

'Yes, I'll bring it back.'

I pick up the file of a Japanese girl. She has been refused and given temporary admission to collect her belongings and return to the port for removal to Calais although she has indicated that she would be willing to pay for her own flight back to Japan. I find this amazing. The Japanese youth do not want to go home. Once they have tasted the freedom from the social restraint of Japan, they dig in. They will use any stratagem to remain here and they will lie without compunction. She is due back at the port tomorrow. On a whim I decide to check her address with the collator at her local police station in Rye, Sussex. 'Oh I remember the lass,' he says. 'We caught her trying to break in to Paul McCartney's house.' I minute the file, carefully guarding for myself the suspicion that we would not see her again. Several weeks later I discovered my suspicions were accurate.

I am now puzzling over this Mantelli chap that Geoff is interested in. Trevor, the IO who tried to get me to join the football team, has had a hand in it and it is not clear what he has done. This is often the case. The IOs do things, take decisions but do not record them on the minute sheets. The next IO has to look through the file at the duplicates of the forms which have been served in order to try to work out what his predecessor did. I am stumped. I can see that Mantelli was released from DHB Police detention but have no idea what happened to him after that. At that moment I spy Trevor's beard wagging in the general office.

'Trevor!' I wave to him. He comes over.

'Ah,' he says, 'I've been looking for that file. It got scooped up and put away before I could finish it.'

'So where is Mantelli?'

'Calais. He went out on the ten fifteen this morning.'

'I can't see any removal directions.' I search amongst the papers. Trevor moves right in to the office.

'No, you won't find any.' He drops his voice. 'He elected to embark.'

'But he has already been refused. He can't elect to embark.'

Trevor drops his voice lower. 'Well he did not exactly elect to embark but he went to Calais this morning.'

I look at him, nonplussed. 'But... he's got no document. He had no passport. He tried to get in on an NPE card.'

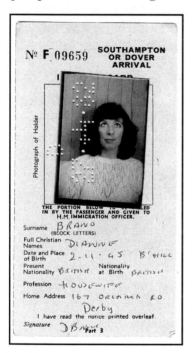

THE NO PASSPORT EXCURSION CARD

Known as an 'NPE card', these could be obtained on the day of travel from the ferry company at the port.

The details were filled in by the holder and no check was made of their veracity.

The NPE card is a special arrangement whereby British citizens can buy a sixty-hour excursion ticket to one of the Channel ports and travel without a passport. The traveller goes to the desk of the ferry company, buys his ticket and is given a three-part No Passport Excursion Card (thus the 'NPE') which he fills in with his details and attaches to it two passport style photographs from the booth in the concourse. He then takes the NPE card with him in place of a passport. At certain stages of his return trip, two of the sections are detached and retained, leaving him with a simple card bearing his photograph and details. This he hands to the IO upon his return to Dover. Versions of this arrangement have existed at various periods since the 1850s.

It did not take long for naughty persons to realise that the system had possibilities for fraud. The technique is that you ask for an NPE card at the counter when you buy your ticket but put it in your pocket without filling it in. You then board the ferry by using your full passport. On foreign soil you meet up at a pre-arranged point with your aspiring immigrant. You take his photograph, stick it on the card and complete the description section with his details. You then both travel back to Dover as if returning from a day trip. You present your passport, he presents the return portion of the NPE card and one more illegal immigrant walks in.

The unpleasantness from the IO's point of view is that when you challenge a suspect, you are inevitably lambasted by some liberal loony in the queue who points out in a loud voice that you are only stopping the man because he is black. Whose side are these people on?

Mr. Mantelli has been unlucky. The IO picked him out and now we have an undocumented Jamaican to try to get rid of. We cannot send him back to Calais without a passport because the PAF – the French frontier police – will not accept black men without passports. Where are the loony liberals in Calais, I wonder?

'Look... you'd better let me minute the file,' Trevor suggests. His manner is almost furtive. I do not understand it.

'How was he removed without a document?'

Trevor stands up and looks through the glass screens into the general office, then he goes to the door and glances up the corridor.

'I took him to the Sealink desk in the booking hall and got him another NPE card.'

'You did–?'

'Shhh. Keep it quiet. I'll fudge it over on the file. The important thing is that he has gone. We would have been stuck with him for months if we had waited to document him properly.'

'But... what did he say about the idea?'

'He was quite happy. It got him out of the police station. We should be quite happy, it's got him out of the country. I've probably saved the British taxpayer thousands of pounds.' He grins at me disarmingly. 'It's lateral thinking,' he says.

I hand him the file. 'You can wipe him off the board then. Geoff was taking an interest in the case. Will you update the inspector or shall I?'

'I'll do it. Geoff's a pussycat.'

'Cats have claws, Trevor, don't forget.'

He grins again and disappears with the file, leaving me gawping in admiration at his sheer cheek. I settle down to a quiet Saturday afternoon in the casework office.

The telephone rings.

'Immigration Dover East.'

'Ah good afternoon, is that Customs?'

'No, this is the Immigration Service at Eastern Docks, Dover.'

'Yes, I think that is who I need to talk to. It's about this guide dog.'

'Which guide dog?'

'The one you have quarantined.'

'This does not sound like anything to do with us but how can I help you sir?'

'Mrs. Fielding went over to France and had her guide dog taken from her under the rabies control when she came back. She says that they asked you before they went if it would be all right for the dog to go with her and you said yes.'

Alarm bells are ringing in my head. 'And what is your interest in the question sir?'

'Well we want to know why the dog was taken from a blind woman. It's ridiculous.'

He's prodding but still not giving anything away. Time for the killer question. 'And who are you sir?'

'Oh this is the news desk at the *Sunday Mirror.*'

Gotcha! I put on a welcoming, indulgent voice. 'I know just the person you need to talk to sir.'

'Oh thank you.'

'The telephone number is...' I read out the number for the Home Office Press officer. 'He will be able to answer your questions.'

The caller is not amused. The newspapers always try it on. They know that they must go through our Press officer and not contact the ports directly but they always like to have a go, just in case anybody falls for it.

Geoff wanders back in with my casework guide in his hand. He's looking thoughtful and is about to say something when the phone rings.

'Immigration Dover East.'

'Ah, hiya. It's Dean at the *Dover Express.* Can you tell me the latest on this guide dog case?'

'Perhaps you can tell me, sir. What guide dog is this?'

'The one in quarantine. You must know about it. Went for a non-lander on the *Panther* on Thursday and was put in quarantine on the way back.'

'Ah that would be Customs sir, not Immigration. I should try them if I were you.' Geoff is questioning me with his eyebrows. I replace the receiver. 'That's the second enquiry I've had about a guide dog. The first was from the *Sunday Mirror.*'

'What did you tell them?'

'To contact the Press officer of course.' I pause for a moment. 'He said the dog was detained on Thursday. I was on office duty on Thursday morning and now I come to think about it, I recall that a P&O hostess rang up to ask if we had any objection to a guide dog travelling on a non-lander and–'

'–What did you tell her?'

'I distinctly remember telling her that we would have no objection because the Immigration Service were not interested in dogs. She would have to ask HM Customs who operated the anti-rabies control. They would have something to say about it.'

'Hmm. I wonder if she did?'

'Who can tell?'

The telephone rang.

'I'll leave you to it,' he said.

'Immigration Dover East.'

'Hello, this is the news editor at the *Sunday Mirror*. I'm following a story on the guide dog which went on a day trip on a ferry–'

'–Yes I have already spoken to one of your colleagues and advised him to speak to the Home Office Press officer. Do you wish me to give you the number?'

'What? Er no... it's just a quick question about the rules on rabies quarantine.'

'I don't know anything about the rules on quarantine. This is not a concern of the Immigration Service.'

'But when the lady went out P&O asked you if it would be all right.'

'All your enquiries must go through the Press officer sir, as I am sure you know.'

'I've spoken to him and he said that it was alright for me to phone you direct.'

I was stumped for a moment. Why would he say that? What was the point of having a Press officer? Unless... 'I think you misunderstood him sir.' That was my polite way of saying, 'you're a bloody liar.' 'Try ringing him again. Goodbye.'

I think I ought to update the casework CIO. I nip up the corridor and recount the narrative to Will.

'What a shower of shits,' he says.

When I get back to my office the phone is ringing.

'This is the Home Office Press officer here, who am I speaking to?'

I give him my name. 'I have had several enquiries about a guide dog. Do you know anything about it? What can you tell me?'

'Well sir,' I begin and then stop suddenly with a thought running through my mind. 'Can you give me your name sir?' He does so. 'And can I call you back on the published telephone number that I have here?'

'You may.'

I put the phone down and dial the official number for the Home Office Press officer. The same voice answers.

'Sorry about that sir, I just had to check that it was not a newspaper trying to trick me.'

'Well done.'

'I've already had the news editor of the *Sunday Mirror* telling me that you said that he could contact us directly.'

'Did he indeed? That's a bit sharp. Now what can you tell me about this dog? I've got Peter Walker breathing down my neck.'

'Peter Walker?'

'The Agriculture Minister.'

I tell him all I know, give him the telephone number of our local office of Customs and replace the receiver with a sigh of relief. The latter action merely permits it to ring again.

'Immigration Dover East.'

'Good afternoon, this is the chief news editor of the *News of the World*. Now, about this guide dog which is in quarantine in Dover–'

'–Who did you say you were?'

'The chief news editor at the *News of the World*.'

'Really?'

'Yes, I really am.'

'I can't believe that. What, the chief news editor?'

'Yes, the chief news editor.' His voice sounds peevish.

'And you want to know something about the guide dog?'

'Yes, that's right. I understand that it was–'

'–But if you were really the chief news editor of the *News of the World* you would know that you should be phoning the Home Office Press officer and not me, wouldn't you?'

'Yes but–'

'–So are you the chief news editor?'

'Yes I am,' he snaps.

'Thank you for calling sir. Goodbye.'

I put the phone down and see Will giving me a big grin and a double thumbs-up from the doorway. That is what I call 'management support'.

Later that year the French unilaterally ended the NPE card agreement at very short notice but not before I was to derive a little entertainment from it. I was sharing blue X, the fixed point on the walkers inwards control, with a colleague one afternoon and together we were processing an almost constant stream of 'buckets and spades' – British day trippers. The surrendered cards were stacking up on the desk and every few hours the clerical officer came down and took them away.

The lady before me was slim, dark haired, in her late forties and wearing a black raincoat over dark trousers and a jacket, white shirt and bow tie. I took her card, checked the photo and waved her through and dropped the card on the pile. As I took the card from the next passenger I happened to glance down and read the details on the previous card. *Julius Caesar Pontius Pilate, born Pompeii, 4AD. Nationality: British.'*

I grabbed my suspect index and stamps, pulled the rope across the gap between our desks and called out to my colleague.

'Mick, work to your left. I've got to check something quickly.' I made a knowing nod towards the baggage reclaim behind us. I quickly dumped my official gear in the on-call room and then hurried through to the baggage reclaim area. I caught up with the raincoat after she had passed through the customs control.

'Excuse me madam.' She turned. 'Is this your excursion card?'

'Yes.'

'What is your name, madam?'

'Julius Caesar. What's wrong?'

'Oh nothing, except that I always thought that Julius Caesar was a man.'

'So?'

That was clever. She was obviously a woman but how do I prove it?

'Do you have any other names apart from Julius Caesar?'

'Pontius Pilate.'

'And when were you born?'

'Four AD.'

'That makes you one thousand nine hundred and eighty years old.'

'Yes.'

'Come with me please.'

I took her back to the customs bench and asked the officer there to search her handbag. I was sure that she was British and, as such, of no interest to me. I really ought to go back to help my colleagues. At that moment an SB officer walked through on his way back from the pub. I beckoned him over and handed him the card.

'She's of no interest to us. I'll leave her to you.'

He grinned sourly. Later that day he came over to my car booth.

'Your loony Roman,' he said, 'lives in Harringey in a council flat. She's claiming supplementary benefit in two different names.'

'Oh yes. And what are they?'

'Julius Caesar and Pontius Pilate.'

'I thought there was something fishy about her. I don't know how I knew.'

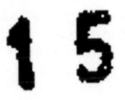

The South Eastern Railway and the London Chatham & Dover Railway companies realised when their lines reached Dover in the nineteenth century that money could be made by providing hotel accommodation for passengers crossing the Channel and so in September 1853 an imposing four storey building was opened practically on the quayside and named, 'The Lord Warden Hotel'.

By the 1930s the hotel was run by Gordon Hotels Ltd., and the guests climbed the steps to its porticoed front door to relax in a *well appointed and very comfortable hotel containing all modern improvements.'* With breakfast at 4/6, lunch 5/- and dinner 7/6 it was not cheap and although it boasted a lift and electric lighting it had no central heating and out of the one hundred rooms available from 8/6 per night to 18/-, only twelve had running water and half of those had no hot water.

More than a century later its stately white bulk frowns haughtily down on the later, less aesthetic erections perpetrated in the docks. It is no longer a hotel; it is the offices of British Rail Southern Region and renamed 'Southern House'. But it still has its views. To the north the rooms look over the busy inner docks with cranes swinging to and fro and trains bursting out of the tunnel from Dover Priory station; the west is dominated by the bulk of the five hundred and seventy foot high, wedge-shaped Shakespeare Cliff, so named from King Lear's description beginning *'...how fearful and dizzy t'is to cast one's eyes so low...';* looking eastward, the eye is drawn inexorably along the graceful sweep of Waterloo Crescent across the harbour to the cliff opposite where sits, in all its defiant immobility, Dover Castle and to the south lies the English Channel and the coastline of France.

I can see none of this as I crouch in the gloom of the corridor and gingerly introduce the blade of my screwdriver into the groove of the screw. It is that time of the year when I decide upon a tactic to avoid night duties and winter boredom. The arrears work that we used to do up at Dover Castle has now moved into a suite of offices on the top floor of Southern House. These would definitely have been the 8/6 rooms with no central heating and no water. The Home Office has leased the western side of this floor and stuffed it, rather than staffed it, with IOs who for multifarious reasons would rather work an eight hour day on flexitime than labour all hours of the night and day.

For this exercise we are now processing files from both B1 (Alien) and B3 (Commonwealth) divisions of the Home Office. The separation is deemed necessary because different immigration rules apply to the two categories and the distinction is marked physically by the file covers: green for alien, beige for Commonwealth. This division seems bizarre to us IOs – at the port we also deal with different sets of rules for aliens and Commonwealth citizens but we apply both as required. I suppose they specialise up at the Home Office because they can. They do not have real people sitting in front of them, they deal with files.

We have organised ourselves into 'smoking' and 'non-smoking' rooms. The 'smoking' rooms are larger and more crowded. Occasionally our attention is drawn to operations in the marshalling yard which is laid out below us like a train set. One day we watched them unloading new cars from a train; the posse of drivers running from the minibus to the train, jumping easily from the platform onto the low-loader wagons and then driving the cars down the train to the ramp at the end and out to the car pound where the minibus awaits them to take them back to the train. One bright pioneer, seeing that his steed was a Land Rover, decided to take a short cut to the platform and simply drove off the side of the wagon. He misjudged his manoeuvre and the front wheel of the Land Rover dropped down into the gap between the train and the platform. We passed an entertaining afternoon watching them sort that out.

Another amusement is provided by a quirk of the automatic telephone exchange that serves our floor. One of the IOs discovered that if you directed an incoming external call to a non-existent extension, then fifteen seconds later it rang again as an incoming call. It is a matter of a moment to ring up the automatic weather forecast recorded in German, redirect it and hang up and wait. When nobody answers the telephone the CIO sighs heavily and lifts the receiver. We know that he does not understand German and hates to lose face. He sweats and bluffs but the woman's measured Teutonic tones do not falter as she continues to talk over him. Aren't we cruel?

At last the screw begins to give and I gingerly withdraw it from its hole in the door. Taking care to allow nothing to rattle, I ease my screwdriver under the brass and prise the door knob away from the olive green paint. Taking the brown bakelite doorknob from my pocket I quietly slot it onto the end of the bare shaft and offer it up to the holes in the door. They match. Brilliant. I pull screws one by one from my mouth and fix it in place. On the other side of the door, oblivious to the criminal activity taking place, the CIO works on at his files. I can hear his chair creaking as he moves. Somebody coming! I straighten up just in time and amble back to my office with a file under my arm, a screwdriver up my sleeve and a solid brass Victorian doorknob from the original Lord Warden Hotel in my pocket. Last week I had swapped a handle from the unused door behind the stationery cupboard with a plastic handle of my own. With this new acquisition I now had a pair. They were beautiful in their smooth simplicity and British Rail's maintenance division was arbitrarily scrapping them and replacing them with plastic or aluminium levers. The rescued pair grace a door in my house and their Victorian craftsmanship remind me daily of the ignorant folly of unconsidered modernisation.

It's Thursday, the day when the files arrive in the van from Lunar House and the cleared files are returned. Pete, the IO who started at Dover East at the same time as me is gazing through the window.

'I reckon he's growing runner beans up on that allotment.' He points to a small square of cultivation clinging to the steep slope of Shakespeare Cliff.

I get up from my desk and move to the window. Any excuse for a bit of exercise. I look down into the compound where we park our cars. It is an area of scrap tarmac laid under the viaduct road which takes all the traffic to and from the Western Docks. Access is obtained via a magnetic card-operated barrier. The Dover West IOs are issued with the cards. We are rationed so the protocol is that if you are followed up to the barrier by a cardless colleague, you leave your card in the slot for him also to push and throw up the barrier again.

'You know old Foster phoned here yesterday and complained that I had parked my car at the top end of the car park thus taking a space near the pedestrian exit and forcing a Dover West IO to walk ten yards further to his office?' I said.

'Poor devils. What did you tell him?'

'I said that it could not be my car because he had refused to issue me with a car park pass.'

'It's nice to know the inspector is busy enough to worry about cars in the car park. Much more useful than focusing on immigration problems.'

'I kept confirming that the number he was quoting was my car and then insisting that it could not be in the car park because I had no pass. He gave up after the fourth try.'

'Prat.'

'Where did you put your car then Pete? I thought you drove past me up towards the gate.'

'I did.'

'A green Austin 1100?'

'Yeah.'

'Where is it now then? Have you moved it?'

'No.'

'Well I can't see it.'

Pete pulled an indulgent face at me and pointed to the car park.

'It's um...' He stared. 'You've got me worried now. I can't see it either. I thought I parked it by that blue MG. I think I'll go and check.'

'I'll come with you.'

We walked up and down the car park. His car was nowhere to be seen.

'It's been nicked.'

'Hold on. Before you report it, we are going to check every corner of this car park. Around the other side of the viaduct as well. Everywhere. It's in your best interests. Last year I had mine nicked from the multi-storey at Dover East and I checked every floor before I reported it which was just as well because three days later it was found two floors higher up with another hundred and thirty miles on the clock. The police reckoned it was a crew member who had wanted a trip up to London.'

Pete's car was not there. We satisfied ourselves fully that it was nowhere in the car park and he reported its loss to the police. Later that afternoon I glanced out of the window and saw a green Austin 1100 near the gate.

'Pete, your car's back.'

He ran down the stairs and returned a few minutes later with a look of utter bemusement on his face.

'Yeah, it's my car. Nothing missing from it. The police will never believe me. They'll say I mislaid it.'

'That was why I made you search properly. I will bear witness to its removal. Not that they will worry – crime solved.'

'Have you seen this denunciatory?' He held up a letter from his file. I shook my head. 'It's a classic. This fifty year old bachelor, British citizen of course, goes over to the Philippines, gets himself a young nubile wife and returns home. Wife gets twelve months code 1 on arrival at Heathrow and told to apply for revocation after twelve months.' He turned a minute sheet on the file. 'They live in marital harmony and domestic bliss for a year and then he submits her passport and gets her conditions cancelled as a spouse.'

'Standard procedure. Has she now gone off with the boyfriend whom she knew was already here?'

'Better than that – poor old hubby, it seems, was bitterly deceived and taken in. He had married a bloke. After a year of 'normal' sexual relations he discovers that his wife has a willy and balls.'

'You're joking?'

'No I'm not. Look.'

I read the letter. I thought that nothing could surprise me anymore but this was one of the attractions of the job – just when you thought that you had seen it all something incredible like this turned up.

'Well that must make the 'wife' an illegal entrant, mustn't it? Obtaining an entry clearance by deception?'

'It's all academic. He/she has legged it with his/her passport so we have no idea where he/she is at all.'

'Another one gone to ground.' I returned to my file. An Iranian had married an Irish girl and applied for the twelve months stay to which he was now entitled. At least the Home Office had raised the file in the correct name. The week before I had dealt with two brothers whose names the clerical officer had copied from their passports – *'marrons clairs'* and *'marrons foncés'*. Unfortunately she had not been familiar with Iranian passports and had read the description of their hair, making them the brothers *'light brown'* and *'dark brown'*.

My Iranian's spouse was a divorcee, submitting her decree nisi along with the marriage certificate and passports. I noticed that her previous husband had also been Iranian. The Iranians who were trying to settle in Britain had plenty of money. Was it any wonder that I would suspect that the woman was being paid handsomely for each nuptial? I felt jaded by this suspicion. My judgement was becoming perverted by the subliminal reminder that many of the Iranians that I had met, I had refused entry to. It was a reinforcement of that prejudice which grows out of constant contact with a thin and unrepresentative slice of a community. What was happening to my sense of humanity? Surely the world was not all that bad?

I sighed a philosopher's sigh and studied the papers. The decree nisi was forged. The original names had been 'snopaked' out, the form had been photocopied to produce a blank form and then the new entries had been written in the spaces and the form photocopied again. What gave it away was that the rubber endorsing stamp had not stood up to the multiple copying and so the forger had inked over it to darken it. But he had not been very skilled with the pen. Or was I perhaps just incredibly perceptive? I tried to phone to discover which name fitted the serial number of the decree nisi but got lost in the many telephonic diversions that these offices use as their defence. The marriage certificate had been forged in a similar manner. Just for fun I took it to our photocopier and with the aid of a pen and slips of paper, I married her off to the eight IOs working in the other room and pinned the certificates to their notice board to remind everybody to be vigilant.

'Bags have arrived,' is shouted down the corridor. 'All hands to the pump.'

Several of the male IOs go down and help unload the van; carrying the leather pouches two at a time into the vestibule. By the former porter's lodge we stack them alongside the large glass-cased maker's model of a Sealink ferry which stands proudly on its pedestal. To add realism, the modelmaker had placed half a dozen Dinky Toy cars on the car deck. These were now over forty years old, pristine and unblemished in their dust free display case and were probably worth a fortune.

When we had unloaded all the pouches from the lift we checked off their contents against the sheets accompanying them. Each pouch contained twenty-five files. We were a hundred files short. That was four bag's worth. We double checked. We searched downstairs to make sure that none had been forgotten by the model ship. Nobody could have stolen them, where could they be? We had verified that the van was empty before it had departed. We phoned up Lunar House and explained the discrepancy. They investigated and discovered that one caseworking group had been unable to find any leather pouches so had put one hundred files into two stout paper sacks and placed them at the entrance of Lunar House to be collected alongside the leather pouches. Oh, they had been collected all right. The sacks that they had used had been pre-printed with the bold instruction, *'Confidential Waste – for burning only'*. Nobody saw those files ever again.

Files are sometimes 'flagged'. This is the pinning of a small piece of paper to the front cover so that it projects above the top. These flags might inform you that the file deals with an 'appeal case' or 'minister's case'. It makes them easier to find in a pile. As I collect my next file from the box I discover a handwritten flag which had been crushed down out of sight. I unfold it and read it aloud: 'The Naughty Norseman?' It meant nothing to me. But it did to everybody else in the room.

'Oh the Naughty Norseman file. Have you got it?'

'Hey, Lloyd's found the Naughty Norseman.'

'I'll swap you for a Turkish sole rep.'

I was amazed because everybody seemed to have heard about this file except me. Apparently an EO in the group in the Home Office had phoned down in advance to tell us to look out for it. It took me some time to work out why. It dealt with the application for an extension of stay by a Moroccan man who had married a British woman. He had been allowed to stay initially for twelve months but by the time that his case was reviewed at the end of this period to decide whether he should be given residence he had acquired a police prosecution and this now had to be taken into account.

He was managing a club in London which had been investigated by the police. He was entitled to work here on the conditions stamped in his passport. It was the police report which contained all the meaty details. Two police officers, one man, one woman, had been sent in plain clothes to investigate the running of the establishment. When asked for his membership number at the door, the officer had said that he was not a member but he was allowed in after a short formality which consisted of a hand coming out from under the counter and feeling his genitalia. This examination apparently being found satisfactory they made their way into the dimly lit interior where they sat at a table and ordered a drink. Several couples were dancing on the floor; they were predominantly men and they appeared to be holding their partners by the unusual embrace of the insertion of a finger into the partner's rectum. On a bench in the corner two men were performing a lewd sex act and so it went on. It was page after page of a catalogue of debauchery. It was no wonder it had been flagged. I felt quite exhausted by the time I had reached the end. By the way, as a result of this clandestine visit, the manager was prosecuted for serving alcoholic drinks without food in contravention of his licence.

In 1946, Cary Grant, who was born in Bristol but held an American passport no: 46083 issued in Washington on 8 March 1946, arrived at Croydon Airport on a Moreton Airways charter flight from Paris. He was accompanied by Sir Alexander Korda. His UK visa had been issued in Los Angeles and endorsed 'in transit to France' whereas he had flown direct to France and then decided to come to England so, strictly speaking, it was not valid. The situation was explained to him and he was given permission to stay for one month and allowed to proceed to Claridge's Hotel. The IO wrote a landing report which was sent to the Home Office. I know, because I read it but I have no recollection now why I dealt with his file.

As I locked up at eight o'clock one evening, I wandered down the corridor, opening office doors and checking that the safes were closed and the lights extinguished. I had been working in the silent building on my own for over an hour. I poked my head around the kitchen door and saw that the tea urn was not still bubbling, I made sure that all the telephone receivers were sitting properly on their cradles. High up on this top floor, the light filtering in through the uncurtained sash windows was reflected up from the road below. The rooms were gloomy and silent. Suddenly my heart rose to my mouth. Those shadows made it look as if there was a body on the floor. I could see the legs sticking out from behind a desk. Fearfully, I crept in. I must be mistaken. I was not. Linda was stretched out on the carpet. It had been her leather boots that I had seen. Christ! What do I do now? I could see no signs of an injury. She was just lying there. Inert. I quickly knelt down at the side of her body and, I don't know why, I put my hand on her forehead. I just had time to register that it was warm when she opened her eyes and jerked into a sitting position.

'What the hell do you think you are doing?' she demanded sharply.

The hurt of her unexpressed suggestion that I was some kind of pervert trying to grope a sleeping woman was washed away by my relief at finding her alive.

'Christ Linda, you gave me a fright. I thought you were dead. All I could see was a body lying on the floor.'

'You are an idiot. I'm going to a party tonight but it doesn't start till eleven. I was just getting a bit of shuteye before, that's all.'

'Well you could have warned me.'

Never a dull moment in today's Immigration Service.

'What's the difference between a man and a shopping trolley?'

The gorgeous Vanessa flashes provocation at me in her blue eyes. Everybody fancies Vanessa, so it is said. I am doing a short spell of relief at the hoverport and half a dozen of us IOs are drinking our morning coffee in the circle of easy chairs which make the focus in the middle of the office. The coffee club is a civilised arrangement whereby we all throw ten pence into a beer mug and then pour ourselves a cup of freshly brewed coffee. When the money starts to overflow then the club treasurer treats us to doughnuts. I even designed a tee-shirt for the doughnut circle which quickly established itself as a fashion design statement.

'The difference between a man and a shopping trolley?' I repeat. She nods, her blonde hair swinging despite the lacquer. 'Let me think... well, they can both be picked up outside supermarkets by women and they both eventually end up carrying the shopping and being pushed around by a woman.' The other IOs laugh.

'No that's not it. The answer is: a shopping trolley has a will of its own.'

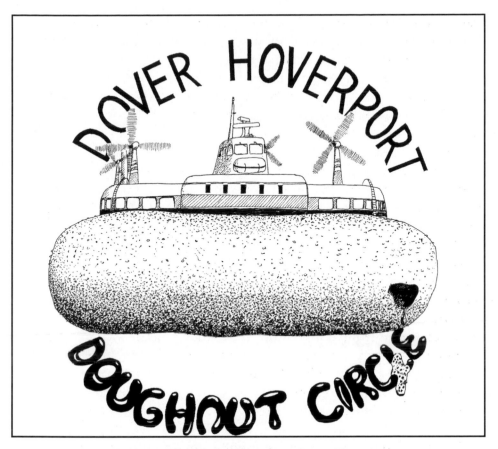

THE DOVER HOVERPORT DOUGHNUT CIRCLE TEE-SHIRT.
Designer: Martin Lloyd.

I cannot think of a better introduction to a disquisition on the failure of the French hovercrafts. The French nationalised railway company, SNCF, had brought into service for the opening of the Dover Hoverport, a French designed and built hovercraft to supplement the *Princess Margaret* and *Princess Anne* which were operated by Seaspeed, the subsidiary of the British Rail maritime division, Sealink. The Sedam N500 *Ingenieur Jean Bertin* was the pre-production prototype which the SNCF put on the Boulogne-Dover service. It was a disaster. The British SRN-4 craft were powered and steered by propellers on rotatable pylons mounted on the roof, one at each corner. As a result they could execute a 360º turn in their own footprint. Don't forget, the hovercraft has no keel or rudder to maintain a purchase in the water – it is skidding around on a cushion of air above it. The Sedam N500 had three propellers mounted in a line across the top of the craft at the stern. They were fixed in position and steered the craft like an aeroplane by blowing their air wash over a set of vertical rudders.

Now, think of supermarket shopping trolleys. Unlike men, there are two basic designs. One has casters on every wheel the other has casters at the front and fixed wheels at the back. The latter is easier to steer since it naturally travels in a straight line and all you need do is pull or push on the handle to swing the nose around and the tail will follow. This is how the N500 was steered. The pilot could run the two outside engines in different directions which created the same effect as a housewife pulling at one end of the handle and pushing at the other in order to swing the nose of the trolley. The British SRN-4 was the trolley with casters on all four wheels – less easy to steer in a straight line since you can never guarantee that at any one time all four wheels will continue to point in the same direction. So, in the supermarket environment, the French trolley is the winner.

Now you leave the level, tiled floor of the shop and start to cross the car park. You encounter a ramp which slopes across the direction of your travel. With the French trolley you pull and push on the handle to prevent the loaded nose from swinging down the incline and dragging you into the dustbins. You sometimes need quite strong wrists to achieve this. When the British trolley hits the ramp all four casters turn in the same direction and it begins to slide sideways. You counteract this by putting yourself lower on the slope than the trolley and pushing the latter upwards against the incline and sideways in the direction in which you want to travel. Once you have achieved the equilibrium, you travel crab-wise across the slope but expend less effort than with the French trolley.

How can this relate to hovercraft – there are no slopes on the sea? Correct, but the equivalent effect is provided by the wind.

The *Ingenieur Jean Bertin* had weak wrists. Those three engines were simply not sufficiently powerful to keep the craft pointing in the desired direction in a strong cross wind. The design meant that the wind had fifty metres of hovercraft to use as a lever against the thrust of the engines. And it transpired that the engines also lacked the basic power to get the craft up onto the ramp at Dover at low tide. On the French side there was no problem because at both Calais and Boulogne the approach was made over flat sand but at Dover the beach shelves steeply. The craft would get half way up and then stick, going neither forwards nor backwards. We once watched it straining in this position for fifteen minutes, waiting for the tide to rise and give it more purchase. Occasionally when it failed to climb the ramp it would slide back down again and go out into the harbour, turn around and take another run at it. Sometimes it succeeded at the third or fourth attempt. One day, arriving on a falling tide and unable to climb the ramp, it had to take its passengers back to Boulogne. Can you imagine what they thought of *Jean Bertin* – getting them to within a hundred yards of their destination and then taking them home again?

Jean Bertin was an engineer who in the early 1960s had designed an experimental hovertrain, *L'aérotrain,* for the SNCF. His company built a half size prototype and ran it at speeds of 180 mph. Part of the projected full scale line from Paris to Orleans was constructed but never completed. The track is still there, rusting away.

And on the beach at Boulogne, the Sedam N500 *Ingenieur Jean Bertin* is doing likewise. It has been stripped of all useful pieces and abandoned by Hoverspeed, as the joint company is now called. As a result of the disastrous performance of the prototype, no orders were placed for the first production model, the *Cote d'Argent* which, having proved itself equally disappointing in its trials, mysteriously caught fire outside the factory one day and was totally destroyed. I bet it was insured at Lloyd's of London.

THE FRENCH HOVERCRAFT DISASTER
The N500 hovercraft prototype *Ingénieur Jean Bertin* abandoned on the beach at Boulogne. It has been stripped of its engines, only the pods remain.

The summer at Dover East had not unfurled without the odd crease or two. At the eleventh week of the miners' strike, Arthur Scargill had tried to get the dockers to come out in sympathy. Such a call could only realistically be answered by those ports still operating within the Dock

Labour Scheme. This was an arrangement to retain dockers on full pay when there was no work, so that they would be available when there was work. Upon reflection, the arrangement did have similarities to the manner in which IOs were paid a salary but spent a proportion of their time waiting for something to happen. The Dock Labour Scheme was not popular with employers and several ports had either not taken part or had come out of it. Dover was one of these ports so, in theory, there should have been no response from the workforce but one small section at Dover found the way to prevent the embarkation of lorries.

The lorry drivers decided that if they were not allowed to travel, then nobody would and they blocked vehicular access to the berths by parking their lorries across them. The port and the town began to choke with lorries. Kent police invented 'Operation Stack' whereby they closed the last section of the M20 at Folkestone and used it as a lorry park. The situation became a little fractious with two hundred lorries parked in and around the docks, schoolchildren sleeping in stranded coaches and the Merry Dolphin running out of food supplies since none were allowed in by the blockading lorries.

At about the same time the French right wing politician, Jean-Marie Le Pen, rallied the coal miners of northern France in support of their oppressed British brethren and decided to march on London. Mrs. Thatcher's government made it clear to him that he was not welcome and supported this declaration with instructions to the police and Immigration Service. When we at Dover learned of the intended arrival of eight hundred coal miners from Calais the contingency plan swung into action. Martin Lloyd and two police officers were despatched outwards on the Sealink ferry with instructions concerning Monsieur Le Pen and his task force. Working at full speed on the return journey we examined and landed as many of the coal miners as we could deal with. The SB officers hovered over my shoulder, hoping to pounce on poor old Jean-Marie should I discover him. It was all a waste of time. As far as the miners were concerned, it was a jolly day out. They had no intention of toppling the government. They draped around my neck one of their specially struck medals, 'in solidarity with the British miners' and we got on famously.

Eventually, everybody saw sense and agreed that it was neither miners nor Mrs. Thatcher who ruled the country but lorry drivers and everything returned to normal.

Sipping coffee in the calm and order of the hoverport is a beautiful contrast. I could retire to this port. It had retained the gentility and

MY GOLD MEDAL
I was supposed to be checking the
French coal miners to make sure
that the politician Jean Marie Le
Pen was not hidden amongst
them but they awarded me one
of their medals.

It declares solidarity with the British
miners in the name of the French
trade union, the CGT, and features a
miner's head before a background
of British and French flags
and a coal face.

humanity that I had remembered from the first three months of its
operations. The office even has its own golf course. A few feet into the
general office there is a small inspection hatch in the floor. To cover it, a
square of matching carpet has been trimmed to fit. It did not take long for
one of the golf enthusiasts in the office to lift this carpet tile, cut a neat
hole in the middle of it and then replace it over the hatch. The sound of
a golf ball rattling into the hole could often be heard between flight
arrivals.

A challenge was invented to tee off from one corner of the tile,
complete a circuit of the pillars in the centre of the office and back to the
hole. The champion had achieved it in three shots. One day I managed it
in two. And I had witnesses. By aligning a chair at a carefully computed
angle, I bounced the ball off the leg around the top end of the pillars
where it hit the base of a row of filing cabinets and then rolled into the
only four square inches of carpet from which, I had calculated, there
would be a straight putt to the hole. It was more like snooker than golf but
as I can play neither, it was with a satisfaction difficult to explain that I saw
my putt roll neatly into the hole.

But office golf was not without its hazards. One day, having completed
his round, Norman, a real golfer, forgot where he was and whacked the
ball back to his caddy as he would on the green. It bounced up onto a
desk and smacked into one of the large double-glazed windows with a
sickening crack. We gazed, horrified, as the jagged spider shot out to the
edges of the frame. Like a guilty schoolboy, Norman had to report the
matter to the CIO. I could hear the discussions in the CIO's office.

'Well what did you think you were doing?'

'I forgot where I was, Ray. It can happen to anybody.'

'We'll have to get Maintenance in to repair it.'

'But what shall we tell them? I can't say that I was playing golf.'

'Well, make up a story about falling against the window.'

'They wouldn't believe that. Double-glazed windows don't break like that. It takes a sharp rap.'

'Like from a golf ball?'

'Yeah.'

'Say you knocked a piece of heavy equipment against it.'

'OK, I'll think of something.'

About an hour later I answered the door bell. In the corridor stood two workmen in overalls.

'Come to look at your broken window.'

'Come in. It's straight through into the general office.'

'On the golf course?' the workman said.

Vanessa is the allocator this morning. The hovercraft is grumbling through the western entrance.

'Nikos and Pedro to cars, the rest to feet,' she says.

As far as I know, I don't have a nickname. We grab our stamps and books and clatter off down the stairs. I choose the desk closest to the on-call room because the light is stronger there. Watching the arrival of a hovercraft is fascinating when there is only a pair of double glass doors between you and the craft. It heaves itself off the sea and onto the pad, the engines take on a harsh tone as their sound reverberates inside the blast wall and then the craft continues on towards you. It gets bigger and closer and noisier and still it comes on. Dust and sand are blown sideways from under the skirt. When the superstructure has disappeared above the window frame and your horizon is filled with black, pulsating, shiny wet rubber, the craft suddenly sinks with a sigh of dying engines and deflating skirt onto the concrete. A blue tractor pushes a fan-shaped ramp out to hitch to the stern of the craft and as soon as the craft's bow ramp hits the concrete, a luggage tractor trundles up into the blackness and re-emerges towing the trolleys to the carousels in the baggage reclaim. The steps are wheeled out, the passenger doors, port and starboard, are raised and red-hatted hostesses lead the crocodiles of passengers from each exit down the steps towards the passenger hall where we are awaiting them. The cars drive out of the stern, away towards the sea, to turn 180 degrees around the end of the blast wall and then race down to the kiosks.

THE VIEW FROM MY DESK
Dover hoverport. The hostess, modelling the summer see-through uniform, is opening
the sliding doors to welcome into the immigration hall the passengers who can
be seen disembarking from the hovercraft on the pad.

'How long are you staying in the United Kingdom sir?'

The Malaysian man is in his fifties with a pad of black hair above each ear and a shiny brown pate between.

'Two, maybe three weeks sir.'

'And what do you come here to do?' I have already noted from his landing card that he is a company director.

'I am going to try to sell my rubber bands to your British Post Office.'

Now that's interesting. 'How many do you think you can sell them?' I ask as I stamp his passport.

'They use two million every day. I can sell them billions.'

'You know what the postmen do with the bands don't you? They just throw them away.'

He grins. 'Good,' he says.

It is the third week in September. This is the time when all the foreign university students return to their studies. Soon the desks resound to the impact of stamps on passports interspersed with the funny rattling noise that an IO's finger makes as it sorts through the coloured blocks of wood in the plastic tray to find the appropriate conditional landing stamp. Mingled in with the students is an organised tour group from Thailand. The first IO to get the story shouts it along the line of desks to his colleagues. 'Three days Strand Palace Hotel then Heathrow for Bangkok.' We stamp, we tick boxes, we note passport numbers on landing cards and write unique numbers into passports. We are down to the last few passengers now.

A tall man in his twenties, fair hair, blue eyes, suntanned, wearing an open-necked shirt and jeans and a welcoming, frank smile.

'Hello, how are you today? he says. I ignore the invitation to tell him about my piles.

'How long are you staying here sir?' I open his green South African passport and check his name against his landing card.

'Aaaw a couple more months. I've just been to Paris for a couple of days, you know.'

I check his name in the book. It is not there. I am not surprised.

'And what are you coming here to do?' I have already noticed that he arrived in the UK a year ago at Heathrow, was given permission to stay for six months as a visitor, stayed for five months and three weeks and then embarked through Dover East for a day trip. Upon his return he was given permission to stay for another six months; five months and two weeks of which have now elapsed.

'Aaw just on holiday, you know. Staying with friends and that.'

'You have spent practically all of the last twelve months in the UK now haven't you?'

'On and off, yes.'

'Four days' absence in twelve months is not really a case of, "on and off" is it? What have you been doing here?'

'Just a holiday, you know.'

'Where have you been?'

'I went to Scotland and York.'

'Where do you stay?'

'With my friends in Maidenhead.'

I look at the address on the card. 'Are they British friends? South African friends?'

'No, they're British. Well, he's British you know and she is from South Africa, a long way back. Yeah.'

'Are they related to you?'

'No, not relations, just friends.'

'And how long have you known them?'

'Aaw, some time, some time, you know.'

'And have you stayed with them all the time that you've been in the UK?'

'Yeah.'

'What do you do in South Africa?'

'Advertising.'

'Who for?'

'An agency in Pretoria, you know.'

'And what do you do for them?'

'Aaw I'm in charge of the street advertising, you know? Bill boards?'

'How much leave have you got from your agency?'

'Aaw there'll be a job for me when I get back, that's no problem.'

'How do you support yourself here?'

'What d'ya mean?'

'How do you pay for your food and lodging and travel?'

'Aaw I'm staying with friends, that don't cost me much and I get money from South Africa when I need it.'

'You've got money in South Africa?'

'Aaw yeah, I've got money there, you know.'

'How do you get it when you need it?'

'My parents can wire it over to me.'

'How much money have you got on you now?'

'Not much.' He grins. 'Bought some booze on the hovercraft.' He holds up a plastic duty-free bag.

'Can you show me how much you have please?'

'Sure, sure.'

He puts the bag down and pulls a wallet from his inside pocket. He opens it and shows me the edges of three ten pound notes. But I have noticed the edge of something else tucked in to the fold. It reinforces my suspicion.

'Have you got any baggage?'

'Yeah, one bag.'

'We'll go and get it then.'

There are only three bags left on the carousel. The other two must belong to the other hold-ups who are still being interviewed by my colleagues. I look in his suitcase and then sit him under the watchful eyes of a Hoverspeed hostess whilst I go into the on-call room to inspect my booty. It is very thin but I am fairly confident that it will serve – a small desk diary.

I derive no prurient interest from delving into the sordidness of the lives of others. Daft really, why am I doing this job? Well, not for the entertainment of reading a stranger's innermost thoughts about loved ones or for the juicy details of how many girls he screwed and in what positions. Some IOs become almost orgasmic about the revelations, reading them aloud for their colleagues in the office to guffaw and giggle over. And the women are as guilty as the men. I am just looking for a lead and some evidence.

I find the lead. Woven into the fairisle knit of a busy social life of parties, outings, sports matches and meetings is an intermittent thread of entries composed of times and initials. The times vary from day to day; the initials are either KH' or 'W&H'. Amongst the telephone numbers written at the back of the diary I find, *'The King's Head'* and *'The Waggon and Horses'*.

I dial the number for the King's Head. A man replies.

'Good afternoon,' I say, 'Is Pete on tonight?'

'Pete? No he's got the week off. I think he went to Paris.'

'I'm trying to get hold of him. When will he back at work?'

'Hang on.' I hear the landlord scrabbling through some paper. 'Monday, from seven. You should be able to see him then. It's usually quiet on Mondays but we've got the darts match that night. Pete will be doubling up with Jen in the Public. Do you want to leave a message?'

'No thanks. You've been very helpful.'

'Cheers.'

I dial the Waggon and Horses. They are expecting Pete to run the barbecue on Saturday as usual. He has been doing it now since last summer. It's very popular when the weather is good. I return to my passenger.

'Right sir, could you open your wallet for me again please? There is something in it I would like to look at.' He shrugs and opens his wallet. I tug at the edge of the paper that I had noticed earlier. 'I see you have a prescription here.'

'Aaw yeah, I've got a rash. I had to go to the doctor.'

'This prescription is dated within the last seven days but it does not show you living at the address you have given me.'

'It doesn't?' His surprise is not that convincing.

'No it doesn't.' I show the form to him.

'Aaw now why would he have done that?'

'Well, you must be registered with him at that address. Is that the case?'

'Aaw yeah,' he admits in a show of sudden realisation, 'my friend did the registration for me. He must have put his address instead of mine.'

I look at him and say nothing for a while.

'I think it would be better for you if you told me the truth about what you are doing here.'

'I told you–

'–I mean about working at the King's Head and doing the barbecue at the Waggon and Horses every Saturday.'

He tries a few blustery denials. I just shake my head sadly at him. He eventually admits that he has been working here for nine months, being paid cash in hand; is signed on at a local doctor's on the National Health as a UK resident at somebody else's address; his 'advertising' job in Pretoria was with a bucket of paste and a brush as a bill sticker on a casual daily basis; that he has been supporting himself solely from his earnings; that he knew that he was not allowed to work here and that, really, he did not want to go back to South Africa at all, he wanted to live somewhere in Europe, preferably England. I refuse him entry and send him back to Calais.

We know white South Africans are trying to get out of their country. We have known it for years. Back up in the office the messenger has dropped an envelope on my desk. It is a note from Geoff, the new inspector at Dover East. He wants me to come and see him.

'What time is the next arrival?' I ask Vanessa.

'The *Margaret* has gone tech, so it will be whenever the *Anne* gets back.'

'And she is still on the pad. I've got to nip across to the East.' I wave the note in the air. 'I'll get back before four.'

'Going over for another bollocking are you?'

'Probably.'

'I hear you have been chatting to surveyors,' Geoff says, smiling up from his desk at my astonishment.

How had he found out? Not that it was of any concern of his. It was obvious to me that I was in a dead end job. No skill that I had developed could be sold outside the Civil Service. For the past few months I had been assessing the feasibility of leaving the IS and re-training in another discipline. I could survive on a part time job and my savings whilst I studied.

'Well... um.' I shut his office door and sit down. 'I enjoy being here Geoff, most of the time, but I can't see me doing this for the rest of my life.' His expression changes from one of amusement to one of curiosity. 'I got talking to the surveyor who looked at our house. I'm interested in buildings and he genned me up on building surveying as a career. I've not done anything yet. I've found out some stuff about courses.' His face now reverts to amusement. 'I would have told you before I handed in my notice.'

'I am pleased to hear that.' He is grinning about some private joke. 'But I was talking about customs surveyors.'

'Customs surveyors?'

'Yes – Peter Purdy. You were shouting off your mouth to him one day on walkers about Customs and Immigration not talking to each other.'

'It wasn't quite that. I said that we knew nothing of their work and they probably had some pretty inaccurate ideas about ours. I thought that we ought to tell each other how we worked, that was all. Don't you agree?'

'Yes, that is why I have put you forward for it. Next Tuesday at the Holiday Inn. Peter Purdy will provide a room full of customs staff. You'll have an hour to spill the beans. Tell them what you like. So what will you tell them?'

This was putting me on the spot with a vengeance. 'Well the first thing I would like is to be able to give them a good look at our General Instructions. They know all about regulations. By seeing ours it will help them understand why we sometimes do silly things.'

'You mean, why some of the things that we do, appear silly.'

'No I don't. Some of our instructions are downright idiotic and you know it.'

'Good,' he said. 'Let me have an outline of your talk by Friday.'

The whole pace of my life was about to change.

After I had done the talk to Customs, Geoff then asked me to prepare a training exercise to show the new entrants how to handle casework. He had been amused and instructed by my private casework guide that he had borrowed. I was to construct a training session and deliver it myself. It felt bizarre for me to be picked out for a task such as this. Up until now I had kept my head down and worked. All the applications for special duties that I had made to date had been made partly in the hope that I could get away from this stupid, disruptive shiftworking pattern. It had not been from a surge of ambition – I had no competitive spirit in me.

I had always made myself available to new IOs when they had asked for assistance and I had hoped that perhaps one day I might get onto the training team. Had I been thinking in my own little way that I could make a difference to the manner in which the IS operated? It sounds implausible to me. I think it more likely that I remembered the terror of my probation period when I had had nobody to turn to and subsequently I felt compassion for my neophyte colleagues.

In the past when I had applied for ECO postings or to do training I had been passed over. I had to presume that the officers junior to me who were receiving the attention were performing better than me. I had watched Karl arrive three years after me, get a three month ECO posting to Lagos and upon his return, be seconded to Dover West so that he could train IOs. One of his trainees was a chap called Jolyon Jenkins who completed the training course and then left and wrote a series of revelatory and scathing articles about the Immigration Service for *The New Statesman*. He went on to become a journalist and radio producer. Clever chap.

'Right then, choose a file, any one you like.' The three trainees all lift a pink file from the day's stack in the casework office. They carefully avoid the file which is three inches thick. They are about to learn the first lesson in casework – the thicker the file, the less work there is left to do on it. 'Today, you three are collectively the casework IO. I shall help you to not make too many cock ups.'

They study the files and tell me what they propose to do on them. In the meantime they have to answer the phones and perform all the other minutiae of the task. Janice has transferred down from Lunar House on promotion. She knows all about files and feels quite at home. The other two brave it out. They have just come from their induction course and already they have absorbed the bravado attitude to ignorance that obtains throughout the Service. I listen as they propose disastrous courses of action and then let them carry them out. I am hoping that today they will understand that if they don't know what to do, they must find out, not just guess. They can ask me, they can look in the instructions, they can ask the CIO, but it saves a lot of bother for everybody if they do it correctly the first time and it is a valuable learning exercise for them and an unbeatable confidence builder. At the end of today, they will come out of this office knowing more about casework handling than IOs with five years more experience than they.

They make mistakes. I allow them to develop into the chaos that I can predict and then I step in at the last moment to prevent absolute disaster. Towards the end of the duty they are discussing cases amongst themselves, coming to a consensus on the correct action and then trying to confirm that it is correct before initiating it. This is tremendous progress in the space of five hours. They are teaching each other but they don't realise it.

Janice answers the phone and her face jerks into shock. She covers the mouthpiece with her hand.

'It's Alex Lyon,' she hisses. 'He's making reps.'

Alex Lyon is a Labour MP. I have a vague idea that he was a Home Office minister when I joined the Service in 1974. I admit that I am really not interested in politics or politicians. An MP making representations on a case invokes a bizarre kow-towing by the IS. As soon as the phone call is received, we have to suspend all action on the file until the written representations are received. Needless to say, MP's reps are usually invoked at the last minute; when we have done all the work, when the subject has been proven to have no claim to remain here and when we have made arrangements for them to be removed from the UK. By stopping the process at this stage, it costs the country the most money possible.

I glance across at the casework board. We have five cases which have been suspended whilst awaiting MP's reps. On one of them we have been waiting for the written reasons for over eight months and nothing has been forthcoming. In the meantime we have to extend to the subject a temporary permission to stay, periodically renewing it after each check which confirms that the 'reps' have not arrived. The Home Office cannot force the MPs to submit their representations within a specific time because they have omitted to state in their guidance notes what that time period should be. And so the MPs procrastinate and we extend permissions to stay. I recall an IO, Reg Toale who once remarked, 'How can an Anatolian hill farmer in Turkey be represented by a British Member of Parliament? Did he vote for him?' I could see his point. The man was not in his constituency, he had not voted for him, why was the MP claiming to represent him? I didn't see much of Reg but whenever he popped up, he always seemed to be saying something pointed.

'That's no bother, Janice, ask him whom he is making reps on and then find the file.'

She does and then I watch her fluster as the state of the file obstructs her progress. She is turning over minute sheets and folding back duplicate forms in an attempt to find the answer to the MP's question. When she has finished I point out to the three of them that all that bother had been caused by the failure of several of their more senior colleagues who had preceded them on the file and who had not done their work properly. The lesson is well learned. There is nothing like a jolly good dose of fear to engrave an argument into somebody's memory.

I finish the session with some conjuring tricks to underline the importance of the minutiae. The trainees have been writing interim progress on scraps of paper and attaching them to the fronts of the files with paper clips so that casting an eye over a fan of seven files laid out on the desk will tell you immediately the state of play on each. I pick the files up casually one at a time, as one would do when working and when I replace them, the notes have changed places. It is so easily done. If you have to attach a note to the front of a file, use a pin, of the nickel plated variety as supplied for the purpose by the Stationery Office. Paper clips can migrate to other files.

Passports if kept in a file should be placed in a securely closed document envelope and laced into the file. I show them something on a file, put the passport back in the envelope but put it unattached in the file and then replace the file in the bookcase. A few minutes later I ask one of them a question, the answer to which can only be found by looking at the passport. He takes out the file. The passport is not there. They are nonplussed. They saw me put it there. 'Look in the rubbish bin,' I say, and there it is. It was a simple sleight of hand to hold the file vertically and allow the envelope to slip silently from the bottom and into the bin below the bookcase. It sounds silly. It's play acting. But it does happen. Passports get lost. They can disappear into thin air if one is careless. I know that I am not doing this training from a sense of magnanimity – it is pure self-interest. If I can teach these IOs how to do the job properly then perhaps it will make my life easier.

I used to be able to read two or three books a week whilst sitting at the desk, waiting for passengers. Now my time is absorbed in working out timetables for training and designing exercises. But I still have the opportunity for some interesting encounters on the control.

One day a saloon car pulls up at my kiosk having just disembarked from France and a woman hands me three British passports. Her husband is driving, she is in the passenger seat and sitting in the middle of the rear seat is her mother. She is fast asleep with her head tilted back on the parcel shelf and her mouth wide open. They have made her comfortable by wedging her in with bags and cushions. A blanket is on her lap. I check the passports, the mother is in her eighties. I am about to hand back the passports when I pause. The woman freezes in terror; the husband gazes through the windscreen in a good imitation of unconcern. How has her mother managed to fall into such a deep sleep in the journey from the ferry to my kiosk? I wonder whether to ask them to wake her up so that I can check her face against the photograph in her passport but I don't – because I know she is dead. Her skin is yellow. She is motionless. She is not breathing. The bags have been placed there to hold her in position. The blanket was used to cover her over in the ferry. She obviously died on holiday and they have decided to get her back to the UK without French interventions. I hand back the passports and let them go. Why complicate everybody's lives?

When I was a boy all my mates were mad about cars. We would sit at a cross roads and test each other.

'What's that coming?'

'Hillman Minx.'

'No, it's a Hillman Super Minx.'

'All right then, what about that black one?'

'Daimler Conquest.'

'No, it's a Lanchester.'

'But it looks just like a Daimler Conquest.'

'Daimler bought them out.'

'Vauxhall Cresta.'

'You sure it's not a Wyvern?'

Occasionally we would do the same at night. The Wolseleys were easy because they had illuminated badges on the radiator. The Jaguars had sidelights still mounted on the top of the wings and headlights quite close together. The Land Rover had them really close together between prominent mudguards.

Riding at the front of the top deck of a bus in Rickmansworth with my chum one day I called out, 'Cor look at that. What is that?'

It was large and dark brown and had double headlights.

'It's a Mk10 Jag with no radiator grille.'

'No it's not. The headlights are not right. And the Jag is bulbous at the side, that car is flat.'

We argued and argued as boys do. Two years later I recognised the Rolls Royce Silver Shadow the moment it was shown. What we had seen was one of the trial vehicles – obviously minus its distinctive grille.

On the Sunday before Rover released their Rover 2000 TC, I saw a dark green Rover coming down Chesham high street.

'What's wrong with that Rover 2000?' I said.

'Nothing, he hasn't closed his bonnet properly that's all.'

'But the bonnet is higher. It's got an extra strip of aluminium along the top of the grille.'

'No, that's because it's not shut.'

As the car went past, we saw that it had the chrome letters 'TC' on the bonnet but when the Rover 2000 TC was announced in the press on the folllowing Monday, I insisted that this was not the car we had seen. And I was right. I had spotted a car testing the Rover three and a half litre V8 engine but disguised as the new 'TC'.

When studying at college I found two versions of the not-yet-released Hillman Avenger parked behind a pub by the Tinsley Viaduct near Rotherham. Their shape had been disguised with cardboard fins which had been taped on and sprayed over. What has all this got to do with my life in the IS, I hear you ask?

Well, I was sharing a car kiosk one day when my colleague pointed out the strange looking car which was approaching him. It was a limousine-sized saloon in a dull dark blue with a simple metal grille. The body had no brightwork on it and the front and rear ends had been very stylishly camouflaged with some excellent cardboard work. He tried to get the occupants to divulge what it was but the driver just smiled pleasantly so he peeked at the steering wheel boss to see if there was a badge engraved on it. No, it just had a nut. As he handed back the two British passports I called across to him.

'It's a Rolls Royce.'

The driver's eyelids flickered. 'Why do you say that?' he asked.

'It's a bit obvious isn't it – using 1900 TU as the registration number? You either use that or 100 LG on test cars.'

His face was a picture. My schoolboy car-spotting years had not been spent in vain.

Not all drivers find our chatty observations to their liking. Long before BMW had ever made a diesel-engined saloon car, I had one such vehicle pull up at my kiosk. It was big and new and shiny, as BMWs tend to be but the characteristic rattle of a surprisingly unrefined diesel was emanating from under the bonnet. I had to show that I had discovered their secret.

'I didn't know that BMW made a diesel,' said I, airily.

The driver scowled at me. 'They don't,' he said through gritted teeth. 'Is there an AA office in the docks?'

That was an unfortunate and erroneous deduction on my part, delivered with an innocent conviction – unlike the waspish jibe levelled by one of my colleagues. The proud driver of a brand new Ford arrived at Mike Conatty's kiosk one day having managed on the first day of the new registration number to not only take delivery of his new car but also go to Calais on a day trip and return so that all could see it. It was some feat, only slightly tarnished when Mike handed back the passports, ran an appraising eye over the gleaming Ford Granada and remarked, 'A Dagenham Dustbin, they look quite nice before they start to rust don't they?'

How did he get away with it?

We often see enormous motor caravans, built on the American scale, which lumber through between the kiosks. Some are the size of small trucks with twin rear axles and with a motor bike hauled up onto a platform at the rear as if it were designed to be used as a life boat. A smaller version of one such vehicle came to me one day and I was chatting as I stamped the passports of the two middle-aged American gentlemen who were coming on a business trip. Somehow, I cannot remember how, the conversation came around to insurance and they divulged that the vehicle was insured for four and a half million dollars. I thought I had misheard.

'It's because of the equipment built into it,' he explained. 'For the business. It's the prototype demonstrator of a satellite navigation system. This vehicle knows where it is on the earth's surface to within one metre.'

'You're joking.' I would not believe that.

'No, it's true. It would register a different location if I pulled forwards to that line there.'

I eventually believed him, however fantastic it seemed then. I could not imagine that twenty years later such systems would be standard fixtures on many new cars. It's lucky that we don't have to insure them for four and a half million dollars.

Almost before I could draw breath from writing an assessment of the casework training days that I had provided, my team leader CIO told me that I was to design a consolidation course for IOs coming off their two year probation. There would be three groups of six officers and I would have to exercise each group for a week. My working life suddenly became a turmoil of challenges ranging from, 'how do I find out what they need to know?' to, 'how do I use an overhead projector?' It was an unusual experience to be challenged by the job that I had been doing for over ten years. Looking back I realise that the feeling was both bizarre and unusual for me because for the first time in the Service, I was being 'managed'. Somebody, almost certainly Geoff, had decided that the reason why I was looking for another job was because I was being under-used and unchallenged in my current occupation. He gambled that with but a little encouragement I would make a greater effort and would generate substantial benefits for all. But my entry in the book of posterity of the Immigration Service was entirely unforeseen by me, although many would propound that it was absolutely true to type.

Part of the visit to ISHQ that I arranged for my three groups was a coffee chat with one of the assistant chief inspectors, Mr. Smith. He sat at the top of the table, I sat at the bottom and the IOs sat three down each side. It was a Big Chief and some little Indians and they were suitably impressed and flattered when he brought them what was on his desk for the day and asked them how we should deal with it. This was Monty asking the advice of the Desert Rats on how to take Tobruk. It was an inspiring process for now they were dealing with the policy and decision making from the other end.

'Right then, at half past eight last night a Nigerian lady with a nine year old child landed at Heathrow Terminal Three. She installed her daughter in the lounge and then got back on the plane and returned to Lagos. What do we do with the girl?'

'Send her back,' was the quick response.

'How? She has no passport.'

'Where is she now?' one of the women asked.

'Good,' Mr. Smith said. 'That is what we need to think about first – her welfare. She is nine years old and alone in a foreign country. At the moment she is being looked after by a chaperone but what power have we to detain her? Who should provide for her maintenance? And at some stage we must establish her immigration status and decide what to do with her.'

And so the discussions continued. Having arranged the meeting, my presence was superfluous but I attended because I was interested to see what advantage they derived from the interchanges. I made a point of not taking an active part – this was their course, not mine. I tended to let my mind wander whilst maintaining an outwardly interested demeanour. On this particular day I must have been deeply immersed in that alternative world which lurks within one's head and seeps into one's consciousness when one is not actively engaged. Up the table they had reached the point where two IOs both knew the answer to a problem but when they tried to explain it, the key word kept escaping them.

'Oh it's... er... Oh I know what it is but... um... You know...'

'Yes, I know what you mean it's the... it's the... Oh...'

They stalled. I was suddenly awoken from my reverie by a wryly amused Mr. Smith who addressed me. 'What was that comment Martin?'

My gaze travelled up the perspective of the table where seven faces were turned towards me, wearing various expressions of astonishment. Oh bum, I thought, I must have spoken aloud. Oh well, put your money where your mouth is, Martin.

'Oh it's the clitoris factor, Mr. Smith.'

'The clitoris factor?' He repeated. I nodded. 'Explain please.'

I pointed at the two IOs who were searching for the word. 'You know what it is but you can't quite put your finger on it.'

Not much useful discussion ensued after that but the expression itself was rapidly adopted by ISHQ where, I am told, it is still used although I am sure that nobody now remembers who invented it.

But when I was not training or writing guidance notes for various procedures I was stamping passports. Earlier in the year Heathrow had put out an urgent call for relief and I had spent three weeks at Terminal Three. I shall always remember cycling around the perimeter road from the Hatton Cross entrance in the six o'clock gloom of a winter's morning, involuntarily crouching over the handlebars as, with landing lights aglow, the incoming flights lowered themselves onto me. No matter how I timed my crossing of the end of the runway, with an arrival every minute, I could not escape the frightening and oppressive feeling as I looked up at the staircase of three or four airliners waiting to pounce on me. One of them, I knew, was going to get me. What actually did nearly get me was an armoured personnel carrier.

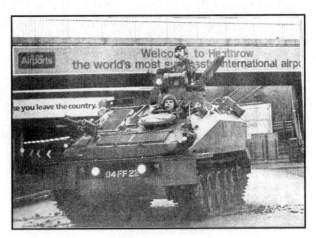

ME VERSUS TANK

The Spartan armoured personnel carrier, complete with 7.62 mm gun, which I bullied on the cycle path.

photo courtesy
Sky Port

The army was running one of their 'routine security exercises' in the airport to reassure the public. Later, we learned unofficially that it had not been an exercise at all but a full-blown operation to stave off an actual terrorist threat but divulging that information to the general public apparently would not have been sensible. As I pounded along the cycle track which led into the service tunnel alongside the carriageway under the runway, I heard a peculiar grating and roaring coming from behind a bush and suddenly the armour-plated nose of a tracked vehicle lurched into view from my left. I blew my horn. When I say 'I blew my horn' I need to qualify that declaration. Having had several near-death escapes from under the wheels of TIR lorries in and around the docks I had firmed my resolve one day and visited our local ships' chandler. There I had purchased a hand-held marine fog horn which was powered by a canister of compressed gas. This contraption I had fitted to the handlebars of my bicycle.

So I blew my horn. The driver, hearing what was obviously a heavy goods vehicle arriving at speed, stamped on the brakes and I scraped through the gap with a thankful wave of my hand.

On my first day on the control, a colleague had taken me into the watch room to introduce me to the duty CIO. It was Bert who had been my mentor when I had first arrived at Dover East.

'Bert, this is–' Bert looked up from his book.

'Hello shit head,' he said.

'Hello turd face,' I replied.

'Oh... er... you know each other then?' my guide observed.

In the corridor we met inspector John who had also been at Dover East. Before my guide could introduce me, John laughed and said, 'I see they're sending all the rubbish up from Dover East.'

'Yes,' I agreed, 'I notice that you got here before me.'

'Do you need me any more?' my guide asked, rather superfluously.

I also spent a month across the bay at Dover West. It was like returning to the prehistoric swamps. The staff seemed more jaded and world weary than before. A sense of a creeping doom pervaded the atmosphere. Rumours were afoot that Sealink were going to pull out of the port; that the rail service was going to be axed.

The offices were drab and reeked of pipe and cigarette smoke. The toilets smelled like toilets. The port was used for induction training of new IOs for our district. This meant that, unlike my generation, they gained no experience of working in an airport. Few of the recruits wanted to be posted to the West. It seemed to be dying on its feet.

This did not affect the enthusiasm of the diehard regulars for the work. They were on God's earth to knock off any passenger that moved. When listening to IOs referring cases to CIOs I felt uneasy at the one-sided arguments often presented, laden with presumed guilt and which were accepted with a nod by complacent CIOs. It fitted the port's image: no duff passengers got through Dover West. They were hardline. I could not subscribe to their head-hunter mentality. It seemed to me that if you were unable to refuse a passenger because the rules did not allow it then bending the rules was not the solution. I should have realised that merely by entertaining that thought I was walking on thin ice.

One day a battered blue Ford Transit minibus crawled off the ferry. On the roof an enormous metal cage had been bolted and into it, oddly shaped bundles and great plastic drums had been lashed. The latter contained cooking oil. Customs began stripping the bus down and we got stuck into the Turkish passengers who had driven from Cyprus.

There was a sprinkling of returning UK residents, whom we dealt with fairly quickly, and then an assortment of others. I interviewed a young Turkish man who, along with several relations, was coming to the UK to attend a wedding. He had the invitation with him and plenty of money, he had a job to return to and was expected at the house where he was going. I would have been surprised if the circumstances had been otherwise for the Cypriots usually get themselves organised.

I was unprepared for the mental assault that I was subjected to by my colleagues whilst we were tidying up our paperwork afterwards.

'How can you justify that landing?' a furious IO stood over me and spat the question at me.

'What do you mean? He was going to a wedding.'

'They always say that. They're knock-offs. A young Turkish Cypriot male? Stone cold knock-off.'

'Who is?' another asked as he came into the office.

'Lloyd's passenger.'

'Oh yeah I saw that one. I was playing the queue for him.'

'But he landed him!'

'What?' The newcomer actually stopped in his tracks and turned to me. 'You landed him? You landed him? He was a bloody knock-off. What were you playing at? This isn't Dover East you stupid ponce.'

I wanted to come back with a stinging retort. I wanted to fling a scorching insult at him. I wanted to punch his face. I just sat there and looked at him. I had obviously blotted the Dover West copybook by landing somebody whom they would have refused.

You find your entertainment where you can. For me, it has often come from the passengers. They do such weird things and sometimes can be made to behave in extraordinary manners. The embarkation control point was three massive wooden desks set athwart a long tiled corridor which ran along the inside of the main station building. Through the window we could see the quayside laced with rails and straddled by cranes and alongside this massive granite wall lay the ship whose passengers we were to embark. This was very much a maritime port. The ships were within spitting distance, and the gulls, bombing distance; the green sea sometimes crashed over the wall and the IOs were all proper men. At Dover East, the spanking new passenger hall had been opened and it made the port look even more like an air terminal. If we stretched on tip toe we could sometimes see the tip of a ship's funnel over the roofs of the lorries but the sea we never heard nor saw.

Whilst the level of traffic at the East meant that embarks was manned continuously day and night; at Dover West the IOs went down to do the embarks once they had finished the landing. You sat on your stool at the desk and waited. The SB officer would be trying to do the crossword behind you and the Sealink man would be wandering up and down with his walkie talkie clamped to his ear. Suddenly he would say, 'Right y'are,' and with a clang and a rattle, the metal concertina door at the far end of the corridor would be pulled, screeching along the metal runners and in

THE VIEW FROM MY DESK
Looking seawards up Admiralty Pier from the car kiosks at Dover West.
The bizarre construction on the left with the covered walkway leading to it from the
side of the Marine Station is the pontoon onto which the Jetfoil passengers alight.

would pour the eight hundred passengers, hot-foot from the train and every one intent on being the first person up the gangplank.

They would spill into the corridor, some outwardly running with their rucksacks bouncing on their shoulders; luggage trolleys would be wielded like battering rams. *Dung-dung, dung-dung, dung-dung,* the wheels would thud over the floor tiles. It was quite a spectacle.

One day as I approached the empty desks at the start of my duty I mused that the set-up looked like one of those optical illusion drawings of M. C. Escher. We had tall brickwork with high arches near the roof. The floor was tiled with cream tiles, the perspective of the long corridor being accentuated by the black mortar. It just needed one of those never ending staircases and a perpetual waterfall to complete the picture. As I walked I stumbled slightly and realised that there really was an optical illusion at play. The visual dominance of the lines of tiles disappearing into the distance disguised the fact that the floor was not flat – it was a series of transverse troughs where the floor had sunk between the girders supporting it. This might explain why some people had problems pushing the trolleys in a straight line.

I stood chatting to the SB officer whilst we awaited the unleashing of the hordes. I looked up. We were to have ultra-violet lamps fitted to the desks so that we could detect forgeries. In order to feed the electricity to the desks, a rubber cable ending in a huge rubber waterproof socket had been run down from the ceiling to each desk. Dover West is a railway station. The ceiling is very high. I took hold of the rubber socket hanging just above my head and gave the cable a swing. It swept out towards the wall, paused and then returned, swishing past me like a stately pendulum to its furthest extent in the other direction. Amused by this, I set the other two in motion.

'Oh stop, you're making me feel dizzy,' the SB officer complained.

That gave me an idea. The doors were rattling open, I could hear the hubbub beyond. I grabbed the pendulums and reset them, swinging in unison. With a rush the vanguard of embarking passengers invested the hall. I jumped behind my desk, and imitating the cables swishing above my head, I began to sway in the contra-direction. I could only imagine what the experience was like for the front rank. They were charging down a long corridor pushing wobbly wheeled luggage trolleys but for some reason these were lurching up and down although the floor appeared flat and when they tried to steer by fixing on a target ahead they found three swaying one way and one the other. They were charging towards me like the chariot race in Ben Hur. They lost it. With a lurch, one trolley veered into another, a Samsonite bounded off and went slithering down the tiles like a piece of wet soap on the bathroom floor; somebody tripped over a suitcase that was being towed along. More trolleys crashed into the pile-up. It was chaos.

'You did that,' the SB officer accused me.

'Not me guv. It's all in the mind.'

I wonder whether it was because Dover West IOs still did 'crossings' that they maintained their communal belief that they were the real IOs doing the real job. A 'crossing' in Immigration Service terminology is where the IO boards the ship at his home port, sails in it to the foreign port and then inspects the passports on the return journey. The most coveted crossings were those between Southampton and New York on the 'Queens' – the *Queen Elizabeth* and the *Queen Mary*. The journey out took four days during which time the IO had nothing to do but enjoy the luxury of his first class cabin and meals in the main dining saloon.

Lee, who had formerly worked at Southampton recounted how on several occasions he had been flown out to Gibraltar to work the cruise ships home on their final leg. He also told me an amusing story about an IO manning the shore control where the disembarking passengers were checked to make sure that they had seen the IO during the crossing. An American youth came off the *s.s.Queen Elizabeth* which had just sailed up the Solent, past the oil refinery and other industrial eyesores. He dropped his passport onto the desk of the soberly dressed, middle-aged IO, looked around him at the peeling paint and endeared himself to his travelling companions by observing in a loud voice, 'Gee, Southampton really is the ass-hole of Europe.'

'Just passing through are you sir?' the IO responded.

The organisation at Dover was, perforce, more prosaic as I was to find out. For my crossing, I was paired to a local IO, Mick, whose job it was to show me the ropes. The first ninety minutes of the duty were spent across  the road, drinking in the Cinque Ports. I opted out of this and occupied my time in getting my book up to date. We then had to present ourselves at a grubby little kiosk inhabited by an employee of Sealink, the ferry company, where we signed a piece of paper, the import of which I never deduced and were given the sum of one pound. This pound, Mick instructed me, was to be laid at the side of our plates in the restaurant on the outward journey because a civil servant could not claim tips as expenses and the waiter would expect a tip. The fact that we were not paying for our meal was irrelevant.

We then took our positions on the desks in the Dover Marine station and embarked the passengers for our ship as they poured out of the trains from London. Once the embarkation was terminated, we boarded and went straight to the restaurant. Whilst eating our free meal the steward would come and take our orders for duty-free spirits to be supplied at crew prices from the captain's bond. Mick was overjoyed to discover that I was a teetotaller with no interest in buying duty-free whisky and so he ordered twice his Customs allowance; only grumbling later when he discovered that I had stupidly filled my official case with official stuff to help me do the job. You were supposed to throw out your General Instructions to accommodate the bottles and baccy.

The outward journey to Dunkirk was uneventful and boring. I had omitted to bring a reading book with me. Dunkirk at one o'clock in the morning is black and bleak. With the usual crashing and shouting and banging and screeching the ship docked and the bars and decks emptied as the passengers scuttled ashore. We were alone on a ghost ship with just the French crew ambling around in a pretence of clearing up. When the first passengers made their way up the gangway, we went below to our control accommodation. This was situated in the bowels of the ship, near the waterline. It was a corridor with a high counter running down one side and a doorway at each end. The principle that the passengers entered through one door and exited through the other was sensible and practical but the result for us was that for four hours both doorways were blocked by queuing bodies and we stewed in a fug of diesel fumes, cooking odours, vomit smells and sweat.

When we wished to detain a passenger we simply impounded their passport and told them that we would see them at Dover. They could not get away from the ship. When it did at last appear, the steely grey sky over Dover was never a more welcome sight for me but any thought that my job

THE VIEW FROM MY DESK

The Sealink Ferry, *St.Eloi*, being pumped up in the ferry dock, Dover West.

was over was soon dashed when I realised that we were a train ferry and had arrived in the ferry dock at Dover. This had been built for the train service to the Continent and was an enormous lock. On the lock side was the pump house which, according to the state of the tide, raised or lowered the level of the water so that the rails on the ship's train deck would match up with those on the link span on the dockside. The tide was quite low when we arrived so with the prospect of another thirty minutes pumping before anybody could disembark, we had to keep on working.

And once we got off we were pounced upon by the early IOs who were just begging for knock-offs. They shared out the impounded passports and grabbed their owners as they appeared. When I crawled into bed later that morning, I was exhausted.

The P&O Jetfoil service to Ostend that I had dealt with in St. Katharine's

Dock when I was at Adelaide House in London had been withdrawn but
Belgian Marine had leased two of the Boeing craft to run a fast service to
supplement their conventional ferries which already ran between Dover
and Ostend. To facilitate this, they installed a pontoon against the quay at
Western Docks, alongside which the craft could dock and in which the
passengers could be processed. It was simply an old ship with the bow and
stern cut off. The inside was arranged for the handling of baggage and
passengers.

It is towards this that I am walking now, in the company of Barry who is
going to the car kiosk.
'I've not seen you around for a while Barry,' I say.
'No you haven't. I've been on annual leave.'
'Oh, did you go away?'
'What I do on my annual leave is no business of yours.'
I grin at his joke. It isn't a joke. He is Scottish and means it. I shrug and
decide not to speak to him again. Ever. I climb up the gangway and
descend the stairs to the control area below deck. I chat to the SB officer
and the hostess. Neither of them tell me that what they do on their
annual leave is none of my business. The Jetfoil curves in through the
western entrance and glides to a halt alongside. I have every admiration
for the crew on these craft. Young ladies in tight skirts and court shoes
secure the craft to the pontoon and usher the passengers ashore. They
look for all the world like simple hostesses but the care of the passengers
is only part of their skills. They are fully registered able seamen, capable
of all work. Once, when I was on a trip to Ostend, the Jetfoil suddenly lost
power and came off its foils to bob on the water in the middle of the
Channel. One of these supposed 'hostesses' made an announcement over
the tannoy and then put on a hard hat, protective gloves and boots and
lifted up an inspection hatch in the floor of the cabin. To the passengers'
astonishment, she grabbed a selection of tools and descended the ladder
into the darkness to effect the repair or adjustment that was necessary.
They must have different trade unions in Belgium.

The two other IOs have joined me now and the passengers are coming
up the escalator. There is a mixture of Belgian businessmen, well-to-do
tourists and backpackers who have travelled from Brussels on the train to
Ostend with onward tickets to London. We settle down to the work.

A black passport with pale yellow pages. A Sri Lankan. He speaks
English. I see from his passport that he has been in Belgium for over a
year.

'Where do you go in England?'

'London. Bayswater Hotel.'

'Have you been here before?'

'No, first time.'

'Why do you come here? What will you do here?'

'Three days sightseeing. St. Paul's Cathedral, Buckingham Palace.'

'Do you have any family here?'

'No, no family.'

'Any friends here?'

He hesitates. 'Not me.' He points to another Sri Lankan being interviewed by one of my colleagues. 'He has friends here.'

'But you don't know anybody here?'

'No, not me.'

'What country do you live in?'

'Brussels.'

'How long have you lived there?'

'Year and a half.'

'What do you do there?'

'Hotel. *Plongeur.*'

I know that this is the washer-up in the kitchen. Had he come from Sri Lanka to wash dishes in a hotel? Sri Lanka was a country which exported manpower, mostly illegally.

The CIO is hovering behind me. I had thought that Bill Ventian at the East was an old lady; this one was a nagging old lady. He worries you and worries at you until you do what he wants. He nods towards the other Sri Lankan.

'These two are together,' he says.

'Yeah, I know thanks.'

'Well, David is detaining his. They are together.'

'OK.'

He walks away, satisfied. I look at the passport. It shows that the Belgian authorities know that the passenger is in their country and that they have given him a permission to stay longer. I think I know why.

'Have you applied for political asylum in Belgium?'

'Yes, political asylum.'

'Has it been granted?'

'They said I can stay.' He points to the Belgian temporary residence stamp in the passport.

'Was asylum refused to you? Have you any papers about this?'

He shows me his return rail/jetfoil ticket and his hotel voucher. He has thirty pounds on him. He does not really know whether the decision on his asylum claim has been made yet. The suggestion from the stamp in his passport is that the Belgians have refused it but given him permission to stay anyway.

'You are away from your job for four days. How can you do this? Don't they need you?'

'It is long holiday in Belgium for the queen. Restaurant is closed.'

I stamp his passport, giving him permission to stay for a month. I take the next passengers from the queue. They are an American couple who had believed the travel agent when he had told them that this was the quickest way to travel from Brussels to London. They are regretting it and the size of their suitcases. We carry on working through the queue. As I land the last two Belgian businessmen, the CIO comes over.

'Where is your hold up?'

'I haven't got one.'

'What did you do with the Sri Lankan?'

'I gave him a month.'

'But David is refusing his.'

I turn to look at him full in the face. 'Yes?' I say.

'Well don't you want to refuse yours?'

'I've landed him.'

'We can get him back off the train. It's still in the station.'

'Do what you like. I've landed him.' I pack up my stuff and hurry through the door behind me to start the embarkation. When I have nearly finished the CIO comes in.

'We've got him. We've got him,' he says. He is triumphant.

'Got who?'

'Your Sri Lankan. You can come and re-examine him.'

'He's not my Sri Lankan. I landed mine. He's your Sri Lankan. I'm going up to the office.'

So he got a local IO to revoke my landing stamp in the passport and refuse the passenger. I have no idea on what grounds. I was so disgusted with the whole affair that I took no further interest in it. What was the point of having relief staff in your port to assist you if you reversed their decisions and made more work for yourself? I suppose that question has answered itself. Without the work created by the high refusal rate, the port would have had difficulty in justifying the staffing levels that it enjoyed. But it was more insidious than that. Was I so out of touch with the requirements of the job? Dover West obviously thought so. Who else shared their opinion?

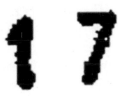

Out in the big wide world of which I took scant notice, things were happening which would eventually impinge directly upon my life. At Dover East we got annoyed every time an MP phoned up to make representations on a case but down on the south coast the problem was very small fry. The majority of cases upon which MPs made reps were from the Indian sub-continent. Along with democracy, imperial Britain had given India a civil service and by golly they were now going to show us with a vengeance that they knew how to use one.

We were 1,278 IOs in the Service and in the previous year we had dealt with 37.5M. people arriving. Of those, we refused entry to about 22,000. The five most refused nationalities were Bangladeshi, Indian, Pakistani, Nigerian and Ghanaian. Half of the country's IO complement worked at Heathrow Terminal Three and it was to this port that the majority of these nationalities arrived. And it was from here that most of them absconded.

The procedure was fairly standard. The IO refused the person admission to the UK and directed his removal. The passenger's sponsor in the UK, be it family, friend or agent, would telephone his MP and ask him to intervene. The MP contacted the Home Office and the IO was directed to give the person temporary admission whilst he awaited the written representations from the MP. By the time these arrived, weeks later, the passenger had ceased to report weekly to the police station to which he had been directed. He was no longer traceable. He had absconded.

Last year (1985) 255 absconded from Terminal Three and ninety nine of those were on MP's 'reps'. By June this year, 269 had already absconded. The Press put pressure on Douglas Hurd, the Home Secretary, to clear up the 'scandal' so David Waddington, the Home Office minister, stood up in the House of Commons and accused twenty three MPs of abusing the system and said that he was considering bringing in a visa requirement for these five nationalities.

Now what effect do you think such a pronouncement would produce in those countries?

But down at Dover East, we were making cinema. Frederick Forsyth and Elstree Studios were going to spend a day shooting the immigration and customs controls for the film *The Fourth Protocol* starring Michael Caine and Pierce Brosnan so Geoff appointed me as the Immigration Service liaison officer for the day. I had already some experience of amateur film and theatricals and knew that the one activity which could be guaranteed would be: waiting. I got permission to park my car in our pound so that I would have a base to retire to when not needed. Not for me the standing around in a duffle coat. Not that I possessed a duffle coat.

The DHB had cordoned off one half of the vehicle lanes through our control points so that the cinema activity would not interfere with the normal traffic of the day. Fourth Protocol Films had advertised in the local press for film extras who were requested to turn up with a car and a passport.

Under the canopy were parked two enormous generator lorries which supplied power to a battery of lamps the size of wartime searchlights. These threw a cold, early morning light onto a customs search bench which they had moved out from inside the shed so that they could work in the open where they had more space to manoeuvre. The famous VW camper van was already in position. This was the vehicle in which an important part of the nuclear warhead was to be smuggled.

I introduced myself to a wiry young lady who was the director for the day and told her that I would be sitting in that car over there when she wanted me. She thanked me and gained my immediate devotion by leaping onto her racing bike and pedalling three hundred yards down to the camera to talk to the men there. I sat in my car and listened to the radio. Eventually they reached the bit where the cars were to pass through the passport control. I accompanied her to one of our control booths which had been allocated to them.

'What would you like from me then?' I asked.

'Can you show me what you would do when a car pulls up?'

'OK.' I mimed taking a passport through the guichet, looking up the name in the book, asking at least one question, stamping the passport and returning it.

'Got that?' she asked the chap standing at the side of her. He nodded. 'OK. Take position.'

I relinquished my chair and stood at the back of the kiosk; he sat down; the director sprinted off to the camera. I looked up the car park. Over on the right, three lanes of cars from the Zeebrugge arrival were being ushered to the passport control by a solitary penguin. In front of me, two lines of locals in an assortment of vehicles were awaiting the signal to start under the caring attention of no fewer than five DHB marshals, standing in echelon up the queue so that each one enjoyed an unobscured view of the camera. Oh the vanity!

The signal was given, the cars were unleashed, the actor handled the passports through the window as I had shown him. After about five minutes the director's minion turned up.

'You'll have to do it quicker,' he instructed the actor. I said nothing. It was their film, not mine.

The cars were reversed up the lanes to their starting positions. The passengers from Zeebrugge goggled at them in incomprehension. The walkie talkie crackled and up came the cars again. The first passport was proffered. The actor snatched it through the window as if he had a vacuum cleaner up his sleeve. He was on the fourth car when the minion arrived.

'It needs to be quicker. We'll put somebody outside to hand you the passports.'

That will only slow it down, thought I, but I said nothing. The cars reversed up the car park. The penguins adjusted their caps and made sure that they were in a good light. The first car could not approach near enough because of the person who had been posted outside the kiosk to hand in the passport. Eventually the passport was passed across, fumbled into the other hand and then thrust through the window where it practically bounced on the desk before being returned. The car crawled away. The next one drew up.

'Got a better idea,' the minion said. 'Why don't they just hold up the passports as they drive by?'

It was an ironic prophecy. Nobody could guess that within five years, this would be exactly our way of working. What was obvious to me was that I was no longer needed. They were not looking for authenticity. It did not bother me. I accept cinema for what it is: a fiction.

The following day we received a letter from the director, Timothy Burrill, thanking us on behalf of Freddie Forsyth for *'our extraordinary effort and cooperation'* and disclosing that he *'had seen the material that we shot this morning and it appears quite excellent.'* Needless to say, none of it was used in the film.

Whilst we were bumbling along at the seaside, Terminal Three was swamped by the extra arrivals as the nationals of the five countries that David Waddington had threatened with visas all rushed to the UK to try to beat the deadline. On one single night, the eleven IOs on duty had to deal with a jumbo-load of Bangladeshis as the Bangladeshi airline Biman cashed in on the crisis with an extra arrival. The majority of these people were worthy of full examination and were accorded it as and when the queue advanced. The IOs were still dealing with them in the morning when extra flights from Ghana and Nigeria deposited another five hundred aspiring entrants. These queued right back to the plane. Eventually passengers were being given temporary admission and told to come back the following day for their primary interview. That is to say, they had not yet seen an IO. If you had been let in to the country of your dreams without having to answer one question would you return to the immigration office the following day and risk the officials sending you back?

But that is not the question which is occupying my mind. It is: why has Geoff asked me up to the office to be ready to take a telephone call from ISHQ? What is cooking? Is it more training they want?

No, they want to send me to Dhaka as an ECO. Dhaka is in Bangladesh where everybody speaks Bengali. I have learned Urdu.

'But I applied this year as I have every year and I was not chosen,' I say to the assistant chief inspector.

'Yes but we have just found one more vacancy and your inspector indicated that you would be available. Are you? There is a flight out on Thursday.'

I try for fourteen years to get an overseas posting and when it does come, they expect me to go at two days' notice. It eventually took them eight days to get my flight organised and real brinksmanship was involved. I was informed that a Thomas Cook rep. would get the Bangladeshi visa issued in my passport and hand the latter to me when I turned up for my flight at Heathrow Terminal Four. I had premonitions that this could go nastily wrong.

The lady at the British Airways check-in desk knew nothing about either my passport or the Thomas Cook rep. I loitered. It was early days at Terminal Four and half the check-in desks were still awaiting tenants. Peering into the gloom of the unused and unlit end of the terminal I thought that I could just distinguish a figure. Could it be my rep? It was. She was standing in the dark by one of the empty desks, a long way from the light and bustle where my flight was being checked in.

'I am Martin Lloyd. I hope you have my passport for me,' I said.

'Ah yes, Mr. Lloyd.' Now read this bit carefully: 'Do you have any form of identity on you?'

I looked at her. I looked at my passport in her hand.

'You've got my form of identity. It's my passport. If you turn to page three you will find an unflattering but fairly accurate photographic likeness of me affixed thereto.'

'I can't do that sir.' She shook her head. 'I'm not allowed to check passports.'

I stared at her. I was tempted to grab the booklet and run but I was intrigued by the possibility of the ridiculous and, although I had little time to play with, I decided to push it to see how far it could go.

'How do you want me to prove my identity without my passport?'

'Well, have you anything else?'

'Such as?'

'Your airline ticket.'

'That will not prove my identity will it? It will merely show that some-body with my name has a reservation on the flight.'

'But the ticket would be held by you.'

'It has no need to be. My passport is not being held by me. You are holding my passport but that does not make you into Martin Lloyd. Unless you would like to go to Dhaka instead of me? Do you fancy that?' She did not.

'Well have you anything with your name on it?'

'Ah yes,' I exclaimed and pulled out my spectacles case. 'Look, inside the lid. It says, *'Martin Lloyd'.*'

'Thank you Mr. Lloyd.'

She relinquished my passport.

I checked in.

I boarded the plane.

Bangladesh is the new name for East Pakistan which was created from the Bengal region of India. To explain it in simple terms: in the middle of the Indian sub-continent lived the Hindus and at the east and west edges lived the Muslims. With the partition of the Indian Empire upon independence from Britain in 1948, the Hindu area retained the name 'India' and the Muslim areas on either side became Pakistan – East and West. This worked in a fragile way until 1971 when East Pakistan decided to seek independence from West Pakistan. At the end of a tangled civil war, East Pakistan became the independent Bangladesh – 'land of the Bengalis'.

Britain is represented by a High Commissioner, as Bangladesh is in the Commonwealth. I was seconded to the Foreign Office to work in the

Immigration Section of the British High Commission in Dhaka. It all sounded very grand and I suppose some aspects of it were but the nitty gritty of the work was simply a concentrated version of what every IO does in the UK – interview people. Whereas in one day's work at a port you maybe said one sentence to hundreds and gave an in-depth interview every two or three days, as an ECO – an entry clearance officer – you chatted to nobody but conducted two or three in-depth interviews every day. You would know about these beforehand since the application would have been submitted and the appointment made probably eighteen months earlier. Our job was to try to reduce that waiting list, or so we were told.

The work was divided into 'settlement' – people coming to join members of their family already settled in the UK, and 'visits' – people wanting to travel for other reasons such as holiday or business.

There must have been about twenty IOs seconded to Dhaka, working alongside the handful of Foreign Office grade nines who had failed to swerve around an appointment to the immigration section. Such work was not considered to be a useful career step for a diplomat but they had to succumb to it at some stage so they might as well get it over and done with; rather like measles. When I was in my last year at school I had attended a careers convention run by the Civil Service for the benefit of those who nurtured aspirations in that direction. I had declared an interest in the Diplomatic Service which at that age I could enter as a grade nine once I had acquired the necessary A-levels. Luckily I was utterly discouraged by the vapid recruiter for that department who, after having enthused about her job for fifteen minutes, had only managed to tell me that she sat at a desk and that all the work came in on one side, she dealt with it, and it went out by the other side. And here I was, twenty years later, working as a grade nine equivalent in the Diplomatic Service. It's a funny old life.

Once thrown into the maelstrom with the other IOs, most of whom came from Heathrow, it became immediately apparent to me that I was the odd one out. The office was packed with a turmoil of frantic head-hunters who had been rewarded by the chance of getting three knock-offs a day and a suntan. I had been posted to Dhaka because Geoff had angrily shouted my eligibility down the corridor to the man who takes the decisions at ISHQ. Geoff thought that I deserved recognition for all the training that I had put in at Dover East.

We started work at seven in the morning and finished at two in the afternoon. The heat was stifling in the interview rooms unless you put the air conditioning on, in which case you could hear neither your

THE VIEW FROM MY OFFICE

The locally employed guards
controlling entry to the British High
Commission, Dhaka, Bangladesh.

interviewees nor your interpreters. The latter hated the cooling air as it played havoc with their throats. The temperature as far as they were concerned, was a fact of life. Why try to change it?

An important part of every settlement interview was to establish the family tree of the person sitting before you and then check in the archives to see if we possessed files on any other family members who might have also made applications. By this method one could cross check the claims to family affiliation and immediately establish a doubt when the name of the fourth male child of the father's third brother turned out to be Haroun Miah on one file and Kaboun Miah on the other. I was told that with the extended family system which obtained within the sub-continent, such an inconsistency spelled guilt since all one family would live in its own compound and they would have grown up with each other and know each other well.

The examination process was complicated by the interviewee's dogged determination to give the right answers, whether they were the truth or not. The reasons for our questions made no sense to them; our refusals were supported by logic impenetrable to the Bengali mind. They saw our interrogation as might a child who swatted up for an examination in a subject in which they had little prowess but were determined to master somehow.

Settlement cases could be of a mind-boggling complexity. Imagine this scenario: a young Bengali man arrives in the UK to stay with his uncle. He is given a job in a restaurant and gets permission to stay. He sends most of his wages back to support his extended family in Bangladesh. After a few years, one of his mates at work asks him why he is not claiming tax relief for his wife so he gets a marriage certificate from Bangladesh and mails it to the Inland Revenue who send him some money as a refund. Next year, this fictitious wife has a child, for which he is given the family allowance. The following year it is twins. It is astonishing how common is the incidence of multiple births among those claiming allowances for fictitious families. All is running along nicely. He is earning money and every year his fictitious wife is producing revenue-earning babies.

Then a problem arises. His mother in Bangladesh finds a nice girl for him to marry so he does his duty on his next visit home and they tie the knot. This is fine until he wants his wife to join him in the UK, as she is entitled to and as, almost surely, her family will be encouraging her to, for this could eventually give their side of the family an opening to settle in the UK as dependent relatives.

Now realwife has to get a passport in the name of falsewife. This might present a problem in the UK. It is no great obstacle in Bangladesh. She then applies to the British High Commission for a visa to join her husband but she is almost certainly a virgin. What about all those children that she has given birth to? What can he do about them? Well the obvious answer is to tout around the extended family for a selection of children of roughly the right ages to impersonate the fictitious progeniture and thus get them visas at the same time.

The IO is now confronted with a selection of family members, all pretending to be somebody else, trying to remember their names correctly and mostly able to concur on the composition of the family tree. He interviews them individually and asks them to explain the discrepancies in their accounts. 'Circles in my head' is a common defence. Any disparity between the dates of the husband's visits home to impregnate his fictitious wife and the stated births of the children is explained by the not so uncommon fourteen month pregnancy which apparently occurs in the Indian sub-continent. If this is not believed, then a new birth certificate is obtained showing a more believable date.

If the IO is able to convince the husband that he can prove that apart from the wife, all the others are fraudulent applicants, then the husband is invited to sign a confession which is sent to the Inland Revenue who then try to claw back the money which they had paid out over the years on the non-existent family.

Variations of this fraud are: presenting the death certificate of the false wife to explain the 'second marriage' – this does not threaten the claimed authenticity of the bogus children; and presenting a genuine first wife with her genuine offspring mixed with a selection of other relations who would also like to live in the UK.

And you might get two of these interviews to complete in one morning. The pace of work was breakneck and the pressure to produce refusals was crushing.

For our introductory fortnight, the new arrivals were given the task of completing the reports of the IOs who had finished their turn of duty and had just been posted back to the UK. This produced much head-scratching as we were writing up papers on a case that we had not conducted and about people whom we had not interviewed. On the first file given to me, leaving aside the difficulty of reading the IO's handwriting, he had interviewed three joint applicants on a 'Q&A' basis – question and answer. That is to say, he had put the same questions to each person and recorded their responses in three columns alongside for easy comparison. His interview notes covered forty seven sides of A4 and towards the end, running out of paper, he had gone around again, slotting in questions numbered out of sequence with the main text as and where he could find space. Having sorted that out, it was now my job to justify within the immigration rules, his decision to refuse a visa. I thought it would be difficult but I soon realised that in Dhaka, refusals were easy; justifying the issue of a visa would prove more challenging. I learned from my colleagues that we were not there to issue visas to these 'bogwits' and 'mud-scratchers'; we were there to catch them in their deceits and send them back, empty handed, to their paddies.

The applications for visit visas were processed in a building situated about a quarter of a mile away from the main high commission. This caused me a minor problem one day when, as the last officer, I was detailed to lock up and leave. I cleared the desks and closed the cupboards whilst my colleagues shot off in their cars to the club. One of my responsibilities was to lock the embossing stamp in the safe. The former was a huge cast iron affair which clamped onto the top of a table and, by the process of the operator pulling down a great steel lever, impressed the design which had been engraved on a metal die, through both the adhesive visa sticker and the page onto which it had been affixed. It was an anti-forgery device to prevent naughty people from steaming off the sticker and inserting it into a different passport. When I lugged this inanimate lump in my two hands to the safe I found to my disappointment that some kind officer had already closed the safe and spun the dials. I had not been told the combination of the safe because I would never need to open it. But now I did. The time was a quarter past two and even the main high commission would be closing. I grabbed the phone and dialled the admin officer.

'Malcolm, it's Martin Lloyd. I'm over at visits, locking up and I need to put the embossing stamp in the safe. What's the combination?'

'I can't tell you over the phone. It's not secure.'

'Well can you come over and tell me?'

'No, I can't leave the office. You'll have to come over here for it.'

'I can't, I'm on my own. Everybody has gone.'

'Sorry, I can't dictate it over the phone.'

'But how do I come over to you if I can't leave the office?'

'You'll have to lock up and come over.'

'But I can't lock up because I can't leave the embossing stamp out and I can't put it in the safe because it's locked.'

This exchange was taking on the cadence of *There's a hole in my bucket, dear Lisa.*

'You will have to bring it with you.'

'I can't carry that on my bike, it weighs a ton. I've got nowhere to attach it. Can you send a car for me?'

NOTICE IN THE BRITISH HIGH COMMISSION WAITING ROOM

'No, I'm on my own. You'll have to take a rickshaw.'

I could hardly believe my ears. I hauled the press onto the front doorstep and locked the office. Leaning back to equiponderate the weight of the hated machine which was pulling my hands out of my wrists, I waddled, bent double, to the corner of the road and hailed a cycle-rickshaw. We wobbled off down the avenue with me thinking that, for the sake of security, I was probably committing the most insecure act possible with this valuable piece of equipment. I told the rickshaw wallah to ride through the gates of the British High Commission and right up to the front door. Keeping one hand on the press, I rang the doorbell with the other. Malcolm opened the door wide.

'Come in,' he said.

'No, I'm not dragging this thing inside. You come out.'

'I can't tell you the combination here. The Bangla might hear it.' He nodded at the rickshaw wallah.

'Can't you whisper it in my ear?' This was *Alice in Wonderland* stuff.

'Too risky.' He shook his head. 'Hang on a minute. I'll write it down.' He disappeared inside and then returned with a scrap of paper which he handed to me. 'You'll have to memorise it. I can't let you have the piece of paper.'

I stared at him for a moment, wondering whether he really was taking the piss. He was not. I read the number, committed it to memory and, as he stretched out his hand for the return of the paper, I solemnly screwed it up into a ball, popped it into my mouth, chewed it and swallowed it.

'If the Russians want to analyse my poo, they are welcome to it,' I said.

'I wouldn't put it past them.'

The applicants in the 'visits' section were more varied than in the 'settlement.' Sometimes we would get the Bangladesh Biman air hostesses wanting new visas; other times we would be dealing with a claimed group of ethnic music and dance performers. I wondered what would have been the reaction had we introduced the trade test that we used at Dover East. Some categories of applicants stood no chance at all. Young males intending a tourist visit to London were refused automatically. Sometimes you decorated your interview with a fatuous dismantling of his proposed itinerary. 'Westminster Abbey' – you're a Muslim, what interest do you have in the Anglican church? 'The Underground' – they've got one in Calcutta, why don't you go there? It is cheaper. One day I refused the official photographer accompanying an arts group because he could not tell me what format of photographic film he used in his camera.

Students also had a hard time. In order to qualify for a visa they had to prove that they intended to return to Bangladesh at the end of their studies. If a student applied for a visa for a computer programming course I was told that it was an automatic refusal because, 'there are not any computers in Bangladesh.' I knew this to be false. We had several computers in the high commission and many of the private European firms used computers. The argument built upon this inaccuracy was that since there were no computers in Bangladesh, then a computer student would have no employment prospect at home and would have no incentive to return. I remember this today every time that I take a call from a computer operator at an Indian call-centre.

A biassed and uncompromising attitude pervaded the operation of the immigration section and was fostered by the declarations of one of the second secretaries who was a Foreign Office man, not an Immigration Service CIO. 'A Bangla only takes twenty-seven seconds to copulate,' was one of his snippets. What relevance he thought this had to our work or judgment I was unable to determine. The trouble with Bangladesh, whose mean altitude over a large proportion of its area was about ten feet above sea level was, according to him, that 'it was ten feet too high.' On another occasion he told me that 'fraudulent applicants ought to be put up against the wall and shot.' It was unpleasant and demeaning to have him throw you a file with the observation, 'this bogwit has been refused before, I want him refused again.' The experienced officer was supposed to find an argument to guarantee the desired outcome. It did not matter to the second sec. – he could say and do what he liked. He knew that he would only be in the job for three years before he was moved on elsewhere. It mattered to me.

But all work and no play makes Jack a dull boy. Any newcomer to the closed world of the ex-pats and diplomats was pounced upon and invited to parties and dinners merely for the distraction of having somebody new to talk to. It could be quite flattering if you let your apparent popularity go to your head. But you had to understand the unwritten social protocol. One expression which I encountered was, 'we must invite you round for dinner one day.' This actually meant, 'there is no way we want to see you again.' Once I had deduced the meaning I would put them on the spot by pulling out my diary and saying, 'yes, how lovely, when would be convenient?' This was where I stumbled across the second line of defence: 'I haven't got my diary with me. Give me your telephone number and I'll call you.' These people were hardened professionals in the social guerilla of graces; you could not beat them.

Sipping a lime and soda at the bar of the British Club in the afternoons after work and eavesdropping on the conversations I gradually realised that the Diplomatic Service section of the Foreign Office was one big travel club. The diplomats were paid in the UK where they bought their houses and leased them out to pay the mortgage. As they were based in central London they qualified for the Inner London Weighting supplement to their salaries. When they were posted abroad for periods of three years at a time, they were paid an additional foreign service allowance which was proportional to the perceived hardship of living in that particular country. Their conversations consisted almost entirely of discussing the financial merits of where they had been posted last, where they were at the moment and where they intended to go in the future.

This could have been galling to me had I been in any way sensitive because I had been sent out on a 'six months plus' posting which meant that I could not qualify for the £87 daily subsistence allowance and so was paid the £9 lodging allowance. The argument was that the cost of living in Bangladesh was very cheap. This was true but my financial situation was not helped by the Home Office gleefully stripping me of the various allowances to which I was entitled while working at Dover and the Foreign Office taking three months to dole out the foreign service allowance which should have replaced them. I was left on my basic salary. By the end of my term I had paid £427 above my income for the privilege of working in Bangladesh.

When I had been 'in post' for about three weeks I was summoned, sorry, invited, to a fifteen minute welcome interview with the High Commissioner. I knew it was to be fifteen minutes because his secretary had whispered, 'fifteen minutes' to me as she had shown me in to his office. He chatted about life in Bangladesh and sketched me an outline of how the High Commission functioned and how my being a diplomat should influence my behaviour.

'One piece of valuable advice I can give you, Mr. Lloyd, and that is: do not gossip. There is more harm caused by gossip and rumour in a closed community such as this than you can imagine.' I nodded obediently. He sat back in his chair, the official duty having been done. 'So which terminal do you come from?

'Which terminal? Oh I'm not from the airport. I'm from Dover East.'

'I wasn't aware that we took in immigration officers from the seaports.'

'Oh yes, surely you remember Putka and Philbrow? They came from Dover East. You must have heard of their exploits.'

These two officers had preceded me as ECOs on three-month postings. Happily spending their £87 a day they had distinguished themselves at the British Club bar, organised drunken rickshaw races down Gulshan Avenue and staunchly supported the local 'gay girl' population.

"Well, I will admit that I have not heard about them. Perhaps you should tell me.'

'Well, I would but I don't like to gossip,' I said.

He pressed the bell push on his desk.

I am not a sportsman so I was not dragooned into representing the UK in cricket or hockey matches but apparently I did possess one skill which had been 'noised abroad.' The video recording of the last satirical Christmas revue which I had written and directed at Dover East had been posted out to Dhaka and had done the rounds. They now wanted me to assist them with the revue for the British High Commission New Year's Eve party.

About ten of us met in a room at the club and they threw in ideas and bandied them around the table.

'We could get Steve from Security. He can play the trumpet.'

'Oh yes good idea.'

'And that Dutch wife of the commercial chappy; she does a fantastic belly dance.'

'How do you know?'

'Never you mind.'

'What about Carol and her guitar?'

'What about Christmas Carol and her guitar? We could do a Dickens spoof.'

'That's a brilliant idea.'

'Yes we could pretend the Chancellor was Scrooge.'

'What about Marley's ghost? Who could we pretend that was?'

'The Deputy High Commissioner?'

'Yes, he won't be there. He always goes to Bangkok for Christmas.'

'No it would have to be somebody more lowly than that.'

They were enthusiastic and bubbled on like this for over an hour at the end of which, of course, they had nothing. They looked at me.

'Who is going to write the script?' I asked.

'Well we all are. Together. You'll help won't you?'

'Help with what? I don't know what you want. Neither do you.'

'Yes we do. We are going to do a sort of Dickens spoof Christmas Carol.'

'What with? You have no material.' I thought this observation was accurate unless they had decided that Scrooge would be a Dutch belly dancer with guitar and trumpet accompaniment. They looked at each other, quite perplexed. They had spent an hour in energetic group discussion and thought that they had chosen a story line and a cast and individually they probably had, but there had been no consensus and nobody had actually committed themselves to doing anything. The success of their venture relied upon the participation of people who were not at the meeting and still ignorant of their expected roles. I knew from experience that a script could not be written by a committee. Was this committee a microcosm of how the Diplomatic Service functioned, I wondered? What was needed was a coup d'état. I looked across at Simon. He was the only one with any worthwhile experience on the stage.

'Do you want to work with me on a script?' I said. He nodded. I looked around the table. 'I'll come back in two weeks and if I haven't got a script by then, you can write your Dickens spoof.'

And I won't have anything to do with it, I thought.

Simon was a long-term ECO in the second of his three years in post.

'What is the format of the party?' I asked him.

'They hire a room at the Sonargaon Hotel and have a dinner then we put on a half hour show and then there is a dance.'

'And who comes to it? Is it just high commission staff?'

'No, it's everybody who can get a ticket. British Airways usually have a table for their crew on stopover; the foreign companies have tables. Loads of people come. It's the highlight of the year.'

'So we need to widen the appeal of the show. Pass me over that telephone directory. Greater Dhaka Power Project, Deep Tubewells Project, Ewbanks – let's see if we can get some of that lot a mention.' I knew that it did not matter what you said about people as long as you said something. There was nothing more insulting in a satirical revue than being ignored.

The show was an uproarious success. I wrote a scandalous scenario based around a fictional corrupt commercial attaché who was stealing food from the commissariat and selling it off to locals. I played the part of a Metropolitan Police officer who had been sent out to investigate the thefts; we also had a cannabis smoking deputy vice consul, an illiterate deputy high commissioner; a lecherous secretary and a Bengali sweeper, played superbly by a Foreign Office grade nine. As each character was assassinated, or company ridiculed, jeers and cheers rang around the room. Easily the greatest tumult occurred when the Bengali sweeper offered to procure the services of a prostitute for the deputy high commissioner in the following exchange:

'You want gay girl? Very lovely lady sahib. I've got nice sister.'

'Do you mind? I'm a British diplomat.'

'Oh sorry, sorry sahib. I've got nice brother.'

The laughter and applause could be heard out in the street.

Simon and I had decided to get out of Dhaka for Christmas. Neither of us was particularly religious and the attraction of the traditional singing of Christmas carols on a roundabout in the middle of the Gulshan district of Dhaka where most of the ex-pats lived was not sufficient to stop us from booking a flight to Khatmandu. It was the best Christmas that I have ever had.

On Christmas Eve we were sitting in an earth-floored guest house, eight thousand feet up in the foothills of Annapurna. Our Nepalese hostess had bedded down her children by the embers of the woodfire which were still glowing by the open front of the house. We sat inside at a long wooden table with two Dutch girls and a rather serious American man. All of us escaping Christmas for our own secret reasons. Our Christmas Eve dinner was to be straightforward *dal-bat* which was the universal meal of rice and chick peas into which was thrown whatever protein that could be found.

'We really ought to dress for dinner when in company,' I observed. Simon nodded agreement and we took our bow ties from our pockets and attached them to our collars. 'What do you fancy for starters?' I said. The Dutch girls laughed. The American stared.

'Oh, oysters,' he replied enthusiastically. 'You can't start a Christmas dinner without oysters.'

'Yes, I suppose you are right.' I fished in my rucksack and pulled out a tin of oysters. 'Got a can opener?'

We opened the tin and savoured the oysters. I had discovered this single tin in the commissariat a few weeks earlier and had earmarked it for a celebration.

'Anybody for champagne?' Simon asked pleasantly as, with a startling pop, he uncorked the bottle he had just drawn from his bag. The two Dutch girls thrust their mugs eagerly forwards. The American was more reluctant to get involved.

Our hostess had managed to find some chicken to put in the rice and we ate this course with some relish and not a little hilarity.

'Of course,' Simon said as the empty plates were taken away. 'Christmas isn't really Christmas without Christmas pudding is it?'

'You're right,' I said, and nodded sagely.

The girls switched their glances from one to the other of us. Waiting for a movement. At length, Simon reached for his bag. The girls craned forwards, eyes sparkling. Even the American was tilting his head to peer down the table. Simon pulled out a small packet.

'Toothpick anybody?'

The audience relaxed into disappointment.

'My sister makes a fantastic Christmas pudding,' I continued to nobody in particular. 'It's a South African recipe she uses. Full of nuts and fruit.' I sighed as I remembered it. 'The best ever.'

'The Christmas pudding, is that the cake?' one of the girls asked.

'No, the cake is with the white icing on the top, like snow,' Simon explained. 'You eat it at tea time. Christmas pudding you eat after the main course with brandy butter or cream.'

'Ah, I have never eaten English Christmas pudding,' she said.

'It's an acquired taste. Some people find it too heavy. What do you think?' I said, as I pulled an aluminium foil package from my bag. Jaws dropped open as I unwrapped my sister's Christmas pudding onto the table. There was no need to issue invitations this time. Bowls were thrust unashamedly forwards. I divided up the pudding and we tucked in. 'Of course, it should really be eaten with cream,' I apologised, 'but I don't know whether I have enough to share with everybody.' I shook the tin of UHT cream and we poured ourselves each a drop into our dishes.

'Gee, you Brits,' the American said, shaking his head. 'You Brits, you've just got class.'

'Well I have never eaten English Christmas pudding before and I have to climb a mountain in Nepal to do so,' the Dutch girl said. 'Wait till I tell my mother.'

Our hostess had tried the champagne with much giggling and was now gingerly picking at a piece of pudding whilst an old battered kettle simmered on the metal plate at the side of her.

Simon rubbed his stomach. 'Well that was OK,' he allowed, 'but where do we take our coffee?'

Coffee back in Bangladesh was difficult to obtain. Halfway up a mountain in Nepal it was unknown. Sickly tea was the universal native drink.

'Ha coffee!' the American said. 'Now that will beat you.'

'Yes, I admit it,' I said. 'It's only Nescafé Gold Blend.' I put the small but precious jar on the table. 'I couldn't get the percolator onto the plane.'

One Dutch girl clapped her hands and screamed in pleasure. The other poked the rueful American in the ribs. He had the grace to laugh.

During the night as I lay on my wooden board bed I heard a muffled thudding and clopping coming from below our window. Voices whispered and sandals slapped on rock. I peered out. Below me, a mule train was silently padding its way down the track to the valley floor below. And in the morning, I lay on my stomach on my top bunk and watched the golden sun as it crept slowly down the south faces of Annapurna and Machhapuchhare.

On the return journey an incident at the airport in Dhaka amused me but infuriated Simon. He had a greater sense of his own importance than I had of mine. The Bangladeshi passport officer took our passports and then left his box and carried them into an office. At that time the UK did not manufacture a diplomatic passport. We were the only country in the world not to do so. We used the ordinary blue passport and on page five would be found an endorsement, *'holder is a member of Her Britannic Majesty's Diplomatic Service'*. Very low key but, paradoxically, just a tad conceited – rather like not putting the name of our country on our postage stamps.

Simon protested to the man's colleague. 'Hey, we're British diplomats from the high commission.'

The man responded by stamping a piece of paper and handing it to him.

'We've been IS 81'd,' I laughed. 'They're detaining us.'

Simon hit the roof. I stood and laughed. It was just too funny. After all those years of holding people up at frontiers, the tables had been turned on us. Perhaps they were looking up our names in their suspect index, after all, the position of 'Passport Control Officer' had been introduced into British embassies and consulates worldwide before World War 1 solely to act as a cover for the activities of the intelligence agents of MI6. We were doing the same job, but without the spying.

But Simon could not see the funny side. We were being made fools of before all the other passengers. He stormed up and down. I chose a bench to sit on. Eventually the man returned our passports.

'You'll probably find that he knew exactly what job we did and was punishing us for refusing a visa to a member of his family,' I said, but Simon just scowled and threatened complaints to the high commissioner.

But he brightened up when my rucksack did not appear on the baggage conveyor. We waited and waited. I grabbed a porter who assured me that there were no bags lying around on the other side of the wall. I chose to disbelieve him and followed him through the door marked *'no admittance'*. He was right. My bag was not there. In my mind there was only one place that the bag could be – in the plane. I brushed aside the security man and carried on walking out onto the tarmac and up to the plane. A man was pulling away the platform onto which they had unloaded the contents of the hold. I clambered up and peered into the

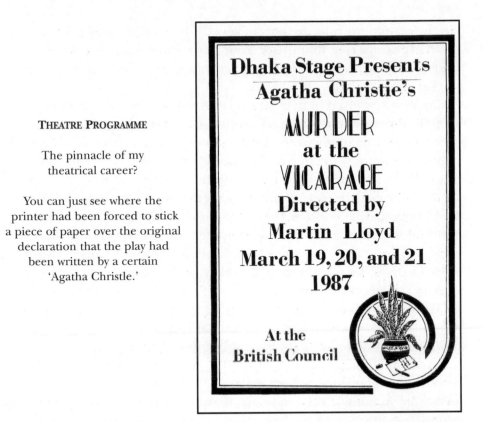

Dhaka Stage Presents
Agatha Christie's
MURDER
at the
VICARAGE
Directed by
Martin Lloyd
March 19, 20, and 21
1987

At the
British Council

gloom of the aircraft belly. How fortuitous it was that my small black rucksack had reflective stripes sewn on it. I caught the glint and pointed it out to the protesting man. He crawled in and, hey presto, returned with my bag in his arms.

And then it was back to work. January and February are probably the nicest part of the year to be in Bangladesh. The skies are clear, the days are warm without being searing and the humidity is low. As a result, this is when all the official visitors arrive. The second sec. issued a three-line whip to attend the high commissioner's garden party (on our day off) in honour of the head of the Civil Service who was on a fact-finding tour of overseas posts. I ignored it on the basis that we would stand around in the scorching heat of the garden, talking to the people whom we worked with every day. I went to the British Club and enjoyed cool relaxation in the deserted swimming pool.

The other visitor who made perhaps more of a mark was the MP for Islington, Jeremy Corbyn. He visited the visa section of the British High Commission and sat in on a couple of interviews to see how we worked.

He then went down to the Jatiya Press Club in Dhaka and made a speech in which he asserted that the present visa regime was 'the outcome of the apartheid policies of the ruling UK government.' He seemed to have got the picture OK then.

I was also involved in the first trial DNA tests where applicants would give a small blood sample whose DNA would be extracted and then compared with that of the family in the UK to whom he claimed to be related. The system would show unequivocally whether the family relationships were as claimed. An intriguing aspect was that the majority of the applicants, once the science had been explained to them, were very keen to take part. This suggested to me that they were sure that the test would prove the genuineness of their claims, but after a few weeks the trial was abandoned. I don't know why. Perhaps the 'official report' might tell us in thirty years time. Perhaps the tests were getting the 'wrong' results.

And very soon it was time to go home. I doubt that I made much mark on the queue of applicants. Over five thousand were still waiting for visas to join their families in the UK. No matter how hard we worked we had reduced the queue for first-time applicants only from eighteen months to one year and as fifty percent of these were habitually refused to become second-tier applicants we were merely delaying the crisis. The rate of work was inhuman, the pressure to refuse was ridiculous and counter productive. Instead of analysing the appeals statistics to discover which adjudicators were giving judgments against us at the tribunal perhaps the management could have spent more time examining why we were losing the appeals in the first place. Could it be that the initial decisions had been wrong?

My biggest enterprise was to direct a play for the local ex-pat theatre group, Dhaka Stage. They had a slot available in March and wanted me to fill it. There would just be enough time to do it before I returned to the UK. The Americans dominated the theatrical scene, putting on American shows at the superbly equipped American School. I decided to give them a dose of Agatha Christie – *Murder at the Vicarage* – the first story in which Miss Marple appears and to stage it at the British Council in downtown Dhaka. 'Nobody will come downtown with the student riots that we are having' I was warned. We were sold out every night, with people paying to sit on the steps to the lighting gallery. The choice of play was dictated by the fact that it was the only Agatha Christie work that I could find in the British Council library. I soon discovered that Dhaka Stage was a serious concern. This was not the fumbling of the diplomats trying to write a Christmas revue. This was big time. At the first meeting they talked about sponsors and publicity and how many production assistants I would need. I eventually settled on two very capable women, one from the Australian High Commission and one from a private company. The set was built by a Swedish professional theatre set designer who was in Bangladesh as a house husband – his wife being the one with the gainful employment. The posters and programme were designed by a professional graphic artist. Everywhere I turned, high quality, professional help was at hand. Naturally, Bangladesh provided a few hiccoughs. The script had to be submitted to the Minister of Culture for approval before we could go ahead. He refused to accept it until it was bound in leather as a book, rather than the stapled photocopies that we were working from. The programmes were delivered twenty-four hours before curtain-up with a spelling mistake on the title page, 'Agatha Christle' They took them back and hurriedly printed 'Agatha Christie' on a thousand slips of paper which they pasted over the mistake. The power went down five minutes before opening on the first night. I heard the generator kick in but no light appeared. I ran out into the darkness and tracked down the muffled thumping of the engine. In a shed a little Bengali man was contentedly watching the generator spewing out fumes. I leaned across and threw the switch and the lights came on. On the second night a tree crashed down onto the roof of the theatre but the show went on.

Leaving aside the work, living in a foreign country rather than passing through as a tourist I enjoyed immensely. One's nose becomes accustomed to the smell of the garbage piled up in the pens at street corners; to the perpetually warping doors and peeling paint; to the insistent attention of rickshaw wallahs the moment you set foot in the street. I had my bicycle air-freighted out to Dhaka for me. Judging by the state that it arrived in, British Airways had put it on a non-stop flight to Bangkok and had thrown it out as the plane had passed over the Bay of Bengal but once I had got it working I found it to be the best way of getting about. I cycled into the old town where the Europeans do not go and meandered down narrow streets full of open-fronted shops and sizzling food stands. I used it to travel to work and to attend social functions.

I met many interesting people; the more interesting being those who worked outside the diplomatic circle: the engineers, the aid workers, the teachers, in short, the people who were actually doing something rather than just talking about it. I shall treasure the memory of a dinner at the house of a Bengali lady interpreter where I was the only European invited and we ate with our hands. I amused myself by trying out my Urdu on our

Pathan chowkidhar who guarded our garden gate.

I was surprised at the enterprise of the businessmen in Dhaka. The copying centre in downtown Banani, for example, had equipped itself with photocopying machines of a much higher specification than were used at the British High Commission where we had to install greenhouse heaters in the paper cupboards to stop the paper from sticking.

And I loved the railways. What a way to travel!

It was thirty-two degrees when the plane took off from Dhaka airport, it was four degrees and raining when we landed at Heathrow.

Welcome home.

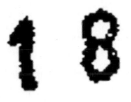

People are a bore when they come back from an overseas posting. I must have been insufferable. I had to stop myself from opening every conversation with, 'when I was in Dhaka,' but it was difficult. I had seen and done so much that was different in such a short span of time. I had met socially and professionally more interesting people in six months than I had in the previous six years and the astonishing aspect of it all was that their opinions of my capabilities were utterly different from those of the management of the Immigration Service. So who was right and who was wrong? I did not know but it caused me to reflect.

I had worked amongst ambitious IOs whose only concern had been the promotion of their career at all costs; honesty, compassion, truth, colleagues, were all pushed aside to achieve advancement. If I did not do something soon I would be left as the only IO still sitting at the desk stamping passports – all the others would be running little empires.

'I want a transfer to the Training Unit at Harmondsworth.'

Geoff looked serious. 'It's not as easy as that.' He was embarrassed.

'I might remind you that on my last annual staff report you said that I was "the most inspired trainer that you had ever met". Doesn't that count for something?'

'And I still believe that, but the decision is not up to me I'm afraid. You have to do at least five years at Heathrow first.'

'Why?'

'It's the rule. You have to do your porridge first. And then you only get a three-year attachment to the Training Unit. And it is not guaranteed that you will get it.'

'So the purpose of the Unit is to provide a rest reward for IOs at Terminal Three?'

'Well, not exactly, but the most of the trainers have done a good ten years at Heathrow.'

'And that makes them good trainers does it?'

'Martin, I can't change the system.'

'Then it is wrong. If you identify someone in the Service who has a skill you need and you do not exploit it then that is just a daft waste of resources.'

He pulled a face and upturned his palms at me. He could do nothing.

It was not a good time at Dover. Whilst I was in Dhaka, the Townsend Thoresen ferry *Herald of Free Enterprise* had rolled over outside Zeebrugge harbour, drowning 188 passengers and crew. Nearly everybody in Dover knew somebody who had been affected by the disaster. Ferry companies were now being pressurised to establish nominal passenger lists for each sailing.

Meanwhile up at Harwich the Home Office was cramming people on board a ferry which was going nowhere. The *Earl Wilson* had been chartered as a temporary detention centre to house the Tamil refugees who were awaiting the decisions on their asylum applications. It was civil war in Sri Lanka, no matter what anybody said.

'Smacks of Dickens to me,' said Reg Toale. 'The convict hulks on the marshes – straight out of Dickens. Mind you,' he added, 'the mystery of today's refugees is more profound a mystery than even Dickens could have dreamed up. Why is it, for example, if people are fleeing a country to save their lives, why is it that they manage to fly across a quarter of the globe to claim asylum in the UK? There are loads of countries nearer to Sri Lanka than Britain. We are not exactly next door. And where are all the families? Why are the refugees all young males of working age?'

'You're a cynic,' I said. 'It could be that it is precisely this section of the populace who are the most threatened by conscription and war.'

'India is nearer to Sri Lanka than Britain. They could go there.'

I was embarking a line of Colombians. They had alighted from their coach and were filing past my desk. Some had been landed on conditions which meant that I had to check and stamp their embarkation card and passport but most had been 'rolled'. They were a group of ordinary looking people, mostly families with young children. Once past me they continued down the long kiosk to the customs officer behind me and then re-boarded their coach. I put my hand out for my stamp. It was not there. A naked inked pad stared at me. Panic. How could I have lost it? I was using it a few minutes ago. I shifted the stacks of blank embark cards about, I moved my suspect index to one side, I looked on the floor. It was nowhere to be seen. At that moment a Colombian lady with a bouffant of dyed blond hair hurried back to my desk from the coach. She was full of apologies in Spanish, at least, I supposed them to be apologies, and was pointing to her six year old son. She handed me my embarkation stamp. The silly child had been playing with it. They got back on the coach and then I remembered the child. He had been standing at the side of my desk by my stamp pad and had been looking at my eyes all the time. He had not been playing, he had been working. The moment that he saw that I was not looking, he had stolen the stamp. He had been trained as a shoplifter. Fortunately, when he had shown his booty to his mother the latter had realised the danger and had hurried back. In fact, the entire group must have been an organised tour of shoplifters on their way back home.

A few days later, in the same position, I was stamping away frantically when I had a momentary vision of the person before me flinching just before my stamp impacted on the passport. But it did not so much impact as splodge. Whilst I inspected my stamp he picked something from the floor which he then returned to me. It was half of my stamp. The hinge had sheared off.

To brighten my life I applied to go on a day liaison course at MI5. Every few years the Security Service would invite IOs to come for a day of lectures and interchange of ideas. I believe their intention was to explain to us what they actually did and how we could help them in their work. If they succeeded in that, then we came away with an impression of having watched a circus of freaks trying to be on their best behaviour.

MARTIN HAS A BRAND
NEW STAMP NOW.

The office was in an anonymous building just off Regent Street. It had no name above its broad window which was draped with about four layers of net curtain in order to obfuscate the interior. Upon entry, my IO's warrant was checked and I was escorted in the lift to the lecture room on the top floor. There were about twenty IOs in the room, all slouched on chairs and trying to swallow the plastic coffee from the machine. Then we had lectures. As somebody who had an eye for presentations, I decided there and then never to emulate our first speaker who fired us with his enthusiasm by declaring in a lugubrious voice, 'this is probably going to be the most boring lecture you'll hear today.'

They talked of 'threats' and 'operations' without saying anything at all. And when it came to question time, any one of us could have answered the questions that we put to them with the responses they gave us. I was about two thirds of the way through one talk before I realised that 'STD' was not

'Subscriber Trunk Dialling' – the automatic telephone system which was being introduced throughout the country – but the Soviet Trade Delegation.

'Because of the restrictions the Soviets have put on British diplomats in Russia, we have imposed similar constraints on theirs in the UK. So we have given them certain designated routes to follow when they leave London. They must not deviate from them. For example, when they go down to their place near Hawkhurst they have to drive down the A21 and turn at the Flimwell traffic lights.'

'But how do you know if they stick to the route?'

The lecturer put on a smugly condescending face and nodded gently. 'Oh, we would know,' she said pompously, suggesting without suggesting that they tagged and followed every Soviet car.

Utterly risible.

Lunch was downstairs in the ward room. This was a dingy basement with the coats of arms of various security services from around the world pinned to the pine cladding. We were broken up into tables and, as if by chance, at each table sat one of the lecturers. We got a horsey woman in tweeds. I decided to have some fun.

'Can you tell me,' I asked ingenuously, 'what is the significance of the single white light bulb in the line of orange bulbs above the bar?'

'What? Oh right.' She turned to study the bar. 'See what you mean.' She frowned whilst I waited for her to tell me that they had run out of orange bulbs. 'Can't say that I've noticed that before.'

Emboldened by her vacillation I developed my enquiry. 'I wondered if it was a signal of some sort, given that it is not the middle bulb in the line but offset to the left by three.'

'Oh.' She pondered some more then leaned to the neighbouring table. 'Justin, why have we got one white bulb above the bar?'

By now the IO from Belfast was kicking my ankle under the table and looking at the ceiling.

Justin turned. 'One white bulb? Where?'

'Look at the line above the bar. They are all orange except for one.'

'And it's not the middle one,' I pointed out helpfully.

'Well, one, two, three.' Justin waved his finger in the air as he counted. 'No, you're right, it's not the middle bulb.'

'So it's not there for decoration,' I suggested. 'It would be in the middle if it were.'

'Yeah, yeah. So what do you think Roz?'

'I had never noticed. I hadn't really thought.'

'Err. I wonder if one of the orange bulbs blew and the barman only had white ones left,' Justin suggested.

I sucked on my teeth. 'Possible,' I agreed reluctantly. 'Possible.'

But more fun was to come my way. I went out after lunch for thirty minutes of fresh air. I don't know whether they suspected that we would make a rendezvous with some foreign power and divulge the content of the morning's lectures but they disapproved of anybody going out at half time, as it were. I braved their censure.

Upon my return, the uniformed security official was busy so he put me in the lift and pressed the button for the third floor and left me to it. I stepped out at my floor and walked down the corridor to the lecture room, thinking as I did so, that I had just got time to get a cup of coffee from the machine in the ante-room. I stood, dumbfounded. They had taken the machine away. Now this was not possible. It must have been plumbed in or something. But it was not there and, more sinisterly, there was no evidence of its having been there.

Well, I could not conjure up coffee from thin air so I shrugged to myself and walked on down to the lecture room. It was not there either. And on the way in this morning I did not recall passing through this automatic blast door which shuts off the back of the building from the front. Ummm. Keep walking Martin, you should not be here. This is not for you to see. In the offices as I passed, people were slaving over files and computers. I needed to find my way back to the lecture room pronto before I ended up in the Tower.

The inevitable happened. Somebody came down the corridor towards me. What do I do now? He was about my age and was carrying two sheets of paper before him. He glanced at me and before the question could form in his mind I went in to the attack. I pointed a finger at him.

'Do you know where you are supposed to be?' I rapped out in a voice of authority.

'Um... er... yes,' he finally decided, his eyes wide with apprehension behind his spectacles.

'Good, then can you tell me where I am supposed to be please? I seem to have wandered into the wrong part of the building.'

Had I said that I had just goosed the Mother Superior he could not have appeared more scandalised. He took me by the elbow and hurried me back through the blast doors to deliver me with a short comment that I did not hear but which seemed to impress the lecturer.

But they never lose the Soviet Trade Delegation on the A21, do they?

It all went a bit downhill after that and when the IO from Cardiff, who had managed to slip out at lunchtime for a couple of pints, fell asleep on the back row during the afternoon session, we took it in turns to nudge him to keep his stentorian snoring at full volume.

Oh no, not Crystal Maria Hartmann. Is she still here? I delve into the pink file that my morning colleague has left in the middle of the desk where I could not miss it. This is just what I want at the beginning of an afternoon office duty. What has she been up to now?

She is a German lady of thirty-five on the long-term casework board. About three months ago the DHB police were called to the Merry Dolphin café in the docks because a customer would not pay for her food. There they found Crystal Maria Hartmann with her rucksack, surrounded by empty plates and scowling waitresses. She had disembarked from Calais a few hours earlier as a foot passenger, had refused to board the bus to the immigration control but had repaired instead to the café for a spot of refreshment.

The police had brought her to our control where she had told the IO that she lived in the big white house across the bay and owned all the ships in the harbour and so did not need a passport. The IO had sat her down and phoned upstairs for a German speaker. When the latter had presented himself, Fraulein Hartmann was nowhere to be found. A phone call to the town police for assistance elicited the enquiry, 'was she likely to be the foreign lady who had just taken a taxi from the docks to the railway station and refused to pay the fare?'

Over the following weeks it became obvious that we were stuck with her. She claimed to be a West German national and so had the right to work here but she was refused on the grounds that she had no document and no money and no intention of working to support herself. The fanciful and irrational answers she gave resulted in her being certified under the Mental Health Act whereupon she was moved to the local mental hospital, St. Augustine's, at Chartham near Canterbury.

I well remember having to drive out there to interview her in an attempt to get her documented by the German authorities. I stood in the hospital grounds on a sunny afternoon; the smell of newly mown lawn was heavy and the drone of the mower could just be heard far down the park. The breeze rustled through the foliage of the ancient trees as I ambled towards the main building, past the chapel and the fire station, complete with miniature fire engine. I paused and gazed at the view over the rolling parkland downs to the valley of the Stour and Canterbury itself and I thought to myself that this was the place that I would like to work in: peaceful, relaxed, pretty and safe. Perhaps I could get myself committed and just forget all the complications of life.

I succeeded in collecting sufficient data to convince the Germans that Crystal Maria Hartmann was one of their citizens and they issued her with an emergency passport in the form of a single sheet of paper which we could use to remove her. That was the story as I had remembered it.

I open the file. What is today's task and why has it been left for me? Apparently we want to remove her to Calais where she came from and not fly her to Germany, but the French will not play ball. 'She is German, send her to Germany,' they say. We point out that she lives in France but when the French learn the reasons for our refusing her they observe that they have enough indigent loonies of their own. My task today is to convince them that one more won't make much difference. Gee thanks.

Searching through the file I uncover the name and telephone number of the Frenchman whom Maria Hartmann had phoned from St. Augustine's. The number was noted as a result of a little initiative of mine in suggesting to the sister at the hospital that the more we knew about Fraulein Hartmann, the quicker we would be able to take her off their hands.

Nothing ventured, nothing gained, I telephone the gentleman who proves to be vague about his relationship with our detainee.

'Does she live with you?

'Sort of.'

'In your house?

'Mostly.'

'Is she related to you?

'Definitely not.'

'How long have you known her?'

'Three years.'

'The problem, Monsieur Dupuis, is that we wish to send her back to France where she lives but the French authorities are unwilling to accept her back without proof that she is resident and able to support herself.'

'What will happen then?'

'If the French will not accept her, then we will have to fly her back to Germany.'

'She hasn't lived in Germany for decades. She knows nobody there.'

'Does she have a residence permit for France?'

'Yes.'

'Where is it?'

'Hasn't she got it with her?'

'I'm afraid not.'

'I'll have a look for it here. Can you ring me back in an hour?'

'I will do that.'

Bruce comes back from his lunch break. 'I left the loony Kraut for you. Two of a kind. You should get on well,' he says.

'Thanks Bruce. When are you going to wash your car?'

Bruce had bought a new Renault 5 two years earlier. Since that time the only thing that he had done to it was to put petrol in it. It was now a dusty grey all over, the windows were indistinguishable from the bodywork but the irony was that because of its coating of dirt, it shrugged off the corrosive seagull poo which would otherwise eat through the bodywork of a clean car. Perhaps he had discovered the ultimate defence.

'I've forgotten what colour it is. I shall have to consult the log book to find out,' he said. 'And if I wash it, I might not find it in the car park.'

Almost at the end of my duty, Geoff wanders in.

'What's the latest on Maria Hartmann?'

'I've spoken to a French chap called Dupuis with whom Maria had sort of lived in his house in Limoges although he was rather cagey about his relationship.'

'So would I be if she were my girlfriend. How does that advance us?'

'He has agreed to bring her residence permit up to Calais to show to the Police de l'Air et des Frontières and to meet her off the boat and guarantee her maintenance in France.'

'What do the French say?'

'If we can arrange it, they will accept it.'

'Good. Well done. Get it sorted out for a day when you are on duty. You will be accompanying her across the Channel to hand her over.'

'But–'

'The sea air will do you good.'

What qualifications and skills do you think you would need in order to accompany a mentally ill German lady across the Channel so as to effect her legal removal from the UK? Well, an ability to speak German would be useful. I speak French. Being of the same sex so that you could ensure that she did not top herself in the toilet could be important. I am a man. A familiarity with nursing procedures and medicines might come in handy. I am not even a qualified first aider. Skill in unarmed combat for when she goes doo-lally would, I suppose, be an unnecessary luxury. So I sit in the onboard cafeteria and buy her coffee and doughnuts from my own purse and try to maintain an interesting conversation in a mixture of French and

English to distract her from the fact that she is being returned whence she came. Inevitably she needs to go to the toilet so I have to hang around outside the door like a pervert to make sure that she does not go walkabout.

At disembarkation in Calais I gallantly hold her arm. It's not gallantry, it's determination. I am not going to be beaten by her getting 'lost' in the port as she did at Dover. The French immigration officers know about her but seem evasive when I ask if they have now taken her over from me.

'Not yet, not yet. Just wait a minute.'

We wait. Eventually a *chef commissaire* takes me aside and makes an apologetic disclosure.

'There has been a bit of a hiccough.'

'But she is being met by her friend, Monsieur Dupuis.'

'Oh yes, he's here. We know all about him.'

'Good.'

'Not good. He's in the book. We've arrested him. He's wanted for non-payment of maintenance to his ex-wife.'

I just stare at him. How often did they look people up in the book? Why did they choose him? Eventually they decide to grant bail to a rueful Monsieur Dupuis who puts Maria in his car and drives her away.

'Supermarket?' the chief says.

I look at my watch. 'I've not got time.'

'Nonsense. It's only five minutes away. Get in.' He points to a Renault estate painted in a decorous blue with matching lights on the roof.

It takes me ages to find the coffee that I want. The chief is surprised that I am not loaded down with wine.

'I'm teetotal.'

'What a waste,' he says. 'We'd better hurry.'

I grip the seat as he turns on his blue lights and siren and we hurtle back to the ship. Three weeks later Crystal Maria Hartmann was found wandering around Dover hoverport. She appeared confused so they put her on a train to London.

The rumbling of the wind had steadily increased to a roaring. Our house was a three storey, late-Victorian pile on the cliff above Folkestone harbour. We had views of the Channel and Boulogne. And we got the weather. But this was something new. Outside, the lamp standards were swaying like trees and the sea was a continuous rumbling of thunder as it smashed over the promenade. Objects, unidentifiable in the dark and storm, skittered their routes peculiar down the road, banging, crashing, breaking, shattering. The roaring was now so loud that we had to shout to each other inside the house. I put my hand on the bedroom wall. It was thirteen-inch cavity brick and had stood for a hundred years. It was vibrating like a drum skin. Then we heard *Hengist* moaning on its siren. A continuous wailing blast that was nonetheless modulated by the thrumming and pulsing of the wind. I peered through the front window. I could see nothing because the glass was covered in dirt. *Hengist* had broken from its moorings alongside Folkestone quay and was now drifting out of control across the harbour. Five and a half thousand tons of Sealink ferry on its way to the rocks. The siren wailed for minutes on end as a warning to everybody that the ship was not under control.

This was the hurricane of 1987. Morning came, bright as it always does after a storm but our front room was as gloomy as a cave. The facade of our house up to the roof was covered in sand from the beach a hundred feet below. I tried to ring the office. The lines were down. I cycled to work. At Capel, the top floor and roof of a house was sitting in its back garden. It belonged to one of our IOs who was on his way back to the UK from a short-term ECO posting. My bicycle could get through where cars could not. I could lift it over fallen trees, I could wheel it around disembowelled bus shelters. The wind had torn through the caravan park on the former airship station. Every field hedge between Folkestone and Dover was decorated with bedding, fridges, clothes and cupboards.

AFTER THE STORM
The Sealink Ferry *m.v. Hengist* run aground on the Warren at Folkestone.

A coaster had sunk in the western entrance to Dover harbour, men were missing. Everybody had a tale to tell. The night duty had had no work because no ships could dock. The IOs were told to stay in the building. One IO pointed out that he only lived a few hundred yards away and was given permission to go home. They saw him leave. Half an hour later he was still spreadeagled against the glass of the booking hall by the wind. They eventually hauled him back inside.

Enormous rollers were tumbling up the beach but the weather was bright and calm. Ships were docking. In the office at Dover East Immigration, the one CIO looked at us three IOs.

'One to blue, one to black and one to embarks,' he said. 'And let's pray that some of the later shifts can get in.'

I went down to black – cars inwards – and sat in a kiosk, waiting for the first passengers to arrive. For once, there were no seagulls. The telephone rang in my kiosk. I could tell from the ring that it was an outside line. This was good news because there were no lines working to the upstairs office.

'Immigration Dover East,' I said.

'Crown Prosecution Service here. I need you to get out a file for me, pronto.'

'Sorry, no can do. I'm on my own.'

'Well you'll have to go and get it.'

'I'm on a fixed point. I can't leave it. Ring back tomorrow'

'But we need it this afternoon. You'll just have to go and get it.'

He was getting in a tizz because he had left it too late to prepare for his case in court. The CPS could be notoriously inefficient.

'Did you have a storm last night?' I asked pleasantly.

'Of course we did.'

'Well so did we. At the moment, there are three immigration officers running the port of Dover, I am one of them. I am sitting in a glass booth on the quayside and that is where I have to be. The internal telephone line to the office where the files are kept does not work and we are on emergency power only.'

'This is important. I am ordering you to get that file.'

'Oh go away,' I said and put the phone down. It was unlike me to be unhelpful. Why had I done it? The satisfaction had been only transitory.

American tourists? We just love them. When you start as an IO you try to interview them. It goes something like this:

'How long are you staying in the United Kingdom?'

'In the united what?'

'In the United Kingdom. Of Great Britain and Northern Ireland.'

'Oh we're not going there, we're going to England.'

So for the next lot you adjust the enquiry.

'How long are you staying in England?'

'Hey, Harvey, the man wants to know how long we're staying here.'

'Is that your husband at that desk?'

'Yeah.'

'Well here is your passport, go and stand with him.'

You are only asking a question to fill in the time whilst you look them up in the book and to establish that you have spoken to them. So you try another one.

'How long are you staying in England?'

'Oh we'll only be here a few days then we're leaving.'

'Back to the States?'

'No, no, no, we're leaving for Scotland.'

Perhaps you could stop confusing them with all the geography. Try this.

'How long are you staying here?'

'Right. OK. So how long am I staying here? Right. What here?'

'Yes. How long are you staying here?'

'Oh we're not staying here, we're going to London.'

After a couple of years of running through the permutations you realise that what you need to ask is a question that they can answer without having to think. Something they will respond to without realising that they have done so. An irresistible reaction. A Pavlovian prompt. I have developed a cracker. They just cannot stop themselves coming out with the correct answer every time and then, *bonk*, down goes my stamp on the passport. It's brilliant.

Before me are thirty students from Syracuse University in New York. We see this group every year. They come over to Europe to study for a term, or a 'semester' as they always call it. Eager-faced Americans in their early twenties, full of the stimulation of having studied abroad but now the term is over and they are itching to get home in time for Christmas.

'Who was the first president of the United States?'

'George Washington.'

Bonk.

'Who was the first president of the United States?

'George Washington.'

Bonk.

Of course one of the girls had to show off and reeled off to me the names of the first twenty presidents but all in all, we landed the group with no fuss and in good humour which made Stewart's subsequent telephone call so much more dreadful. Had I heard about the plane crash in Scotland? I had but I knew no more than what I had seen on television. It had been a Pan Am flight from Heathrow to JFK. It had crashed near the town of Lockerbie. No survivors. At that point we only knew it as an unexplained disaster; a terrorist attack was only one of the several possible explanations being put forward. What had this got to do with me? Did I remember landing the group of American students on walkers? Yes I did. They were from the Syracuse University. In fact, they had been on their way to Heathrow to.... Oh no. No.

I could still see their faces. I could hear their voices. I remembered joking with them and I had stamped their passports and sent them on their way to flight PA 103.

One problem with working unsocial hours, overtime and on public and bank holidays was that you earned more money than people who did not do these things so if you decided to transfer sideways into another department you became a standard EO – executive officer – and earned an EO's salary. To give you some idea of the difference; the next grade up, the higher executive officer (HEO) earned about £1500 p.a. less than an IO so it made sense for an IO to hang on and hope to get eventual promotion to CIO. But I was not sure that I wanted to be a CIO. At that time, most vacancies were for control CIOs, working at ports, taking references from IOs wanting to refuse passengers and once a year writing staff reports. I did not want to do that; all the fun in the job came from dealing with the public not from bitching about your colleagues.

Nigel Andrews, the IO who had studied Urdu at the same time as me, had taken promotion to HEO and was now working in London. Here, on behalf of the Home Office, he composed and presented arguments at the Appeals Tribunal to support the refusal decisions taken by IOs. The appeal cases were brought by various organisations or firms of lawyers on behalf of those passengers who did not agree with the decision to stop them from coming in to the country. And of course, we have already seen that not every IO notified the passengers of their right of appeal and the process by which they could exercise it.

Such a job as this would drive me around the bend but I continued to trawl through the Home Office notices, hoping to find that elusive and attractive opportunity which would not involve me sitting behind a desk all day long. I was tempted by a posting in a department which inspected friendly societies. It was advertised as covering the whole of the UK, including Northern Ireland and needing candidates who were prepared to travel. This sounded more like it. I phoned up the officer in post.

'Can you tell me something about the job?' I asked.

'What do you want to know?'

'Well, this requirement to travel, for example...'

'Oh they are not too strict on it. You don't have to if you don't want to.'

'Oh no, I don't mind travelling. How long have you been in the post?'

'Just over four years.'

'And how many times have you been sent to Northern Ireland?'

'Where? I've never been to Northern Ireland.'

'It says in the recruitment notice that you must be prepared to travel.'

'Oh yes, you have to do that.'

'So where have you been then?'

'Well most of my jobs are in south London.'

'Have you ever been out of London?'

'I don't think I've ever been north of the river.'

I did not bother applying for that job. Another post that interested me was HEO in a small department which acted as liaison between the Home Office and the European Commission. Here, I was expected to travel out to Brussels and I would have to use my French. I made an appointment to visit the incumbent in Croydon. He outlined the job which was mostly administrative. That part would be no problem to me and the recording and reporting of meetings held in French would similarly be within my capabilities and might even enable me to develop some useful extra skills. It was the travelling function which turned out to be the grit in the oyster.

'So, if I have got this right, on a Thursday I work until five in Croydon then I beetle off down to Heathrow and take a plane to Brussels, which would normally incur about four hours of overtime. But this I do, unpaid, in my spare time?' He nodded pleasantly. 'I then attend the meeting on the Friday and fly back to London on the Saturday morning, which is my day off, also unpaid?'

He nodded again, but less enthusiastically. I suspect that he could see that making such a proposition to an officer who could claim travelling expenses to drive across the harbour from Dover East to West would be a non-starter.

I then jumped in and applied for HEO trainer in the Home Office in Central London and was a little disconcerted when they called my bluff and invited me to an interview. This was getting serious.

I walked into the room, turned to close the door and stood with my back to the interview panel for a few seconds whilst I memorised the layout of the wall. They had chosen the classic set-up of a room with two identical doors side by side. One lead to the corridor, the other to a cupboard. The nervous candidate flustering his way out would infallibly choose the latter. I did not intend to give them that entertainment.

Behind a barrier of two tables set lengthwise across the room sat four men.

'Good morning gentlemen,' I said.

'Sit down Mr. Lloyd,' the bald man said and indicated the solitary chair set before them. I thought his action quite superfluous unless it was to reinforce in my mind that he was the 'chairman'. I did not share this observation with the board. I dragged the chair backwards from the table by about four feet, so that they could see all of me, then I sat and laid the palms of my hands gently on the tops of my thighs in the submissive, 'I am a woman and I want to be caressed' position. By chance, I had just read a book on the subconscious movements and acts of humans and what they betrayed. I was hoping that this opener would disarm them a bit.

They introduced themselves and I immediately forgot their names because they were all written on those 'Toblerone' blocks on the table before them. The head of the training department was the man sitting at the left end of the table. As far as I was concerned, the others were of no importance. He was the man I had to impress. And off they went.

'If you were Home Secretary, Mr. Lloyd, what would be the first thing you would do?'

'Resign and get myself a decent job. I don't want to be the Home Secretary, I'm applying to be an HEO trainer.'

'What do you think is on the Home Secretary's desk this morning?'

'I suppose you don't want the 'cup of tea' answer?' I looked along the blank faces. 'No, I thought not. Well, whatever is on his desk won't be dealt with for ages will it?' They looked, and waited. 'Isn't he in the West Indies at the moment?'

'Oh, he might be.' They looked at each other for confirmation. 'Well, let's just say that he is here. What do you think would be his concerns?'

I threw up an organigram in my mind. What else did the Home Secretary have responsibility for?

'He is not just there for immigration matters,' I said, playing for time. 'It might be the overcrowding of prisons, the undermanning of the police force, the difficulty of recruiting for the Probation Service or the rumbling threat of another strike in the Fire Service. I have no idea. Have you?'

'Tell me Mr. Lloyd, to what do you attribute the low morale in the Immigration Service?'

'What low morale?'

'Are you saying that morale is good?'

'No, I am asking you how you have established that there is low morale in the Service.'

'Well, let us presume that there is. What is causing it?'

'Whatever you wish. You have invented the low morale. Do you want me to invent a fictional reason for its being there?'

'So you don't see low morale?'

'No.'

'I would like you to think of a training session which you have attended recently, either as a trainer or a trainee, and comment upon it.'

I talked about my visit to Box, leaving out the orange light bulbs and my getting lost in the corridor.

'What did you think of it?' the head of training asked me.

I paused whilst I pushed my honest opinions into the background.

'From a technical point of view I think they committed the mistake that many organisations make and that is to employ the experts to deliver the expertise. This technique is fine if their expertise includes an ability to communicate'

'Go on.'

I looked at the other three members of the board. They were leaving it to him. This bit was his party. One of them was writing something on the paper in front of him.

'Let me tell you a story,' I said. They all looked up, the pencil went down, they leaned forwards. I shot a quick glance at the head of training. I didn't quite wink at him but he had seen what I had done. With six words I had captured their attention.

I ran them through the 'this is the most boring lecture you will hear today' section via the STD which we thought was telephones and the lecturer with the indecipherable accent. I did all the voices and intonations. I had that board in the palm of my hand. From the corner of my eye I could see the head trainer smiling quietly to himself.

'You see,' I concluded, 'if you want to get your point across, you do not necessarily need to use the expert who has the knowledge of the subject. An expert trainer can learn the text and present it much more effectively. You save the subject expert until later to answer the queries at question time. That is where he uses his expertise.'

'But that would require a doubling of manpower.'

'It is no saving to use one person in order to fail.' I knew they liked little epithets like that.

We chatted on. During one rambling summary I glanced up at the wall behind them and then stopped talking.

'No, sorry, I've lost it,' I admitted. 'I've forgotten what I was going to say.'

'Oh that's all right Mr. Lloyd.' They shuffled their papers to cover my supposed embarrassment.

'I was looking at that architrave up there.' I pointed at the wall behind them.' It's unusual isn't it? Here we are in a modern office block built, what, in the sixties? But this room has a decorative moulding running around it, a bit like a 1920s sitting room. I wonder why they did that.'

Eyebrows danced as they peered up at the walls. They agreed with me that it was unusual but could offer no explanation.

I had been told that the interview would be scheduled to last twenty-five minutes. It lasted forty-five minutes. Did I have any questions for them? There was only one to ask. I turned to the head trainer.

'Is there anything that I have said or done today that suggests to you that I am not capable of doing this job?'

He put his papers down, sat back and looked me in the eye.

'Mr. Lloyd, I have complete confidence that you are capable of doing this job.' In other words, if you don't get it, it will be because of the other three, not because of me.

Then we came to the end and the chairman thanked me. I put my hands on the arms of the chair as if to rise but I remained seated and looked at them. Ha! Gotcha! Where is the final question thrown at the candidate as he leaves? They looked at each other in alarm. I was not playing the game. I waited. They waited. I made a move.

'Ah Mr. Lloyd, one last question.' I sat back in the chair and stretched my legs out comfortably before me. 'If you were prime minister would you get rid of the New Year's honours system?'

'No I don't think so. It doesn't do any harm does it? And I would quite like an MBE, wouldn't you?'

Of course, one of the bloody Toblerones already had one.

When their rejection of my candidature was communicated to the port, Henry, the inspector who had replaced Dennis, called me in to his office. He was an inconsequential man whose obsessive concern with trifles ensured that he always missed the main course. He put on his stern face and pulled the sheet of paper importantly towards him.

'The board have sent a report about your behaviour.' He glowered at me. 'I shall read it to you and then ask for your observations.'

'Go ahead.' I raised my eyebrows and shrugged.

He started to read the committee's explanation of why they had not offered me the job. It was of academic interest as far as I was concerned. They had said 'no', that was all I needed to know, wasn't it? As he read the account, his disapproving tone made it sound like a litany of my shortcomings and transgressions. Why had the board bothered to send me this? I thought about the practice of reporting in the mainstream Civil Service as compared to the accusatory drubbing that passed for the same in the Immigration Service. The ethos was completely different. The Home Office was interested in developing its staff and getting the best out of them; the Immigration Service needed to keep its staff in its proper place. Then a light dawned on me.

'Just a minute, Henry.' He choked at my interruption. 'This isn't supposed to be a bollocking, you know. They haven't sent that report so that you can tear me off a strip. It's what is called 'feedback'. They are giving me some important advice about how to conduct myself at interviews. It's not a discipline matter; they are trying to help.'

'Well, yes,' he stuttered a pained agreement to my forceful proposition. He sounded rather disappointed at not making me grovel.

'And what they have said is, "Mr. Lloyd displayed all the qualities, skills and knowledge necessary to succeed in this job but he would not act like an HEO." I can't help that. I am what I am,' I declared, thinking to myself that I sounded a bit like Marcel Proust.

But why was I trying to find a way out of the Service anyway? What was prompting me? It could surely not be ambition. It transpired that it was something more sinister than that.

'Come on mate, give us a smile. Look at him, scowling like that. It won't crack your face to smile you miserable bugger.'

I am in pain. I don't feel like smiling. It is astonishing how rude the public can be to absolute strangers if they are civil servants. I understood early in the job that the last thing that a holidaymaker wants to do on his way home is to queue up and show his passport. He wants to go straight through to pick up his baggage, smuggle his extra duty-frees through customs and then get on his coach or train home. We were an obstruction and, to most people's eyes, a useless one. In the flood of returning British tourists we have allowed husbands in on their wives' passports and vice versa; we have failed to notice when a passport has expired or was unsigned; but we have let the people in. That is an important part of our job. To let in the ones who should be in, as quickly as possible.

A couple arrived at my kiosk one day and the man handed me two passports – a British visitors passport in the name of Mr. David Turner and a Spanish passport in the name of Maria Elena Gonzalez-Turner.

'How long is Maria Gonzalez-Turner staying here?'

The man leaned across the seat, narrowed his eyes and clenched his teeth. 'This woman is my wife. She lives here.'

'This is not apparent from her passport sir.' It had been issued in Spain and showed that she had been landed twice as a visitor.

'If you were any good at your job and knew anything about Spanish surnames you would know that a married woman takes her husband's surname as the last part of her own.' His scorn was withering. His voice was acid.

'She could be your sister-in-law, sir.'

'I don't have a brother.'

'Do you happen to have your marriage certificate with you sir?'

I could not have hit a more tender spot had I insisted on *droits de seigneur* over his spouse. I was a useless, pettyfogging, petty minded, idiotic, stupid... He eventually paused for breath. I had had enough of this. I stamped the passport.

'I have given this lady permission to stay for six months as a visitor which is the maximum I can do in the circumstances. If you wish her to stay here longer you will need to send her passport to the Home Office in Croydon. Here is a form telling you how to do it.'

He snatched the passports from my hand and drove away. Had he spoken to me more civilly and answered a couple more questions I could have given his wife permanent residence there and then but instead, I had condemned him to months of wrangling with the IND in Croydon. I once was able to rise above this unpleasantness but now I was becoming as tetchy as they were.

Saturday afternoon, I am on a spare blue duty which means that I spend all day on the walkers control. We have wall to wall Colombians from Medellin on shoplifting tours of Europe; twelve desks available, only eight occupied. Where were the other IOs? Down the pub. We, the idiots, worked on. At half past two some IOs wandered back, accompanied by a CIO. I held up my hand to the marshal, packed up my stuff into my case and walked out. The CIO glanced at me and pulled out his maywork to see where I was going. It was not my meal break but I went to the rest room and made myself a cup of tea. I propped my legs up onto an empty chair to ease my aching joints. I contemplated the view from the window – a jagged necklace of coaches waiting to unload, a steaming pan full of cars with their engines running, an intermittent trail of lorries and cars filtering through embarks. The telephone rang. That would be the CIO looking for more staff. I ignored it. The port fouled up. I sat and drank tea in beautiful solitude. After an hour I returned to the walkers control.

'Where have you been?' the CIO asked.

'I've been down the pub,' I replied.

He looked at me and grinned. 'No, come on, where have you been? You should have been on blue this last hour. It's been heaving.'

'I've been down the pub.'

'You should have been here.' He was getting angry. 'Where were you?'

'I've been down the pub.'

'But you don't drink.'

'I've been down the pub.'

He eventually saw the light. I had realised that I could make myself immune from sanctions by claiming to have been 'down the pub'. If they challenged my lie, it would throw the spotlight on the absenteeism during working hours by the hardcore drinkers in the port, of whom he was one. He was furious. I had taken out one hour. One hour in fifteen years.

It is ten o'clock on a Friday night and I am sitting on cars embarks. The newly designed port facilities have superimposed the embarkation control on the inwards control. Vehicles leaving the country now climb a ramp to our kiosks and then scoot down the other side to ground level to get to the ships. The ramp is steep and gets greasy from the perpetual passage of vehicles. We sit in the general office and watch the occasional articulated lorry slithering slowly backwards down the slope with its wheels turning forwards. Underneath, the cars entering the country are navigating a pin-ball route through the supporting pillars. Two of the kiosks cannot be used by cars towing caravans – the pillars are in the way. One caravan can hold up the cars trying to leave six kiosks. The IOs sit and wait, the passengers fume. I install alongside my guichet a handwritten notice which reads, *'This port was designed by architects, not by me.'* It turns many an angry protester into an indulgent complainant. 'Not your fault, mate, but it's bloody annoying.'

Ten minutes past ten. My relief is late. I need an urgent visit to the toilet. High above the port before me, a solid line of TIR lorries slowly edges its way down Jubilee Way – the road which flies off the cliffs of Dover and into the port. I have been timing how long it takes them to get to me. The present delay is about twenty minutes. At the beginning of my hour I had waved through a French lorry on the far kiosk to my right. He had raised his hand in acknowledgement and driven on through and then skidded to a halt. Well, from where I sat I could not see that the harbour board had left the barrier down. He had taken it with him. He was annoyed at the dent on his lorry. I shrugged and said sorry. It was not my responsibility to raise and lower barriers.

I phone the office to see where my relief is. The phone rings on unanswered. I phone the on-call room with the same result. I try black X, down on cars inwards. No reply. I phone foot embarks.

'David? It's Martin out on cars embarks. Whom did you relieve at ten?'

'Percy. He's gone over to the Albion.'

'Have you got today's maywork there? Who is supposed to be my relief?'

'Archy.'

'Is he sick today?'

'No, I've just seen him in the Albion, drinking with Swanley.'

'Is Swanley the night CIO?'

'One of them.'

'Who is the other?'

'Dunno.'

'I've got lively bowels. I need to go to the loo.'

'I don't wish to know that. Kindly leave the stage.'

By half past ten I am writhing on my chair and have phoned all around the port. It would appear that there are only the three fixed-point officers running the show. At ten forty-five I abandon the embarkation control, switching off my kiosk light and ensuring that all the barriers are in the up position. If you want to leave the UK, I'm not stopping you.

The following afternoon Swanley calls me in to the CIO's office.

'You abandoned the embarkation control last night,' he accuses me.

'I was not relieved.'

'You have to wait for your relief. It is a fixed point.'

'I needed to go to the toilet.'

'You should have got somebody else. You can't just walk off like that. They could have covered for you.'

'I tried. The only people who were answering phones were all on fixed points like me.'

'That's atrocious behaviour. The whole security of the country depends upon us.'

I look at him. Am I really hearing what I am hearing?

'Do you recognise the irony of this situation?' I say.

'What do you mean?'

'Well I was in the port. You weren't.'

'What has that got to do with it?'

'Quite a lot in my book. You were drinking in the Albion with the officer who was supposed to be relieving me and you are telling me off for abandoning my post?'

'You walked off the control—'

'—You weren't even in the port. And you were drinking with the IO who should have been on embarks. You should have been sorting out my relief, not drinking with him.'

'Don't you tell me my job,' he shouts. He is red in the face and his fists are clenching convulsively. 'I can run Dover East from the bar of the Albion.'

Yes. He really says that. 'I can run Dover East from the bar of the Albion.'

'Well patently you cannot,' I say.

It all came to a head some weeks later. I was the fixed point on cars and was sitting in the kiosk reading a book. Nothing was due in for about ten minutes. A woman in overalls came walking down the empty car lanes towards my kiosk. She looked like a cleaner. I kept a vague eye on her to see where she was going. She walked past my kiosk. I shot open the guichet.

'Just a minute,' I called.

'What?'

'Where are you going?'

'I'm going to catch my bus.'

'This is not the way out. It is the immigration control. The way out is over there.'

'I always go this way.'

'Can you come here please?'

'I shall miss my bus.'

'This is the immigration control. Do you have a dock pass?' She fished in her bag and pulled out a pass which showed that she was employed by the cleaning company. I pointed across the front of the kiosks to the docks exit road. 'The route you take is over there and out via the staff exit gate. That is the way you go.'

'I always go this way.'

'Well you mustn't.'

'I've never been stopped before.'

'Well I'm stopping you now. This is the immigration control for passengers arriving. You are staff. You go out via the staff gate and your pass will be checked by the DHB policeman. I am sure that you know that.'

'But this is quicker. I go this way to catch my bus.'

'Look, I don't want to have to tell you again. You can't go this way; it is not for staff. It is a security control.'

'But I shall miss my bus.'

I gave up. 'Oh piss off.' I waved my hand and shut the window. What was the point?

Half an hour later a CIO came down to talk to me. 'I've just been over to the DHB police station. They've had a complaint.'

'Oh not the cleaner?'

'Yes. What happened?'

'She tried to come through the control. I pointed out the correct route. She argued. I pointed out the correct route. She argued. I pointed out the correct route. She argued.' Up until then he had been with me. 'So I told her to piss off.' He sunk his head in his hands.

'She has put in a formal complaint about you.'

'Brilliant,' I said. 'So she was in such a hurry to catch her bus that she stopped off for half an hour at the police station to fill in a form? What are we supposed to do? Leave the gates open for everybody?'

'You're not supposed to tell them to piss off.'

'She wasn't taking notice of anything else that I said.'

The following day I was called in on my day off to be interviewed by Henry. He was still smarting from my refusal to take a bollocking for failing a promotion board.

'This is very serious,' he said.

'I agree. The control is like a colander. The security in this port is abysmal. People seem to think they can walk in and out as they please. What are we going to do about it?'

'You will have to go and apologise to her.'

I think I must have blinked. 'Apologise to her?'

'For being rude.'

'Oh yes, I shouldn't have told her to piss off but she should not have been walking through our control.'

'She has been told that.'

'I told her five times myself. She already knew it. They all know it.'

'I don't know how I am going to stop this from going up to Estabs.'

This was a threat. A visit to Estabs went on your personal file and knocked back your chances of ever doing anything nice. I looked at him, sitting there behind his desk, trying to wield his power. When would the management in this place ever stick up for its staff? Customs would probably have strip-searched the woman and what do we do? Try to castigate the IO for his attempt to maintain the security of the port within the published instructions. Then I realised my strength. I would call his bluff.

'OK, let it go to Estabs.' I leaned over his desk to make my point more forcefully. 'What can they do to me? I am immune. I am a Dover East IO. I work in this dump. What can they do to me? – give me a disciplinary transfer to somewhere nicer?'

It didn't go to Estabs.

I apologised to the woman.

And she continued to walk through our control.

19

Apparently the disease was called 'Sticklerism' or the 'Wagner-Stickler Syndrome' and all of our family had suffered from it from birth. It is a genetic deficiency in the constitution of the collagen in the body. The collagen, as I understand it, is the matrix from which the body makes all the soft tissue for skin, muscles, organs and such. I had accepted the total blindness of my mother as a child of seven would. When other eyes in the family had begun to fail it was because we had 'weak eyes'. We were utterly unaware of Sticklerism. The dislocation or hypermobility of joints were just characteristics of our clan.

When the various medical specialists began to examine us as a significant sibling group upon which they could do genetic research, then we began to suspect that perhaps our bodies did not work properly. Why did nobody in our family ever squat? Because it felt as if your knees would burst, of course. How long do you sleep for? Until your joints start to sting. Why do you sit crookedly like that? To ease the pain on your hips.

Nobody can know what it is like to live in another person's body but it became apparent to me that living in my body hurt me. From the doctors' observations I have deduced that the reason why I know I have legs is because they have been aching since I was eight years old. But if all your joints ache, and have always ached, you cannot recognise it as pain. It is just living. I didn't know it was pain until I was told so. Sometimes I inwardly rail against this revelation. But it can have a funny side to it. After a recent hospital operation, whilst I was still benefiting from the residue of the general anaesthetic, the nurse who had to complete the post-operative report asked me, 'How do you feel?'

'Bloody marvellous,' I replied with genuine fervour. 'I could do with one of these every day.' For the first time in my life, my body was just there for me to use. I could lift arms, bend legs, flex shoulders and I felt nothing. It was paradise.

'Patient is reticent about pain,' the nurse wrote on the form. She had no idea!

At other times I try to read back into my past, inventing 'what if' scenarios: would I have performed better at my school examinations if sitting on a chair for three hours at a stretch had not been so painful? Could I have run faster in athletics if my hips had not clicked and jarred at every movement?

Enough of this! Such postulation is unproductive. Sticklerism is hereditary, progressive, irreversible and untreatable. You've got it and you're stuck with it. It will make you blind, deaf and crippled. You managed the first thirty-eight years in ignorance of this; what are you intending to do now that you have the knowledge? What can you do?

There was nothing the NHS could provide although my GP managed to wangle some sessions with a private physiotherapist. I still start my every day with twenty minutes of physio exercises on the bedroom floor which are necessary to set up my body for the day. I was determined not to rely upon painkillers – I saw that as a dangerous slope.

How could I organise my working life? It would be difficult to change as the knowledge that everything I do, every movement I make, hurts me, only complicates the scenario. Silly little things are dangerous. If I am sitting on a swivel chair and a person leans on the back as they talk to me or moves it as they pass by, that slight and innocent action can mislocate my joints causing me gasping pain. But it would be considered petty in the extreme to ask somebody not to touch your chair and inexcusably offensive to refuse to shake hands but that greeting can cause me a physical hurt that will last a week.

I went in to the inspector, put the diagnosis report on his desk and told him that as from that day, I would do no more night duties. It was a good time to be making a nuisance of myself; mainstream Home Office practice was beginning to filter through to the Immigration Service. Shock horror, they were now talking about married women being able to job-share and even the possibility of employing disabled people. What was the world coming to?

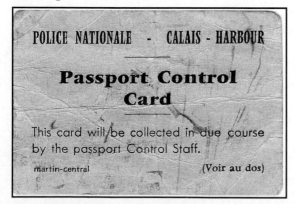

POLICE NATIONALE - CALAIS - HARBOUR

Passport Control Card

This card will be collected in due course by the passport Control Staff.

martin-central   (Voir au dos)

BOOKMARK
The French immigration officer crossing on the ferry with you places this card inside your passport to show that he has checked you.

I take it out and use it as a bookmark.

Now that I was an awkward unit, they would try to get rid of me. The only port in the district where the officers did not do night duties was Dover hoverport – the port to which I had tried and failed to get a transfer when it had opened ten years earlier. He would find me a place when the next vacancy arose.

Every port keeps a refusal register. It is a ledger whose pages are divided into columns in which are recorded the details of every passenger refused entry at the port. The last column across the page shows the port to which the passenger was removed and the identity, time and date of departure of the vessel or aircraft. Somewhere in an immigration office I have been shown a refusal register for the wartime years. For two of the refusals the resolution of their cases in the final column was defined in one word, 'shot'. They were German spies who were discovered, taken up to London and interrogated. They refused to work for Great Britain and so were executed.

In October 1940 the government took over the Royal Victoria Patriotic Schools in Wandsworth and IOs were instructed to send certain classes of persons there for interrogation by MI5. It eventually became known as the London Reception Centre and was the responsibility of the Home Office with the staff and guards supplied by the War Office. Any foreigner who was suspected of espionage, however, was removed from the LRC to 'Camp 020' which was Latchmere House on Ham Common. This was where they were really 'grilled'.

I am outside Latchmere House Detention Centre now, sitting in a Vauxhall Astra, waiting for the guards to unlock the gate and allow me in. I am going to 'interrogate' a Nigerian in order to apply for a Nigerian passport for him so that we can remove him from the UK. It is a familiar story; he came in as a student on his Nigerian passport and applied for a council house which he divided up and sublet. He then obtained a British visitors passport in a false identity, moved to a different borough and was given another council flat, and so on. He also dabbled in the odd bit of cannabis importation and was suspected of involvement in a fraudulent arrangement at the GPO sorting office where he selected interesting looking parcels, stuck a pre-addressed label over the original destination and had them delivered to his private unpacking centre. Naughty man.

The gate opens. I drive in. I am driving the second car that I had tried from the pool today; the first car had only one working headlight.

'That's no problem,' I was told. 'You'll be back before dark.'

'With an endorsement on my licence? Not likely. I'll take another car.'

The detention centre has been spruced up a bit since World War 2 but the layout of huts and roads is redolent of that era. When the contractors were renewing the ceiling in the main block they discovered some old wiring whose purpose was not immediately apparent. It was identified as part of the secret microphone network which was used to eavesdrop on the suspected spies in their rooms. The technique was to install a microphone behind a grille covering the ventilation duct on the wall furthest from the window. The apparatus of the time was bulky compared to that of today and was nowhere near as easy to conceal. Inevitably a suspicious spy would examine his room and discover the microphone and so whenever he wanted to converse with his room mate they would both move to the window, as far away as possible from the eavesdropping microphone. This was exactly what was intended, for the real microphone was hidden above the curtains by the window.

'Mr. Donald Adolabe?'

'Yessir.'

'Sit down. I am an immigration officer and my job today is to fill in this form so that we can apply for a Nigerian passport for you.'

'Yessir.'

'You understand that you have been refused permission to stay in the United Kingdom and recommended for deportation?'

'Yessir.'

'Well, we can't remove you without a passport so that is why I am here today.'

'Ah have got a passport.'

'Where is it?'

'Da Immigration have got it.' I search in the file and pull out the slip of folded beige cardboard. 'Dat is my passport.'

'This is a British visitors passport which you obtained in a false identity.'

'Yessir.'

I open it out to show him the details of the holder. 'That is not you.'

'Dat is me.' He points to the passport.

'No it is not.'

'Dat is me.' He stabs his finger on the photograph. 'Dat is me.'

'Yes, the photograph is of you, but the name and personal details are not you.'

'Yessir.'

'Where is your Nigerian passport?'

'Ah have lost it.'

'That is why we have to get you another one. You don't want to stay in here longer than you need to do you?'

'Ah want to go home.'

'To Nigeria?'

'Yessir.'

'Good. Well we are both working to the same goal then.' I pull out the application form from the Nigerian High Commission. 'Now what is your full name?'

'Donald Ijuma Adolabe.'

'When were you born?'

'Twenty fifth of March, nineteen fifty six.'

'What is your place of birth?'

'London.'

'No, you were not born in London.'

'Dat is my place of birth.' I shake my head. A look of sudden realisation illuminates his face. 'Ah, you mean my place of birth in Nigeria?' I nod encouragingly. 'My place of birth in Nigeria is Kano.'

'Thank you Mr. Adolabe.'

It's an interesting concept, isn't it – two different places of birth? But not as strange as that proposed by a Nigerian at Dover whose name and date of birth the IO had found in the book.

'That person is not me,' the passenger insisted. 'It is my twin brother.'

'Your twin brother? But not only was he born on the same date as you but he bears exactly the same name as you – all three names are identical. That must be confusing for everybody. How on earth do they tell you apart?' the IO enquired, not unreasonably.

'That is easy. My brother was born in Lagos. I was born in London.'

Try arguing with that.

I am on a month's relief because I applied for another spell of duty in central London. The Immigration Service has had a shake-up in the finances and some budgets have now been allocated locally. The only possible reason for this is to save money. It cannot be to provide greater autonomy to the districts, no matter what they say. In the London District they have apparently decided to economise on office rent. The office has moved from Adelaide House and the salubrious environs of London Bridge and has infested, rather than invested, a pokey, misshapen office block south of the river near Stamford Street. Isis House has none of the grandeur of neo-classical high ceilings and no stupendous panorama of the River Thames, HMS *Belfast* and Tower Bridge. At Adelaide House I could walk up the entrance steps and pretend that I was somebody in the City; here I skulk over cracked paving slabs to a grotty street door like a furtive businessman visiting a brothel.

I arrived on a Sunday to start my first duty that afternoon.

'Hi, I'm Mo. You're with me. We're doing visits.'

'Hello Mo,' I said. She was about ten years younger than me with bleached hair and spiky mascara.

'Do an IU check on those would you?' She threw two Home Office files onto the desk before me. 'I've got a report to finish before we go out.'

I fought my way through the zigzag of desks to one of the two computer terminals and tried to log on. This is a technical procedure designed to stop unauthorised persons from accessing the data. It involves numbers. No matter how many times I tried, the machine would not let me in. There is nothing more frustrating than the blank refusal without explanation that is the defence of idiots and computers. 'Wrong'. Tell me what I am doing wrong. 'Wrong'. But I am doing it the same way as I do at Dover East. 'Wrong'. Why don't you let me in? 'Wrong'.

I checked my password. I checked my warrant number. I could not fathom it out.

'What are you playing at?' Mo swaggered up.

'I can't get on to the computer. It won't let me in.'

'Dumbo, let me show you. This is a computer. Com-pu-ter, get it? Don't you lot know anything?' Apparently the Adelaide House attitude had not been lost in the transfer. She tapped at the keyboard and the screen welcomed her. 'See? Easy.'

'Just a minute,' I said. 'You used the number keypad at the end of the keyboard. Why don't you use the numbers on the main keyboard?'

'Cos it doesn't work that way, Dumbo.'

'Well it does at Dover East.'

She shook her head in pity and walked away. Do you know? I was not really happy with her attitude towards me, a colleague, of whom she knew nothing. But I need not have worried, because she did not care.

'Here's the map.' She threw an A-Z onto the dashboard. I reached forward to take it but missed as she let in the clutch and I was hurled back into my seat. 'Yeah baby, baby,' she sang and turned up the radio. 'Heard this track first in the States last year.' She tapped the rhythm on the steering wheel as we scattered a group of pedestrians. 'Peasants! Yeah me and Cindy – Do you know Cindy? We backpacked across the States.

Brilliant. Got put in the choky for a night 'cos we'd crossed the state line with half a bottle of brandy on us.' I hung onto the seat as we turned a corner and then braced my feet as she slammed on the brakes. 'They do a great cocktail in that wine bar.' She pointed at a red-painted shop front decorated with hanging baskets. 'Got coconut in it but they won't say what else. Two of those and you are under the table.' She flicked her hair from her face and lifted her foot from the clutch again. The seat hit me in the back and the tyres screeched. 'The big cop fancied himself. Threatened us with the District Attorney and all that crap. We told him to go fuck himself and he left us alone. The cheapest night we had in the States and it was courtesy of Uncle Sam.' She slowed down suddenly. 'It's along here somewhere.'

I made a successful grab for the A-Z. 'Where are we making for?'

'Ah, over there,' she said and drove across the three lanes to stop at the kerb. A car behind hooted at her, she gave it two fingers. 'Leather jackets,' she said. 'The cheapest in London. Gotta have one. We're on double yellows but, hell, it's Sunday. You'll be alright here for a while poppet.' She got out and slammed the door. 'Read the files whilst you're waiting. Make yourself useful.' She walked into the shop.

What fuel was this woman burning? She was treating me as if I were a doddering old fool. I felt resentful. The rest of the duty passed in a cacophony of non-stop noise from the radio and non-stop drivel from her. I tried to analyse the situation and treat it rationally. I should have been flattered for her behaviour seemed to emulate that of an insecure woman frantically trying to impress a man. I wasn't flattered but battered. Battered and flattened. I didn't give a toss what she had said to the Ghanaian who was lying to her or the Algerian who wanted her phone number; why couldn't she just shut up for five minutes?

Did London make people like this or was it that London attracted them? Several Dover East IOs had transferred up here. Willie was already dead from a heart attack. Douglas the woman-hating Scots IO had got a CIO board on appeal, passed it, and as my caseworking CIO one day, I found him to be a proper IO's CIO. He stood up for you, tried to help you in your job and was not out to trip you up at every opportunity. I would never have expected him to take to working in London but life in the metropolis had not made him into a screeching, shopaholic moron like Mo.

And then there was Aubrey. From the very first I had thought there was something wrong about him. He was a thin, weasel-faced Glaswegian who had come to Dover East from the Public Enquiry Office in Croydon. This was the office that I had visited as a trainee where I had sat next to the clerks as they had processed the applications for extensions of stay. The problem with somebody coming from this environment was that every person they saw in the PEO was a 'case.' They were people whom the IO had either told to visit the Home Office for an extension or who had deceived the IO from the start as to their intentions. When the officers working in daily contact with this raw material get transferred to the port they somehow expect the same proportion, i.e. 100%, of passengers to be 'cases'. They are not. It is something like 0.3%. Aubrey became the knock-off king of Dover East. He would get a case every day. He would come in for an A duty at ten past six in the morning and by the time that the rest of the shift had stamped on at the correct time of six-thirty, he already had a hold-up. It could not be right. If one officer could find so many refusals then the other one hundred and twenty IOs in the port must have been slacking. I did not believe that to be statistically possible. Surely, some of his refusals must have been morally wrong if not factually inaccurate? Yet they all had been authorised by a CIO.

I considered Aubrey's attitude to be simplistic, unhealthy and immature. I remember an instance of sharing a car kiosk with him. A Spanish registered Fiat had stopped at his guichet.

'Do you speak English?' he asked.

'Yes. Little.'

'How long are you staying?'

'Three weeks.'

'Why do you come here?'

'My... er... seester is work here.'

'What does she do?'

'Er... she go... I no speak English.'

'Oh I'm not having that. I can't trust what you are saying. First you say you speak English and now you say you don't. I shall have to detain you.'

I stared at him, astonished. It was a slight language difficulty which could be overcome with a modicum of goodwill on his part; it was not a case of wilful deception suitable for detention. But detained they were.

When in the casework office, heaven help you if you were handed one of his files. He wrote down every word that he said and every word that the passenger said in a minute spidery script that ran from edge to edge of the paper, ignoring the margins. It was so dense that you had to follow the lines with your finger along the top edge of a ruler in order to read them. He was intense, he was obsessive and I thought that he needed help before he did himself and the Service an injury.

But I did get some fun out of him. We were chatting around his desk on blue X one day as we waited for the ship to unload. In his serious tone he divulged that it was his birthday that day. I surreptitiously pulled a blank embarkation card from the stack and wrote clearly on the back. *'It is my birthday today. My name is Aubrey.'* When the walkers' bus began to discharge its load we scattered back to our desks and I folded back the bottom half of the card and stood the card up on the ledge below the front of his desk where he could not see it but the public could. I knew that he would treat every returning British holidaymaker as Lord Lucan in disguise and this would surely give somebody in the queue time to read it. The results exceeded my expectations.

'Happy birthday.' The first passenger greeted him. He took the passport and studied it assiduously for clues as to who the person was and how they had known it was his birthday.

'So how old are you today then Aubrey?' the next one said.

In the meantime I had managed to pass the word along the desks to my colleagues. We watched him getting more and more desperate.

'Happy birthday Aubrey.'

'You are doing this, Lloyd,' he pointed an accusing finger and called across at me. 'I don't know how you are doing it, but you are.' By now his face was a bemused grin but he was still clearing the passengers at just the correct cadence so that each had time to read the card.

'Don't know what you are talking about,' I lied.

It took twenty minutes to clear that queue and by the time we reached the end, Aubrey was resigned and acquiescent. He had the goodness to grin when the ruse was exposed to him.

But here at Isis House, things were going deep. He was so involved in an operation investigating the Yardies that the Met. police had loaned him one of their cars. He was just the type of manic, one-track, obsessive investigator that they would believe in. I never actually met him at Isis House. The next time I saw him it was as the subject of an investigatory programme on television after he had been suspended.

It was at Isis House that I conducted my first political asylum interview. In the world as it is now, where nearly every knock-off seems to whisper 'asylum' as soon as they realise that their attempt to fool the IO has failed, it seems bizarre to be able to remember the first asylum interview you did but they were not a commonplace occurrence back in the eighties. The applicant was an eighteen year old Ghanaian, which was unexpected since at that time we had a ship full of Tamil asylum seekers all on hunger strike. This Ghanaian knew as little about political asylum as I did. To ensure that the IO asked all the correct questions and collected the necessary information the Home Office issued a questionnaire to use as a framework for the interview.

I filled in the form and asked no supplementary questions. The applicant said that he had been told to apply for asylum by his mother. He did not know what it meant. He could not quote any instances of fearing for his life because of religious beliefs or ethnic origins, so we left it at that. I often wonder whether his claim succeeded. Looking back on it now I realise that I conducted an appalling interview; it could have been of no use to anybody.

Although the work at Isis House was supposedly the same as it had been at Adelaide House, to me it seemed just a bit grubbier. Perhaps it was the dowdiness of the office that was rubbing off on the work. I thought that some of the tasks could easily have been done by cheaper clerical staff: it took me half a day in the Nigerian High Commission trying to get a passport issued. Why pay me all that money for doing the job of a courier? Where, before, I had found the work challenging in its novelty, now it was depressing in its mundaneness and nobody seemed to worry if a job was left undone or poorly executed. I was glad when my term was over. I would not go there again, I decided.

But before I left Isis House I enjoyed a morning of entertainment. I was given the task of serving a form at Horseferry Magistrates' Court. I rang up Nigel Andrews whose office I knew was near there.

'Can you leave your appeal statements and come and have coffee with me?' I asked.

'Yes, easy, I'm on a report-writing day. I'll meet you downstairs.' He was waiting for me in the street when I got there. 'Come and have a look at this,' he said, leading me off through a maze of pavements and shops. 'Netball.'

'Yer what?' I said. 'I can't stand sport.'

'Wait till you see this. It's a regular league with teams from the offices of the district.'

'Oh yawn, yawn.'

I plodded along behind him, my leather case banging against my legs. We each bought a plastic mug of something at a kiosk window and I followed him towards a plaza where I could hear cheering, cries and calls and the occasional blast of a whistle.

'What do you think?' He grinned.

Well, what did I think? A netball post had been erected at opposite ends of the paved square and around it stood the spectators. In the middle a bevvy of young women, squeezed into shorts and tight shirts were leaping and running about playing netball. Most of the spectators were men and it was not the bouncing of the ball which held their attention but the bouncing of youthful female anatomies. I revised my opinion of sport there and then.

'Have you finished your coffee?' he asked.

'No, I think I can still find some in the bottom of the cup.'

It was a wonder we got to Horseferry Magistrates' Court at all. I showed my warrant and was escorted down to the cells. I found our detainee and the court official opined that bail would not be granted in his case. I served the form on the police; I was not going to get caught out by believing the opinions of an usher. Having done that we went upstairs to watch the fun.

Nigel and I kept a low profile as we waited amongst the lawyers and other members of the public so that we would not get involved in any of the cases coming up that morning. If there is one phrase you dread to hear, it is, 'Your honour, to settle this point, I believe there is an immigration officer in the court today.'

But I knew from experience that it was very difficult to hear what was going on in court because the actors in the drama just talked to each other; they were not there to deliver to the gallery, so as soon as the door was opened, I elbowed my way forward and we got seats right at the front. Nigel and I quickly appraised our neighbours and exchanged a look that we both understood to mean, 'all these people look as if they should be down in the cells.'

The dock itself was a three-sided construction of wrought iron surmounted by a wooden banister rail. It was directly in front of us. Beyond it stretched the benches for the counsel, the tables for the clerk and then the dais supporting the magistrates' bench.

'May the court be upstanding.' The usher's voice rang out loud and clear. A door at the far end opened and in walked John Cleese. He did the Ministry of Silly Walks sketch to his chair, leaned over the table, looked down the court, gave me a pantomime wink and then sat down.

We also sat, Nigel and I holding our breath to prevent an outburst of laughter. The magistrate turned and winked at the clerk of the court and proceedings commenced.

I thought it was unfortunate that the representative of justice should look like a well-known comedian, have an awkward gait and a nervous tick; it was deadly for us. We were sucking in our cheeks and rubbing our noses to hide our reactions. And as you are well aware, in circumstances as formal as those, the more you try not to laugh, the more difficult it becomes. But we had been hardly tested yet.

The first contestant was brought up from the cells and prodded into the iron corral by a rotund police officer. He was a man in his early twenties, dressed in jeans and a tee shirt. He gazed around the court vacantly and his jaw slopped and slapped as he masticated his gum. The clerk began to read out the charge.

'...that on Sunday the 14th of this month, you did, in the locality of the Lancaster Hotel, use language and behaviour likely to cause–'

At this point the police officer suddenly jerked towards the accused and in a stentorian voice bellowed, 'Are yeeoo choooin'?' The youth paused with his mouth open. Then he snapped his jaws shut.

'Yeah.' He nodded.

'Well git it art then.'

The lad looked for a moment as if he was going to argue but thought better of it and pulled the gum from his mouth and began to roll it in his fingers prior to lodging it somewhere. He looked down at the banister rail and then up at the court. Every eye in the room was upon him. He looked right, he looked left. Eventually he shrugged and thrust his hand into his trousers pocket.

The charge was read and the magistrate asked for the evidence. A police constable sitting by the top table stood up and began to read from his notebook.

'I was on duty outside the Lancaster Hotel on the day in question. At approximately half past ten in the evening Mr. Haynes and his wife came out of the hotel and stood under the porch to await a taxi. The defendant was heard to remark, "Cor, look at the fucking state of her. Look at the fucking state of her." I asked him to moderate his language and he replied, "yeah but look at the fucking state of her."' This was delivered in the caricature of the police evidence accent that you have heard in every Ealing comedy.

I dared not look at Nigel. I wondered if I could discreetly stuff my handkerchief into my mouth. Oh why had we sat at the front?

'You have heard the evidence. How do you plead?' the magistrate demanded.

'I dunno what you mean, "how do you plead? How do you plead?" Wodjer mean, "how do you plead"?'

'Well do you plead guilty or not guilty?'

'Wodjer mean, "plead"? I dunno what you're talkin about.'

The magistrate sat back, gave another pantomime wink, jerked his head backwards and then sighed.

'You have to plead either "guilty" or "not guilty".'

'Wodjer mean?'

'Well you heard what the policeman said. Did you do those things?'

'Oh yeah I done that.'

'Well then you are pleading guilty.'

'No. No, I don't wanna be guilty.'

'But you just said that you did those things.' The magistrate's voice rose an octave.

'Yeah I done that but I don't wanna be guilty.'

'Enter a plea of "guilty",' the magistrate said to the clerk. 'Fined twenty pounds.'

The lad was manhandled away and replaced by a man in his fifties wearing the jacket of a lounge suit over jeans.

'Loitering on the highway,' a clerk announced and then a man sitting next to the policeman who had given evidence, shot up from his seat like a jack-in-a-box.

'Tea towels,' he said and sat down abruptly.

'How do you plead?'

'Guilty your honour.'

'Fined fifteen pounds.'

He shuffled out and another man took his place.

'Loitering on the highway,' said the clerk.

'Ice creams.' The jack-in-a-box popped up and down.

'Anything to say?'

'Just the usual meaningless excuses Guvner.'

'Fined twenty pounds. Next.'

'Loitering on the highway.'

'Fluffy toys.'

And on it went. We deduced that we were seeing the collection of unauthorised street-traders who had been arrested over the weekend.

BOOKMARK
Please have this card ready. It will be collected at the gangway.
And then used by Martin as a bookmark.

After the four saffron-robed Hari Krishna disciples had trooped out, ('singing and chanting,') having tried to sell a copy of their book to the magistrate, Nigel and I made our getaway in case we became a 'snorting and guffawing' prosecution.

Ever at a loose end in London? Go to a magistrates' court.

Back at Dover East and world history creeps into our car kiosk. My colleague taps his newspaper. 'I see Rudolf Hess has committed suicide.'

'Shall I cancel him in my suspect index?'

'Better wait for the official notice. If they thought he was a risk to the security of the UK when he'd been safely locked up in Spandau prison since 1946, then they will probably be scared of his ghost. He must have been nearly a hundred.'

' *Born 1894'* it says here. That makes him ninety-six. Do you reckon that there are any really dangerous people in this book?'

'Who knows, my son, who knows? Aye oop, cars.'

An enormous black slug of a Rolls Royce limousine slides up to me. The chauffeur hands me two British passports. I can already see the SB officer hurrying across from the other lane.

'Could you lower the rear window please? I can't see in.' The darkened window slides down to reveal a venerable old lady in black – Lady Diana Mosley.

Geoff collared me pretty smartly in the office and set me to work updating the carriers' liability file that I had designed. The Carriers' Liability Act had been introduced in 1987 to try to stop the airlines and shipping companies from bringing to the UK persons who were patently not qualified for entry. One might think that the mere fact that in a case of refusal the carrier was already obliged to pay for the removal of the person from the UK would be sufficient deterrent but often this cost them little – they merely put the person back on one of their own aircraft or ships – sometimes successfully selling them duty-free goods on the return journey as well. The government decided to fine them one thousand pounds for every offending passenger that they brought in. Suitability was to be measured on a simple yardstick such as, 'this passenger needs a visa for the UK, he has none. You should not have brought him here.'

That sounds straightforward but how does the airline find out if the passenger has a visa? What right have they to demand to see the passport? How can they tell whether the visa is genuine? The carriers complained, not without reason, that the government was trying to outsource the immigration control and earn money from it. They began to challenge our proof. How do you know that the passenger came on our ship? Where is the evidence? This was sometimes impossible to produce because those who wished to claim asylum would destroy all their documents in the toilets between disembarkation and the passport control. Immigration offices had to set up teams of surveillance IOs who watched the passengers as they stepped off the planes. It was all very expensive in manpower terms. The IS had to provide training for the carriers' staff so that they could interpret the stamps that we used. When several years later new visa stickers and redesigned stamps were introduced, the Carriers' Liability Unit of the Immigration Service, because obviously we had another empire by then, published a super full-colour brochure explaining and illustrating clearly all the changes. The brochures were issued to the airline check-in staff but not to IOs. It was the world turned upside down. We could produce full-colour brochures to instruct the layman but we could not train our own staff.

From the procedural point of view, the IS approached the challenge of the liability of carriers and the imposition of fines with its usual arrogance. We can do anything. It can't be that difficult to organise. Before the instructions were released, Geoff got hold of a copy and gave them to me. He told me to take two days off the control and work out how the requirements of the Carriers Liability Act were to be implemented at Dover East. It certainly was a challenge, for now we would be required to take certain actions within set time limits. This in itself was not an unfamiliar concept, but we had to record the name of the person taking that action and the time and date that they did it otherwise the demand for payment would not be valid. For that proportion of the personnel who still managed to complete an office duty without ever writing on a file, this obligation would appear as revolutionary as it would distasteful.

I digested the instructions, scratched my head and sketched on paper. Taking a simple paper file cover as the base, I managed to print the instructions in the correct chronological order, with guidance notes and references to relevant official circulars and with spaces where the officer taking the action had to record his name before he could enter the next stage, in such a way that once you had the blank file you had the instructions, the guidance on how to proceed, the record of what you had done and the legal wording of the Act all on one folded A3 document. And this I did with a typewriter, drawing pen and ruler. It never occurred to me that I was doing work of several grades higher than that for which I was being paid. I did it to make my job easier to perform. Mistakes cause extra work and I am lazy at heart.

But not too lazy to take off my tie on the day that the BBC radio announcer declared that this was the hottest July on record. I had been standing in full sun behind a sheet of glass for thirty minutes. I had already hung my jacket on the back of my chair. The Brits. filing through the hall were wearing the absolute minimum to retain decency. Some wore even less.

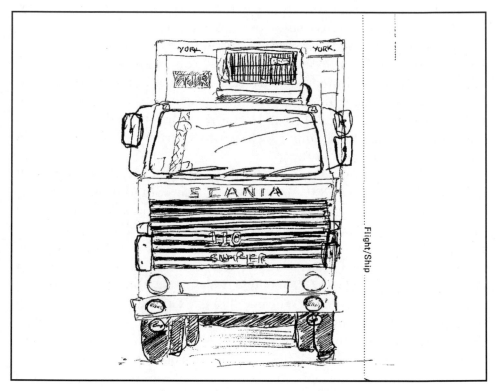

THE VIEW FROM MY OFFICE WINDOW
A TIR lorry waiting in the queue at the freight control, Dover East.

I dealt with a British coach driver at the window and watched him return to his coach to pull it forwards to the police gate. As he put the coach in gear he looked up into his rear view mirror. I saw his lips move. My days of guiding coaches around Paris flooded back to me. He was speaking to somebody at the back of the coach. I grabbed the phone at the side of me and rang the police gate.

'Exit.'

'Immigration here. Check inside that coach that is approaching you. I think he has someone hidden at the back.'

'OK.'

A few minutes later a rather sheepish British coach driver and his mate were presented at my window by the DHB police officer. His mate had lost his passport and rather than have to explain it all to me had decided to hide below the back seat. I gave them a warning, which was actually without any weight since I was satisfied that he was British, and then let them proceed. It was more important to let them know that we had our eyes open. Just in case the next time it was a couple of illegal immigrants that slipped below the seat.

'Where is your tie?' the CIO suddenly said from behind me.

'In my pocket,' I replied as I handed back a passport.

'Put it on.'

'It's too hot.'

'Put your tie on. You are not properly dressed.'

I was wearing a crisply ironed, short sleeved white shirt with the top button left undone and grey flannel trousers. The passenger sweating in front of me was squeezed into a microscopic pair of shorts and a loose singlet. The CIO was standing in the shade.

'No, I'm not putting my tie on. It's too hot.'

He stormed off. About five minutes later Joy appeared at my shoulder.

'You're relieved,' she said.

'It's only twenty to.'

'I was on office duty. I've been told to take over your duty and you are to replace me in the office.'

'What a prat,' I said. 'Not you, Joy.'

'I know who you mean,' she sighed as she dumped her book and stamps on the desk.

I sat in the cool of the office and idly flicked through the one file that was 'live' for that day. Downstairs the passenger hall was bursting at the seams. Oh well, if that's the way they want to play it.

After about half an hour the CIO came up to give me a bollocking. He ranted up and down the office whilst I watched him in bemusement. He was becoming red in the face with his passion. The Immigration Service was not a discipline force like the police. We did not have uniforms, we did not salute or have parades and inspections. The whole ethos of the job was for us to be inconspicuous and non-threatening. A couple of years earlier some discussion had been noised about giving us uniforms after an IO had claimed for the ruin of his sports jacket by a Stationery Office issue ball point pen which he had secured in his breast pocket by the clip on its cap. The pen had slipped out of its cap and leaked its black ink through the

Harris Tweed. The Stationery Office's defence had been that the clip on the cap was not actually a clip for attaching the pen to pockets but a crafty device to prevent the pen from rolling from the desk. The pen was not faulty and the IO was just careless.

The question of uniforms for the Immigration Service was next considered within the context of the Prison Service being kitted out in new togs and the Home Office consequently finding itself with a shed full of old uniforms. What could they do with them? Why not make the IOs wear them? That's the way things are done in high places. Find a solution then search for a problem for it to solve.

'So what have you got to say for yourself?' the CIO said. 'This will have to go to the inspector.'

'I am thirty-eight. I know when I can take my tie off.'

'You've not heard the last of this,' he threatened me.

And neither have you, I thought.

Memo from HMI Dover East
To: Mr. M Lloyd.

I have received a note from the CIO that he told you to put on a tie when you appeared on the controls, but you refused. As a result you were instructed to continue your duty in the Ops room and one of your colleagues had to work on the passenger controls.

I am told that you told Mr. Smith that you considered yourself old enough to be able to decide whether to wear a tie or not. I should like to make it absolutely clear that the instructions on wearing a tie when dealing with the public apply to all ranks. Any dispensation can only be granted by an Inspector or a CIO if he considers the conditions warrant it.

I trust that I have made the position quite clear and in future you will abide by the instructions.

I photocopied the memo and put it on the general noting file for all to see. Four IOs immediately took off their ties. I followed it with a copy of my response:

Memo from Mr. M. Lloyd
To: HMI Dover East.

I was recently ordered by the CIO to put on my tie and when I refused I was sent up to the office and was replaced by a colleague. At that time there were eight IOs on the control with me and only five of them were wearing ties. The three not wearing ties were all women and none of them was asked to put on a tie. The IO who replaced me was also a woman and was not wearing a tie.

Any repetition of this action by you or any other member of management I will consider to be an act of discrimination within the terms of the Sexual Discrimination Act 1975 (as amended) and take it to a tribunal.

I trust I have made myself clear.

Well, the spade really hit the trifle then. The natural reaction of the management was that I was taking the mickey. They could not believe that they were discriminating. You see the problem at Dover East was that although we now had plenty of women IOs, we had no women CIOs. The idea was laughable. A woman CIO? How could she possibly boss men about? And of course the male CIOs had no idea how to deal with the women IOs. At the same time that I was being castigated for not wearing a tie, we had a woman trainee turn up for work wearing paint-stained jeans, a tee shirt and fur coat. Did they say anything to her? No, of course not. And she wasn't wearing a tie either.

To keep our official keys secure, male IOs had to attach their key chains to their clothing. Women IOs were allowed to pin the chain to the lining of their handbags. How safe is that? How many times have you heard a woman in the office say, 'Now where did I put my handbag?' I would propound that it is more times than you have heard a man say, 'Now where did I put my trousers?'

Luckily the whole thing escalated into absurdia with IOs wearing high-necked jumpers so that nobody could see whether they were wearing ties, or knotting them so low down on their chest as to make them invisible under the jacket. I decided I would buckle under with a vengeance. The daft thing was, I actually liked wearing ties. So I combed the charity shops for the most hideous ties that you could imagine: Indian shot silk in pink, a batik affair that looked like split intestines, 1960s kippers in paisley. The only one I could not find was a tie with a nude woman on it. Shame. Colleagues joined in the hunt and I would find a gaudy tie in my pigeon hole with an anonymous note attached to it, *'bet you wouldn't dare wear this one.'* I always did. Eventually I managed to excite a response from the travelling public and submitted an official memo to notify my CIO that a passenger had complained that I was wearing a tie.

After that, we wore what we liked. They were almost treating us like adults. Which was just as well, because the job that we were supposed to be doing sometimes had serious ramifications.

'What's happened to that Samara chap?' I asked as I relieved the morning office shift.

'What Samara?'

'The one on the–' I looked at the casework board. 'Oh, he's been rubbed off.'

'What was he?'

'An Arab of some denomination, I think. I wasn't involved in the case.'

'Well he's not here now.'

An hour later I got a call from our compound.

'Do you know anything about somebody collecting the car of that Arab chappie?'

'No, I don't. But what is his car doing here still? He's been rubbed off the board and his file has disappeared.'

There was a shuffling and mumbling at the other end.

'OK forget it. Nothing to worry about. I'll tell you later.'

Samara was a member of the PLO squad who had assassinated an Arab journalist a few weeks earlier in London. He was whisked away by SB to Paddington Green police station which is one of the top security sites. The car was covered and trailered away by MI5. A couple of weeks later Douglas Hurd signed a 'not conducive to the public good' deportation order for him and he was kicked out.

Well I hope that the Dover East IO who picked him out was wearing a tie – what would the man have thought?

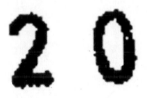

'Paul Daninos,' I say.

'Paul who?' Andy challenges me.

'Daninos. He wrote *Les Carnets du Major Thompson*.'

'Never heard of him.'

'That's because you're a philistine.'

'I never touch the stuff. Anyway he doesn't count if you are the only person who has heard of him.'

'He embarked through Dover East in a dark grey Daimler V8 250. He had brought it over for a service because it is cheaper here.'

'Doesn't count.'

'He came back and insisted on signing an embark card for me as a souvenir. A bit embarrassing really.'

'Don't care.'

'All right then... Richard Adams. Arrived in a Rover 3500.'

'I've never–'

'–He wrote *Watership Down*. You must have read that.'

'Yeah I've read it but I didn't remember his name.'

'His occupation in his passport was *'schoolmaster'*.'

'Doesn't trump my Harry Secombe. Yours are all very literary aren't they? Poser.'

'I landed Kate Adie down on walkers last week.'

'Who?'

'I'm not having that. You know Kate Adie – the TV news reporter. Full name Kathleen, born in Blackburn.'

'I've got a Harry Secombe.'

'Alan Simpson and Ray Galton in a Burgundy Bentley Continental and before you profess your utter ignorance, they wrote most of *Hancock's Half Hour* and invented *Steptoe and Son*.'

'I've got a Harry Secombe, on a Friday night, at Gatwick. Beat that.'

'Tracy Ullman at Terminal Three when I was on relief.' Andy pulls a rude face at me. 'All right, I'll admit that I didn't know who she was until I saw a photograph of her in the *Sunday Times* on the following day.

Apparently she is a comedienne.'

'Harry Secombe.'

'David Frost off Concorde.'

'You never saw him.'

'No, you're right, but I know somebody who did.'

'Cheat.'

'All right then, this'll beat you. Princess Anne and Captain Mark Phillips on nights. Drove through in a Range Rover with a police car leading them. She was picking her nose.'

'She wasn't picking her nose she was rubbing her face and I was there as well so that's snap.'

'Oh bum, you win. Let's go down and do the craft.'

I fitted in to the work at Dover hoverport with an eagerness lubricated by a decade of anticipation. Here was a port where I had my own space; a desk of my own. It sounds terribly petty but when the work you are trying to do is subject to random and inescapable interruption from arriving hovercraft, the facility to simply put down your pen on the paper and return an hour later to find it in the same place and everything untouched is a valuable component of efficiency. In some environments, 'hot desking' does not work – it's a rubbish idea thought up by self-promoting management gurus to sell to penny-pinching employers.

A small port, a 'dinky port' as the Service pejoratively refers to them, is a very rewarding and useful place to work. I have found that IOs who transfer in from a dinky port always know more about the mechanics of the job. At Dover East we had an army of clerical staff to sort out the reports, landing cards, circulars and other paperwork. All we were required to do was to stamp passports. In a dinky port, you have to do it all yourself.

And it is pleasant to be able to chat to a hostess or a baggage handler or a bus driver whilst waiting for the passengers to arrive. It makes me feel almost human.

On my first day at work I put a bottle of champagne in the office fridge and told everybody that it was needed to celebrate my first refusal. They thought I was joking. Well, those who did not know me, did. Two weeks later, he arrived. Recently I had been told on a senior IOs' course that IOs were not allowed to 'stereotype' passengers. Most of us bridled at this. What was the use of our experience if we were not permitted to apply it? You might as well employ untrained staff straight from the employment exchange. Oh what a prophetic observation! We were also sanitised to fall within the requirements of the Race Relations Acts. Trainers were not allowed to single out nationalities for particular treatment. They could no longer tell trainees to look in the back of a Tunisian passport in order to find where the French always put their refusal stamps. 'Rubbish!' we all cried. 'Tunisian is a nationality not a race. We are not picking them out for special comment because of their ethnicity but for their allegiance to a country.'

So when this twenty-eight year old Japanese man came up to my desk and proffered a passport which showed that he had been in Europe for eight months my racially biassed, prejudiced stereotyping mind told me that he was not going back to Japan and, as a Japanese he would not consider it dishonourable to tell lies to me, a European. He was a wealthy young man on an extended holiday in Europe. No he was not. He was a cook with a complete set of chef's knives hidden at the bottom of his bag along with the references from the restaurants in France and Germany who had employed him illegally. He had arranged work for himself in a Japanese restaurant in London and was going to settle here. I refused him and then nipped back up to the office and returned with a tray of sparkling glasses and the champagne. The control area took on the aspect of a diplomatic cocktail party as a couple of Hoverspeed hostesses, the customs officer, the operations manager, a cleaner and the Japanese chef stood around toasting each other and exchanging pleasantries. We all waved to his glowing, beaming face as he was escorted back to the craft for removal to Calais.

Maybe he thought that this was the standard procedure for refusal in the UK because he tried again two weeks later and was refused at Newhaven. He didn't get any champagne there. I checked.

THE VIEW FROM MY OFFICE WINDOW

Three hovercraft parked on the pad, the Jetfoil on the right, arriving from Ostend and still on its foils making its way to the pontoon at Admiralty Pier, and the wide blue yonder of the English Channel.

Throughout the nineteenth century a multitude of proposals to cross the English Channel by rail were put forward. Most of them involved tunnels, some, bridges and one, turning the Varne sandbank into an artificial island but the surprising aspect for me was that most of these schemes were dreamt up by French engineers. Why? The French did not want to visit Britain – it was cold and grey and wet and the food was awful. The vast majority of passengers crossing with Charles Dickens on the Folkestone Packet to Boulogne would also have been British; why did the French want to facilitate their passage? – because they spent money. Even now it seems that the cross Channel links are run largely to allow the British to visit the Continent and not vice versa.

Construction of a Channel tunnel was started several times in the nineteenth century and all of the projects were financed by railway companies, after all, they had the most to gain. By the middle of the century more than a million passengers were already crossing the Channel annually on their ships. The French sunk a shaft at Sangatte in 1874, not far from where the present Channel tunnel terminus is sited. The British started out to meet them from Dover itself, at the foot of Shakespeare Cliff. But it was not to be. When about two thousand feet had been dug from both ends, a parliamentary committee met, deliberated and decided that it would not be expedient to construct a tunnel under the Channel. The military, in its various guises, were afraid that once built, it would permit an easy invasion of England. This was despite the fact that egress from the tunnel would have been by hydraulic lift to raise each carriage individually to the surface and that the tunnel site was covered by a specially built battery which had been constructed on the Admiralty Pier in Western Docks with its cannons facing inland so that it could bombard the exit if required. The tunnel was bricked up. The guns are still there.

In the 1960s the Channel Tunnel Study Group met and drew up a recommendation to the British and French governments that the tunnel should be a twin rail tunnel financed by private enterprise. This was a bit of a blow for Kent because British Railways had purposefully neglected to improve the lines down to Folkestone and Dover on the understanding that when a tunnel was built then the government would give British Railways lots of money to pay for the new route. So whilst passengers on the rest of the network reclined on their seats in air-conditioned trains with automatic doors and running on silent long-welded rails, we in Kent froze on upright benches, peering through the dirty rattling windows in our noisy slam-door, *clack-clack, clack-clack* trains.

Then in the late 1970s, suddenly it was 'on'. Fields around Dover were sown with rows of huts to accommodate the workers, the boring machines arrived along with the drug dealers.

The Immigration Service had to devise a system to check passengers which would please the politicians, the operating companies and the travelling public whilst remaining within a sensible budget. The europhile politicians wanted free passage for everybody through the tunnel with no passport checks at all; the operating company supported this vision, the ferry companies did not. They did not need a competitor on the cross Channel market who not only would have no problems with the weather but could also guarantee no delays at control points. The ferry companies' revenues were already under threat by the proposal to revoke the 'duty-free sales' arrangement. More than once I had heard it said that the duty-free shop on the Townsend Thoresen ferry *Free Enterprise I* had paid for the construction of *Free Enterprise II* and so on through the fleet with the assurance of a logarithmic progression. The profits from 'duty-free' sales were enormous because once the duty had been lifted, the seller could add a margin of several hundreds of percent and still appear to offer a bargain. My father was the manager of an off-licence in Chesham called Climpson's. When I was helping him in his shop at Christmas 1966 he had advertised Teacher's Scotch Whisky for sale at 2/6 ($12^1/_2$p) a bottle plus tax. Shoppers had thronged in and slapped their half crowns down on the counter. 'Forty seven and sixpence please,' my father had said. They could not believe that of the full sales price of £2.37p, only 12p was allocated to be shared between the producer, wholesaler and retailer with the remainder going to the Exchequer. But it was true.

The dream of a control-free tunnel faded and the next problem was to devise a system wherein the frontier authorities of the respective countries could carry out their checks without hindering the operation of the tunnel. The traffic through the tunnel fell into two classes. The through express trains were to be called 'Eurostar', and would carry only foot passengers. They would depart from a specially converted area at Waterloo station in London and pass through the tunnel area without stopping. The Shuttle trains which would carry no foot passengers but all the motorised traffic – cars, coaches, lorries – would run only between the terminals of Coquelles and Cheriton; the width of the train being too great to be accommodated on the standard railway systems of the two countries. Passport control on Eurostar could easily be undertaken at the terminal stations: Paris, Brussels, London and the intermediate stops at Ashford, Kent and Lille, France with any operational 'filling in' which might be needed being provided by IOs travelling on the trains. This would be the equivalent of the 'crossing IOs' on a ferry.

The motorised travellers for the Shuttle would converge on the terminals from all directions via the road network and would have to be checked at the terminal. This would create the problem of queuing. Vehicles disembarking from ships at Dover East could easily spend forty minutes waiting at the immigration and customs control points. This could not be allowed at the tunnel for it would create a backlog of trains waiting in the tunnel to be cleared. The solution was 'juxtaposed controls'. As France and Great Britain were more interested in checking the people wishing to enter their country than those wishing to leave it, why not put the French controls in England and the British controls in France? This would mean that travellers only queued to enter the tunnel. At the tunnel exit, having already passed through the control points of both countries before entering the tunnel, they would simply drive onto the motorway.

It was within this context that the hoverport immigration office acquired the Channel Tunnel Unit which was formed in order to thrash out some of the problems posed by the imminent inauguration of the UK's first real international land border. It was inevitable that the team would be foisted upon us because we had the newest and most comfortable accommodation in the south east. The IOs were all local; we knew them, they were no trouble. The CIOs kept out of the way. The inspector was one of those people whose work was so important and pressing that he would walk into the general office already talking to the person he wished to address regardless of whatever they were doing or saying. He was a steamroller. Steamrollers are powered by steam. Steam is just a load of hot air which has become rather wet.

One morning he erupted through the doorway, talking at me over an important telephone call that I was taking in French, slapped a sheet of paper down on my desk and told me that he needed it translated into English before ten o'clock. I was not in his team, I was a control IO but to keep matters sweet I fitted his 'request' in to my busy morning. When my translation was still lying untouched in his in-tray after lunch and he still had his snout in the trough somewhere I relegated him to the lowest stratum of importance in my world and thereafter co-operated with him accordingly.

The empire I did want to join was the Telecoms Unit. It managed the budget for the Immigration Service countrywide and was run from the hoverport by an inspector, a couple of CIOs and some of the control IOs in their 'down time'. Within a few months of my being transferred into the hoverport, an IO in the unit moved out and I was given proud responsibility for radio pagers throughout the Service. At this time we had a contract with BT for them to supply a pager called Le Bleep. It looked somewhat similar to those cheap French cigarette lighters and my task was to assess applications from the various ports and allocate the equipment. Pagers at that time were 'zoned' and you paid according to how many geographical zones you wished your pager to function in. With Le Bleep, we also could pay a surcharge for additional differentiated 'bleeps' to allow the user to know which person was calling him.

Needless to say I received no training in procurement skills; I was supposed to know how to negotiate with telecommunications companies. As it happened I had studied contract law at college which served me well when I later forced Vodafone to alter one of the conditions which was printed in 2pt grey type on the back of all their standard contracts. You were not supposed to read them. I took the job seriously and did. The clause declared that in the event of Vodafone failing to provide the service contracted for, the customer would compensate them. And all their other customers had signed it.

Any mobile technology provided by the Service was considered to be a status symbol. A port applying for pagers would insist on having full UK coverage although they would only be used in say, Middlesborough, because it made them feel important. But the representations made to me were nothing as compared to those made to my colleagues who were in charge of mobile phones. It is difficult to believe today but in the 1990s we were supplying mobile telephones which cost £1,000 each. To carry one of those on a job meant that you had real status. 'Health and Safety' was an increasingly popular lever employed to try to prise a telephone out of us. Suddenly it had become dangerous for an IO to go into the London docks without being able to contact their home port at every instant. Or confidentiality was cited – it was unreasonable to expect an IO to use the telephone in a police station when reporting back on an interview. Then they tried the 'greater efficiency' mantra – being able to contact the IO wherever he might be in his duty. This argument I considered to be disingenuous since the first place any office would look for (and find) a missing IO was in the pub.

A useful contribution that I made at this time was to concoct an Immigration Service telephone directory. I taught myself to use Wordperfect, which was the word-processing package which came with our computer and I compiled a directory which allowed any officer to dial straight to the extension number he needed and to speak to the person he required. Why did not such a directory already exist? It seemed a bizarre oversight to me. I got permission to have it printed and distributed country-wide. It saved me a lot of time. It must have economised years of man-hours throughout the Service.

I had managed to strike a good deal with Vodafone for a block of pagers which could display a short text message on a small screen and I started to replace the Le Bleeps whose facility was restricted to informing the receiver that he needed to telephone somebody. One of the first applicants for a new Vodafone pager was Barry Lipscomb, an HMI at headquarters. He had a reputation for amassing all kinds of 'status' equipment. He did not have a Le Bleep but had already justified his need for a mobile phone, a secure fax machine, a scrambler landline telephone and a remote electric lock on his office door. How would a pager improve his efficiency? The answer, of course, was that it would not. It would solidify his belief in his own image. Nobody else at ISHQ had managed to qualify themselves for a mobile telephone and a pager. The CIO telecoms told me to supply it so I did. I was annoyed several months later to discover that Mr. Lipscomb had contacted Vodafone direct and insisted upon all the options available being assigned to his pager. The deal that I had negotiated had been for a uniform but nevertheless useful set of options for the entire block of pagers. This had got us the good price. He had effectively rescinded that contract and incurred the Service in extra costs. I rang his pager but got no response. I rang his secretary who told me that he was in Manchester but the pager was locked in his safe.

'What is the point of that?' I asked. 'It's no use in a safe. Does he ever take it with him?'

'Well, I don't know. It has been there since he got it.'

Nikos, the mobile phone supremo IO, was taking some interest in my call.

'Why don't you phone him on his mobile?' he suggested. 'He declared that he needed one of our latest Motorolas. We only had three.'

'Are they any good?' I asked.

'About the best we have got.'

'Do you want it back? Give me his number.' I rang his mobile telephone. 'Will it work in Manchester?'

'Yeah, no problem.'

He was right.

'Hello. Lipscomb,' the voice replied.

'Hello?' I said. 'Hello?'

'Hello, Barry Lipscomb.'

'Hello? Hello?' I turned slightly away from my phone but remained close enough for Mr. Lipscomb to hear what I was saying. 'His stupid phone isn't working.' Nikos raised his eyebrows in disbelief. I turned back. 'Hello? Hello? Is there anybody there?'

'Hello. It's Barry Lipscomb here. Who's that?'

'Hello? Hello? No, the thing isn't working.'

'Hello?' The inspector's voice sounded a trifle irritated now.

'Hello? Hello?' I turned aside again. 'What phone did you give him then? A Motorola? But they're crap, you know they are. Why did you give him one of those? Hello? Hello? No it's no use. I shall have to try his pager.'

He was still saying 'hello' when I rang off. I repeated this trick several times over the next three weeks and the Motorola phone was returned to us, accompanied by a terse note demanding a better performing model.

Rather belatedly the Home Office realised that some of the Telecoms team would need to be trained in their new automated system of paying invoices. This was a computer-based system where all the payment details were entered upon the database in the correct format and once the authorisation was given, the payment was automated and unstoppable. A machine somewhere in their system typed out the cheque, inserted it into an envelope and despatched it. So it was back to the classroom for me at Lunar House where I had trained so many years before.

It only took me eleven hours to cycle to Croydon from Folkestone, for which I was paid 6.2p per mile travelling allowance. Had I used a noisy, fossil fuel-burning, atmosphere-polluting, road-damaging motor car I would have been recompensed to the tune of 43p per mile. It was a three day course so I stayed with Joy whom I had known as an IO at Dover East and was now a CIO at Gatwick. She happily pointed out that the building opposite her house was the trading headquarters of the Ann Summers organisation and that they sometimes did the video shoots of young ladies modelling their lingerie in the offices on the top floor. I threw many a random glance through the window but was never rewarded. I do not know to this day whether she was teasing me or not.

In the classroom I showed myself to be the dunce that I had for so long been able to hide. There were about sixteen of us trainees, each sat before a computer which was linked to the trainer's computer and a display screen at the front. We were given demonstrations on the screen of how to fill in invoices and then made to complete exercises where the invoices which appeared on our screens were missing certain entries. Our task was to use our new found knowledge and skills to discover the missing information and insert it into the appropriate boxes. Time and again the dozen or so IOs in the class were shown up as laggards by the three clerical officers and one HEO from the mainstream Home Office who, presumably, spent more of their time on computers than we did. The HEO was particularly competitive and the sound of her clear voice smugly ringing out with the correct answer was particularly galling; especially as the trainer had intimated that he had expected a sharper response from these IOs who were clever people and paid for their supposed knowledge.

'Right, this is the next problem coming up now. We need to know the date on the invoice and the record time for finding the answer so far is one minute and twelve seconds.'

Miss Clever Clogs set a new record; I was still trying to find the answer when they went on to the next problem.

'OK. Well done. Here is the next one.' Up on my screen came an enquiry from the Longfield Trading Company – one of the fictional companies that they had used several times before. 'You have to find the invoice and tell them how much the total is. And the record for this is fifty five seconds.'

I buckled to. The reputation of the Service was at stake.

'Two thousand and ninety three pounds and fifty three pence,' I was the first to shout out.

'What?' the trainer gasped and looked at his watch. 'That was twenty two seconds. It can't be done in less than forty seconds. It's impossible.'

I sat back. 'Well is it the right answer?'

'Yes. But you cannot do the key strokes and screens in that time.'

'Well come and look at my screen.'

'Yes, Two thousand and ninety three pounds and fifty three pence,' Miss Clever Clogs rang out.

I glanced pityingly at her.

'I don't understand it,' the trainer muttered as he tapped at my keyboard. 'You went straight to it.'

'Yes,' I said airily.

'But how did you get straight to the correct invoice? You can't do that unless you know the answer already. How did you do it?'

'It is the Longfield Trading Company isn't it?' He nodded. 'And you've used it three times before.'

'Possibly.'

'I noticed that the reference numbers for the exercises have been composed of the initials of the fictional company plus a series number so

I just tapped "LTC-4" into the trainer's box at the top right and hey presto.'
  'That's cheating,' Miss Clever Clogs sniffed.
Yeah but it's the way an IO's mind works.

DEATH OF A HOVERCRAFT

The *Prince of Wales* caught fire
and burned out on the
pad one day.

   On the operational front, Hoverspeed were now running just the two
stretched SRN-6 hovercraft: the *Princess Margaret* and the *Princess Anne*. The
smaller craft, the *Prince of Wales*, had been sitting on the pad awaiting a
buyer for the last two years but one Friday morning it decided it would
wait no longer and it burst into flames. At this very minute it is being
scrapped by the simple process of hiring a JCB and a skip and smashing it
all up to take away.
   The new owner of Hoverspeed, Alan Sherwood, had introduced a
catamaran service also running from the hoverport to Calais. The 'Seacat'
vessels were built in Tasmania and he had managed to wrestle the Blue
Riband from the USA by achieving a crossing of the Atlantic Ocean in three
days and seven hours in *Hoverspeed Great Britain*. The service needed some
positive press for its early days were most inauspicious. The 'Fastest Way
from Portsmouth to Cherbourg' as the Seacat timetable had claimed in
1990, made the entire Press contingent sick on a trial cruise, because of its
unsettling motion and inevitably got dubbed the 'Vomit Comet'. The
timetable was printed but the service did not run in 1990. Eventually they
decided that the short sea route from Dover to Calais would suit the

catamaran better and the passengers agreed.

A dedicated berth was built for the craft alongside the Prince of Wales pier at the end of the hovercraft pad. I crossed on the Seacat several times with my bicycle and found it to be bearable on a moderate day and, frankly, no worse than the hovercraft. Neither the hovercraft nor the Seacat, it has to be admitted, were as steady and stable as a ferry. The advantage was supposedly that any discomfort that was to be caused by the weather conditions would not last as long on the 'fast ferries' which had some truth in it although when the sea was rough, the craft had to reduce speed to prevent damage, thus prolonging the crossing. The hovercraft captains were also instructed not to 'buzz' the Seacat. Passengers paying the supplement to travel on this super fast luxury catamaran were complaining that half way across the Channel they were being overtaken by the hovercraft which had departed Calais after they had.

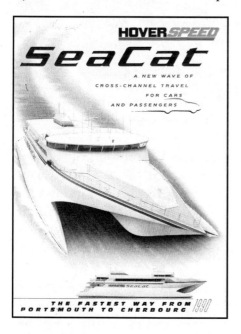

A WORK OF FICTION

The 1990 timetable published for the Seacat catamaran service from Portsmouth to Cherbourg.

It did not run.

I was still cycling to work on a daily basis, come rain or shine. One stormy night I was lifted bodily from my bicycle and dumped on the verge by the updraft where the road runs close to the edge of the cliffs at Capel le Ferne and on a snowy morning when I tried to put my feet down at a road junction I discovered that my snow-encrusted shoes were frozen to the pedals. At work I was able to park my bicycle in an unused car kiosk which I reached by cycling across the seaward side of the pad. To regulate the passage, a traffic light had been installed on the corner of the terminal building to control vehicular access to the pad and often I would have to wait for a hovercraft to park before I was given the 'green' for my bicycle.

Apart from the mental advantage of clearing my mind of work matters on the ride home, the exercise was a positive aid to my maintaining my mobility. The total distance that I could comfortably walk in a day was diminishing; stairs were a slog, standing was painful. I had been examined by a specialist who had talked of my 'subluxation' – explaining that this was spontaneous partial dislocation of joints – and had opined that it would be quite safe for me to take twelve aspirins per day. I demurred at this, deciding to put up with the pain for the sake of conserving my stomach lining. I have no way of knowing whether this was a wise decision or a show of obstinate stupidity. I managed to hide all these depredations from my colleagues who, seeing me cycling around, imagined me a fit and sporty chap. When, one day my hip mislocated and I got stuck on the toilet and missed a hovercraft arrival I apologised and declared that I had misread the timetable. When my various joint pains became too much to bear I would find an unused room in which to hide whilst I mastered the discomfort.

As an IO on the Telecoms team I was given managerial responsibility for the clerical officer who helped us. This was unusual; IOs rarely got the opportunity to manage any staff as they themselves were the lowest in the rank order. The clerical staff at a large port were supervised through clerical line managers. We had no such luxury at the hoverport so I jumped at the opportunity of learning something more useful. And for this reason I was sent on a short residential course in a hotel in Eastbourne to learn how to manage staff. I took my bicycle in the back of my van so that in the evening after classes I could go for a ride and get some exercise and fresh air.

The group was a mixed bunch of civil servants, all of them in the same boat – having to manage staff for the first time. We were divided up into groups and set various tasks at which we always seemed to fail in some way. By the end of the first day I had deduced that the tasks themselves were always impossible; the aim was to encourage us to work together. Once I had decided upon that, then I could discuss the task-solving proposals from members of the group which, before, I would have immediately dismissed as unworkable. It did not matter – we were going to fail anyway. The important thing was to listen to them and let them know that their voices were being heard.

But the sitting in lecture rooms and the moving about at the beck and call of others was beginning to take its toll on me. On the Wednesday, just before lunch, we were set a treasure hunt in Eastbourne. In our group we were five IOs, two clerical officers and one scientific officer.

'Listen,' I said, 'we need to think about what they are going to challenge us with. They have told us that somebody has got to go out now to find the first clue which will expire before lunch is over. That's the first thing. When does that person eat? And by the time that they come back the rest of us will have eaten and be ready to start. They are splitting us up. We are going to have problems of communication and transport. We need to establish lines of communication and investigate means of transport.'

The trainer who was sitting in on this discussion nodded her head thoughtfully. I was on the right track and she knew it. But I could have spared my breath. The IOs grabbed the list of clues, bolted their food, and then dragged us as a group around the town. I stumbled on behind them, tripping over paving slabs and jarring myself on kerbs. The two clerical officers chatted happily about their holidays and the scientific officer did not open her mouth. After the first three clues had been solved I never saw the clue sheet again. It was passed back and forth between the vanguard with an excited, 'Come on, this way,' and we would lurch off in another direction. We had to split the group. The distance was too far. We could not communicate with the others. My hips were sore, my head was thumping because my neck was out of joint, my knees were stinging and all I could do was to mutter, 'you stupid buggers' under my breath. I had a radio pager and a bicycle – communication and transport, but IOs always know how to do everything, so we did that.

When we got back to the hotel I told the trainers that I was going straight to bed for a rest. I lay on the floor of my hotel room – the bed was too soft – and I cried with the pain. Eventually the aspirins took effect.

On the last day of the course we all had to answer a test paper and plot our score on a graph. The head trainer looked at our graph on the flip chart. It was a mountain range of peaks and valleys.

'Whose is the red line?' he asked.

'Oh that's Martin's,' they laughed.

They would. My line was half way up the scale and crossed the graph horizontally with neither a dip nor a peak.

'Very interesting,' he said. 'That is the profile of the ideal civil servant.'

What a benediction! But I did learn a very important lesson from all the games that we had played: there was little point in my learning to manage staff when I had not yet learnt to manage myself.

Andy is sitting on the desk to my left. In between passengers he occasionally taunts me by hissing, 'Harry Secombe'. I pretend to ignore him. The CIO on duty is Snow White. I never did learn how she earned her inappropriate nickname. She was nothing like a princess for heaven's sake – she was from Dover West. We were getting a lot of their staff on attachment now because they had nothing to do over there. The port was dying. It was being run down, the ferry services were transferring across to the East or simply being withdrawn. Soon, the *Nord-Pas de Calais* rail freight service would be the only ship using the port.

The knock-off-anything-that-moves mentality had stayed with the West IOs. One day I had used one of their IOs to interpret in Spanish whilst I interviewed a Venezuelan. When I thanked the IO she was scandalised to learn that I intended to land the passenger.

'He's not a landing, he's a stone cold knock-off,' she exclaimed. 'Give me the passport, I'll knock him off.'

For the sake of experiment I handed the document to her. She beetled off and rustled up a Dover West CIO who was also working at the hoverport and they refused the passenger. I was bemused. It was almost an orgasm she was building up to. I suppose I should have been concerned for the rights of the passenger but, frankly, I did not care. One Venezuelan more or less made little difference in the great big scheme of things. It was important to her though, but I suspect it was important for the wrong reasons.

The problem with Snow White was that she would not leave you alone. She wanted to meddle in your case. I have seen her stand behind an IO's desk and fire questions over his shoulder at the passenger whilst the IO was trying to interview him. It destroys any logical construction that you might have introduced into your enquiry. And it is bloody rude. If she wanted still to interview passengers then she should have stayed as an IO.

A small dark-skinned man walks up to my desk and hands me a French *Titre de Séjour*. It is the blue passport with two diagonal gold lines across the corner. Its significance is that the holder is unable to obtain a national passport from his own country. In practice, it means that he has been granted political asylum. If you have fled your country for fear of persecution you can hardly walk into your country's consulate in order to renew your passport – it would invalidate your claim.

The man was born in Sri Lanka. He is obviously a Tamil refugee. I take his document, check the details, turn it to the page which I would stamp if I landed him and then place it face down on my desk.

'How long are you staying here?' I ask.

'For a holiday.'

A hand sneaks over my shoulder, grabs the passport and disappears. I turn in surprise. Snow White is wandering down the hall leafing through my passport. I wait. She continues walking away from me.

'Wait here please,' I say to the passenger. He nods. I pick up my book and stamps and walk into the back office, leaving the passenger standing at an empty desk. I sit down in an easy chair and pick up a discarded newspaper. About three minutes later Snow White pokes her head around the door.

'Oh, you're not on the phone then? What are you doing with your passenger?'

'Which passenger?'

'The Tamil standing at the desk.'

'You can do what you like with him.'

'What are you doing with him?'

'Nothing to do with me – he's your passenger. I was interviewing him but you took the passport.'

'I was just having a look.'

'I naturally assumed that you were taking over the case. Why else would you snatch the passport away from me?'

'No, no, I wasn't. Can you come and deal with him please?' She hands me the passport. I take it and walk past her without a word. She has not apologised. I don't think she even realises how rude she is.

Reg Toale is stamping on for the afternoon shift when we get back up to the general office.

'Have you heard about Dover West?' he asks. 'It's closing. The IOs are being transferred to the East and to here.'

'What about their CIOs?' I pull a face.

'Same thing, I think.'

'Don't mind him,' Andy says. 'He's sulking because I beat him at Happy Families.'

'What with?' Reg says.

'Harry Secombe at Gatwick on a Friday night.' He answers with the smug satisfaction of a worthy victor.

'Oh yeah?' Reg unlocks his case and drops an embarkation card to the table. 'I've trumped you. Sylvia Kristel, born 28.9.52, Dutch, embarked through Dover East two nights ago.'

'Ha! You can't beat that.' I am gleeful. Snow White is banished from my mind. 'Emmanuelle on nights. Brilliant!'

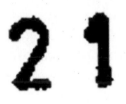

21

It was too good to last. Our office became a magnet for departmental squatters. Our locker room was turned out and made into an office for the assistant director. He was the boss of our South Eastern Region. He smoked cheroots shaped like the toggle buttons on his duffel coat.

All around the country, ports were setting up their own enforcement units, working in liaison with the police to deal with the foreigners who were already in the country. So the enforcement unit for our region was foisted upon our office. We had spare desks, apparently. We became a minority within our own territory, squashed into one side of the room. Luckily it was the side with the view of the pad so we could at least see the craft arriving.

We had always been told that we were 'investigating officers' and so did not need to administer the official caution before interviewing a passenger, unlike customs officers who were 'prosecuting officers' and took their own cases to court. Now we all had to be prepared to administer the caution should we encounter people facilitating illegal entry; remembering importantly not to use the cinema version: 'anything you say will be used in evidence against you.' The enforcement officers swaggered about quoting paragraphs of the immigration rules that us lesser IOs did not know even existed. They tested discreet radios for surveillance purposes and put 'tails' on suspects – not always successfully. One suspicious lorry driver shook them off by driving up the exit road, onto the roundabout and then straight back down onto the motorway again. They dared not follow him for fear of 'blowing their cover'. They did not think of making a complete circuit of the roundabout and then following him.

The running down of Dover West had started when I had been doing a month's relief there to cover IOs on annual leave. With an almost demonic glee a pair of IOs had enthusiastically obeyed the instructions from ISHQ and set about destroying the set of suspect circulars. These were files containing the reasons behind a person's entry in the suspect index. When you identified somebody 'in the book', you sat them down and then went up to the general office and found his or her circular in the safe and read up the background. Dover was one of the original 'approved ports' under the Aliens Act of 1905. It had a complete set of circulars dating back to 1908. This was real history; exactly the type of history that should have been submitted to the Public Record Office for archiving under the Public Records Act 1958 so that future generations would not have to read this book to find out what life in the Immigration Service was really like.

I grabbed the oldest volume from the safe and read it avidly as the clock of doom ticked away. It was a fascinating contemporary witness to the political fears and economic requirements of the time. The forerunners of the IOs – the aliens officers – were instructed to beware of international card-sharpers working the liners between New York and Southampton; Armenian Jews running the white slave trade to north Africa; Bolshevik revolutionaries carrying subversive material; Sicilian pickpockets coming to Ascot racecourse and 'consumptive paupers' from the Ottoman Empire. After the Great War, the IOs, as they were by now called, were required to check up on German maritime pilots who intended to work around the coast of Britain and to honour the special passports issued to those making pilgrimages to the war graves of their sons in northern France. The instructions issued to IOs from the Home Office reeked of moral self-righteousness in a time when dogma went unchallenged. One of the decrees I thought outrageous, if not illegal. A certain number of French women 'of dubious morals' had contracted marriages with British men and obtained British passports. This was their right. But on arrival at a UK port they were to be refused entry and their passports confiscated. How was the IO supposed to do that? 'Excuse me sir, the Home Office says that your wife is a prostitute so I'm keeping her passport and sending her back to France, even though she is British?'

Dover West is now unstaffed and Bill, a Scots IO of venerable age and beard has been put in charge of emptying the office. The rare ships that arrive at Dover West will be dealt with by the officers now based at the hoverport. Into the skip goes furniture and equipment and every day, cars drive up the Admiralty Pier and return loaded down on their springs. That skip must be magic because no matter what is put in it, it never overflows.

'What's that you've got there?' I ask him as he lugs a grey steel box onto his desk behind me.

'It's the 'secret box' from Dover West. It was at the bottom of the safe.'

'What are you going to do with it?'

'You know, I'd quite like to open it. It's got something in it.'

'So why don't you?'

He gives me a pitying look. 'I'm just a foot soldier, laddie. You don't think that they told me the combination do you? The secret box was for the generals.'

'Oh, the 'need to know' principle. Very wise. So have you asked them?'

'Och aye. Over the last two days I've phoned around the district to every CIO and inspector who was serving at the West when it closed. None of the buggers can remember the combination.'

'And of course we are not allowed to write down the numbers, we have to commit them to memory, don't we? That makes it a bit awkward doesn't it?' I give a rather unkind laugh. 'You can hardly chuck the thing away if it is full of state secrets.'

'I've got one last hope.' He picks up the telephone and rings a CIO who retired five years earlier. He waits while the man goes into his lumber room and digs out old diaries in which, of course, contrary to regulations, everybody writes down the safe combinations.

We crowd around as Bill eases the combination lock back and forth, counting carefully as he does so. He hauls up the lid with a creak and we peer in. Mimicking the lyrics of *The Sound of Music*, it contains one of Julie Andrews' favourite things – a brown paper parcel tied up with string. On the paper is inscribed in block capitals, '*To be opened only on receipt of special instructions from HM Chief Inspector or on the outbreak of war.*' Bill lifts it out and places it on the desk.

WHAT BILL FOUND IN THE SECRET BOX.

'Do you reckon it is firearms?' Reg Toale says.

'And ammunition. It's heavy enough,' I say. 'I vote we open it.'

'And what about the special instruction from the chief inspector then?' Bill appears uncertain.

' *"Or on the outbreak of war"* it says. It doesn't specify which war,' Reg observes. 'I mean, they are fighting in Bosnia, in Zaire, in just about everywhere really, so war has broken out.'

I produce a pair of scissors and snip the string. We rip off the paper. The parcel contains a block of booklets entitled, *'Instructions to HM Immigration Officers on the Outbreak of War'*.

'Oh goody, something to read.'

I take a booklet and put my feet up on my desk. The others do the same. At the end of half an hour Reg says, 'Well that's reassuring to know that we are prepared. Just think, we get the four minute warning of an impending nuclear strike and throughout the country, officers rush to the secret box in the safe–'

'–which in our case took two days to open.'

'Precisely. They then sit down and read a thirty-two page booklet on what they must do. Brilliant. By that time they and the booklet are a little pile of radioactive dust.'

'I wonder how long they have been in there?' Bill says.

'Well surely the Civil Defence Corps was disbanded in the 1960s wasn't it?' I say.

'And when did we stop using London telephone numbers which had letter prefixes?' Reg asks. He flicks the booklet back onto Bill's desk. 'Well you've got a lot of confidential waste to get rid of now. All those booklets are secret.'

'And pointless,' I add.

And another pointless thing is the manner in which we are roped in to act as rent-a-crowd for the AD. We are directed to attend a conference in the general office at Folkestone. It is not an invitation, it is an order. The AD has a vision of how he will run the district and he is going to explain it to us. His vision is the 'light touch' which will make it quicker for the ordinary public to move through the port and allow the IOs to concentrate their efforts on the problem passengers. It is not a discussion. He stomps back and forth across the creaking wooden floor, waving his arms about and writing figures and percentages on the flip chart. The cynics are already thinking, 'if we are now to be allowed to wave people through without looking at their passports, why are we there at all?'

The chairs are uncomfortable, I am in pain, I don't want to be here. We are a press-ganged audience for a speaker who just wants to show off his prowess with figures. We have been bludgeoned with percentages of this and ratios of that. He is explaining how, as part of his plan, an inspector has studied the car control at Dover East and very cleverly negotiated with the harbour board for a marshal to check the cars in the queue and if the passengers have not filled in landing cards, to hold them back until they have done so. This will speed up the control.

I've had enough of this tosh. 'No it won't,' I say loudly.

'What?' He stops in mid flow. The audience stirs with a ripple of interest.

'You are going to hold the first car in the queue until they have filled in their landing cards? How will that speed up the control?'

'Well obviously it will save the IO's time. He can concentrate on those who have filled in their cards.'

'And where will those people be? Behind the car which has not filled in the cards. Or are you going to feed several lines in the queue at once? You'll need extra marshals for that.'

'Well this can be sorted out with the harbour board.' He dismisses me. I will not be dismissed.

'The vast majority of landing cards filled in by passengers are destroyed locally because they are only needed for stats purposes. If an IO gets a car with four French passengers in he marks a blank card, *French, 4*' and date stamps it. It takes him about five seconds. Your system will take about three minutes. You are going to make the IO wait whilst the passengers fill in cards that he is going to put in the bin under his desk? That's daft. The only cards that need to be filled in for the IO are those of people whom he puts on conditional landings and he can fill in those far quicker and more accurately than they can.'

'Well I think we can–'

'–What percentage of passengers are conditional landings?'

'I can see what you are getting at.'

'Good. So what is the percentage? We have had the percentage of nearly everything else this morning.'

'Nigel?' He turns to look at the inspector.

Nigel looks down at the papers on his lap. 'It's not a large percentage I'll admit,' he says.

'Well did you find out?' I ask. Nigel looks embarrassed. 'It's surely important to know what percentage of passengers actually need to fill in cards before you make everybody fill them in, isn't it? Did you find out?'

'Er... no I didn't but it is not a large proportion.'

'How do you know if you didn't find out?'.

The AD now thunders in with flat eyebrows and pinched mouth.

'Are you saying that Nigel doesn't know his job?' He jabs a finger at me.

I look at his scowling face and offensive finger. He obviously believes that the best form of defence is attack. I glance across at bemused Nigel. My knees are stinging, my head is aching. I think to myself, 'why am I bothering with these plonkers?'

'Oh carry on, carry on,' I say, and look pointedly out of the window.

I obviously made a mark. When the AD got back to the hoverport he gave me the job of organising his confidential filing system. In it I read a paper from an inspector who had been an IO on the same Urdu language course with me so many years earlier. I knew he had been promoted to CIO because I had seen him once sitting at his desk in Lunar House when I had passed down the corridor.

'Ben,' I had said, 'good to see you. How are you getting on?'

His head had come up from his papers and he had looked at me and frowned. 'Yeah, don't tell me, um, Dave, isn't it? Terminal Two?'

I got the message.

So when he had reached inspector he had been given access to the IO's confidential appraisal reports in order to assess the functioning of the system. In an attempt to entertain, he had inserted sarcastic personal observations into his analysis, one of which ridiculed an idiosyncratic observation which I had written in the space provided on my annual

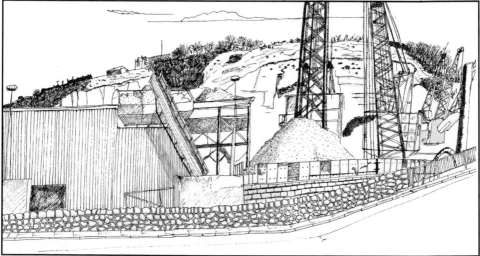

THE VIEW FROM MY DESK
Sitting in the car embarkation control kiosk you could watch the sand and gravel being unloaded from the dredgers.

report. He had raised a doubtful laugh rather than evaluate the important criticism about the reporting system that I had been making. He was safe and his comments pampered to the prejudices of ISHQ; he had mentioned no names and he knew I could never see the paper. He was wrong.

Over the years the image of the hoverport had altered. It had opened in a blaze of publicity as the fast and luxurious route for crossing the Channel. It was more expensive than ferries but quicker. It purposefully catered for the 'jet-set'; the check-in procedure imitated that of the airports; every passenger was guaranteed a seat and whilst ensconced therein could be served with drinks and duty-free goods by uniformed hostesses.

It was now looking a little shabby. The man who stood on the pad and waved at the craft with the ping-pong bats to tell it where to sit down had been sent packing; the captains could judge the distances quite safely without him. Next to go had been the porters; passengers could carry their own suitcases. Then the staff canteen was deemed unnecessary. The complement of on-board and ground staff which had always fluctuated with the seasons was reducing year by year.

The monied travellers were moving to the ferries which were more reliable, more frequent and more fun. The hovercraft and the Seacat could never compete with the ferries in the realms of the space provided for passengers but somebody in Hoverspeed decided that they could compete advantageously for the day-trip traffic; after all, a return trip on the hovercraft could be completed within ninety minutes. This fact was quickly appreciated by the teams of traders whose sole purpose in travelling was to purchase vast amounts of duty-free beer and tobacco. Several years earlier at Dover East we had laughed at our first encounter with a pick-up truck from Essex loaded with forty-five cases of cheap foreign beer which, because of its low alcohol content, fell within the duty-free personal allowances of the driver and his mates. Within a few months the gangs had divided up the market and were importing thousands of pounds of duty-free alcohol daily on their personal allowance. It was always for a family wedding or a birthday, of course. By the time that Hoverspeed had decided they wanted a slice of the action, the factions were conducting a running battle in Dover and Folkestone with the rented bedsits which they used as warehouses being raided by rival gangs and, in one case, torched.

Using the hovercraft increased the speed at which you could get booze into the country. We saw the same people three times a day with their shopping trolleys or sack barrows. They would go out on the first craft, buy their beer and baccy and upon their return rush out to the car park and stash it in their van and then get back on the craft for another trip. Other gangs would visit the car park towards the end of the day to break open the doors of their rivals' vehicles and drive off with the booty. It was all very unsavoury.

And it was not only the booze cruisers who switched to the hoverport. A yellow Luton van came in one day but not at my kiosk. One of my colleagues landed it. Customs looked in the back and noticed that the load space appeared foreshortened. It was. A compartment had been built behind the driver's cab and in it had been placed five Pakistanis and the whole lot then rivetted up and painted over. Very naughty, but it proved that illegal immigrant traffickers would try any route. I wondered how many times they had already done it.

We rarely saw a Rolls or an Aston Martin on the craft nowadays but I remember a rather flashy Maserati. In it were a man and woman, both travelling on British passports which at that time were still the blue version. They were well presented and seemed to represent that very class of traveller that was deserting Hoverspeed.

The woman's profession was 'solicitor' and she had been born in Oldham. I never trust solicitors and this one had altered the date of birth in her passport. She had very cleverly matched the blue ink of the original Passport Office entry and amended the figure three to an eight, altering her year of birth from 1943 to 1948. This still left her nearly ten years older than her male companion. The following revelation may sound bizarre but the women of this age whom I had already caught changing their dates of birth had always made themselves older. The rationale had been explained to me by a lady from Birmingham.

'I work in a night club in Dusseldorf. I look after the girls but the German clubs always look for somebody a bit older for that job so I just changed my date of birth. Everybody does it.'

Checking the British passport of what appears to be a genuine traveller takes an IO about three seconds. In that time I had registered a suspicion that the document had been tampered with.

'What is your date of birth madam?' I asked.

'Third of February, nineteen forty eight,' she said smartly. She was very good. She was very convincing. But I had detected just a slight flick of her eye-lid as she had spoken.

You've got to be courageous to delay a UK citizen presenting what appears to be a valid passport. Had it been tampered with? Was I sure? I bit the bullet.

'Just pull your car through there please madam and I will join you in a minute.'

'Is there a problem?' Her voice was tart and cutting, designed to intimidate me.

'Oh I shouldn't think so.' I smiled disarmingly and pointed to the buffer car park between the passport control and Customs.

'Our passports.' She held out her hand.

'That is what I am going to check.'

'What's the problem?'

Oh well, here goes.

'It appears to me that the date of birth in your passport was originally entered as nineteen forty three and has since been altered to forty eight.' This suggestion interested her toy-boy who turned his head to take a closer look at her. An inspection which did not pass unnoticed by the solicitor. 'Have you altered it madam?'

'No I have not.' Short. Succinct. She does not trust herself to use long sentences.

'This won't take long.'

She parked her car and I went into the ops room and studied her passport under the microscope. I could clearly see the two different inks present in the same digit. As I put the passport into the photocopier the CIO came in.

'Are you holding up those Brits. in the Maserati?' I nodded. 'What's wrong with her?'

'Altered date of birth in her passport.'

'Is that all?' His eyes turned upwards in derision. 'You can't detain her for that. Let's have a look.' I gave him the passport. 'Well I can't see anything wrong with that. You've got a copy?' I nodded. 'Send her on her way.'

I shrugged. Her smile was victorious when I returned the passports to her. To my mind that sealed her guilt. During the patches of free time that afternoon I ran checks on her. The passport office said it would take a couple of days to find her application form so I suppose that it was a good job that I had not detained her but they were able to confirm from a hand-written register that the date of birth upon issue had been nineteen forty three. I had taken an address from her and so I rang up the local police and asked them if they knew anything about her.

'Oh her? She's as bent as a nine bob note. We've been trying to pin something on her for years. What's she done now?'

'Made an unauthorised alteration to her passport.'

'Can you do her for it? We'd love to see her banged up.'

I knew I couldn't. I sent a report to the Passport Office, explaining what she had done and enclosed a photocopy of the passport because I thought that she might now cover up her offence by throwing the passport away and asking for a new one. What a nasty suspicious mind I have.

A British passport slightly altered by a vain lawyer was chicken feed in the real world. Europe was awash with duff documents. In any violent civil upheaval, no matter where it happened, the government offices were always invaded. Whilst the thugs and hooligans are smashing the windows and wrecking the furniture there will be a small band of enterprising souls quietly taking possession of the stocks of blank passports and the equipment needed to issue them. And shortly after that, the documents will start turning up at our desks because, no matter what politicians and trendy pressure groups try to tell us, immigrants the world over target Britain as their number one destination.

Zaire was a persistent problem because they would issue diplomatic passports seemingly to anybody. The country was in chaos and I suspect that the Zairean Foreign Minister had little control over his diplomatic staff, some of whom were supporting themselves by selling passports. South American drug dealers would acquire stolen Italian i.d. cards; Indians would use Dutch documents and claim to be of Indonesian descent. In Western Europe there was a population of immigrants floating back and forth across frontiers, changing identity and nationality as it did so in order to keep ahead of the police forces.

I was once standing in a tram in Brussels with a fellow IO when the ticket inspector got on. The West African lady sitting below us opened her handbag to show her Belgian family travel discount card to the inspector. Frank and I looked at each other and shrugged resignedly. In that snapshot of time during which her bag had been open we had both identified a Zairean diplomatic passport, a Portuguese passport and an Italian identity card.

If the world was changing, so was the job. When I had started I had understood in my simplistic way that the job of an immigration officer was to deal with passengers going in and out of the UK. I was aware that some lucky IOs went abroad to issue visas and some ran training courses but by and large our tool was a landing stamp. Diversity was provided by the occasional chance of performing summer relief to another port; a bounty which was doled out in a strict priority order. Then 'after entry' work began to assume a greater importance and every district had to have its enforcement office. The number of appeals rose as did the proportion of

HOVERPORT AT NIGHT
This was often the view when I got on my bicycle to ride home.

cases which were pushed to judicial review. The casework load increased exponentially but the staff available to do it did not. Our procedures in dealing with the cases were shackled by compulsory time scales which were designed to provide protection to the passenger; laudable, but easily exploited to prolong delay. The 'bum's rush' – removing the refused passenger before he had time to think – was no longer permitted and so we had to lock up more detainees. The capacity of Harmondsworth detention centre opposite Heathrow airport had long since proven insufficient. We were now taking over complete wings in prisons. The Home Office had even built a detention centre at Campsfield House in Kidlington, Oxfordshire which was designed solely to house immigration detainees.

The diversity of appointments in the Immigration Service was brought home to me when I compiled the IS telephone directory. I could understand that we now had to have IOs working in groups such as the Detention Management Unit and the Asylum Liaison Unit but what the devil were the Professionalism & Communications Team and the Scrutiny Implementation Scheme? And who was I to ask? Was I not in the IS Telecoms Unit?

Around the coast at Folkestone, the Channel tunnel terminal was nearing completion and soon would need staffing. We were a mobile grade when it suited the Home Office and had to go where we were sent. The 'crown transfer' package, whose attraction included a very remunerative interest-free bridging loan, which had been handed out whenever an IO was transferred out of his district, had now become quite rare because government departments had been made to cut costs. This falling incidence of compulsory transfers had lulled the IOs into forgetting that they were a mobile grade. The AD was about to remind them. And a transfer to the Channel tunnel would earn them little extra money. Some tried to fight.

There were IOs who were genuinely nervous of travelling through the tunnel twice a day to work at the juxtaposed controls in Coquelles. The fear of a train crash or a terrorist bomb exploding ten miles into the tunnel was a terrible nightmare but cut no ice with the AD. Unease was not settled by the circular we received from Eurotunnel telling us that all workers regularly using the tunnel were to be subject to a compulsory ear examination because of the danger of damage to their hearing. There was no risk to the travelling public of course, we were assured of that, but all the workers had to be tested. Presumably the travelling public had stronger ears.

I have never been very lucky with hearing tests but it is genuinely not my fault. When I submitted to one at the local hospital the man carefully closed me in a soundproof booth the size of a telephone kiosk and then said, '   .' I looked through the window at his soundless lips. They agitated again but more wildly. Eventually he opened the door. 'I said, "put the headphones on".'

'Sorry,' I replied, 'I couldn't hear you. This booth is soundproof. Didn't you know?'

I slotted my Channel tunnel hearing test into a gap between hovercraft arrivals. I jumped on my bike and pedalled off up the Folkestone Road to the ghost town of huts which had been built as the workers' village for the tunnel construction. The wind was pushing strongly behind me as I swooped down the road to the security barrier. Inside the booth to which the red and white pole was attached sat a man, a steaming mug and a copy of *The Sun*. As I squeezed my brake lever, the cable snapped and I hurtled into the barrier at 15 mph. The cabin was wrenched through ninety degrees, the man fell off his chair, the tea went one way and *The Sun* the other.

'What the bloody hell do you think you're playin' at?' he shouted as he picked himself up from the floor.

I unwrapped myself from the pole. 'Sorry mate, I've been sent for a hearing test.'

'Hearing test? You need a bloody eye test.'

I helped him resite his hut and I collected as many pages of his newspaper as I could find and then continued on down the road to the hutted site. Up the deserted hillside I climbed, peering at the terraces of huts, all numbered, all unoccupied except one. I had to find that one. It was the hut at the very top on the right, as you would expect. Inside sat a lady in a white coat. She perched on a stool in the middle of the room and asked me if I had ever been in the Army ('not to my knowledge') or been near any loud explosions ('never heard them if I had'). She sensed that my attention was elsewhere.

'Are you feeling all right?' she enquired.

'Yes, fine thanks, I was just watching that spider behind you.' As indeed I had been. It was a real Miss Muffet job – big and hairy and lowering itself from the ceiling of the hut by a single strand.

'What?' she shrieked. She jumped up. Papers went one way, the stool went the other.

Well, at least there was nothing wrong with my eyesight.

Back at the hoverport men in red overalls were loitering on the foot passenger control. Two were examining an industrial vacuum cleaner, a couple more were cleaning windows. One was on a step ladder. It was that time of the year again and MI5 had to spend what remained in their budget or lose it. They stayed for five days, ostensibly looking for an Irish terrorist, then they went back home. I never feel particularly secure when surrounded by armed personnel. Train a man to fire a gun and he will want to fire it.

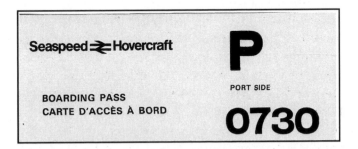

BOOKMARK

The port-side passes were pink, the starboard, green.

Seaspeed ⇌ Hovercraft

P

BOARDING PASS
CARTE D'ACCÈS À BORD

PORT SIDE

0730

My work at the hoverport was well regarded by management. I was now getting top marks in my appraisal reports. I was happy and efficient because I could, to a large extent, organise my working day to suit my physical condition. I was not the IO that you would find gazing into space; I always found something useful to do and enjoyed doing it. One day I achieved something of an extraordinary rarity. It happened like this.

My knowledge of foreign languages was singular in that I only spoke

French – my Urdu was useless. Most of my colleagues spoke at least German or Spanish as well. My expertise in German was restricted to those bizarre phrases that a schoolboy could remember from his war story picture comics wherein lantern-jawed British commandos biffed and bopped their way through coal scuttle-helmeted Germans whilst snapping out expressions like, 'Take that Fritz.' The Jerries' ripostes provided my entire German vocabulary, to wit: *Donner und Blitzen, Schweinhund Englander, Gott in Himmel* and *Achtung Spitfeuer.* I think you will readily agree that they are not phrases that could find any useful place in the vocabulary of a British immigration officer of the 1990s.

One quiet, sunny, summer's afternoon I was gazing dreamily out at the English Channel from a car kiosk when the first car disembarked from the hovercraft. It was a large green Mercedes driven by a large, square-headed German accompanied by his equally substantial wife. The electric window slid down and a huge fist was thrust at me, gripping a pair of green passports. A more archetypical pair of Germans one could not have met. I inspected their passports and just as I was about to return them I was distracted by a noise and movement to seaward. I squinted into the sunlight and there, burbling along above the southern breakwater on its way to the Shepway Air Show down the coast at Folkestone, flew a lone Spitfire.

I just could not resist it. I pointed to the plane.

'Achtung! Spitfeuer!'

The Germans flinched, snatched their passports and drove away. OK, so I should not have said it, but, be honest, wouldn't you have done the same? Just think, how many people today can honestly claim that they have had legitimate reason to say, *'Achtung! Spitfeuer!'* to a German?

Language of whatever sort was always the essential component of our work. It was what we did. We asked people questions and we listened to their replies. There was an occasion when I interviewed a passenger without speaking at all. A little Indian-looking lady came up to my desk and presented a Mauritian passport.

'How long are you staying?' I asked.

She waved her fingers at her ears and mouth and shook her head. Deducing that she did not understand English I asked her if she spoke French. She nodded and silently mouthed the word *'oui'.* It was then that I realised that she was deaf and dumb.

I pointed to my lips and said in French, 'Can you read my lips?'

She could, but I would need to be able to understand her replies. Could I also lip read in French? I had never tried. There was no necessity for me to speak the questions out aloud since she would not hear them and I did not need to, so I interviewed her silently. We got along famously. She worked as an orderly in a hospital in Paris and was coming to visit her sister who lived in Bromley. I enquired about her money and tickets and when she would return and what family she had living in Paris and how long she had lived in France. I was so engrossed in the challenge of lip-reading in French and disconcerted by the surreal aura of the silent interview that I had not noticed that the level of noise in the passenger hall had dropped markedly. The passengers and the other IOs were staring at us, trying to work out how we were communicating.

I stamped her passport and wished her a happy holiday and sent her on her way. The next time she arrived at the hoverport she ignored the directions given by the hostess and made a beeline for my desk.

And sometimes the language difficulty is completely one-sided.

He was twenty two, she was nineteen. They were Swiss and she was rather shy, holding his hand whilst they stood at my desk. I could tell from their passports that they almost certainly spoke French, rather than German, Italian or Romansh so I started straight off in French.

'How long are you staying here?'

The girl looked anxiously at the man, waiting for his reply.

'W... w... w... we.....er....mmm.' He threw his head about irritably and took breaths and started again. 'G... g.... g... go.... ers... ers... ess.' I looked at the girl for a reply. Her eyes pleaded with me and then filled with compassion and anxiety as they switched back to the man. She glued her eyes on him, willing him to speak. Even I could feel the power in her look. It was almost supernatural; it made my scalp tingle. But still he stuttered. I could ask him to write down his answers on a card but that was not what she wanted. I decided to wait. 'Z... Zj... Azerj... Azerjust... oo weeks.'

'Just two weeks?' I confirmed. He nodded and expelled a lungful of air as he released the effort that he had been expending. His face softened a bit as he relaxed and then the muscles tensed up again as he prepared himself for my next question. 'What do you come here to do?'

'Ahug... erhug... eny... erhug... eny...' He stopped and looked at me. Beaten. He brought the girl's hand up to the desk with his and pointed to their gold rings. He was giving up too easily.

'So what do you come here to do, sir?' I repeated. He pointed to the rings. I shrugged incomprehension. The girl was clinging to him, as if trying to empower him with her abilities. I had noticed that when he tried to speak he crouched slightly forwards as if he was ashamed of himself. As if he wanted to hide his attempts from all around him. I realised that I too was leaning forwards, complicit in this subconscious concealment.

Suddenly I sat up straight on my stool and pulled back my shoulders. 'What do you come here to do?' I repeated. The abrupt movement startled them.

'Erg... Gunny... Honeymoon. Honeymoon.' He straightened up to face me.

'Ah, honeymoon. And where do you go?'

'Erl... erl... London.'

'Where will you stay?'

'H... hotel. P...Piccadilly.'

'So you're staying in a hotel in Piccadilly. Is this your first time to the UK?' He nodded. I wasn't accepting that, not after the progress we had made. I could feel the girl's eyes burning into me. She had chosen this man and married him. They had been man and wife for twenty-four hours and this was just the beginning of the rest of their lives together. She believed in him and she was determined to prove to him what she already knew: that he was better than he thought he was. I repeated the question. He looked at me, nonplussed that I had not accepted the nod.

'Yyyes. First time,' he said, pulling his shoulders back.

I could land them now if I wanted to. I was satisfied under the Immigration Act. I was not satisfied for myself or for them.

'And what country do you live in?'

'Ssswitzerland.'

'Where do you go when you leave England?'

'Switzerland.'

'Back to Switzerland?' I suggested.

'Yes, back to Switzerland.' He was standing up straight. His face was relaxed.

'What do you do in Switzerland?'

'What do I do? For work?' He was prolonging the interview himself now. 'I am a–' He closed his eyes and pushed the tip of his tongue against the back of his upper teeth. '–technical draughtsman.' I stamped their passports. 'Tell me please,' he began. The woman's eyes opened in alarm. 'Where will w...we find our suitcases?' The look of pride and love in his wife's eyes was overwhelming. This was a sentence that he had initiated.

'Just through there sir.' I handed the passports back.

'Thank you,' he said.

As they walked through, his wife looked me directly in the eyes and said gravely, 'I thank you, sir.' I had never known anyone able to convey so much heartfelt gratitude in such a short sentence. I can hear her voice now as I write these words. She knew what I was doing and she had been willing her husband to prove himself capable now that somebody had taken the trouble to give him the opportunity.

This is the best part of the job, I thought. We don't have to be nasty to everybody.

```
POLICE DE L'AIR ET DES FRONTIERES          CALAIS LE 30.10.91 à  M. 30.
                                                      (date)    (neure)
    DU PAS DE CALAIS
*****************************************
*                                       *            Sexe : M/F
* AVIS de REFOULEMENT en GRANDE BRETAGNE.*
*                                       *
*****************************************
Nom :  SHIHT                citoyen(ne) ... Britanique ....
                                              (nationalité)
Prénoms :  Rood             Domicile : ... 112 rue de Luerpool
Né(e) le 27.12.1962 à  LONDRES  à LIVERPOOL.
                                Destination prévue ......
Profession : ... Ignoree
Arrivé(e) à CALAIS le  20 Juin 91  par (SEALINK - P.O. - HOVERSPEED)
n'est pas autorisé(e) à entrer en FRANCE.
MOTIFS : (obligatoire) Défaut de document transfrontiere . Trouble à l'ordre
Est placé(e) sous la responsabilité de la compagnie (SEALINK. P.O. HOVERSPEED) qui devra  public
assurer son retour à DOUVRES/FOLKESTONE par son premier départ.
· La compagnie susnommée voudra bien transmettre à l'IMMIGRATION BRITANNIQUE le présent avis,
ainsi que (mentions à rayer si cette deuxième transmission n'est pas NECESSAIRE) le document
désigné ci-dessous :  Demuni de document
PASSPORT/C.N.I ........ N°......... DU ............... AU .........
        (nationalité)
QUALITE  NOM et SIGNATURE        POLICE NATIONALE    GRADE  et NOM du FONCTIONNAIRE
de l'AGENT de la COMPAGNIE :     CALAIS-PORT          de la P.A.F :
                                 3 0 JUIN 1991           I.P
                                 0 575 P.A.F.A.F
```

REFUSED BY THE FRENCH
This Liverpudlian male was refused entry at Calais by the French authorities for a public order offence and for not possessing a passport. In the absence of proof, they had to accept the name he gave. I suspect it was not his correct name.

Bolts, in the traditional sense, usually come out of the blue and this one certainly did: we were no longer to run our telecoms budget. It was not a job for untrained IOs, and certainly not officers paid weekend overtime and language allowances whilst doing it. No, the Accommodation Unit in the mainstream Home Office who were trained in that sort of thing, and, incidentally, paid less, were the right people for the job. They would take over this responsibility as from the beginning of next April. This was bad news for me. My telecoms duties each week had allowed me to schedule my work so that I was the most comfortable and thus, most efficient. Take those away and everybody loses. But I had not realised how sinister was this unwelcome development.

Eventually the Accommodation Unit staff came down from London and gazed longingly at the view from our windows as they listened to our various exposés of how we each ran our section.

Hardly had we absorbed our disappointment than it was decreed that as the telecoms work would be going and passenger operations at the hoverport were diminishing with the gradual withdrawal of the hovercraft, then the port would be overstaffed and some of the control IOs would have to be transferred elsewhere. I was in the frame.

I sat back in my chair and thought hard. Crozier, an inspector at Dover East, had targeted me the moment that the planned withdrawal of the telecoms responsibility had been announced. He wanted me back in their port to run the casework office. It was a mess. He had made occasional dark hints that my time at the hoverport was coming to a close, I was required elsewhere. I realised now the sinister import of these observations. The reason I had won a transfer to the hoverport in the first place was that I had wanted to avoid night duties. But if I was scheduled for daily casework duties, he pointed out, there would be no night duties. I thought of the casework office at Dover East. It was about the most aggressive environment that I could think of. The desks were hemmed in by zigzag walls of filing cabinets so that people were forever squeezing past your chair; nowhere could you take more than three steps without having to sidestep or turn through ninety degrees; the lighting was by fluorescent tubes valiantly flickering through yellowing diffusers; the ceiling was two feet above my head when standing and from it issued the continuous hiss and moan from the ventilation.

I knew where I would prefer to work. In the brand spanking new office at the Channel tunnel terminal had been established another empire especially to liaise with European police forces and border controls. If I were transferred to this European Liaison Unit I would be able to carve myself a safe space and, incidentally, exercise my command of French for the benefit of the Service. Crozier's response to my disclosure that working at Dover East would cause me physical pain was refreshingly untainted by compassion. He said that he, 'could live with that.'

So I went to prison.

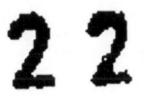

In 1874 a prison was built high on the hills above the city of Rochester in Kent, overlooking the valley of the river Medway and near the village of Borstal. In 1902 it became the country's first youth offender prison in an experiment to educate the inmates so that they would be equipped to deal with life upon release otherwise than by the traditional system of being coached by the old lags in all the tricks of criminality. The prison gave its name to the 'borstal' system.

In a twist of fate, by 1994 HMP Borstal was no longer a borstal but a 'category B' establishment called Rochester Prison. Within its walls, the IS were detaining eighty-three foreign nationals pending solutions to their cases and IOs were posted there on temporary relief to administer the casework. I volunteered for a three month period of relief. I had no real idea what the work entailed nor what the conditions in the prison were like; I was given an outline of the hours I would have to work and was expected to get on with it.

One of the outgoing IOs took me in to the prison on my first day to work alongside him. He was about fifteen years my junior and knew it all.

'Of course they wouldn't let me stay on because of the threats to my life.' He dangled this carrot before me.

'Oh yes?' I responded with blatant incredulity.

'Yeah, Security uncovered a plot. The inmates were going to riot at meal time and storm the hospital block. The Algerians were going to take me hostage and then negotiate.'

'Waste of time,' I said. 'The IS would never pay a ransom for the return of an IO, they would just dock his annual leave for the time out of work.'

'No, yeah, well these were serious. Nasty dudes these Algerians. They had got it all planned.'

'Well I shall have no problem. I'm not important like you are.'

'No, of course not.' His concurrence was entirely without irony despite the scrapyard full that I had employed.

He took me 'down to the wing', to update one of the detainees on the progress of his case. 'Sadiq, get your arse in here,' he called to the man.

I sighed. Why did jobs like this attract idiots of this calibre?

The other two IOs who started with me were Paul, whom I had mentored as a trainee at Dover East, and Lindy, whom I had yet to meet. We immediately got on well, which was very important because we were living in each other's pockets. To serve as an office we had been given a room in the hospital wing. In it were squeezed three desks, three chairs, a small table for the fax machine and a filing cabinet. With a filing drawer open, nobody could leave the office; I could not leave my desk if the office door was open; Lindy could not get to her desk if Paul was sitting in his chair. If we had visitors they had to stand in the middle. There was not sufficient space for two people to pass each other; every move had to be pre-authorised by the occupants of the room. The window was small and barred and looked out onto a blank white wall.

We set to work with a will. Whatever the outgoing IOs had been doing they had not wasted their time in organising the paperwork. The office was awash with requests from ports for us to interview their detainees and faxes from IS Casework in Croydon and scribbled notes on odd bits of paper about what various detainees had requested to be done on their behalf. It was chaos. We started by raising a local file for every detainee. We were scandalised that this had not already been done. This action led to a discovery. Many of the detainees were known under three different names. It was understandable that the prison staff would not be as familiar with the vagaries of foreign names as would IOs and so they would often misspell or rearrange a name. Thus the port would know their detainee by one name; when he arrived at Rochester Reception, the prison officer recorded him with his interpretation of that name and when he arrived on the wing the officer there chalked his version of the name on the cell door. Thus if you wanted to see Ahmed Oualid Dada you might have to ask for 'Wally'. It was essential to record his prison number on the file so that we could accurately identify the subject on official prison forms.

We were nominally within the responsibility of Gravesend immigration office and we had plenty of work to do but as their management rarely paid us a visit, we just went ahead and did it without supervision. Working within the prison system was certainly different for us. I was astonished when our first batch of mail arrived, all opened. We can't have this, I thought. I know that the Prison Service and the IS both come under the Home Office but our official circulars and the correspondence regarding the detainees are all confidential. I spoke to the lady in the Discipline Office who told me that they always opened every letter and then put them in the respective trays for distribution. It was the rules.

Paul pointed out that I was worrying about nothing since every prison officer and every official visitor who was issued with a key wallet at the gate effectively had a key to our office and if they were so minded they could come and poke their noses into our work any time that they desired. Our only security was a lockable filing cabinet for which we held the only two keys.

'So these civilians who wander about and say they are from the Board of Visitors can unlock our office door?'

'Yup.'

Lindy immediately got up and put the tea bags in the filing cabinet.

'Security precaution,' she said.

On the other hand, when we needed it, the Discipline Office would photograph and fingerprint our detainees for us. This was a great burden lifted, for fingerprinting is messy and has to be done in accordance with strict procedures and, in any case, where could we have done it? Certainly not in our office nor on the wing. So we decided amongst the three of us that henceforth we would interpret our regulations liberally and apply a sensible dose of give and take. If the Prison Service wanted an IO to interpret at a discipline hearing which was nothing to do with the IS then we would pop along and do the job. If we needed fax rolls we would get them from the prison store; photocopying we would do in the medical secretary's office.

I rather liked working in the prison. For a start, it was quiet. We were surrounded by high brick walls which kept out all but the noise of occasional aeroplanes. It was a bit like living in the Giant's Garden. If you could remember to order yourself a lunch at the canteen it would be well cooked, cheap and substantial. Enjoying a proper meal at a proper mealtime was quite a novelty for anybody in the IS. The journey to work, involving a forty-five minute drive up the motorway, did not take any longer than my nine mile cycle ride to Dover and the extra cost was covered by our claims for travelling expenses. All in all, if you liked challenging work in a weird environment then it was just the ticket. There was even a chance that if you visited Cookham Wood prison next door you could be served a cup of tea by the Moors murderess, Myra Hindley.

But I had a hankering after changing some things. I did not like the attitude of the prison staff to our detainees. They would taunt them. They shouted at them as a matter of course. This was made more harsh by the echo that was always present on the wing. On one occasion I had seen an officer push a man behind the knees without apparent reason so that he would stumble through a doorway. When I became more familiar with the prison environment I asked myself whether this attitude was caused by the inevitable monotony which derived from the system. Every day was timetabled; you knew what was going to happen. Any rupture in the routine would be welcomed. If, by tripping up a detainee some sort of violent reaction could be provoked then the men from Security would have to be called in and they were fully kitted up with helmets and shields and ready to rush to any part of the prison at a moment's notice to settle all disturbances. What they really liked was to get their teeth into quelling a decent riot. This behaviour, born perhaps of monotony, was akin to thrusting a brand into the haystack so that you could call out the fire brigade.

What had not been explained to the prison officers by our predecessors was that the people whom they were 'banging up' for twenty hours in twenty four, unlike their usual charges, had not been imprisoned because they had been convicted of a crime. The behaviour of the IOs whom we had replaced had done little to alter this misunderstanding. Many of our immigration detainees were not criminals in English law.

It must have been very confusing for the prison officers to leave a wing full of convicted thieves, fraudsters and practitioners of violence and walk across the yard to D wing where the immigration cases were housed and be expected to treat them differently. I know that I raised a few eyebrows by talking to the detainees respectfully and addressing them by their proper names. Gradually the prison officers realised that when an IO was present on the wing, then they had to tone down their behaviour. The result, not unsurprisingly, was that much of the tension disappeared, the detainees cooperated more, and everybody's job became easier.

And nobody was taken hostage.

We IOs naturally stood out because we wore our own clothes; we were not a uniform service. This was useful for us because in the detainees' eyes it made us visually distinct from the people who were locking them up. Whilst in the prison we were expected to wear our warrants in a visible place upon our person. When I joined the Service the IO's warrant was a printed slip of paper pasted into a blue cardboard cover which sported a small gold crest embossed on the front. It declared that the holder was an immigration officer under the Immigration Act 1971 and held the powers given to him under that act, or something like that. Nobody ever read it because we never had to show it to anybody. We were a discreet, almost secret, service. When IOs began to perform more 'after entry' work which involved having to identify themselves to householders on

I certify that the officer named is an Immigration Officer for the purposes of the Immigration Act, 1971.

H.M. Chief Inspector
Immigration Service
Home Office

23 June   19 80

If found please return to: H.M. Immigration Service HQ, Lunar House, Wellesley Rd, Croydon or hand in at the nearest Police Station

IMMIGRATION SERVICE

Name .... Martin J. LLOYD ....

Rank ... Immigration Officer ....

Signature ....

N⁰ 1260   IS 241

MY IMMIGRATION OFFICER'S WARRANT
This was version No.2 which now included a photograph so that
the officer could actually use it to identify himself.

doorsteps and gain admission to custody suites in police stations it was realised that a card without a photograph of the holder at the very least was useless as a proof of identity. It is rather ironic that the service which deals with checking peoples' identities all day long had not quite assimilated that fact.

The warrant that we use now is a plastic card with photograph, bound into a leather wallet which is decorated with a heavy enamelled badge and with this clipped over my belt I walk down the corridor to our office. A young man is cleaning the floor. He is an inmate from the criminal wing and is trusted with small tasks such as this.

'Cor, what a smell of pork,' he says as I approach him.

'I beg your pardon?'

'Pork. I can smell pork.'

I stop and sniff. I can only smell a slight waft of disinfectant from his bucket.

'No, I can't smell pork.' I sniff again.

'Definitely pork innit?' His voice is a sneer.

'Perhaps that is what you are having for lunch, although I would be surprised if we could smell it from here.' I shrug and walk to our office.

'Smell pork,' I hear behind me.

When I recount this bizarre conversation to Paul he opens my eyes for me. 'He was taking the piss. He thought you were police.'

'Eh?'

'In civvies? With a warrant on your belt? He was telling you that he knew you were a cop. A pig. Smells of pork. Gettit?'

'Oh. Well I never.'

A few minutes later I walked back up the corridor to the gents' toilet. The man was still there and as he watched me go into the toilet I got the feeling that he was marking time, waiting for something. I went to the cubicle, closed the door and stood to pee into the pan. I have long legs and, on a whim, I managed to keep one leg well behind me with the heel of my shoe flat on the floor. I heard the outer door open and then there was a tremendous crash as my cubicle door was kicked open. Unfortunately for the inmate, it bounced harmlessly on the heel of my shoe and returned to smack him in the face.

'Oh dear, are you all right?' I asked. He was holding his hand to his nose. 'It was a good job that it happened here. You are in the hospital block. They might be able to do something for you.' I walked past him. 'You know, I still can't smell pork.'

One day I was sitting in a large room furnished with rows of easy chairs upon which sat the various inmates with their visitors. Along the back wall had been constructed several windowed cubicles each containing a table and three chairs. These were designed to give some privacy for those needing to discuss confidential matters with their legal representatives. I was waiting for a solicitor and his interpreter to turn up so that I could conduct an asylum interview with his client. I had already booked my cubicle and was sitting at the top table chatting to the officer in charge of the room. He had the lists of inmates and every time the bell rang one group was marched out and their visitors escorted back to the gate and then another group came in. Most of the men had their wives or girlfriends visiting them; one or two were talking earnestly with men who looked bigger crooks than they were. I wondered whether they were planning their next big job. I would never know, but it amused me to speculate.

We were chatting about something inconsequential when I found I was distracted by a movement at the periphery of my vision. It had been going on for some time, I realised, and now I was curious to identify what it was. Several rows back, a large Jamaican lady visitor was sitting on her husband/boyfriend and they were kissing and joking in a playful manner. Except that... he was slouched down in the chair, almost lying on his back and the lady's repeated action of leaning forwards to kiss him and then sitting back had a sensual rhythm to it. All decency was preserved by her enormous flowered skirt that she had spread over them both like a tablecloth.

I turned to the officer at the side of me. 'That couple two rows back on the left – the lady with the yellow flowered skirt. Have you noticed them?'

He glanced across. 'Oh yeah.'

'Well...' I did not really know how to put this. 'Er... Is it all as innocent as it looks?'

'You think she is screwing him?' he said. 'Is that what you mean?'

'It had crossed my mind.'

'Yeah, she is, but no harm done. It's all decent and under cover and it'll keep old Charlie boy happy for a week or two so why make a fuss?'

Every afternoon we would visit the doctors in the hospital wing in case any of our detainees were being treated. Sometimes it would be a minor wound as a result of a fracas but our long term residents were usually hunger strikers. We were not allowed to call them that, they were termed more accurately, 'food refusers'. These were usually men who had spent years going through every process of the immigration appeals system and were now awaiting removal from the country. In what was supposed to be a desperate last ditch attempt to appeal to any vestige of humanity that might be discovered within the Home Office they would refuse to eat.

**ROCHESTER PRISON
D WING**

Photography is
forbidden in
prisons.

They forgot to
tell me.

They were then put in the hospital wing and kept under observation in individual cells. They continued to take water to keep themselves alive but became weaker and weaker.

I would always make a point of speaking to them in their cell. They usually faced the wall and refused to answer but I would chunter on about all kinds of things, touching now and then upon their case, just to ensure that they had felt some human contact. I do not know how long a person can survive without food but I was surprised to see *'day 72'* chalked on one door. The medical prison officer opined that the inmate was getting food somehow but I could not see from where.

No food refuser died when we were there. That is not how the process worked. When the food refuser had got everything in place then, on a Friday morning, he would refuse water. These men were frail already. A refusal to take water would kill them so if they had not drunk anything by Friday night they would be transferred to the local hospital. The prison was short-staffed over the weekend and could not afford to detach an officer to sit at the bedside; they would hand the responsibility for the prisoner over to the hospital authority. The latter would make it clear that its job was not to lock people up but to cure them. On the Saturday morning the prisoner would discharge himself and walk out into the welcoming arms of his friends who would drive him away to their house. And then we would start the business of trying to find him and get rid of him all over again from the beginning.

My time in Rochester Prison was one of the most fulfilling periods of my career. The three of us had gone into what was a mess and had come away with an unsolicited letter of thanks and recognition from the prison governor for what we had achieved. However, our biggest challenge was still before us – getting the Home Office to refund our expenses. The TSR file which Nigel Andrews had introduced me to so many years earlier was now quite familiar to me. Before starting the period of relief I had worked out how much subsistence and travelling expenses I would be entitled to and had applied for an imprest for that amount in advance. This meant that the Home Office would lend me the money and I would refund the loan by submitting an expenses claim once the work had been done. So far, so good. But my imprest did not materialise.

I phoned up the relevant department and they declared that my request for an imprest had not been received by them. I had every confidence that Norman, our clerical officer, would have forwarded it to the proper place, he was a retired police inspector and was thorough and reliable, so I could only fault the efficiency of the expenses section.

I followed their instruction and submitted another claim. I had been two weeks at Rochester when I received a notification from them that the request had been received but that now the period of the relief work had started, no imprest was permissible. I would have to submit an expenses claim at the end. So much for my idea of not financing the government.

I mentioned this to Paul and he remarked that the same thing had happened to him. He had applied for an imprest but they had held on to the form for so long that he had become no longer eligible. 'That's funny,' said Lindy, 'the same happened to me.' We grumbled and thought no more about it.

I carefully filled in and sent off my expenses claim. A couple of weeks passed and then it was returned to me as 'incomplete'. I scoured it and could find nothing lacking so I phoned them up.

'You haven't put your national insurance number on the form.'

'But it doesn't ask for it. It never has done.'

'It was a rule introduced this month.'

That was bizarre. I had not noticed this instruction in the circulars. I meticulously inscribed the number on the form and returned it. Three weeks passed and the form was returned with a duplicated note attached to it informing me that my claim had been refused because I had used the incorrect form. This was daft. There was only one form. I went to see Norman and he issued me with an expenses claim form. It was identical to the one which they had just refused so I phoned them up again.

'The form you must use is the one with the box printed on it for you to insert your national insurance number,' they said.

'But I wrote the number on the form.'

'Yes but it's the wrong form. It has been redesigned. You must use the new form.'

I tackled Norman again. He assured me that these were the only forms that they possessed but he phoned up the expenses section and asked for a new batch which featured the box for the national insurance number.

'They've not come in yet,' they said. 'We'll send you some as soon as they arrive.'

The forms arrived at the end of March which meant that the previous four months' expenses claims which had been rejected could now be paid... in the new budget period. The IS had already spent its budget by November so somebody had invented this delaying tactic of losing the first application for an imprest, delaying the second until it was out of time, returning the expenses claim with a request for the NI number, refusing the returned form because it had been superseded in the interim and then being 'unable' to supply the new forms until the next budget year was due. I bet the bloke who thought out that trick got an MBE. But my problem was not solved yet. Before paying up, expenses section now asked for sight of my motor insurance certificate to prove that I was covered for business use.

I sighed heavily and photocopied the certificate for them. Just a minute, when I looked at the clauses which applied to my insurance cover, clause K, which was the business-use clause, was not on the list. I checked and double checked. When I had changed insurance companies I had not received the same cover as before. Expenses section would now clap their hands with glee and refuse to pay out. After all that I had been through I was not ready to accept defeat. Especially not after the underhand treatment that we had all been subjected to. I studied the typeface of the letter K. It was not one that you would find on a typewriter so I photocopied the certificate and cut out the letter K from the photocopy. I then pasted this onto another photocopy of the certificate, adding it to the list of clauses applicable to my insurance cover. I then photocopied this paste-up and, abracadabra, I had a certificate showing the correct level of insurance cover. I was gambling that the personnel of expenses section would not be as well trained as IOs were in forgery detection. I was right.

Back at the hoverport the atmosphere is sober as, from the shrinking portion of the office allotted to us, the remaining control IOs pack up their affairs and prepare to move elsewhere. We finally hand over the telecoms responsibilities to the Accommodation Unit who collect our files and equipment. Within three weeks the EO who had taken over compiling the telephone directory phoned up to ask me how I had achieved the page layout.

'I did it all in Wordperfect,' I said.

'Yes but how did you get the telephone numbers to line up one above the other?'

'Are you familiar with Wordperfect?'

'Oh yes, I am trained in it. I went on a five-day residential course.'

'Lucky you. They wouldn't train me. I had to teach myself in my spare time. I can't remember how I did the page layout but if you've been trained then you can work it out for yourself can't you?'

After all, they were the experts, we had been told. We were just untrained amateurs.

My three months' prison sentence has only served to postpone the decision as to where I was to be posted and Crozier is on to me the moment that I return.

'We won't have any vacancies at the European Liaison Unit.' He contorts his rubbery face into mock compassion. He is desolate as he shakes his head sadly. 'What we can offer you is a three month trial at Dover East in the casework office, just to see how you get on.'

'I was transferred out of Dover East specifically because the working environment was antagonistic to my condition,' I remind him civilly.

He drones on, eroding and erasing. Crozier beats his opponents by attrition. After five minutes of his bumbling and buzzing, he returns to the same point and you realize that no progress has been made in the discussion and you are in for another lot of drone. And he will continue, just as a brainless fly will batter and buzz at a window, until you give in and open the window and agree. He is wearing me down. Perhaps I could try it just for a few months. They have redesigned the office, he says. Why can't he just shut up and leave me alone? If I say yes will he stop badgering me?

I open my mouth to agree and am hit by a bolt of self concern. Why am I being coerced like this? Is it really that difficult to transfer me to the place I want to go to? It is then that I realise my problem. He knows where I want to go and his delight is to prevent anybody from doing what they desire. He just loves to rule and spoil.

'I think I ought to ask the Personnel Management Unit what they can offer,' I suggest. Without realising it, this is a brainwave.

'Oh we don't want the PMU all mixed up in this,' he assures me with celerity and some more feigned compassion. 'We can do this all locally. It's much better to keep these things amongst ourselves.'

I nod thoughtfully. 'Well let me think about it,' I say but I am already thinking. He does not want the PMU involved. I cannot understand why. When I telephone them and explain the situation they ask for a summary of proposals from the inspector and then plump heavily in favour of my suggestion of going to the ELU. This reassures me.

Crozier meets me a few days later, his brow furrowed in well-meaning anguish. 'The trouble is,' he explains, 'the PMU don't realise that there are no vacancies at the ELU. Now if you went to Dover East–'

'–Why are there no vacancies? Other IOs are being transferred there.'

'Well that is why, you see. The quota is full.'

'How inconvenient. Leave it with me for a few days,' I suggest.

He nods and smiles. He has sensed victory. I am shaking with tension and anger. For a reason I do not understand they do not want to involve the PMU. I am being bullied because I am vulnerable. Well, what I need now is a bigger bully on my side. I think of the stabbing finger and angry eyebrows of the AD when I had crossed him at one of his pep talks. I beard him in his den.

'The PMU has agreed with my proposal that sending me to the ELU would be the best for me and the IS. That is good news isn't it?' I say pleasantly.

He looks at me, cigar paused in mid puff. I have caught him unawares and he does not know how to react. If he says that it is not good news, he knows that I will ask why.

'Yes. That's good.'

'Right, well get Crozier off my back. He is insisting that I go to Dover East. I'm sure he'll see reason from you.'

'How would you like to go to Folkestone?' he says out of the blue.

'How long for?'

'Until there's a vacancy at the ELU.'

'OK.'

That was easy. Too easy, as it turned out. They had side-stepped the PMU proposal and got me to accept something outside the original offer and it had all been arranged locally so they were still in control.

SEALINK FAREWELL
m.v. Hengist leaving Folkestone on closure of the service.

Folkestone Channel packet port came into being by a stroke of fortune. In the nineteenth century the South Eastern Railway Company were nearing completion of their line from London to Dover and William Cubitt was busily excavating the clay from what is now Kingsnorth Gardens in Folkestone to manufacture the four and a half million bricks which he would use to construct a splendid viaduct to carry the line around the north of Folkestone and on to Dover. However, negotiations with the Dover Harbour Board over how the line was to approach their port were not progressing easily. In 1842, the company which was trying to improve and develop the silted-up harbour in Folkestone went into liquidation and the South Eastern Railway snapped up the harbour for £18,000. They cleaned it up and by 1843 they were carrying passengers from London to Paris in just twelve hours. Overnight, almost, Folkestone had become the premier Channel port of England.

By the time I got there, it was on its last legs. If I had thought that Dover West was moribund then Folkestone was a corpse that nobody could be bothered to bury.

I walked in to the general office and put my case on a desk. 'Not that one, that's mine,' somebody said. I shrugged and moved it to another. 'And I sit there,' somebody else complained. I took stock of the office. It was effectively a shack built above the railway station and passenger hall. In the office were forty two desks for twenty one IOs – but there was not one for me.

The pace of life was relaxed in the extreme. With often four hours between arrivals, IOs would wander off to the pub or go home to mow the lawn or do a bit of plumbing and then amble back in time for the next ship. Having no telecoms work to occupy my 'down time' and as no administrative work was delegated to me, I caught up with some reading, sometimes with my feet on the desk watching the seagulls wheeling above the town; sometimes sitting on a harbourside bench eating an ice cream whilst the fishing boats bobbed in the sunshine. I had only been there three weeks when it was announced that the port would close at Christmas.

The traffic at Folkestone could be quite interesting because it had the rail link from Paris via Boulogne which brought us impecunious passengers from the Mediterranean and North Africa. With the general office being alongside the station, the warning to man the embarks control was usually the office vibrating to the thudding and trundling of the train from London as it ground to a halt outside our door. When we heard the chugging of the diesels then we knew that we were in for a treat because this heralded the arrival of the Orient Express. British Rail no longer possessed any electric locomotives which could run on the 650v Southern Railway system which served Folkestone Harbour and would be powerful enough to haul the heavy Pullman coaches up the steep incline which the South Eastern Railway had been obliged to construct, so many years earlier, to get their trains down from the viaduct to sea level and so now a pair of diesel locomotives had to be used.

It was quite a nostalgic sight – the luxurious chocolate and yellow carriages leaning into the curve of the platform whilst the uniformed attendants helped the passengers to alight and directed them to the passport control. The assistance they provided was often needed since these revellers had been drinking and eating since they had left Victoria and looked as if they had every intention of continuing all the way to Venice. It was great fun watching them stagger through the control; the ladies wobbling on high heels in fancy dresses and outlandish hats and the men gently bouncing from the walls as if they were balls in a slow-motion pinball machine. One of those balls turned out to be someone quite famous. I am useless at recognising people. I just have no memory for faces. Even when examining the passport the name rarely meant anything to me. But this chap I recognised. He walked carefully up to my desk placing one foot before the other with the exaggerated concentration of a man on a tightrope, his eyes firmly fixed on the exit door as if afraid that it would disappear the moment his gaze was averted.

Later that evening I was at a theatre club meeting. They were all waffling on knowledgeably about people of whom I was ignorant or plays in which I was unversed when I suddenly had an inspiration.

'Well, as I said to Sir Peter Ustinov only this afternoon...' All the conversations stopped and all eyes turned to me. 'Thank you sir.'

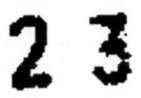

I've made it. I am at the Channel tunnel and it is a brand new experience. Everything is different. It is a port with no passengers; all the IOs work at the French end of the tunnel. Passports are examined and passengers refused in the British Control Zone at Coquelles. We have no complicated procedures for removing people – we simply give them back to the French authorities to dispose of as they think fit. This often means that they release them just outside the port gates so that they can have another go at getting in to England. Only on the rare occasion when the case cannot be decided in Coquelles is casework brought back to England.

I am in the general office at the Cheriton end of the tunnel. All IOs working in Coquelles have to come here first to collect their equipment and take a pool car to go through the tunnel because no walking traffic can access the tunnel at Cheriton, only cars, lorries and coaches. Foot passengers have to travel by train on Eurostar from Waterloo or Ashford. They are not our concern. We do not see them. My duties are divided between dealing with the ELU enquiries and handling the casework which has been brought back to Cheriton. It soon becomes apparent to me that I have an extra role in the functioning of the office – that of assuring continuity. I am here five days a week; the other officers mostly bounce in and out. Messages to be given to staff who will be stamping on later in the day can be thrown over the shoulder to Martin as you leave the office, he will make sure that they get them. The advantage of continuity in handling casework is that of efficiency. Familiarity with a case file saves time and within a short period I become familiar with all the long term casework. The other IOs might be given an office duty perhaps once a month. This gives them little opportunity to learn what statistical returns are needed and how to compile them nor how to update any standing instructions. I make sure that I know how to do all that.

The purpose of the European Liaison Unit, it transpires, is to assist the Home Office in removing difficult cases to countries who either do not want to, or cannot for technical reasons, accept them. Technical reasons usually revolve around documentation. If the person has no passport he cannot travel. We have to apply to the country of which he is a national and persuade them of his identity and encourage them to issue a document of some sort to allow us to remove him. This can be upset if the person denies being a national of that country in order to remain unremovable. Once the document is secured we then have to convince the receiving country that they should accept this person back.

I suspect that the rationale in co-opting IOs to assist was that they were likely to be versed in foreign languages and were knowledgable about foreign immigration procedures. By the time I was posted here, the unit had established good working relationships with the various foreign border control authorities and had started to shift the sticky long term casework which had been gumming up the system. This success was not without repercussions. When you have succeeded in persuading the Netherlands to accept back a Ghanaian to whom you refused entry four years earlier and have only just concluded his case it becomes difficult to refuse a reciprocal request from the Netherlands to accept back a Jamaican who has been in prison in their country for eighteen months on drugs charges, having originally arrived from Harwich. But by and large, the results weigh very heavily in our favour. We are ridding the country of casework which is costing the British taxpayer money, for Britain is accommodating many of these people in local housing or prison and paying them to live here.

Our working environment is rather swish. The office is in the Passenger Services Building. It is an up-to-date suite, carpeted, air-conditioned and non-smoking. Those who wish to smoke have to go and sit on the balcony which is shared with the other users of the building. From the office we have entertaining views through bizarrely shaped windows into the concourse of the commercial area below us on one side and panoramic presentations of Eurostar trains whooshing towards the tunnel portals on the other. The canteen is just along the corridor and every time that they burn the toast, the entire building is evacuated and we have to await the arrival of the fire service before re-entering. They eventually solve this problem by removing the toaster from underneath the smoke detector.

'Martin?'

'Yes Sid?'

Sid is our office manager. 'This request for a strafoplan board that you made. Crozier has rejected it.'

'Why?'

'Says we don't need it.'

CHAPTER TWENTY THREE

ENGLAND AS SEEN FROM FRANCE
The sun is setting behind the passenger services building at the Cheriton terminal of
the Channel tunnel near Folkestone. The white board by the open gate is the notice
forbidding entry to the French Control Zone. I am standing at the top of the steps in
this zone in order to take a photograph of England as seen from France.

'I spend half my casework duties trying to catch up on things that have
been missed because nobody knows what the state of play is. If we had a
board there, on that wall, everybody would be able to see at an instant
exactly where we are and what needs doing.'

'Well, Crozier says no.' He looks at me with a meaning in his eyes.

I realise my mistake. What I should have done was to have told Crozier
that on no account did we want a strafoplan board and then he would
have directed that we were to have one.

'What do you suggest?'

'Well, if you ask me to supply one, my job is to supply it, isn't it?'

'Thanks Sid.'

'There's the catalogue. Work out the size and format and let me know.'

Sid has come from the army and has a pragmatic streak in him, thank goodness.

I answer the telephone and a voice says in French, 'This is the *Police de l'Air et des Frontières* at Menton.' I know this to be on the French-Italian border near Nice. 'We have a man here with a British visitors passport. Can you check it for us?'

'What do you suspect? Has it been tampered with?'

'I don't think so. We are not convinced that he is the rightful holder.'

The British visitors passport is the beige cardboard tri-fold document which can be obtained from some post offices in the UK. The level of security of issue of these documents is, understandably, less than that of a full passport. We know already that they are to be phased out shortly.

'Is it the version with the little blue and red flecks in the cardboard?'

'Yes monsieur.'

'Do you have an ultra-violet lamp handy? Those flecks should fluoresce under UV light.' There is a shuffling at the other end of the line. 'Do they?'

'They are no brighter than before.'

'Then the document is a counterfeit. Can you give me the number?' I reach for the computer keyboard and tap in the number. 'Yes that is one of the numbers used on a series of counterfeits which the police have found in the hands of criminals here. Does he speak English? Have you a good English speaker there?'

'He is black.'

I am momentarily stalled by this disclosure. The suggestion is that he cannot be expected to speak English because of his colour.

'Well I'll leave it to you.' I cannot get involved in their interview. 'Could you send me a fax of the passport? I will see if the police know anything about him. They may be able to pin him down from the photograph.'

As I am writing a note in the log Trevor comes in.

'You're early,' I say, looking at the clock. This is not an inconsequential observation – Trevor is an experienced practitioner of the last minute arrival.

'Has Macdonald stamped on?' He looks sharply around the office.

'No, you're the first.'

'Thank Christ for that.' He hurries to the box file containing the car keys. 'I'm going to lunch but I've booked out the car, OK? I've taken the keys.' He wiggles them in the air. I nod. 'Make sure that Macdonald knows that.'

'Yes I will. And I'll tell the rest of the shift as they arrive. They will be relieved.'

Macdonald is a mad Scotsman with spiky hair and wild staring eyes. He is probably the worst driver in the office. The first man to arrive on a shift usually books out the car and drives the others to the Shuttle and over to France. Nobody wants to be in a car driven by Macdonald so whenever he is on duty somebody in the shift makes sure that they get here before him to prevent him from booking out a car.

I am quite pleased that I do not have to be driven around by some of my colleagues. I have seen them coming off the Shuttle and reaching seventy mph within the terminal. Perhaps I am too old now but I am not thrilled by riding in a speeding car handled by somebody who has held a driving licence for six months. One of the cars has already been damaged by an officer who wrecked its suspension by crashing straight over a roundabout in Coquelles. His claim that the brakes had failed was laughed off by his colleagues pointing to the black skid marks on the tarmac. The only thing that had failed was his driving skill.

I pick up the latest notice from the Home Office. Oh no, not another statistical return to be made! Every time that some plonker gets up in Parliament and says, 'can the honourable member tell me how many... etc.?' then we end up having to count and record things. What is this one all about? Oh, it appears to be a home-grown carbuncle. An HEO in the Home Office has been analysing the outcome of interviews where the passenger has been accompanied by a legal representative and now wants us to submit a weekly record of observations on the behaviour and performance of any attending solicitors. I look at the 'points for guidance' on the notice and they set me thinking. What can possibly be the purpose of this statistical return? Self-agrandissement for the HEO? The whole idea is poorly thought out and downright dangerous. I can already hear, 'can the honourable member tell the House why the Home Office is compiling an intelligence database of the performance of immigrants' legal representatives?' No, we don't want to get involved in this. I carefully feed the notice into the shredder.

'I've just taken a call from the French,' the CIO says. 'They've got two refusals.'

'Nationality?'

'Brit.'

'OK. I'll go over.'

The CIO is Walter. He has also transferred from the hoverport. We call him Walter in honour of the fictional character Walter Mitty because he really does live in a make-believe world of his own concoction. He will speak of someone as being 'a very good friend of mine' and yet if, by chance, you meet them, you will find that they cannot remember him. They have no idea who he is. He once said to me, 'Of course, I only do this job for fun, you know. I don't have to work. I've got a private income.' However, for all his whimsies, he was harmless. He had caused me no trouble. That was to come.

Just as we hand back our refusals to the French in Coquelles, so the French hand back their refusals to us in Cheriton. I pick up my official case and walk down onto the service road. At a tall chain link fence I go through the gate by the notice which reads *French Control Zone. No Entry* and I climb the steps to the kiosks of the French Police. There, a rather irate British man is holding out a form and arguing with the French policeman. His wife is sitting in the car, a strained expression on her face.

'Look, it says here on the back of my insurance certificate, "valid for all countries in the EU". It's even written in French. See.' He points it out to the policeman who shrugs and says, *'non'*.

'Good morning sir. I am a British immigration officer and I understand that you have been refused entry to France.'

'Oh, thank goodness you have arrived. You tell them,' he says. 'This chap says that I've got no insurance for the car. He wants a green card but we don't need a green card anymore. I checked and in any case the insurance company refused to issue one. Even they said that I didn't need one. They don't issue them anymore for Europe. You tell him.'

'Actually sir, I am only here to let you back into England.'

The man stares at me in confusion. 'But I haven't been anywhere yet.'

'No, but if the French refuse you permission to enter France then I have to check that you have the right to come back into Britain.'

'Eh? This is stupid. Are you saying that I can't go to Calais?'

'No sir. The French Border Control are saying that. I am here to let you back into England.' I take the British passports from the French policeman and quickly inspect them. 'That's fine,' I say to the cop, 'They can go.'

'You told him we could go,' the man says. 'So–'

'–I was telling him that you could be allowed back into Britain. We are in the French Control Zone here. I cannot challenge their decisions. It is their law which applies.'

'But we don't need a green card. I checked.' The man is outraged and rightly so because he has the law on his side. And my knowing this does not make my task any the more enjoyable.

'So we can't go? Just like that. They say 'no' and that is that.'
'I'm afraid it is, sir.'
The French policeman hands him a form and points to a dotted line.
'What do I do with this?' he asks me. 'Do I sign it?'
'Has it been explained to you and do you understand it?'
'No, of course not.'
'Do you wish to sign a form that you do not understand?'
'No.'

I shrug at him. The French policeman also shrugs and takes back the form. He squiggles his pen on the dotted line intended for the man's signature, ticks the box which states that the passenger does not want to exercise his right of appeal and benefit from a delay of twenty-four hours before the decision is implemented and then he slings it through a hatch into the back office. I think back to my training days at Heathrow when the IOs 'forgot' to hand the appeal form to the refusal. This is several stages further on from that. And they are getting away with it every day.

The man shakes my hand, gets in his car and is directed back down to the site exit. His day has been ruined and I can do nothing about it.

When I get back to the office the telephone is ringing. It is a CIO from Dover East.

'Oh Martin, the inspector has asked that you come over here to help out in the casework office. We are two IOs short today.'

I am dumbfounded. I stand there shaking my head as if to clear it.

'But I am a Cheriton IO,' I say lamely.

'We are all one now, you know, the South East District.'

'Yes I know that. But I work at Cheriton, not Dover East.'

'But the inspector has told me to ask you to come over and help us.'

'I can't. I've got work to do here. You'll have to find somebody else.'

I put down the phone deep in thought. And I had believed that I was safe. Crozier does not like losing.

There is a lot of animated discussion in the office about the Schengen Agreement and the concept of open borders. The consensus within the IS is that if the UK signs the Agreement our job will consist of waving at all the dross of humanity as it beats its path to the benefits office. Despite what the liberals may believe, signing the Agreement will not stop the French from refusing harmless Brits for not being able to show a document which the law no longer requires them to possess. Cheriton and Coquelles have already climbed to be amongst the top performing ports in the French Police. Their refusal rate is phenomenal. Any British lorry driver is

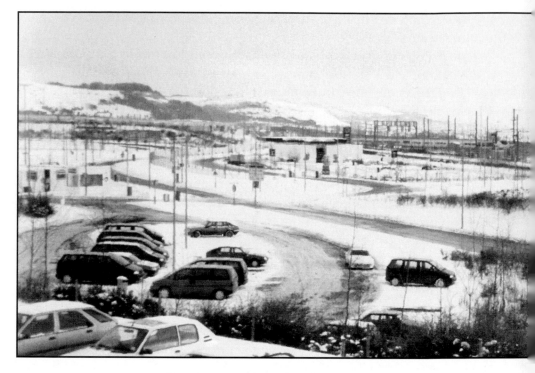

THE VIEW FROM MY OFFICE WINDOW
A winter's morning with the snow lying on the North Downs and on the cluttered layout
of the Channel tunnel terminus making the scene look even bleaker than usual.

peremptorily refused entry at Cheriton if allowing him to proceed would
mean he would be driving on a day upon which lorry traffic is banned. In
vain the drivers plead that they intend to park up on the other side
to await Monday morning. And as for the police's expertise in forgery
detection, it is unsurpassed throughout Metropolitan France because
every passenger refused by a British IO for using forged documents is
handed back to the French who then examine him and 'discover' the
forgery for their own statistics.

Out in the fields behind Coquelles the International Red Cross have
occupied a hutted camp in which they house the immigrants who are on
their way to the UK. As evening falls, the Afghans, the Albanians, the
Kossovans make their pedestrian way to the port and later star on the
security camera videos as they scale the perimeter fences and sprint to the
departing freight trains in order to gain a foothold on a wagon before it
reaches too high a speed. If they can make it through the tunnel they
hope to drop off in the marshalling yard at Dolland's Moor, just inland
from Cheriton and claim asylum. The unlucky ones drop off en route and

In the middle of the picture the tail of a Eurostar train can just be seen as it
makes its way into the tunnel *en route* to France.

their mangled bodies are found beside the track. As morning dawns, those
who have failed to find a train make their way back to a Red Cross
breakfast to await another attempt. For some reason they do not wish to
claim asylum in France. It is so kind of the Red Cross to look after them
for us. As Reg Toale observes, 'what sense can David Blunkett make of all
this – a blind Home Secretary? If nobody describes to him exactly what the
nightly rush to the trains looks like, how can he know?' I have no answer.

The Home Office minister, Ann Widdecombe visits us one day in
company with the AD. He walks through the door with a lighted cheroot in
his hand. He really is an oaf.

'Oh minister, look at this, we have the French...' He cannot remember
the name as he punches at a keyboard, scattering cigar ash over the small
greenscreen VDU. We have one telephone line at Cheriton which is on the
France Telecom network. On this we have a Minitel unit. It is a very early
system for retrieving information online and we can use it to look up
addresses and telephone numbers of French nationals. Ann Widdecombe
glances at it with the disdain of a woman watching a man playing with a

toy train set and continues into the office. The AD abandons the machine in mid search because he has never learned how to operate it and hurries after her. 'What would you like to see, minister?' I have never seen him so unctuous.

'What about a cup of coffee?' she suggests.

'Yes, yes.' He becomes authoritarian. 'One of you girls,' he points at the female IOs in the office, 'would you get some coffee for the minister?'

I did say that he was an oaf, didn't I?

'One of you girls?' Ann Widdecombe turns on him. 'One of you girls! That's so very sexist.'

'Oh I'll get the coffee.' Malcolm stands up. He used to be a steward on the Sealink ferries. The AD is completely unaware of his crass behaviour.

We don't sign the Schengen Agreement and so remain outside the 'Europe without Frontiers' arrangement. One Sunday afternoon I take a telephone call from a senior principal in the IND. I have to verify with him that he is what he says he is. What is he doing phoning the port at any time, let alone on a Sunday afternoon?

'We have a protocol with the French Ministry of Justice and their Home Office regarding persons whom we have refused entry to but been unable to remove for administrative reasons.'

'Yes?' I say cautiously, knowing that I am not privy to the product of such high level negotiations.

'They have sent me a fax which explains the changes they intend to bring in as from Monday.'

'This Monday?'

'Yes. Tomorrow. The duty officer has faxed it to me at home because he thinks that it might be important.'

'I see.' I am lying. I have no idea what he is talking about nor where the conversation is going but I am impressed that this man has a fax machine at home.

'Do you have a French translator on your books that you could get hold of? Obviously all ours are at home.'

'We don't use translators. We sometimes use interpreters at Coquelles but we don't need them here, and we wouldn't use them for French, only for Turkish or Arabic or languages such as those.'

'Oh dear,' he says. The poor lamb seems lost.

'Why don't you fax it down here and let me have a look at it?'

I spend a distracting hour and a half translating into English a document written in French administrative jargon and then fax it back.

He is incredulous.

'You've done it? Just like that?'

It was no great hassle to me but it brought home to me that the wealth of experience and knowledge that was in the IS was unknown to the mainstream Home Office. They had no idea or appreciation of the intellectual resources that they were paying for and this was dangerous because if they did not know what they were paying for, then they would haggle over the bill. With the movement to drive down costs, IOs were now being recruited who had no aptitude or interest in languages. This meant that the IS did not have to pay them a language allowance supplement to their salary. The core of knowledge was bleeding away as the experienced IOs retired and they were being encouraged to do so by the various early retirement packages which were announced from time to time. These were a bonus for bean counters. You get rid of an experienced senior IO who speaks three languages and is earning his maximum salary with the performance-related enhancement and you replace him with a recruit on his basic starting salary. It makes good economic sense doesn't it?

Using interpreters is not without hazards. I was conducting an asylum interview in the police station one day with a Sri Lankan. He had brought with him his solicitor and an interpreter. I was about ten minutes into the meat of the interview when the solicitor's interpreter challenged ours.

'He didn't say that the police found drugs in his house, he said that they found guns.'

I recorded the challenge in my notes and asked our interpreter to put the question again. This time, he interpreted the answer as 'guns'. I had no idea what was going on in Tamil but decided that the only equitable course was to terminate the interview there and then and reschedule it with a different interpreter.

On several occasions my casework duties obliged me to interview our detainees in Rochester Prison but it was not the same. Things had changed. They now had an additional one hundred detainees to take charge of. Malcolm, the deputy governor had left on promotion and the atmosphere was slipping towards what it had been before.

Crozier at Dover East was still nibbling away at me. One day I had to deliver to them a casework file which they needed urgently. I presumed it was not too urgent because I could not physically get into the small Japanese runabout that we were supposed to use and the cycle ride from Cheriton to Dover East took me over an hour. I delivered the file and as I stood chatting to a young lady IO whom I had not met before I was astonished to notice that she was using my casework guide.

'You can't use that,' I said. 'It is over ten years old. I know, I wrote it.'

'You wrote it? Oh great. We think it's brilliant. It's our bible.'

'But most of it is out of date. When I was here I kept it up to date. Nobody has amended it for a decade. Everything has changed. Bits of it must be wrong.'

'Oh we know that,' she explained, 'but we can understand your guide. We can't fathom out the instructions.'

I was assimilating the revelation that they would rather use a manual which they could understand but which they knew to be inaccurate than refer to the current instructions which they knew to be right but found indecipherable, when the CIO came in.

'The inspector says that you may as well do the interview now that you have brought the file,' he said.

'I have delivered the file. It's your casework. You do the interview. I picked up my anorak and left. When was Crozier going to give up the pressure?

'Did you hear about the Hungarian lad?' The IO asks me as I relieve him. I shake my head. 'Yesterday a fourteen year old Hungarian lad arrives at Coquelles in a car driven by his British uncle. Coming to visit a friend in London. Nasty suspicious IO doesn't like the look of the uncle so starts asking questions. Uncle admits that he is not a blood relation, only a friend. Passenger is detained whilst they try to contact the parents. Meanwhile SB do a check on the uncle and discover that he has a conviction for a sex offence with a minor.'

'And this Hungarian lad is a minor?'

'Yeah, he's fourteen. So they bring him back through the tunnel whilst the police continue their investigation.'

'Would they have landed him otherwise?'

'Oh yeah. He had money and was staying for the two weeks of the school holidays and it was pretty certain he would go back afterwards. We managed to contact the lad's mother in Hungary. The parents are divorced. She knows all about this pervert and is happy for her son to go with him.'

'I don't suppose she referred to him as a pervert.'

'No, probably not.'

'What was the boy's reaction to all this?'

'He seemed quite happy to be with the chap. So the CIO says, "land him".'

'Well, he was travelling with his parent's permission.'

'I haven't finished yet. That fiery police officer, the one they call Fishtail, God knows why, he gets his teeth into it with a vengeance and does a check on the friend they are going to visit in London. By the way, this lad does not know him. He has never met this guy and yet he will be staying with him for a fortnight and, would you believe it? It turns out he's another pervert. Got two convictions for sex offences.'

'So what happened?'

'Well I learned all about it from Fishtail. He was sitting in the kiosk swearing and blinding. "The Guvnor told me to drop it" he says. "Always the bloody same with these perverts. You get so far and then somebody upstairs tells you to drop it." It wasn't the first time it had happened, apparently.'

'But had any offence been committed? I mean, the lad was travelling with his mother's permission and was going willingly.'

'I don't think it was that aspect that was upsetting Fishtail it was the 'orders from on high' bit that got his goat. He didn't actually say it but the suggestion was that somebody high up in the force was torpedoing child abuse investigations.'

'Ah, we're back to the perfidious influence of Masonry in the police force, are we? But you can't go about accusing people of sex abuse just like that. You've got to have proof.'

'That's the point he was making. They were being prevented from looking for proof.'

'Come to think of it, my grandfather was a freemason so why am I still an IO?'

'Because you're useless, that's why.'

'Oh yes, of course, I hadn't realised that.'

'QED.'

Scandal on the Eurostar. Luckily it does not touch us at Cheriton. Eurostar pay the Home Office to provide IOs to work on board the trains from Waterloo to Paris and Brussels. This is a modern version of the 'crossing IO' on the ferries. Unfortunately the Sunday newspapers have got hold of stories of IOs taking drugs and having sex on trains and pestering passengers and fighting. All good stuff for a Sunday morning read. I know nothing of sex on Eurostar but I was once travelling in the Shuttle when the couple in the vehicle in the front of us started to get amorous. The preferred vehicle for the 'one mile under' club is the small camper van; for the obvious practical considerations of comfort, space and equipment. In this case the car was a Ford Escort convertible. This is a not unimportant detail since, at some stage in their manoeuvres and for reasons utterly unfathomable to those behind them, they decided to put down the electrically powered folding roof. I can only believe that this must have been an inadvertent action on their part but the result was farcically catastrophic. Suddenly the entire hood of the car reared upwards like a prancing horse, exposing to the world the state of their progress towards a blissful goal. But the designers of the Shuttle had not allowed sufficient headroom to accommodate a folding convertible roof and it jammed against the ceiling of the carriage in the vertical position, jerking up and down on its baulked electrics in an insolent parody of the couple it had just uncovered. How we laughed.

But nobody laughed when the AD announced that the ELU was to close. Reg Toale observed that I was transferred to the hoverport and they closed it; I went to Folkestone and they closed it and now I had come to the ELU and they were closing it. Where did this jinx intend to go next? He would like to know. Crozier, of course, was grief stricken for me because he would now have to transfer me to Dover East.

'Why?' I asked.

'Well, there is no work for you here. You don't go through the tunnel to Coquelles as other control IOs do.'

'But I do the casework and I deal with the French refusals and I conduct asylum interviews in the police station.'

'That is not a full week's work. Once the ELU work has gone, you will have little to do.'

'That is just not true. You will never find me sitting here twiddling my thumbs. Look around the office now. Who is the IO with work in front of him? Me. There are three IOs in the kitchen drinking coffee, Mike there is gossiping with Sid, Len is out on the balcony smoking a cigarette and Brian is over there by the window in an easy chair, reading a magazine. I am working.'

'What are you doing?'

'I am compiling the stats returns.'

'But Sid can do that.'

'No he can't. He has to ask an IO how many asylum applicants we have outstanding; how many unresolved cases are detained, how many on temporary admission. At the moment we have daily, weekly, fortnightly, monthly, three monthly and annual returns of various bits of information to amass.' I didn't add that we were short of one return because I had shredded the instruction. 'Yes, he can fill in the forms but he cannot collect the data; that has to be done by an IO reading the files and completing the logs.'

'Well he's got this guidance form he can follow.'

'Yes, he has. And where did it come from? Not from ISHQ. I composed it to help him do his job. Just as I compiled and keep up to date the operational guide that you can see the CIO consulting at this very minute in his office over there.'

'Well that is all very laudable but we need to look at your future now that the reason for you coming here is to disappear.'

And so the AD came over for a 'confidential chat' which had to take place on the public balcony so that he could smoke two cheroots. He spoke at me for forty minutes. There was no discussion – I managed about seven interjections. The one observation that I took home with me was, 'you really ought to be looking for a job outside the Civil Service.' When I later asked the Personnel Management Unit if this meant that I was being made redundant then the firework show started but the AD didn't care. He had already got his early retirement package agreed so he knew that he could say what he liked.

The ELU work was being taken back into the mainstream Home Office so that the IS could concentrate on its core business. We would not need such a large office so we transferred across to a smaller building by the French control kiosks. This shortened the distance I had to walk to deal with their refusals. One idiosyncrasy of this office was that the services were remotely controlled. There were no light switches, only sensors, and the heating and ventilation were regulated by a central unit in the terminal control building. One of the new IOs warned us that this was not good news. She had worked in a branch of WH Smith where the level of heating in their branches countrywide had been determined by the weather at head office in Swindon.

But we coped. Late one evening an IO walked into the office where I was working on the computer. He stooped and picked up a paper aeroplane from the floor and then walked to the kitchen. By the time he had reached it he had three more aeroplanes in his hand.

'What's with the aeronautics?' he asked, waving the darts above his head before he threw them into the bin.

'Ah,' I said, 'that's because I have been here on my own now for over two hours, working on the computer.'

'Oh, you get bored?'

'No, it's not that. The lights are on a movement sensor and I have not been moving, so every fifteen minutes the entire office is plunged into darkness as the lights go out but if you throw a paper aeroplane up it switches them back on again.'

'Ah, the wonders of modern technology.'

Just recently, one of my friends who has not yet retired, announced that when tidying a desk drawer in the office somebody had discovered two pieces of chipboard marked *plank no 1'* and *plank no 2'*. Did I know anything about them?

They were not modern technology. I would have classified them more as artisanal but they functioned perfectly.

'You know very well I do,' I said. 'Are they still used?' but he appeared nonplussed and requested elucidation. 'Well,' I explained, 'the builders left behind these two offcuts of chipboard so I grabbed the parcel marker pen, labelled them and put them in the drawer. They came in useful on several occasions. I remember one day trying to explain something to one of the inspectors. It was about the procedure for removing a failed asylum seeker to a third country. I went through it twice and he gave me an order which showed that he had not understood it at all. So I tried again and he insisted on another bizarre course of action which could only fail and cause more problems. At this point, I opened my drawer and put plank number one on my desk. I went through the explanation with him again, showing him the relevant Home Office circulars. I really could not put it any more simply but he still could not understand so I put plank number two on top of the first. "What's that?" he said. 'That,' I explained, pointing to the pile of wood, 'is two short planks.'

OK, it may have been in questionable taste but don't forget, I was having to explain important procedures to the person who was paid to tell me what to do. He was two grades higher than me but could demonstrate no evidence of possessing the intellect necessary to grasp what I was telling him and I am not a defective communicator.

At about this time I saw a notice announcing that there was a great need for CIOs and inviting applicants for the shortlist. I had never really been interested in working as a CIO because I liked dealing with passengers, not trying to manage IOs but the variety of tasks now allotted to CIOs in the various empires within the Service meant that I would be able to find a job for myself. In my early days you could not apply for promotion, you had to wait to be invited. You could always appeal against not being called to a board. Now that the IS was having to do things properly, or more like the mainstream Home Office at any rate, it had issued a list of requirements that the candidates needed to satisfy in order to be put on the shortlist for interview. I glanced down them, mentally ticking them off as I went. I realised with a start that I possessed all the qualities. Even the jokers like, 'ability to manage a budget' and, 'experience of managing staff,' neither of which fell within the job experience of a standard IO, I could satisfy from my work in the Telecoms Unit. 'Well, why not?' I thought. They had guaranteed that all those qualifying on paper would be called to interview. I qualified on paper. It would be a trip to London if nothing else. I had been marked 'fitted for promotion' for the last seven years. I had nothing to lose.

Except my eyesight. I can recall as a little boy, sitting outside Aylesbury hospital in the car, not understanding what we were doing there. Playing guessing games to pass the time. Listening to the barking echo of a farm tractor as it took a run up the hill. Sometimes they would get Mummy to wave to us waiting children from the window. I could never see her but I always said that I had. And then she came home and she was blind. Later, as an adolescent, I remember my brother being gently driven up to Moorfields Eye Hospital in London by our optician who was also an opthalmic surgeon. 'Just my luck,' Peter said. 'The only time I ride in a Jag and he wouldn't drive over thirty miles per hour.' The doctor was driving with caution to preserve Peter's sight. The retina had detached in one eye and the task was to get him to hospital as smoothly and as gently as possible. He is now partially sighted.

We were brought up with warnings about seeing 'floaters,' 'satellites' and flashing lights in our eyes and what to do about them. It was all part of the package of suffering from Sticklerism so as soon as I noticed the rippling in my vision and the spot where I could not see, I went to the hospital. They confirmed my self-diagnosis: my retina was detaching. In our family this was bad news because although the needle and thread surgery of the 1950s had now been replaced by highly technical laser welding, the deficiency which causes our retinas to detach in the first place also acts against their successful repair. The NHS did not delay. I was taken in that day and operated upon. That prompt action almost certainly saved my sight.

I had not bothered you with my deteriorating physical state because I hate to read about other people's ills and diseases. For this reason I hid my symptoms from my colleagues as best I could. Why burden them with the unpleasantness? But it was not easy. One of my tasks required me to lie on my stomach on the floor in order to tap on the keyboards of two computers fitted at ankle height under a shelf in a tall cupboard. The clerical officer who one day responded to my whispered request to help me get up again was solicitous and compassionate but I would rather I had not been obliged to seek help. On a couple of occasions I had realised from the reactions of my colleagues that the pain I was experiencing was showing on my face and I resolved to be more careful in future. Some had worked it out for themselves. When I was returning to the office from an interview in the police station one day, Brian, a CIO, had taken one look at me and hurried over to the office door with the practical question, 'What do you want me to do?' 'Just take that file,' I had replied, thrusting it at him, and I staggered into the rest room to recover. I was pushing myself too hard. It was not fair on my colleagues.

With the disappearance of the ELU work I now had to find reasons to keep myself here. After many months of barracking I finally managed to be put on the team of duty compilers. This had been the exclusive reserve of union officials because it gave them power over their colleagues. Whilst Crozier was pointing out, with great sadness and regret, that there were no jobs for me here I riposted by explaining that if I were compiling duties it would free up an IO one day a week to land passengers.

The duties were compiled upon a great planning board fitted with slots to receive T-shaped cards in various colours chosen according to the duty and the day of the week. It took half a day to set it up and then half a day to take it down again. The bending and reaching necessary to accomplish these two tasks caused me acute pain for several days afterwards. I could not go on like this. I had fought to be allowed to do this job and it was killing me. I cursed my stupidity but the stimulus of pain destroys procrastination. I discovered that I could do the whole job in four hours with three sheets of paper and a pencil. I had saved half a day of IO time, I didn't need the board and we didn't need a special room set aside for duties. The union reps, of course, still took a whole day to do the job.

My days now consisted of getting up and doing my physiotherapy exercises to get me into shape to be able to go to work; going to work; coming home and recovering. It was a struggle.

We had an interview booked at Haslar Detention Centre near Portsmouth. The main interview had been conducted; we knew all his story. We only needed the answers to a few supplementary questions and then we could decide. I talked the case over with Walter, the CIO.

'Should we get a local IO to do the interview on Thursday?' I asked.

'No, they are short staffed. We've tried three times now to do this interview. We must not waste any more time and resources on it. Can you go and do it on Thursday?'

'There and back in day? It must be about three hundred miles in all.'

'The interview won't take long. We all know he's a knock-off.'

'How do I refer it? The interview is at three. Will you be here for a referral from about half four?'

'Yes, I am working two till ten on Thursday. I'll be in the office all day.'

'OK, I'll get it set up.'

I phoned the IOs who were doing the same job at Haslar as I had been doing at Rochester Prison. We booked an interview room in the prison and I asked if they could supply a North African Arabic interpreter locally as the detainee was Algerian. It made sense to use a local interpreter; it reduced the chances of his being delayed by traffic.

I drove down to Haslar, arriving at one o'clock. I ate my sandwiches on the seafront and then turned up at the office. The IOs gave me a table to work on and I read the detainee's local file and updated our port file as necessary. Then I waited for the interpreter. At three o'clock I was still waiting.

'Can you ring your interpreter and find out where he is?' I asked.

'I've tried twice. She doesn't answer so she must be on her way. Discipline have just rung. They want to know if you still want this room for interview?' the IO said.

'Yes, of course I do. Tell them I am awaiting an interpreter.'

'OK. They've got Saeed ready but not brought him across yet.'

I waited. Half past three and still no interpreter.

'Right, OK. Ask Discipline to see if the detainee will agree to do the interview in French,' I said.

I phoned Walter and put him in the picture. We both agreed that an interview in Arabic would be preferable but if the interpreter did not appear in time then I was to do it in French. The detainee agreed to an interview in French. I got ready to go in and then he changed his mind.

'You know they close 'Visits' at half past five, don't you?' the local IO asked me. 'And it's four o'clock now.'

'Can we go and get this interpreter? Or send a taxi or something?' I was getting desperate.

'What? To Ealing?'

'Ealing? Your interpreter lives in Ealing? That's a hundred miles away. I thought she was local.'

'She's the only one we know.'

I stared at the ceiling in frustration. What could I do?

Half past four. Still no interpreter. The prison wanted to know if we still needed Saeed for interview. I asked them if they could put him on the phone to me. They could if I would take it on an internal line. I found a telephone on their circuit and spoke to the detainee. He understood my French easily. I apologised for the delay and explained that we were still awaiting an interpreter.

At five o'clock Discipline phoned. He would like the interview in French.

'Take all your stuff with you,' the local IO said. 'We'll be gone when you get back. This office will be closed.'

I grabbed my bag and hurried down to the prison gate.

'We've put you in here sir, if that's OK. We really need him back at six or he'll miss his tea.'

'OK. Thanks.'

I started the interview. At twenty past five I suddenly had a thought. I recalled my time at Rochester. I grabbed the phone and dialled the swtichboard. I automatically fell into the jargon.

'Can you put a nine on this line before you go please?' I knew that the switchboard would close at half past five and then the only link to the outside world would be on direct lines, not extensions. I needed them to allocate me an outside line now. I was just in time. Without it I would have been completely isolated.

At five to six the prison officer turned up.

'Are you going to be long? We need to take him back.'

'I've just got to speak to my CIO. I'll be two minutes.' Walter was right. He was a refusal but of course, I needed his authority to serve the papers. The phone rang unanswered. It rang and rang. I tried all the lines in the Cheriton office. Nobody replied.

'I'm sorry sir. I must take him now.'

'Just let me have one more try. I can't get an answer.'

The prison officer looked at his watch and frowned. He made a call on the wall phone and then came back.

'You can have till six fifteen then I really must take him back.'

'You're very kind. Thank you.' I knew I was being a nuisance. I was upsetting their timetable and mucking up their staffing. At thirteen minutes past six I still was CIO-less. Keys were being jangled outside. I refused the detainee and served the papers on him. I would explain it all to Walter when I got back. After all, he had already told me that the man was a refusal

The traffic was slow up the M3 and stop-start on the M25. It was not the pleasantest of journeys. When I walked into our office I was tired. In one day I had done eight hours of motorway driving and run myself frantic in the middle, trying to arrange and then carry out an interview. That I had succeeded had been due largely to my ability to speak good French, my knowledge of prison procedure and the complaisance of the officers; the last being not something to be assumed as automatic.

With a sigh I sat down and started to write up the case notes. At a quarter to ten, Walter walked in.

'Ah, I've been trying to contact you to refer that case. I couldn't get an answer,' I said.

'Oh, I had nothing to do so I went with the IOs down to Folkestone for the freight arrival.' This was a new service which had been introduced as an attempt to reopen the traffic between Folkestone and Boulogne. The vessel was staffed with Polish seamen. It did not last long. The French seamen's union made sure of that.

For an instant I just looked at him. He had been missing at six o'clock when I needed him. Where had he been for nearly four hours? I thought I could guess. And what was all this about his having, 'nothing to do'? He had sent one of his officers one hundred and fifty miles away to do an interview and refer a case to him and he had, 'nothing to do'?

'Oh well, that explains why I couldn't get hold of you.' I said at last. 'Anyway, you were right. He was a refusal. I knocked him off and served the papers. I'm just writing it up.'

'Who did you refer it to?'

'Well, I've put you down as the CIO.'

'Oh I can't accept that,' he said. 'I didn't take a reference from you.'

'I couldn't get hold of you to refer it. You didn't answer the phone.'

He picked up his case and made for the door. 'I can't authorise a refusal after it has been done. No, you've acted outside the law. Somebody will have to do the interview again.'

I think I must have stared at the door for five minutes after he had gone. I could not believe that he had done that to me. I was still sitting there when one of the CIOs returned from his Coquelles duty. He was a man who had never forgotten what it had been like to be an IO.

'What's the matter with you?' he asked.

'I, er... I....' I just didn't know where to start. He realised that an incident which had left me, of all people, without a vocabulary had to be serious. He pulled up a chair and sat down.

'Tell me,' he said.

And then it all poured out. He sat and listened.

'What a wanker that man is,' he shouted angrily. 'He's scared of his own farts. You referred the case to me. Put me down as the CIO. What a wanker.'

Why couldn't we have more CIOs like him?

Well they weren't going to have a CIO like me, because I did not make it to the shortlist. I was not too bothered. It had been a punt on my part. But, hang on a minute. How could I have not have made it to the shortlist? I had shown that I qualified on every count and it had been confirmed by my team leader. According to the recruitment notice, I would be called to interview. What had happened? Curiosity got the better of me. I rang them up. And do you know what the answer was? You won't believe this.

'We had such a large response that we decided to put on the shortlist only those whom we thought would be successful at interview.'

Just read that again and think about it.

Whilst I was thinking about it I got a call to attend the French control and land a Brit. refusal. It was a corker. He had been refused entry to France for having a cracked glass in his door mirror. From all the crisis points on the globe, young men were converging upon Calais and fighting to get into the UK to claim asylum. We were inundated. They could steal, murder and rape here and we could not get rid of them yet the French could turn away a man for having a cracked glass in his car mirror.

The jinx worked again. It was decided that duty compiling for Cheriton and Coquelles would now be done by the Dover East team. Crozier was almost in tears as he told me.

'With the transfer of this work to Dover East that leaves less reason for you to stay here.'

'Apart from casework, French refusals, office duties.'

'Those can all be done by IOs on their way through to Coquelles.'

'I can't see the port successfully handling casework on the basis of an IO doing it as he walks through the office on the way to somewhere else. It is a recipe for disaster.'

Crozier was heartbroken, I could tell. Despite everything he had done for me things just had not worked out as I had wanted. 'The trouble is, Martin, you are a luxury we cannot afford.'

'OK,' I said. No point in arguing.

He smiled reassuringly and left.

I sat at the desk and thought. Twenty-four years experience was a luxury they could not afford. I know that everybody remarks eventually that the job is not what it used to be but I am not one who does that with a dose of nostalgia or regret. Change is inevitable, I accept that. A job and its practicians have to adapt to the demands of the evolving world. I had started work alongside men who had worn hats to the office and had checked passports at Croydon airport. In those days the officers promoted to CIO and above had served their time as IOs; they knew the job but were bloody awful managers. Now we were recruiting from outside the Service people who had been trained as managers but knew nothing about the job. The future would show us whether this was a wise policy.

A sleek yellow Eurostar slid noiselessly past the window into its burrow under Castle Hill. I could not hear it. The office was air-conditioned, sound-proofed and double-glazed with solar reflecting glass. It was not the piercing sun at five in the morning, boring like a gimlet into your eyes through a broken venetian blind in an unheated car kiosk which smelled like a stale ashtray and had a loose fitting perspex window which rattled in the wind and gave your lungs unbridled access to a poisonous cloud of carbon-monoxide gas.

The people were fun. The job could be as boring as you would like to make it or as fascinating as you could desire. You could predict with ninety percent certainty what the passenger was going to say and you would be wrong ninety percent of the time. You never knew what the next person would present you with. Is he really going to visit the Queen? Do all those children belong to that lady? Would you come here to buy wallpaper? Shouldn't a doctor coming to work here be able to speak English? How many pages are there in a Brazilian passport? Where the hell is Burkina Faso?

I recalled a radio-telephone message I had received at the office one evening. 'I'm going to be late for my night duty tonight. We are becalmed twenty miles west of the Scillies.' It beat the 'flat tyre on my bicycle' excuse. I had been to a retirement party where the officer's personal file, which is so confidential that throughout his career he is denied access to it, was obtained from the personnel section and snippets read out from it to amuse the audience. I had been to a funeral where a landing card of the deceased officer had been withdrawn from Traffic Index and the notes which she had written on the back displayed to the mourners to substantiate the truth of the eulogy. I had worked with sportsmen and linguists, drunkards and perverts; scholars of hieroglyphs and avid stamp collectors. Some had gone off the rails: forging immigration stamps and ending up in prison; shoplifting and being promoted. Some had died before their time. Some had just gone.

'Martin, I'm going over to the canteen. I'll be back in half an hour. Tell the CIO would you?'

The door slammed behind him.

Yes Martin would do that. Good old reliable Martin.

Martin who applies his twenty-four years' experience fully and continuously to trying to make things work better for everybody.

Martin who is a luxury they cannot afford.

I put my pen in my pocket.

I got up from the desk.

I took my coat from the rack and I walked out of the office.

And I never went back.

Martin Lloyd
HM Immigration Officer
16 April 1974 – 28 February 1998.

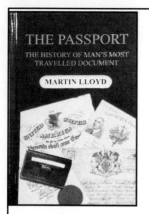

THE PASSPORT

*The History of Man's Most
Travelled Document*
by Martin Lloyd

THIRD EDITION, REVISED AND ENLARGED
Hardback, 294 pages & 83 illustrations

The passport is a document familiar to many, used and recognised worldwide and yet it has no basis in law: one country cannot oblige another to admit its subjects simply by issuing a document. But the state, by insisting on the requirement to hold a passport, provides for itself a neat, self-financing data collection and surveillance system. This well illustrated book tells for the first time the story of the passport from its earliest origins to its latest high-tech developments. Handwritten documents adorned with wax seals, modern versions in plastic covers, diplomatic passports and wartime safe conducts, all drawn from the author's collection, complement the exciting exploits of spies and criminals and the tragic real life experiences of refugees. Whether recounting the birth of the British blue passport of the 1920s or divulging the secrets of today's machine readable passport, Martin Lloyd has written an informative and engrossing history book which is accessible to everyone.

'*...a lively and thoughtful book...*'
SUNDAY TELEGRAPH

Published by Queen Anne's Fan ISBN: 9780 9573639-2-2

Hunting the Golden Lion

a cycle safari through France

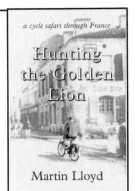

a cycle safari through France

Hunting the Golden Lion

Martin Lloyd

Having recklessly declared in a previous book that it must be possible to cross all of France staying only in hotels called the HOTEL DU LION D'OR, Martin Lloyd is challenged by his critics to prove his assertion in the only way possible – by doing it.

Surely it will be a straightforward and leisurely ride through France? As long as the hotels are no more than a day's cycle ride apart, of course. And if your bicycle has been constructed this century, and if you remember to take with you all that you need... and if your name isn't Martin Lloyd.

Is this why, on the the first day of his safari, he is standing in his pyjamas on a pavement a thousand miles from home, clutching a broken bicycle with a bleeding hand?

Published by Queen Anne's Fan ISBN: 9780 9547 1506 9

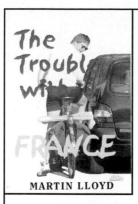

MARTIN LLOYD

The Trouble with France

Martin Lloyd's new international number one blockbusting bestseller

"...makes Baedeker's look like a guidebook..."

When Martin Lloyd set out on his holiday to Suffolk why did he end up in Boulogne? What caused Max the Mad Alsatian to steal his map and what did the knitted grandma really think of his display of hot plate juggling? The answers to these and many more mysteries are to be found in THE TROUBLE WITH FRANCE

THE TROUBLE WITH FRANCE contains no recipes and no hand drawn maps. It does not recount how somebody richer than you went to a part of France that you have never heard of, bought a stone ruin for a song and converted it into a luxurious retreat which they expect you to finance by buying their book.

Nor is it the self satisfied account of another ultra fit expedition cyclist abseiling down Everest on a penny farthing but Martin Lloyd attempting an uneventful ride on a mundane bicycle through an uninteresting part of France... and failing with outstanding success.

THE TROUBLE WITH FRANCE is destined to be a worldwide success now that Margaret's Mum has been down the road and told her friend Pat about it.

Published by Queen Anne's Fan ISBN: 9780 9547 15007

The Trouble with Spain

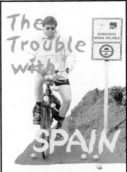

FROM THE BESTSELLING AUTHOR OF
THE TROUBLE WITH FRANCE *COMES*
THIS EAGERLY AWAITED SEQUEL

MARTIN LLOYD

'*...makes Munchausen look like a liar...*'

Still smarting from his brutal encounter with Gaul as detailed in his much acclaimed book, THE TROUBLE WITH FRANCE, Martin Lloyd drags his bicycle over the Pyrenees to pursue the twin delights of sun and breakfast.

What factor will defeat his proposed headlong plunge into raw hedonism? Will it be his profound and extensive ignorance of Spanish history or perhaps his coarse insensitivity to the culture of the peninsula? Or would it be the damning condemnation that he is just too lazy to learn the language?

Read THE TROUBLE WITH SPAIN and you will discover nothing about bull fights and enjoy no colourful descriptions of sensual flamenco dancing but you will learn why you cannot train goldfish to be guard dogs and you will clearly understand why even Martin Lloyd's trousers ran away from him.

CAUTION

This book contains moderate use of humour, some expressions in foreign language and a short but ultimately frustrating scene in a lady's bedroom.

Published by Queen Anne's Fan ISBN: 9780 9547 15014

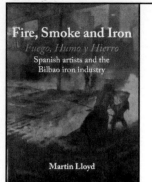

Fire, Smoke and Iron
Fuego, Humo y Hierro
Spanish artists and the
Bilbao iron industry

Martin Lloyd

Fire Smoke and Iron

Fuego, Humo y Hierro

Spanish artists and the Bilbao iron industry.

66 pages, 95 colour illustrations and 35 black & white.

Richly illustrated in full colour

Bilbao in Spain has been producing iron for centuries, drawing in workers from all over the country. Its rapid industrialisation in the nineteenth century was helped in no little measure by British capital and entrepreneurship. Ships carried Welsh coal to Spain and brought back Spanish pig-iron for the steelworks of South Wales. By 1985, it was all over. But the rise, heyday and demise of the Bilbaoan iron industry has been forever fixed in oils, water colours and bronze.

This book shows how iron is made into steel; illustrating the machinery involved and explaining the processes used.
It then illustrates the evocative paintings by which Spanish artists have recorded this industry in its various stages and explains and interprets the activity depicted.

Published by Queen Anne's Fan ISBN: 9780 9573 639-3-9

Every Picture

Every
Picture

Martin Lloyd

'... a tender and engaging love story...'

When the son of an earl meets the daughter of
a coal miner in the doorway of the art college he
does not tell her that he is a viscount.

Why should he?

How was he to know that their paths would cross
and recross and that he would fall in
love with her?

And once that has happened, he finds it impossible to
tell her the truth for fear of losing her. At the very
moment that they finally admit their feelings for one
another, the relationship is wrenched asunder as their
lives take a violent and unpredictable turn, casting their
two destinies onto divergent courses.

Will they ever meet again?

Published by Queen Anne's Fan ISBN: 9780 9547 1505 2

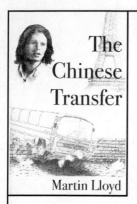

The
Chinese Transfer

a thriller romance that you will
not want to put down

'...this is storytelling as it used to be...'

Paris in the 1970s – student demonstrations, union strikes and oppressive heat. Coach driver Simon Laperche is sent to Orly Airport to pick up a Chinese group and take them to their hotel in the city. A run of the mill job. He could do it with his eyes shut. It was a pity about the guide, but then, he could not expect to please everybody.

Abruptly, things go wrong. The plane is diverted to Lyon and Laperche is ordered to drive his coach south to meet it... and he has to take that infuriating guide with him. Unknown to them both, a terrorist unit has targeted their group and is intent upon its destruction.

Stalked by the terrorists, the driver and guide continue to bicker as they struggle to bring their group safely to Paris. Will the mutual respect which eventually begins to grow between them prove strong enough when the test comes?

Published by Queen Anne's Fan ISBN: 9780 9547 15021

Rue
Amélie

Rue Amélie

Martin Lloyd

another fast-paced thriller from Martin Lloyd.

Following the success of *The Chinese Transfer*, Martin Lloyd takes us back to the seedy side of Paris in the 1970s. Joel LeBatard, a driver for a small-time crook, loses his boss's car and his position. With no job and soon to be thrown out of his bedsit, he accepts a commission from a woman he meets at a funeral, to find out where her father had invested his secret pension.

LeBatard discovers that others are on the same trail – a ruthless big-time gangster whom he has already been stupid enough to upset, and an ex-colleague from his army days who now heads an undercover squad in the Ministry of Defence. They will stop at nothing to get their hands on the very thing that he is looking for, but nobody can tell him what it is.

The hectic action takes them to the four corners of Paris. Whilst pursuing his relentless search, LeBatard struggles with two difficulties: is his new employer telling him the truth and how, in the face of such energy and charm, can he uphold his vow never to get mixed up with another woman?

Published by Queen Anne's Fan ISBN: 9780 9547 1507 6

No Harm
in Looking

A beautifully bound hardback with
nine colour plates.

being a collection of

TALES OF EROTIC FANTASY

for the delectation of

LADIES AND GENTLEMEN ALIKE

*especially illustrated
and published in this edition
for the author's friends.*

K. T. Yalta

Published by Queen Anne's Fan ISBN: 9780 9547 1508 3

The Impetus Turn

In the 1980's a civil engineer is sent to work
in Bangladesh and is thrown into a world
of stark contrasts; of povery and disease,
of diplomatic parties, corporate power
and corruption.

With a naivety aggravated by his stubbornness,
he begins to uncover a fraud which threatens to
cause devastating repercussions in the
political arena and exert a disastrous
influence upon his career.

Should he continue?

Published by Queen Anne's Fan ISBN: 9780 9573 639-5-3